Coping in Young Children

Early Intervention Practices to Enhance Adaptive Behavior and Resilience

by

Shirley Zeitlin, Ed.D.

Psychologist and Private Consultant
Loch Arbour, New Jersey

and

G. Gordon Williamson, Ph.D., O.T.R.

Director
COPING Project
Pediatric Rehabilitation Department
John F. Kennedy Medical Center
Edison, New Jersey
and
Associate Clinical Professor
Columbia University
New York, New York

·P A U L·H·
BROOKES
PUBLISHING Cº

Baltimore • London • Toronto • Sydney

Paul H. Brookes Publishing Co.
P.O. Box 10624
Baltimore, Maryland 21285-0624

Copyright © 1994 by Paul H. Brookes Publishing Co., Inc.
All rights reserved.

Typeset by Brushwood Graphics, Inc., Baltimore, Maryland.
Manufactured in the United States of America by
The Maple Press Company, York, Pennsylvania.

Permission to reprint the following quotation is gratefully acknowledged:

Page 191: A numbered list from National Center for Clinical Infant Programs. (1989).
Four critical junctures: Support for parents of children with special needs. Arlington, VA:
Author.

Library of Congress Cataloging-in-Publication Data

Zeitlin, Shirley.
   Coping in young children : early intervention practices to enhance adaptive
behavior and resilience / by Shirley Zeitlin and G. Gordon Williamson.
        p.   cm.
      Includes bibliographical references and index.
      ISBN 1-55766-127-8
      1. Handicapped children—Services for—United States.   2. Handicapped
children—United States—Development.   3. Handicapped children—Education
(Preschool)—United States.   I. Williamson, G. Gordon.   II. Title.
HV888.5.Z45   1994
362.4'048'083—dc20   94-19030
                                                                     CIP

British Library Cataloguing-in-Publication data are available from the British Library.

Contents

About the Authors

Shirley Zeitlin, Ed.D., is a psychologist in private practice. Her early work as a school psychologist generated awareness of the impact of coping style on learning and the need to identify and help children with special needs before they failed. This led to her interest in the young child and the development of federally funded preschool and infant and toddler demonstration coping-related early intervention programs. Dr. Zeitlin developed and implemented a graduate program in early childhood special education at Montclair State College in Upper Montclair, New Jersey, and also taught educational psychology and directed the research-oriented child study center at the State University of New York at New Paltz. She has lectured throughout the United States, Europe, and China. Through her many activities, including active involvement in national organizations, she makes many contributions to the emerging specialty of early intervention. Dr. Zeitlin's publications include *Kindergarten Screening—Early Identification of Handicapped Children, Personalized Learning Plans for Young Children, The Coping Inventory* (observation and self-rating forms), *The Early Coping Inventory,* and many journal articles and book chapters.

G. Gordon Williamson, Ph.D., is an occupational therapist and special educator who directs two projects at the Pediatric Rehabilitation Department of the John F. Kennedy Medical Center in Edison, New Jersey, an interdisciplinary department that he originally founded and developed. The COPING Project, funded by the U.S. Department of Education, offers training and technical assistance to support the provision of family-centered early intervention services that enhance adaptive functioning. The Social Competence Project, previously funded by the Robert Wood Johnson Foundation, is a model demonstration program to foster the interpersonal skills of children with disabilities. Dr. Williamson is also Associate Clinical Professor of Occupational Therapy in the Rehabilitation Medicine Department at Columbia University in New York. He is a member of the board of directors of Zero to Three/National Center for Clinical Infant Programs and the Academy of Research of the American Occupational Therapy Foundation. Previously he chaired the Parental and Child Health Advisory Committee of the New Jersey Department of Health and served as treasurer of the Division for Early Childhood of the Council for Exceptional Children. Dr. Williamson is on the editorial board of numerous professional journals and has lectured extensively throughout the United States, South America, and the Middle East. Recent publications include the *Early Coping Inventory, Children with Spina Bifida: Early Intervention and Preschool Programming,* and many articles related to human adaptation. His research focuses on the study of the coping resources of children and their families.

authors is then discussed in detail with particular emphasis on coping resources and the elements of coping transactions. In Chapter 3 the coping process is reexamined as it relates to young children. The development of coping ability is described in infants and toddlers with recognition of the critical importance of parent–child transactions. Since this frame of reference is family centered, information regarding the family as a system is provided in Chapter 4. Many facets related to families are addressed including family structure, cultural diversity, functions, life cycle, and subsystems. There is also consideration of the influences of a young child with special needs on the family system.

Chapters 5 through 9 provide the pragmatic structure for translating the coping-related theoretical base into effective intervention practices. Chapter 5 sets the stage by discussing critical aspects for program development. Intervention is defined and the authors' views regarding service delivery, staff roles, and parent–professional collaboration are shared. A personalized decision-making model is then introduced for program planning. Chapter 6 discusses assessment from a coping perspective, with methods for examining each of the child's coping resources. A procedure is also described for observing and analyzing transactions between the child and significant others. Chapters 7 and 8 focus on intervention strategies and activities to increase the resilience and adaptive functioning of infants and toddlers. Lastly, Chapter 9 describes ways to support families and to help them enhance their coping resources.

In Chapters 10 and 11 the personalized decision-making model is used to develop IFSPs with a coping orientation. Information from the preceding chapters is integrated into effective implementation plans through decision-making questions that guide each step of the IFSP process.

The experiences and outcomes of the COPING Demonstration Project are described in Chapters 12 and 13. Case studies are presented of four families who were actively involved in the initial development of the program. Included are follow-up interviews that were conducted 3 years after their children left the early intervention program. (To protect confidentiality, some changes were made in the descriptions of the children and families in the text.) Chapter 14 completes the volume with a discussion of staff coping with the demands of providing early intervention services and managing change in a fluid professional environment. In conclusion, this book presents validated intervention practices that enhance the adaptive behavior and resilience of young children and support their families.

REFERENCE

Connor, F.P., Williamson, G.G., & Siepp, J.M. (1978). *Program guide for infants and toddlers with neuromotor and other developmental disabilities.* New York: Teachers College Press.

Acknowledgments

The development of this book reflects the contributions of many individuals and organizations. We were fortunate to receive grant funding from the Office of Special Education Programs in the U.S. Department of Education and to have the support of James L. Hamilton, who was then Chief of the Early Childhood Branch. Lee H. Coleman, our project officer, was always available when assistance was needed. Jane DeWeerd, originally in the U.S. Department of Education and later Head Start, encouraged our activities from the beginning.

The primary work of the COPING Project was conducted at the John F. Kennedy Medical Center in Edison, New Jersey. Ongoing support came from John P. McGee, Chief Executive Officer of the medical center. Thomas E. Strax, Medical Director of the JFK Johnson Rehabilitation Institute, and Scott Gebhard, Vice President of Rehabilitation Services, generated a climate in which creative development could thrive. Patricia Munday, Director of the Pediatric Rehabilitation Department, was instrumental in ensuring the continuation of coping-related intervention programs at the medical center. Her clinical and administrative leadership consistently promoted best practices. Staff members of the department were actively involved in designing new therapeutic and educational activities. Families participating in the program were most generous in providing direction for the COPING Project and suggestions for program development. Their efforts were expanded and reinforced by feedback from early intervention programs across the United States where COPING training was implemented.

Special acknowledgment is extended to the professionals who participated in a series of grant-supported projects—the COPING Project, CONNECT, and COPING OUTREACH. As the first project coordinator, Margery Szczepanski provided seminal ideas regarding the conceptual model for assessment and intervention. She was also a coauthor of the Early Coping Inventory, an instrument to assess the coping styles of infants and toddlers. Kathleen T. Quinn was especially generative in identifying intervention methods and strategies. William Rosenblatt helped to define supportive services for families. Richard N. Baumwoll contributed his expertise with parent discussion groups. Jane D. Hochman developed coping-related training materials. Linda Bruene focused on expanding our understanding of how staff cope with change. To all of these remarkable individuals, we are most grateful.

Andrea Quigley deserves singular recognition for her insightful suggestions at each stage of book preparation. She played an important role in determining procedural guidelines for integrating the personalized decision-making model into the IFSP process. Ms. Quigley worked closely with us in the task of refining intervention principles and techniques. She also provided critical feedback on content issues as she field tested the information through outreach training.

Evelyn Katrak was imaginative and proficient in her preliminary editing of the manuscript from her home in Jerusalem. Joan E. Goddard was tireless in typing the many initial drafts, and Donna Gasser patiently typed the final manuscript.

It was a pleasure collaborating with the talented team at Paul H. Brookes Publishing Company. Melissa A. Behm, Vice President, provided helpful professional guidance during the evolution of this project. Victoria P. Thulman, Acquisitions Editor, and Tania Bourdon, Copyeditor, were stellar in editing and preparing the manuscript for publication. Ken Foye, Production Coordinator, was skillful in managing the myriad complexities of the book's format. We are truly indebted.

To the very special people who help us cope:
Jack Gardy
Georg Fleischer
Wrenetta and Gaston Williamson
Lynne, Stephen, Thomas, and Andrew Hale
June Zeitlin, Howard Chernick
Norman and Rachel Chernick Zeitlin

Coping in Young Children

CHAPTER 1

Introduction

A major task during childhood is transforming early adaptive behaviors into a mature coping style (Lipsitt, 1983). A child must acquire developmental skills and learn to apply them functionally to manage daily activities. A child's early experiences of interacting with the environment are essential for the emergence of an effective coping style and a positive sense of self. A developmental delay, disability, or at-risk condition may impede this transactional process. Therefore, from the perspective of this book, the goals of early intervention are:

> To enhance the life outcomes of young children with special needs by increasing their developmental and coping capability
>
> To enhance the coping resources of families of children with special needs

Goals serve as the foundation for planning and evaluating services. The goals above emphasize functional outcomes and are based on the following research-supported assumptions:

> The more effectively a child copes, the more effectively a child learns (Bricker & Cripe, 1992; Greenspan, 1992; Werner & Smith, 1991; Williamson, Szczepanski, & Zeitlin, 1993). For the child, developmental skills are the building blocks for growth. Coping is the integration and application of these skills to functional living and mastery of new learning.
>
> The more effectively families are able to cope with the demands of daily living, the more able they are to provide support and nurturance and to achieve a sense of well-being (Beckwith, 1990; Dunst, Trivette, & Deal, 1988; Gallagher, 1990; Holahan & Moos, 1990; Lipsky, 1985).

THE FRAME OF REFERENCE

This book presents a validated frame of reference for planning and implementing early intervention services. It has three unique components: 1) a theoretical model based on the transactional coping process, 2) a decision-making model for personalized planning, and 3) intervention options that expand coping resources and support effective transactions in daily living. These components are interwoven into an intervention approach that is flexible and practical. It can be tailored to meet the needs of children with a range of special needs and families of diverse socioeconomic and cultural backgrounds. The components are adaptable to programs with differing philosophies, resources, and curricula. The decision-making process is used by parents and staff to develop and implement service plans for the child and family. Likewise, this framework facilitates team building and fosters parent–professional collaboration.

The Theoretical Model

There is growing recognition of the importance of having a theoretical rationale for early intervention, especially one that incorporates an ecologically based systems approach (Fenichel & Eggbeer, 1990; Sameroff & Fiese, 1990). This orientation, which views the person interacting with the environment, considers the transactions within the family as well as those of the family within the community. As a frame of reference for intervention, the model of the coping process provides a relevant theoretical foundation for linking child, family, and environmental interactions. The model emphasizes the enhancement of coping resources that enable the child and family to manage current and future challenges and opportunities. This approach has a positive theme, focusing on adaptation and growth rather than pathology.

The Decison-Making Model

Perhaps the most dramatic change in the field of early intervention is the trend toward collaboration between parents and service providers. Currently, parents and professionals are moving away from the role of the professional who directs and controls events toward the achievement of true partnerships. For this approach to be most effective, new skills are required of all participants. The decision-making model described in Chapter 5 uses a sequence of facilitative questions as a structure to foster communication and mutual problem solving. The model can be applied in many ways, ranging from program planning to supporting informal exchanges. It is particularly helpful in the development of individualized family service plans (IFSPs), which were mandated in Public Law 99-457, the Education of the Handicapped Act Amendments of 1986, and its subsequent reauthorization, Public Law 102-119, the Individuals with Disabilities Education Act Amendments of 1991. These plans designate the goals and outcomes that are desired, the services the child and family are to receive, and the activities used to achieve them.

Intervention Options

The field of early intervention is shifting from a primary focus on the remediation of isolated deficits to an emphasis on the integrated, functional application of skills in daily living. This practical orientation is based on the importance of effective transactions to support coping and learning. Therefore, intervention within this context addresses the concrete realities of everyday experiences and involves the following options to enhance the adaptive competence of the child and to support the family: modifying demands, expanding coping resources, and providing contingent feedback. Developmental skills— a critical coping resource—are taught in ways that foster adaptation (e.g., assisting the child to manage new or difficult situations). There is concern about the fit between the individual's resources and environmental demands and expectations. Intervention services draw from a whole range of methods and activities to achieve an optimal fit.

HISTORICAL TRENDS

To appreciate how this frame of reference for planning and implementing early intervention services evolved, it is helpful to review certain historical trends that have influenced its development—changing views of infancy, the shift to family-centered intervention, and the role of government in early intervention.

Changing Perceptions of Infancy as Related to Professional Practice

Modes of intervention reflect the ways young children are perceived by adults. Around the turn of the century, infants were viewed as essentially helpless and incompetent. Their needs were considered primarily biological and medical. The main focus, therefore, was on the delivery of health care. For example, the specialty of pediatric medicine emerged during this time and hospitals created nurseries in which to isolate newborns, minimizing their risk of infection.

Over the years this concern became more targeted to the needs of premature newborns. These infants first received care in a "station" at the Sarah Morris Hospital in Chicago in 1922. The unit was provided with specially trained nurses as well as incubators to regulate the body temperature of the infants. The first city-wide program for preterm infants was developed in Chicago in 1934. By 1970, intensive care units for infants biologically at risk were established throughout the United States (Zeitlin, 1984).

Concurrent with this movement, theorists in child development, such as Gesell (1940) and Piaget (1952), began to pay increased attention to the period of infancy and demonstrated that the greatest growth in physical, cognitive, affective, and linguistic skills occur during the first 5 or 6 years of life. This insight lent support to the need for intervention as early as possible. Behaviorists, such as Skinner (1953), provided a technology for arranging the child's environment to increase and enhance development. Sameroff and Chandler (1975) recognized the importance of the transactional effects of familial, social, and environmental factors on the child's development.

The relevance of these findings to early intervention lay in the growing awareness of the interplay of external and internal factors. It was recognized that some developmental delays can be traced to environmental causes, and that the severity of physical damage can be ameliorated by modifying the environment. With this expanding appreciation of development, there was increased recognition of the range of children and families who can benefit from early intervention. This population can now be described in three categories.

1. *Children with established risk* are those with developmental disabilities, such as cerebral palsy, Down syndrome, or spina bifida, or those with functional delays in specific areas of development.
2. *Children who are biologically at risk* are those who have early health factors that are known to be a potential threat to their developmental outcome. Common risk factors include small-for-gestational-age, neonatal seizures, symptomatic drug withdrawal, and perinatal asphyxia.
3. *Children who are environmentally at risk* are those for whom the postnatal physical or social environments are a vulnerability. Examples are infants who are abused or neglected, whose parents have mental illness, or who are living in conditions of extreme poverty.

These categories are not mutually exclusive. For example, children with physical disabilities also may be environmentally at risk if their parents are teenagers and unable to understand or manage their medical condition. Infants with low birth weight may at some point be diagnosed as having a disability if developmental delays persist. In this book, the term *children with special needs* is used to refer to children in all three categories. The coping-related approach is equally appropriate to each of these groups of children and their families.

Shift to Family-Centered Intervention

Intervention programs have shifted from an earlier focus on the child to a more family-centered perspective. The child-centered programs of former years emphasized primarily the achievement of developmental skills. In some programs, the staff provided all of the services and the involvement of parents was limited to such activities as transporting the child, providing information regarding the child's history, and receiving professional reports pertaining to the child's status and progress. In other programs, the opposite was the case—parents were expected to assume the major responsibility for intervention activities. The parent became the child's teacher and therapist with the guidance of professionals.

During this period, parents also played a very important role in advocating for services at the local and national levels. They were catalysts for the development of such organizations as United Cerebral Palsy and The Arc. Individually and through these organizations, parents were active in generating public awareness, raising funds, and lobbying for legislation.

Over time, programs started to provide other family-oriented services, such as parent support groups, educational workshops, and specialized activities for siblings. Although these services were regarded as worthwhile, they were viewed as supplementary in nature and separate from the child's program. Families were frequently treated as a homogeneous group with similar resources and needs. Consequently, whereas intervention strategies with the children were numerous, only common program-wide goals were developed for family involvement. Predetermined activities were conducted in which all families were usually expected to participate, with the assumption that each would benefit equally. This approach often left both the family and the staff frustrated.

With experience and changing legislation, a more diverse family-centered approach has evolved. The child is now viewed within the context of the family unit (Dunst, Johanson, Trivette, & Hamby, 1991). Thus, in the development of the family service plan, the concerns and priorities of all family members are considered. Activities are directed toward functional outcomes for the child and family. In addition, parents are collaborators in the planning and implementation of services as well as recipients of these services. Furthermore, activities are increasingly in naturalistic environments in which the community works together with the family.

Role of Government in Early Intervention

The thrust for change often requires legal mandates with accompanying financial support. During this century, a series of federal initiatives contributed to the establishment of a diverse service delivery system for young children and their families. The legislation reflects over time an increasingly family-centered approach. In the area of maternal and child health services, three legislative actions are of particular relevance. In 1912, the Children's Bureau was established by Congress to address concerns related to child welfare, such as physical health, infant mortality, and factors associated with disabling conditions. Next came passage of the Social Security Act in 1935 (Title V), which authorized the funding of three programs still active today—the Maternal and Child Health Services, Services for Crippled Children (now known as Children with Special Health Care Needs), and Child Welfare Services. In 1965, the Medicaid provisions of the Social Security Act implemented the Early and Periodic, Screening, Diagnosis and Treatment (EPSDT) Program to provide accessible medical and developmental services for children living in poverty. The emphasis was on prevention and early identification.

The first educationally oriented federal program for preschool children came in 1965 with the establishment of the Head Start program for children from economically disadvantaged circumstances. (In 1972, Head Start's services were extended by a congressional mandate to ensure that 10% of the program's enrollment would be available to children with disabling conditions.) In 1968, with the passage of Public Law 90-538 (the Handicapped Children's Early Education Assistance Act), the government authorized funds to create model demonstration projects to serve exceptional children under 5 years of age and their families. The Handicapped Children's Early Education Program (now renamed Early Education Program for Children with Disabilities) has played a seminal role in the development and dissemination of innovative practices.

The passage of Public Law 94-142 (the Education for All Handicapped Children Act) in 1975 was a legislative landmark. It ensured a free and appropriate public education and related services for all children of school age with disabilities. Although the law did not require children under 6 years of age to be served, financial assistance was provided to states to encourage the establishment of preschool programs.

In 1986, Public Law 99-457 amended Public Law 94-142 to include two main provisions. Section 619 of the law required states to provide the services mandated by Public Law 94-142 to eligible children from the age of 3 so they may qualify for any federal preschool funds. Part H established a discretionary program for states to develop a comprehensive, coordinated, multidisciplinary, interagency service delivery system for infants with developmental disabilities or delays and their families. States were then allowed to choose whether children who were biologically or environmentally at risk were eligible for services. A lead agency and interagency coordinating council were major vehicles for implementing this system. Families were recognized as recipients of services, with the individualized family service plan (IFSP) replacing the traditional individualized education program (IEP). Case management (i.e., service coordination) and procedural safeguards were also required. This law was updated in 1990 with passage of the Individuals with Disabilities Education Act (IDEA), Public Law 101-476. The new law extended the benefits of the earlier legislation. Changes in wording and expansion of some services reflected the importance of the family and the provision of services in natural environments to the maximum extent appropriate, including the home and community environments in which children without disabilities participate. An important coping-related change in wording is the replacement of the term *self-help skills* as an area of concern with the term *adaptive development*.

This brief historical overview highlighted evolving trends in early intervention focusing on children, families, and the role of government. Table 1.1 provides a summary of the changes that have occurred—and are still occurring—in the field of early intervention. It is generally believed that these changes represent a movement toward recommended practice; however, there is diversity among states and programs in their interpretation and implementation.

PROGRAM DEVELOPMENT

Three primary areas need to be addressed for program development: 1) law and policy, 2) the early intervention program, and 3) the IFSP. Because they are interrelated, these three areas must be considered individually as well as collectively and addressed along with the historical trends noted in Table 1.1. Federal law, particularly Public Law 99-457 and its subsequent reauthorization, provides directives for states to develop their early

Table 1.1. Evolving trends in early intervention

From	Toward
Focus on the individual	Focus on child–family–environment interactions
Uncoordinated services	A comprehensive interagency system
Isolated programs for special needs	Community-based services and activities
Child-centered intervention	Family-centered intervention
Professional decision making	Collaborative parent and professional decision making
Individual practitioners	Team approach that includes parents
Focus on deficits	Focus on strengths and resources
Outcome measure: Developmental skill acquisition	Outcome measure: Functional competence and well-being

intervention service system. States in turn formulate policies and evolve rules and regulations on the basis of which individual institutions establish their early intervention programs. In other words, program development occurs within the context of specific legal and policy requirements. Yet, within the parameters of this framework and the resources available, individual programs establish their own philosophy and develop a structure that is responsive to the characteristics, concerns, and priorities of the families they serve. Staff and family generate meaningful IFSPs when they achieve a good fit between family priorities and the resources of the program and community.

To facilitate an optimal fit between individual families and the services they desire, there is a need for theoretical and pragmatic approaches that build from and extend evolving concepts of best practices. This book responds to that challenge by providing models and processes that can guide personalized program development and implementation.

CHAPTER 2

The Coping Process

The birth of a child places many new demands on a family. The parents must adapt physically and psychologically to the added responsibility of providing care and nurturance for their infant. At the same time, they typically have a host of other demands, such as earning an income, maintaining a household, and attending to their personal concerns and those of others in the family. Likewise, siblings discover that daily routines and family dynamics are changing.

All family members, including the infant, bring their own needs, resources, and vulnerabilities to each interaction with the other members. How each person copes reciprocally influences the family system. From these moment-to-moment experiences, family members develop beliefs about themselves and the world, and their beliefs influence subsequent transactions. When there is a match or a good fit between individual and collective demands on the one hand and the family's resources to manage them on the other hand, there is a higher probability for successful adaptation.

A child who has a disability or who is at risk may generate even greater demands on the family (Gallagher, Beckman, & Cross, 1983; Hanzlik, 1989). It is important to recognize the impact of these additional demands, because the way in which the family copes will influence how the child develops, the family's overall functioning, and the parents' feelings of satisfaction and effectiveness as caregivers (Beckwith, 1990; Zeitlin & Williamson, 1988).

The family can be seen as one kind of group; as in any group, the members differ in their coping styles, levels of coping effectiveness, available resources, and the stressors in their lives. Support and help to the family enhances its chances of dealing adequately with the demands of life. Likewise, working collaboratively with family members to teach the child to cope is an important aim of intervention. Once resources have been developed to address a specific issue, they can then be generalized for use at other times. Through such efforts, families are more effectively enabled and empowered to care for their children with special needs and to maintain a quality of life for themselves. Furthermore, the children have the encouragement and support needed to develop their capabilities optimally.

To establish a common basis for personalized intervention planning, this chapter provides information about coping and the reciprocal coping transactions that influence living and learning. Some historical and theoretical background is given. In addition, key concepts are defined and a clinically useful model of the coping process is presented that describes coping from an individual perspective. The model is then applied to a coping transaction that shows the reciprocal interactions between the coping efforts of two people. The transactional model of the coping process is used as a basis for the observation and analysis of child and family interactions. Information can be collected about individual coping resources and vulnerabilities, and the impact of one on the other. This information is used for development of the individualized family service plan (IFSP). The model is also used to help family members understand how they cope with stress, to counsel families when difficult problems arise, and to help service providers be more aware of their own coping behavior and its influence on others. Also discussed is the concept of goodness of fit. This concept, which is based on the effectiveness of coping transactions, is applied in intervention planning.

The process of coping is universal and is equally applicable to everyone, including family members, staff, or any other person. Chapter 3 focuses on how these concepts apply to young children. Although the general process of coping is essentially the same for young children as for adults, there are developmental differences that need to be considered.

HISTORICAL OVERVIEW OF STRESS AND COPING

Present knowledge of stress and coping has evolved from diverse theories and research in medicine, psychology, and sociology. According to Lazarus and Folkman (1984), the term *stress* was used as early as the 14th century to mean hardship, straits, adversity, or affliction. In the late 17th century, it was used in the context of physical science regarding the impact of forces on objects, such as the stress of a bridge span. By the 19th century, the term had acquired a medical connotation—the impact of stress on the body had come to be viewed as a cause of ill health.

Cannon (1953) made a major contribution to the study of stress by describing the impact of environmental conditions such as temperature extremes on specific adaptive responses of the body. This work was later extended and popularized by Selye (1974, 1976), a physician who used the term *stress* to mean the way the body defended itself against any form of noxious stimulus, including psychological threats. He called this reaction the "general adaptation syndrome."

During this same period, concepts related to stress were perceived by psychologists as an organizing framework for thinking about pathology. They used the term *anxiety* rather than *stress*; the latter term first appeared in the Index of Psychological Abstracts in 1944. Sociologists, however, were interested in societal stress. They viewed riots, panics, and other social disturbances (e.g., the increased incidence of suicide, crime, and mental illness) as consequences of stress at the societal level.

Interest in coping evolved from an examination of how psychological stress was managed. While stress is an inevitable part of the human condition, it is coping that makes a difference in human functioning. It is the link between the two—coping with stress—that gives functional meaning to the two individual concepts.

The concept of coping provided an organizing theme for clinical descriptions and evaluation in the 1940s and 1950s and is currently the focus of an array of psychotherapies and educational programs that have a goal of developing coping skills. Coping is also a frequent subject in the media and in self-help books. Despite the popular fascination with coping, there is little agreement in the field regarding its definition, its assessment, or intervention practices.

In psychoanalytic theory, coping is defined as realistic and flexible thoughts and acts that solve problems and thereby reduce stress; the focus is on the person. Individuals have been classified according to coping style for the purpose of making predictions about how they would cope in most encounters. For example, a person may be classified as a conformist; an obsessive-compulsive; or a suppressor, repressor, or sublimator (Loevinger, 1976; Vaillant, 1977).

Another orientation, a behavioral approach, initially used the concepts of secondary and acquired drives to explain coping behavior (Dollard & Miller, 1950). Later, these ideas gave way to a view that emphasized cognition and motives (Bolles, 1974; Dember, 1974). In the earlier behavioral approach, drives were viewed as propelled by emotion. The shift came in viewing emotions (and stress) as deriving from the cognitive way a person perceives what is happening.

Stress and coping research prior to the mid-1970s was concerned mainly with adults in atypical circumstances of stress (Dohrenwend & Dohrenwend, 1974) or in laboratory-based situations (Lazarus, 1966). As early as 1952, Lazarus suggested that the analysis of stress in relationship to performance should take into account differences among individuals and their differing responses to task demands (Lazarus, Deese, & Osler, 1952). This was the initial stage in the development of what, during the next 30 years, Lazarus called the *transactional model*. This development paralleled a gradual movement in psychology from normative research to an increased emphasis on individual differences.

Much of the coping research has focused on adults, although there are some key studies with children. Early investigators—for example, the W.T. Grant Foundation, which commissioned a study in 1937—acknowledged that individuals differ in the way they make adaptations and sought to identify the characteristics of lifestyle and personality associated with successful outcomes.

One result of early work in coping was identification of some of the many mediating variables, or factors, that relate to adaptational differences. These mediating factors include social support (Moos, 1976); cognitive processes and specific beliefs (Bandura, 1986; Beck, 1976; Ellis & Greiger, 1977; Lazarus, 1966); anxiety, positive affect, self-concept, physical health, income, and locus of control (Antonovsky, 1979, 1987; Rutter, 1983); specific coping-related behaviors (Murphy & Moriarty, 1976; Zeitlin, 1985); and a host of specific personality characteristics. In addition, Holmes and Rahe (1967) identified and ranked life events that are traditionally viewed as stressful, such as death, divorce, relocation, and birth of a child.

Lois Murphy and her colleagues at the Menninger Clinic were among the first to study coping in children. They conducted an 18-year longitudinal study of the coping behaviors of a sample of 60 middle-class children in Topeka, Kansas (Murphy & Moriarty, 1976). Information about the children was collected over time through observations and formal and informal assessment. Analysis of the data identified the behaviors most closely related to effective coping, as well as the behaviors and situations that tended to increase the children's vulnerability.

Another important longitudinal investigation (Werner, 1989; Werner & Smith, 1982, 1991) was of the children born in 1955 on the Hawaiian island of Kauai—an island whose people are mostly poor and have many risk factors in their lives. Examples of risk factors included perinatal stress, parental psychopathology, and disruptions in the family unit. Major follow-up reports on these high-risk children were conducted when they were 18 and 32 years of age. This research was more information-oriented, identifying factors in the lives of these children that generated invincibility or vulnerability, such as age, sex, birth order, family make-up, and a number of specific risk factors. Two trends were noted in this longitudinal study: 1) the impact of reproductive stress diminished with time, and 2) the developmental outcome of practically every biological risk factor was dependent on the quality of the caregiving environment.

Children living in chronic psychosocial adversity, such as children of parents with schizophrenia, have also been investigated (Garmezy & Rutter, 1983; Greenspan, 1981). There was an interest in understanding why some of these children seemed resilient, while over time many others developed problems such as school failure, delinquency, and drug abuse. Results of these studies suggested three major protective factors that promote healthy outcomes: 1) a positive disposition, such as an engaging personality; 2) a responsive family milieu; and 3) external social support for the child and family. Of particular importance was the availability of at least one consistent primary caregiver who buffered the child from stress and provided essential nurturance.

The authors conducted a large, field-based study of the coping characteristics of children with and without disabilities (Zeitlin & Williamson, 1990). The sample consisted of 1,035 children with developmental delays or disabilities and 405 children without disabilities, all of whom ranged in age from 4 to 36 months. The coping ability of the group with disabilities was significantly less effective than the coping ability of the group without disabilities in all three categories of the Early Coping Inventory (Zeitlin, Williamson, & Szczepanski, 1988)—sensorimotor organization, reactivity, and self-initiation. The infants and toddlers with disabilities tended as a group to have minimally to situationally effective coping styles, whereas the children with typical development coped effectively more often than not. The coping styles of the children with disabilities tended to be more erratic, inconsistent, and inflexible.

However, both groups of children demonstrated the entire range of coping effectiveness. This finding confirms that the presence of a disability does not necessarily imply that a child will have an ineffective coping style. Instead, it suggests that a child with special needs may be more vulnerable to the stress of daily living.

A comparison of the most and least adaptive coping behaviors of the two groups is also of clinical interest. Both groups were relatively competent in their ability to accept warmth and support from familiar persons and to respond to a variety of visual and auditory stimuli. For the group without disabilities, the least adaptive coping behaviors were:

Finding a way to handle a new or difficult situation
Managing frustration
Using behavior appropriate to situations
Bouncing back after stressful events

The least adaptive coping behaviors for the group with disabilities were related to self-initiation, such as the ability to:

Change behavior when necessary to solve a problem
Enter new situations with ease or caution as the occasion demands
Try a new behavior on one's own
Balance independent behavior with necessary dependance on adults

It is important to note, however, that even the least adaptive coping behavior of the sample without disabilities was in the range of functional competence. In contrast, the least adaptive behavior for the group with disabilities ranged from minimally to situationally effective. Of particular relevance to clinical practice is the finding that the most significant difference between the two groups was in the area of self-initiation. As a group, the infants and toddlers with disabilities tended to be passive or demonstrated a poor quality of self-generated coping.

In this study, the sample without disabilities was further divided by family income above and below $10,000 per year. The children without disabilities from economically disadvantaged circumstances were significantly less effective than their peers without disabilities from more affluent families in the three categories of the Early Coping Inventory. They were relatively less skillful in their ability to anticipate events, engage in reciprocal social interactions, generalize learning, enter new situations appropriately, and be persistent during activities. This finding supports the need to monitor the coping status of children living in poverty because they may be at risk regarding their adaptive functioning.

THE COPING PROCESS MODEL

Foundations of the Model

The concepts underlying the coping process model and its application to intervention were derived from field theory and perceptual, humanistic, and cognitive-behavioral psychology. Lewin (1951) used the term *field* to describe the combination of two elements: the person and his or her environmental context at a given moment in time. He viewed behavior as an outcome of the interaction of these two elements. A change in either influences the whole field. According to perceptual psychology, "human behavior is always a product of how people see themselves and the situations in which they are involved . . . . Our perceptions of ourselves and the world are so real to us that we seldom pause to doubt them" (Combs, Avila, & Purkey, 1978, p. 15). The recognition that individuals experience their own subjective perception of events provides a starting point in the attempt to account for the unique differences in the ways people cope.

The following are some additional critical assumptions drawn from the perceptual literature (Purkey & Schmidt, 1987):

Perceptions can exist at many levels of awareness.
Individuals can be highly selective in what they choose to focus on, and they are quite unique in their selection.
What individuals choose to perceive is in great part influenced by their past experiences, present motives, and expectations.
People tend to believe that others see events as they do.
Effective helping and communication depends on a mutual understanding of the other's perceptual reality.

Contributions in humanistic psychology provide further important insights (Maslow, 1954; May, 1972). Rogers (1961) stresses that all individuals, from the infant to the oldest among us, have a desire to enhance their ability to adapt successfully to their environment. In general, humanistic psychology highlights the following features: 1) the uniqueness and "wholeness" of every individual; 2) an emphasis on "here and now" functioning; 3) a belief in the individual's potential for growth, responsibility, and self-actualization; and 4) a focus on mastery through the enhancement of strengths, resources, and abilities.

Cognitive-behavioral psychology recognizes the vital role that beliefs, cognitions, and perceptions have in influencing both behavior and emotions. Psychologists such as Lazarus (1966), Beck and Emery (1985), and Meichenbaum (1985) described how individuals use cognitive appraisals to manage physical, emotional, and mental experiences. These appraisals are the way an individual construes the significance of an event to his or her well-being. Cognitive appraisals are used to give meaning to internal and external tensions, guide decision making, influence adaptations, and evaluate the outcome of any coping effort. This cognitive-behavioral approach also helps focus attention on the personal resources available to the individual for use in the process of coping. In the words of

Lazarus and DeLongis (1983): "People are rarely passive in the face of what happens to them; they seek to change things if they can, and when they cannot, they use cognitive modes of coping by which they may change the meaning of the situation" (p. 248).

Key Concepts

There are many different definitions of coping and stress, as well as ways to conceptualize their relationship. The reader is referred to the professional literature for further discussion of the various theoretical orientations and their divergent perspectives (e.g., Antonovsky, 1987; Dohrenwend, Dohrenwend, Dodson, & Shrout, 1984; Fine, 1991; Hobfoll, 1989; Lazarus & Folkman, 1984). On the following pages, the two concepts are defined and discussed within the frame of reference of this book.

Coping   Coping is the process of making adaptations to meet personal needs and to respond to the demands of the environment. In the coping process, personal resources are used to manage the routines, frustrations, threats, and challenges of daily living in ways that seek to maintain or enhance feelings of well-being.

Coping involves learned adaptational actions. It can be placed at the middle of a continuum that ranges from reflexes present at birth at one end, to automatic (habitual) responses at the other end that are so well learned and integrated that they no longer require active effort. Much that individuals do to adapt is habitual and does not necessarily involve stress or effort. Thus, the process of coping is viewed as being directed to the generation of effortful responses and does not include reflexive or automatic behaviors. Coping can therefore be considered a subset of the broader concept of adaptation. Although this distinction is not always clear, especially with infants, it prevents the pitfall of defining coping so broadly that it includes everything that an individual does when relating to the environment (Compas, 1987; Williamson, Zeitlin, & Szczepanski, 1989).

Whereas coping is a process, *coping efforts* are the specific actions taken to manage tension-generating events. They are cognitive or behavioral strategies used to manage perceived demands. The effectiveness of coping efforts may range from being consistently ineffective to consistently effective across situations. In contrast, *coping style* refers to the way an individual routinely uses certain types of strategies, rather than others, to manage the world. Although the term portrays a characteristic way of behaving (i.e., typical behavioral patterns), it does not describe the specific actions an individual will use in a particular situation.

Stress   Stress is a tension experienced when an event is perceived as being harmful, threatening, or challenging to one's feelings of well-being. It may be experienced cognitively, emotionally, or physically; usually there is some combination of all three elements. From the perspective of the authors, stress results from the initial perception of an event and is not the result of failed coping. Stress interpreted as harmful or threatening tends to have a negative inference; stress perceived as a challenge, however, is often associated with positive, energizing emotions.

Whereas stress is a reaction, *stressors* are the actual events that elicit the reaction. Stressors can be events in the external environment or internal events such as thoughts and physical sensations. An event can have different meanings for different people or the same person at different points in time. Elliot and Eisdorfer (1982) classified stressors into four types:

1. Acute, time-limited stressors, such as waiting for the results of a medical test, rushing to an appointment for which one is late, or trying to find a lost toddler on a playground

2. Stressor sequences (i.e., series of events) that occur during an extended period of time as the result of an initiating event, such as divorce, bereavement, or job promotion
3. Chronic, intermittent stressors, such as conflict-filled visits to in-laws, recurring hospitalizations for orthopedic surgery, or finding new child care arrangements
4. Chronic stressors that persist over time, such as living in poverty, managing the impact of a disability, or trying to lose weight

In this book, stressors are broadly defined and not limited to major adverse events. They are often reflected in the rather ordinary demands of daily living. A sibling experiences stress when his or her repeated requests for attention are ignored while the parent is changing the baby's diaper. Both parent and child experience stress the first time a child is left with a new babysitter. A toddler experiences stress struggling to retrieve a ball that is out of reach, from the pain of a scraped knee, or from learning to ride a tricycle.

Events are perceived as threatening when one feels that personal resources are inadequate to manage them effectively. Because of this perception, negative expectations and emotions may be evoked. Events are interpreted as harmful when similar situations have already damaged one's feelings of well-being. However, events are viewed as challenging when one feels that one's resources are sufficient. Challenging events are seen as being generative in nature, as facilitating mastery and creativity. Such experiences often elicit positive expectations and emotions.

In actuality, many events generate some combination of feelings of threat and challenge. For instance, a young couple may experience both threatening and challenging forms of stress when they give their first big party for their extended family. They may be excited about showing their new apartment (challenge), but anxious that everyone may not get along or that the meal may not be very good (threat). An example from a toddler's perspective is learning to bounce down stairs on her buttocks. She may be eager to undertake this motoric adventure (challenge), but fearful that she may hurt herself (threat).

Steps in the Coping Process

Each person copes with stress in his or her unique way. However, the overall process is the same for all, regardless of age, culture, life experience, or the many different variables that influence coping efforts. Because of the complexity of these variables and the interrelationships among them, a systems approach is used to describe the coping process.

Stress may be experienced physically, mentally, or emotionally—or in all three ways simultaneously. But in each instance coping efforts of the individual are guided by a sequence of cognitive appraisals and emotional reactions. The cognitive appraisals give meaning to internal and external tensions, guide decision making for coping with the stress, and evaluate the outcome of the coping effort. During the coping process, emotional reactions influence cognition and vice versa. Even very young children make appraisals, in accordance with their level of development.

The coping process is transactional—behaviors result from ongoing interactions between people and their environments, each acting on and reacting to the other. The coping process model, however, describes the coping efforts of only one party in a transaction. In the model, coping is delineated as a four-step process: 1) determine the meaning of the event, 2) develop an action plan to deal with it, 3) implement the plan (the coping effort), and 4) evaluate the effectiveness of the outcome. (See Figure 2.1.) No step is independent of the others; all steps are interrelated.

Step 1: Determine the Meaning of the Event The first step in reaction to an event is to address the following questions: What is the meaning of this event?, and How does it

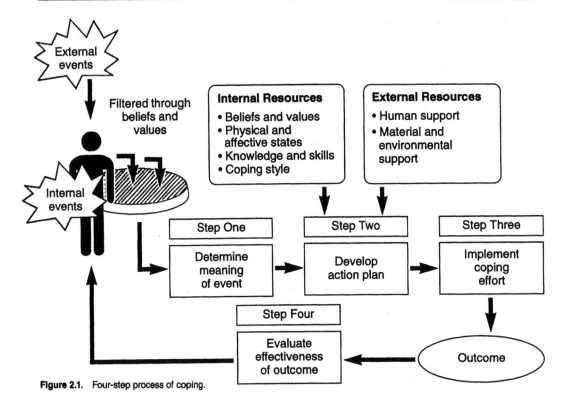

Figure 2.1. Four-step process of coping.

affect my well-being? The event may be a situation or demand in the environment, an internal feeling or physical change, or some combination of the two.

No external or internal event is inherently stressful, although some very traumatic events, such as serious illness, the death of a loved one, or an earthquake, are almost universally perceived that way. Meaning is given to the event through the filter of a person's beliefs and values. Beliefs are what one thinks is true; values reflect what one wants or prefers. Together they provide a structure for the individual's perception of the world and shape personal expectations for outcomes.

Events that generate feelings of stress may be perceived as being threatening, harmful, or challenging. Whereas threatening and harmful events have a negative connotation, challenging events are perceived as being generative in nature, facilitating mastery, creativity, and positive emotions. Families experience this whole range of feelings. A family's perception of stress may reflect the reaction of one of its members to an event, the reactions of other family members to the event, and the reactions of family members to one another. Perceptions of stress are filtered not only through individual beliefs about personal function, but also through beliefs about the family as a unit.

Step 2: Develop an Action Plan   In the second step of the coping process, one asks such questions as: What can I do?, What will managing this stressor cost me in terms of time and effort?, and What do I expect to be the outcome?

Decision making, both immediate and long-term, is influenced by such factors as the amount of stress perceived, what other stressors the person is having to cope with at the time, social and situational constraints, expectations for outcome (including personal and social consequences), the probability of success, and the personal cost of the effort. Critical to decision making are the coping options provided by the person's internal and external resources—personal beliefs and values, physical and affective states, coping style, knowledge and skills, human supports, and material and environmental supports (Lazarus & Folkman, 1984; McCubbin & Thompson, 1991; Turnbull & Turnbull, 1990; Williamson et al., 1993). (These resources are discussed in greater detail later in the chapter.)

Step 3: Implement the Coping Effort The third step in the coping process is to act on the decision, making either a coping effort or a reappraisal of the event. Reappraisal is the result of a changed belief because of new information or new perceptions (Lazarus & Folkman, 1984). For example, a child's disability may become less threatening to his parents when the parents acquire knowledge that encourages them to believe they can do something to help their child.

Coping strategies are intrinsically neither good nor bad. Their value is determined by the outcomes they generate. For example, parents who are experiencing stress because of lack of information about their child's condition may consult a specialist or read an appropriate book. Either strategy has the potential to generate an effective outcome.

Coping efforts may be classified as problem-focused, emotion-focused, psychological, physiological, or some combination of the four. Efforts are directed to responding to the requirements of the situation and also to one's feelings about what is happening. Problem-focused efforts are task-oriented and directed to managing or altering the source of stress. They include seeking information or help, formulating a plan, trying different solutions, or even preventing an event or action from taking place. Emotion-focused efforts manage the feelings related to the stress. They include expressing feelings by showing anger, distress, withdrawal, amusement, and so forth; seeking emotional support from others; or doing something to make oneself feel better.

Psychological efforts are aimed at reducing stress by redirecting thinking. A person defends against having thoughts that are threatening or harmful. For example, a father left alone with his baby for the first time may feel tension about his ability to handle the situation if the baby starts to cry hysterically. He may then rationalize that there is nothing to be concerned about or deny that he really experienced these thoughts. When this rationalization or denial occurs, no further action is taken. These defenses may be successful for alleviating distress in the short term, but they may inhibit the mobilization of long-term coping resources and the generation of effective coping efforts.

Physiological efforts include management of physical tension through such action as the use of relaxation techniques, physical activities (e.g., walking, exercising, running), or sleeping. Another form of coping may be the development of somatic symptoms such as headaches, allergies, or pains. Each type of coping effort influences the other and may facilitate or impede the outcome.

Step 4: Evaluate the Effectiveness of the Outcome Coping efforts may generate outcomes ranging from totally ineffective to fully effective. The effectiveness of a specific coping strategy can be judged only by its developmental appropriateness, its suitability to the situation, and the outcome it generates. Effective coping leads to desired outcomes that reinforce a person's sense of competence and encourage future coping efforts. Ineffective coping often generates an unwillingness to try to manage similar situations, brings additional stress, and creates feelings of inadequacy.

To cope effectively, a person must have the resources to change what can be changed or to make the best choices in response to what cannot be changed. Effective short- and long-term outcomes reduce tension, generate a successful adaptation in the individual or the environment, help to maintain a positive self-image, and foster satisfying relationships with others. Long-term effectiveness sustains health, morale, and social and psychological functioning. The outcome of family members' coping efforts has an impact on the child's development and coping efforts. The following is an example from daily living:

➡   Mrs. Rodriguez has difficulty coping with and completing her daily routine of house-
      keeping and meal preparation. She does not have time to play with Louisa and she may
      hurry Louisa's feeding. For Louisa, this generates a feeling of tension and contributes to
      a belief that the world is neither a safe nor satisfying place. As a consequence, Louisa is
      cranky and less responsive. Mrs. Rodriguez then feels more tense and develops a belief
      that she is not an adequate parent. In addition, extra demands created by Louisa's dis-
      ability are either ignored or responded to curtly.

As can be seen in this example, the outcome of each coping effort adds to the individual's life experience and influences future coping efforts.

    Although the coping model is depicted in four separate steps, no part of it is independent. There is a constant and reciprocal interrelationship among the parts. Action in any part of the system has consequences for other parts of the system. Thus, breakdown can occur or change can be initiated at any point in the process.

    This model of the coping process is a practical one that can be used for three distinct purposes: education, planning, and intervention. Educationally, it is employed to help parents and staff understand the dynamics that influence their coping efforts. In the program planning phase, the model is used to analyze transactions and collect information about coping strengths and vulnerabilities. Intervention to enhance child or family coping can proceed from any step in the process where difficulties exist. Intervention activities are directed toward reducing stressors and/or enhancing one or more of the six personal resources that influence coping efforts, which are discussed below.

COPING RESOURCES

Coping outcomes are influenced by available resources. In different situations, cultures, and age ranges, some resources contribute more than others to effective coping. Because of their critical importance, each resource is discussed.

Beliefs and Values

Beliefs and values not only give meaning to a tension-generating event, but they can be either a resource or a cause of vulnerability in decision making (i.e., beliefs and values can either help or hinder the coping process). *Beliefs* concern what a person thinks is true, regardless of what he or she likes or approves. They are developed from life experience and often reflect the customs and values of society. Beliefs relevant for coping seem to be of two broad types: beliefs about personal control over events and religious beliefs.

    Beliefs about personal control include beliefs about one's ability to master new learning, personal effectiveness, self-esteem, and sense of self in the world. Beliefs shape expectations for the outcome of actions, provide a source of hope, and are part of the effort to create meaning from life. Therefore, they significantly affect the whole coping process. When family members believe they will be able to influence the outcome of their child with a disability, they are better able to cope with the demands of an intervention program. People with rigid or extreme beliefs often ignore options available to them and engage in behaviors that may have self-defeating emotional and behavioral consequences. When a parent believes that his or her child's condition is a form of personal punishment for some previous behavior, such as taking drugs or maintaining an inadequate diet, interactions with the child may be hampered. For example, the parent may avoid eye contact or be uncomfortable cuddling the infant. Beliefs may be rational (i.e., based on reality) or irrational (i.e., stemming from a misperception). When family members or professionals working with the family have very different belief systems, communication about the meaning of or reaction to particular events may be difficult.

Values reflect a person's desires or preferences. They contribute to setting personal goals and motivate a commitment to achieving those goals. Events that are strongly related to held values are interpreted as being important if they threaten or enhance those values. For families, the birth of a child with a disability may require shifts in long-standing commitments. For example, a family that values high academic achievement may find it more difficult to cope with a child with mental retardation than a family who values each member being happy doing the best he or she can without a predetermined standard of achievement.

Physical and Affective States

As a coping resource, *physical state* includes one's general health and current physiological condition (e.g., level of hunger or fatigue). It is easy to appreciate the deleterious impact of a headache, a cold, or lack of sleep on coping. The relationship between stress and illness (real or imagined) is well established (Antonovsky, 1987). A parent's long-term illness may threaten his or her self-esteem, particularly when the parent is unable to participate actively in the family routine. As a consequence, the parent may be unclear about his or her role as an individual and within the family. All family members are likely to feel the impact of one another's physical and affective states.

Affective state refers to an individual's emotions and moods. It influences a person's evaluation of an event, how the person looks and acts, and the way others respond to that person. Affect may be a source of strength or of vulnerability in the generation of coping efforts. For example, feeling anger may generate awareness that leads to appropriate actions to solve a conflict, or the anger may be turned inward in a self-destructive manner that may lead to chronic depression. Feelings of depression make it difficult to generate the energy to do daily activities. Thus, depressed parents may have problems caring for their children.

The display of a positive affect fuels interaction and engagement.

➡ Kenny, a young infant in a chronic care hospital, had a limited ability to relate. However, he had a very warm, friendly smile. As a result, the staff interacted with him in preference to other children who tended to display a flat affect.

Knowledge and Skills

The acquisition of knowledge and skills takes place with the unfolding of the developmental process. Although there is an overall similarity in sequence of development, each individual has a personal timetable and unique pattern. *Knowledge* is a body of information gained from formalized learning and life experience. *Skills* can be considered an application of knowledge. They range from relatively simple, concrete abilities, such as the ability to brush one's teeth, to proficiency in a particular area, such as solving advanced mathematical equations.

Initially, most parents of infants with special needs have minimal information about their child's medical condition. They have little knowledge about what to expect and, therefore, may feel particularly vulnerable in this situation. They typically want additional information as early and quickly as possible.

Coping Style

Each individual has a personal repertoire of coping characteristics and behaviors. They are expressed in what is called a coping style—the way the person habitually uses certain behavioral patterns instead of others to manage events interpreted as threatening, harmful, or challenging. These coping behaviors develop from birth and they evolve over time. They are shaped by the person's temperament, pattern of development, level of competence, prior experience, and specific values, as well as the demands of the environment (Murphy & Moriarty, 1976).

Behaviors related to effective coping include task-oriented behaviors, such as staying with an activity until it is completed; interactive behaviors, such as reacting to social cues in the environment; emotional behaviors, such as being able to express anger or love; and psychological behaviors, such as asking for help when it is needed. Children with effective coping styles generally have a positive self-concept, tend to achieve their goals, and attribute their success to their own efforts (DiBuono, 1982; Kennedy, 1984; Larson, 1984; Zeitlin, 1981).

Human Supports

Support from others helps to modify the tension of people who are experiencing stressful physiological and psychological events. *Human support* is obtained from interpersonal relationships that involve at least one of the following: information giving, tangible support involving direct assistance, and emotional support that contributes to the feeling that one is loved and cared about.

Support ranges from that provided by intimates, such as parents, spouses, or close friends, to the support given by community agencies and various professionals. Being part of a social network does not, in itself, ensure the receipt of support. Networks may be nonsupportive for many reasons, including differing beliefs and values, and attitudes about disabling conditions. Interpersonal problems may limit an individual's ability to establish and maintain relationships with supportive people. It is important not only to have people who are willing to give support, but also to be able to receive support.

Changing life events may alter or eliminate a person's support system. Having a child with a disability may contribute to isolation from people who were previously supportive and may create a need for new resources more sympathetic to the changed circumstances. Parents may develop meaningful new friendships as a result.

Material and Environmental Supports

Material support, such as money, offers improved security and the ability to purchase goods, services, and supportive technologies. Material resources are necessary for basic comfort, to support the quality of life, and to enable an individual to purchase what is needed when it is needed. The need may be actual, potential, apparent, or fantasized. It is an added source of stress when the material needs of one family member deprive other members of desired comforts (e.g., when a sibling cannot go to summer camp because the family has extensive medical bills).

Environmental supports are based on the physical condition of an individual's surroundings. For example, a person can cope better in an environment that includes fresh air and ample space and light. In contrast, one may not cope as well in an environment of poverty in the inner city, because it is often crowded, violent, and lacking in basic amenities. The multidimensional stress of everyday living is greater in these urban neighborhoods.

COPING TRANSACTIONS

The Transactional Process

As noted previously, coping is a transactional process. It is affected by the demands and reciprocal coping efforts of another person. The reciprocal exchanges occurring within a family are critical for all members of the family. Within transactions, the child and adult learn new behaviors, acquire specific beliefs, modify existing behavioral patterns, and adapt to new experiences. The quality, quantity, and character of the child-parent-family-environment transactions greatly influence the development and coping behaviors of each party in the exchange.

Many theoretical models have been proposed to explain how human transactions affect those involved. Although the models vary, some critical elements are shared by all. First, the transaction is not one way (linear), but circular. Second, each transaction is reciprocal. A stimulus event generates a demand that the child reacts to by making a coping effort. The adult then makes a responsive coping effort that may support (or not support) the child's management of the demand, give evaluative feedback, or generate a new demand. Each participant internalizes his or her perception of the outcome of the experience.

A transaction may consist of a single interaction or many interactions generated by a chain of events. The word *interaction* is used to refer to a single exchange between two individuals. It can be considered a reciprocal action or influence. The *transaction* is the entire process and refers to carrying on or conducting an activity to a conclusion or settlement. Each transaction consists of a demand generated by an internal or external event, a coping effort to manage the event, the environment's response to that effort, and the evaluation and internalization of the experience (see Figure 2.2).

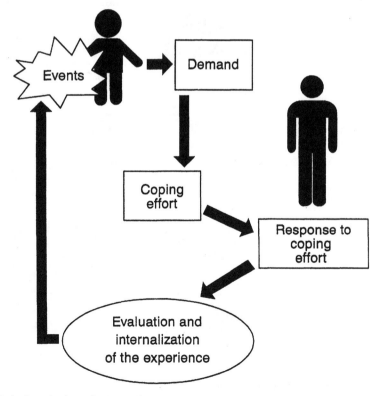

Figure 2.2. Basic elements of a coping transaction.

The following illustration shows how transactions can influence the child's adaptation to daily living. A preterm birth may produce a small, weak newborn who, with adequate nutrition and a responsive environment, is able to develop normally. Whereas some parents respond to a fragile infant with solicitude, others become impatient with the difficulties in feeding. They may stop the feeding sessions too early and thereby provide less than adequate nutrition. The result is a miserable baby who is not available for social interaction. Even a single incident may set up a transactional chain. For instance, a baby that has a severe choking episode when bottle feeding may tend to reject the bottle on subsequent occasions.

Reciprocal coping efforts are the basis for analyzing transactions. Figure 2.3 describes a transaction with numerous coping efforts. The coping effort of the observed person is the event that establishes a demand for the responsive effort of the other person. This

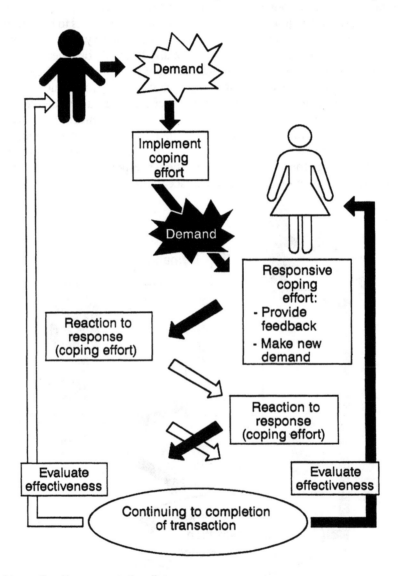

Figure 2.3. A transaction with numerous coping efforts.

individual may cope by providing supportive or evaluative feedback and/or by making a new demand, which, in turn, becomes the event requiring an additional coping effort by the observed person. These reciprocal coping efforts may continue until an outcome is achieved.

Goodness of Fit

The most effective coping outcomes are generated when there is a "good fit" between the demands a person has to cope with and the resources available to manage the situation (Thomas & Chess, 1980; Williamson, 1993; Williamson et al., 1993). "Goodness of fit" does not necessarily imply an absence of stress and conflict, but rather the availability of resources to manage stress and conflict. "Poorness of fit" can occur if the environmental demands and expectations are excessive, even for an individual with good resources. As illustrated in Figure 2.4, there is a good fit in the transaction when the following conditions are met.

- Demands are appropriate in that they are congruent with each individual's capability to meet them.
- The individual has the personal resources to make an effective coping effort.
- The environment provides appropriate supportive and evaluative feedback.

When there is more than one demand in the transaction, conflict may occur (e.g., when a service provider wants the child to perform a particular activity and the child wants to do something else). Conflict is defined as the simultaneous presence of two demands requiring contradictory responses. The essential problem in conflict is that the goal of one of the participants in the transaction is endangered by that of the other or threatened by the other's gratification. A transaction that is effective for both parties cannot occur unless there is some resolution of the conflict. Sometimes an adult must make a demand that at that moment conflicts with the child's wishes. This usually happens when the adult believes the child will benefit over time from the transaction. The demand may also reflect some special need of the adult.

The concept of goodness of fit provides the basis for categorizing major approaches to intervention. These options, discussed in greater detail in Chapters 7 and 8, this volume, involve the following guidelines.

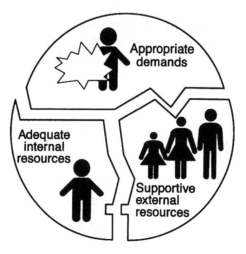

Figure 2.4. Goodness of fit.

- Modify demands so they are congruent with the individual's ability to meet them.
- Enhance internal and external coping resources.
- Change the environment's response to the coping efforts.

    For intervention purposes, the impact of the transactions and the coping efforts of each of the participants should be considered. In most early intervention programs there are four key transactions to be considered: 1) between the child and other family members, 2) between the family as a whole and the service providers, 3) between the child and the service providers, and 4) between the child and other children.

ASPECTS OF COPING

In conclusion, the following is a summary of the various aspects of coping:

- The components of the coping process are the same for all individuals regardless of age, sex, culture, or intelligence; however, the specific strategies for implementing coping efforts vary.
- Coping outcomes are influenced by available internal and external resources. In different situations, cultures, and age ranges, some resources contribute to effective coping more than others.
- Coping is an integrated process related to but different from any single contributing variable, such as intelligence, language, temperament, or social competence.
- The coping process is transactional—the transactions are between persons or between the person and objects in the environment.
- The coping process is circular—actions generate reactions that in turn generate new actions.
- Coping styles are relatively consistent for most people.
- A coping style can be identified when a person is observed over time in a variety of transactions.
- Coping strategies are learned; therefore, they can be acquired, changed, or eliminated through personal experiences.

SUMMARY

This chapter highlights the key coping concepts and the theoretical base that supports this frame of reference in clinical practice. The coping process and its functional application through transactions in daily living provide the foundation for intervention.

CHAPTER 3

Adaptive Functioning in Young Children

Children develop through the unfolding of their genetic characteristics in transactions with their environment (Sameroff & Fiese, 1990). Coping is the process they employ to manage these transactions. Development progresses from a globally undifferentiated state to one of increasing refinement of motor, affective, and cognitive skills. The child evolves from a state of near total dependence to one of greater interdependence and autonomy. The process begins at conception, with rapid and profound changes taking place during the first 3 years of life. This process is applicable to all children—whether they have disabilities or are typically developing. For children with disabilities (depending on the degree of involvement), the pace may be slower and the changes less noticeable.

This chapter addresses issues related to coping in young children. First, it discusses the adaptive capabilities of very young infants, emphasizing their temperamental characteristics. Next, development from a coping perspective is examined. The acquisition of motor control in infancy is used to illustrate how increasing skills in this developmental domain influence the child's adaptive functioning. Then an integrated view is presented of the developmental expansion of coping competence in the initial 3 years of life. Next, the model of the coping process is reviewed as it pertains to young children, with special emphasis on their coping resources. Finally, coping is placed within the focused context of transactions between child and caregiver.

ADAPTIVE CAPABILITIES AT BIRTH

From the moment of birth, an infant responds to internal and external events by a predetermined genetic program of reflexes, fixed behavior patterns, and temperamental characteristics. The impetus to act and receive information from the environment is based on the child's genetic characteristics and the functioning of the central nervous system. The following are universal adaptive capabilities that typically developing infants demonstrate at birth.

- An infant is born with *fixed behavior patterns and reflexes*. These are sensorimotor patterns that are activated to aid in adaptation and survival. A partial list includes: sucking, head turning, head lifting, thrashing, smiling, sound production (e.g., grunting, cooing, crying), grasping and touching, sneezing, coughing, yawning, and hiccoughing.
- Early *emotional expression and communicative abilities* are seen in an infant's responses to pleasurable and unpleasurable feelings or events in the environment. The young infant communicates through sounds, facial expression, and other body language.

- *Attentional abilities* of the infant include the capacity to focus (particularly on the social environment), to observe, and to be curious about what humans do.
- The infant has a *perceptual capacity* to manage sensory stimuli. The child takes in information from the senses (e.g., visual, auditory, olfactory, tactile, and vestibular) and begins to organize it into sensorimotor schemes through the process of assimilation and accommodation.
- The infant's *cognitive ability* begins to link perception to meaning. The child starts to transform perceived information from the senses to representations of the external world. This ability to transform and process information is the basis for obtaining meaning from the environment.
- *Social relationships* (attachments) with other human beings are initially developed by maintaining eye contact, producing the reflexive smile, vocalizing comfort sounds, and exhibiting curiosity and interest in human activity.
- Infants show evidence of having *memory* to store experience. They use past experience to react to similar situations.
- *Temperament* seems to be an inborn characteristic from birth. Each infant has a self-regulated response pattern to internal and external stimuli. The temperamental attributes of the infant account for the rate and intensity of responses as well as for the general activity level.

Of the eight adaptive capabilities of the infant, temperament is discussed in greater detail because of its special relationship to coping and the diversity of interpretations of its meaning and impact.

Temperament

Temperament is particularly important because it influences how a child copes and, therefore, how others respond to the child's coping efforts (Williamson & Zeitlin, 1990). Although temperament is defined in differing ways, most definitions reflect some variation of that originally postulated by Allport (1937):

> Temperament refers to the characteristic phenomena of an individual's emotional nature, including his susceptibility to emotional stimulation, his customary strength and speed of response, the quality of his prevailing mood, and all the peculiarities of fluctuation and intensity of mood; these phenomena being regarded as dependent upon constitutional make-up, and therefore largely hereditary in origin. (p. 54)

There is general agreement that temperament is evidenced in behavioral tendencies rather than in specific, discrete behaviors. Theorists emphasize its biological base and recognize the relative continuity of these behavioral tendencies over time. It is recognized, however, that the expression of temperamental attributes is shaped and modified as a consequence of experience. The impact of temperament is most direct and evident in infancy when idiosyncratic coping styles are developing.

A more comprehensive discussion of the current theories of temperament and how they differ is provided in the literature (Bates, 1987; Goldsmith et al., 1987; Lamb & Bornstein, 1987). Theorists vary in their conceptual definitions and the set of dimensions they consider temperamental in nature. For example, Buss and Plomin (1984) define temperament as a set of early appearing, inherited personality traits (i.e., emotionality, activity, and sociability). Goldsmith and Campos (1986) consider temperament to reflect individual differences in primary emotions and arousal, as expressed by the intensity and duration of behavioral responses. In the view of Rothbart and Derryberry (1981), temperament refers to constitutionally based differences in reactivity and self-regulation. By reactivity, they mean the biological sensitivity of the individual's response to changes in the environment. Self-regulation involves the attentional and behavioral patterns of approach and avoidance that are used to modulate this reactivity.

The work of Thomas and Chess (1977, 1980) deserves special note because of its influence on the study of temperament and its use in clinical practice. They conceptualize temperament as the stylistic component of behavior—patterns in *how* actions are performed in contrast to the *why* (motivation) and *what* (content) of behavior. Thomas and Chess describe the following nine dimensions of temperament. Although these dimensions are not definitive, they provide a useful frame of reference when considering a young child's temperament.

1. *Rhythmicity*, or regularity of body functions (e.g., hunger, excretion, sleep, wakefulness)
2. *Approach/withdrawal* in response to new situations
3. *Adaptability* to new or changed situations
4. *Threshold of responsiveness*, or amount of stimulation required to evoke a response
5. General *activity* level (i.e., high, medium, variable, or low)
6. *Intensity*, or strength of reactions
7. *Distractibility*, or the degree to which extraneous stimuli alter behavior
8. *Attention span and persistence*, or the amount of time devoted to an activity and diligence in the face of obstacles or interference
9. *Quality of mood*, or the amount of pleasant, friendly, joyful behavior as contrasted with unpleasant, unfriendly, unhappy behavior

In addition, Thomas and Chess (1977) describe three behavioral clusters that they designate respectively as easy, difficult, and slow-to-warm-up temperaments. They emphasize, however, that a substantial percentage of infants do not neatly fall into any one of the three categories. *Easy* children are rhythmic, positive in initial approach, adaptive, mild in intensity, and positive in mood. They are regular in their habits, positive in their responses to new situations, quick to adapt to new foods and people, and generally cheerful. They enjoy learning new games and taking part in new activities.

Difficult infants are irregular in rhythm, negative in approach (tend to withdraw), slow to adapt, intense, and negative in mood. These children display great irregularity in eating, sleeping, and eliminating. They tend to withdraw noisily or protest vigorously when exposed to any new stimulus or situation (e.g., unfamiliar food, clothing, people, or places). Although eventually they adapt, initial exposure to new demands, such as going to a nursery school or a birthday party, typically elicit howling or other negative behavior.

Slow-to-warm-up infants are low in activity, negative in approach, slow to adapt, mild in intensity, and negative in mood. They adapt cautiously and tend to withdraw from new situations, but with little or no fussing. As infants, they are likely to respond to a new food by letting it dribble out of their mouths. In nursery school, they stay on the sidelines for several weeks. In kindergarten, if pushed to take part in some new activity, they struggle quietly to escape.

These dimensions and styles of temperament were derived from an investigation of a small number of children who initially participated in the New York Longitudinal Study (Thomas, Chess, & Birch, 1968). This seminal effort generated an array of research that examined Thomas and Chess's results. In general, their nine dimensions of temperament do not emerge in factor-analytic studies using scales designed to measure the dimensions (Hagekull, Lindhagen, & Bohlin, 1980; Lerner, Palermo, Spiro, & Nesselroade, 1982). There is some consensus in the field that the salient variables of temperament are fewer than nine in number and are related to activity, reactivity, emotionality, and sociability (Goldsmith et al., 1987).

There is also a lack of agreement regarding the concept of "difficult temperament." In part, this debate addresses whether the concept "difficult" is an inherent characteristic of the child or merely a social perception. Although Bates (1987) and Carey (1986) have varying definitions of difficult temperament, they both provide support for the validity and relevance of this construct for study and clinical practice. Research findings are mixed regarding the question of whether children with disabilities are more prone to be temperamentally difficult.

Temperament as a Factor in Coping

The relationship between temperament and coping is complex and not well understood. It appears, however, that temperament may influence coping in at least four ways. First, it may influence the child's exposure to potentially stressful situations. For example, an infant with a high activity level may explore the environment vigorously and therefore be confronted with a greater number of potential stressors. Second, temperament may determine the child's range of sensitivity to stress. An infant with strong sensory reactivity and arousal may have a low tolerance to environmental stimulation before becoming distressed. Third, temperament may influence the characteristic pattern of the child's coping efforts. For instance, it may modulate the latency, duration, and intensity of the infant's behavioral responses and emotional expression. Finally, temperament may affect the willingness of caregivers to assist the child's coping. Certain temperamental attributes tend to evoke social support and nurturing parental practices; others foster rejection.

Werner and Smith (1982) found in their longitudinal study that certain temperamental characterisitics played a role in influencing a child's resilience to stress and ability to cope. Activity level and social responsiveness were attributes that significantly differentiated resilient infants from those that later developed problems. The resilient children tended to have a positive socioemotional affect and an approach-oriented behavioral style. In contrast, nonresilient children tended to have a negative socioemotional affect and a withdrawal or ambivalent approach-withdrawal style.

Carlton (1988) studied the relationship of temperament and coping effectiveness in young children with and without disabilities, using the Toddler Temperament Scale (Fullard, McDevitt, & Carey, 1978, 1984) and the Early Coping Inventory (Zeitlin et al., 1988). She found that there were no significant differences in the temperamental qualities of the two groups except for activity level. However, the group with disabilities was significantly less effective in coping-related behaviors that involved sensorimotor organization and self-initiation. There were some correlations between dimensions of the two instruments. For example, in both groups, higher thresholds of responsiveness tended to be related to more effective coping. Likewise, in both groups persistence was related to high effectiveness scores in self-initiated coping.

Thus, temperament contributes to the infant's constitutional responsivity to the environment and self-regulation. For instance, temperament may affect the ability to cope with an unfamiliar situation by influencing the degree of sensitivity and susceptibility of the infant to new stimuli. It may also shape the timing and intensity of the child's coping efforts (e.g., the latency and vigor of crying, reaching out, or crawling away). An appreciation of the child's temperamental attributes enables parents to modify their caregiving to encourage adaptive functioning. For example, flexible schedules may be useful for the arhythmic infant and the older child who has a low attention span and high distractibility.

For the toddler who adapts slowly and tends to withdraw, parents who offer advance warning of changes provide time for him or her to adjust.

Although temperament is important, it is only one factor influencing the coping behavior of a child. Even an infant with a difficult temperament may cope successfully if caring adults are responsive to the child's unique coping style. Individual temperamental features may change as children grow older, but such features still play an important part in determining individual–environment transactions.

DEVELOPMENT FROM A COPING PERSPECTIVE

At birth the human brain is only partially mature, with rapid growth occurring in the first 3 years of life and full maturation being completed during adulthood. During the course of development, the brain's maturation, in conjunction with the child's transactions with the environment, results in a progression through fairly predictable phases. These developmental phases, or stages, are marked by the child's capacity to perform more differentiated acts and to demonstrate increased self-control over what were initially reflexive or fixed behavior patterns. The infant's coping mechanisms and functional capabilities change as the child acquires experience in the environment and as the central nervous system matures.

Development is commonly subdivided into areas—motor control, communication, cognition, social-emotional skills, and so forth. Coping entails the integration and application of these developmental skills into daily living. To demonstrate the relationship of coping and developmental skill acquisition, this discussion concentrates on skill acquisition in a single area—motor control—and addresses both typical and atypical development. This section then provides a more comprehensive, integrated overview of the first 36 months of a child's development.

The area of motor control was chosen for discussion because of its critical role in the sensorimotor stage of development. The intent is to show how this developmental domain influences the coping capacity of both typical and atypical children. A reciprocal relationship is evident because expansion of motor control increases coping options. Likewise, coping helps to motivate, enhance, and refine the child's motor competence. When a child has a physical disability, significant compensatory adaptations may be needed for the child to be optimally functional.

The Acquisition of Motor Control

Motor control as a developmental skill does not develop in a vacuum, but within the context of a child learning to cope with daily activities. One of the most crucial achievements of the infant during the first year of life is to learn to deal with gravity (Williamson, 1987). A normal infant is born with all of the basic movements. The young child can extend (straighten), flex (bend), move laterally (side to side), and rotate (twist or turn). However, two important elements are missing: 1) the *postural control* necessary to assume increasingly advanced developmental positions against gravity, and 2) the *coordination* to use a wide variety of movement patterns in order to accomplish a task (Campbell, 1989; Gilfoyle, Grady, & Moore, 1990). Thus, the challenge for the infant is to develop the control of posture and movement that will enable the child to discover the world and manage it successfully.

The development of postural control against gravity proceeds in a cephalo-to-caudal direction (i.e., from the head toward the feet). In this process, the infant acquires coordination of movement in a predictable sequence—extension, flexion, lateral movement, and rotation (Bly, 1983; Hall, 1990). Progressive acquisition of this control expands the child's repertoire of available coping strategies. The infant's gradual control of extension against gravity is quickly counterbalanced by emerging control of the opposite movement pattern—flexion. Only when extensor and flexor movements are coordinated together does the infant demonstrate the organization of lateral movements that allow weight shifting of the body from side to side. Rotation is the most sophisticated movement pattern and is therefore the last to be mastered in infancy.

During play, the infant practices these movements and learns to organize them for functional use. By observing an infant in the prone-lying position (i.e., lying on the abdomen), one can readily see the head-to-foot development of controlled extension (see Figure 3.1). At 1 month, the child rests in a curled posture and has the arms tucked under the body. By 2–3 months of age, however, control of extension progresses to the mid-back, enabling the infant to lift the head and chest off the mat and bring the arms out to the sides of the body. Gradually, extension progresses to the low back, allowing the infant to use extensor muscles to raise the buttocks off the mat (the playful "bottom lifting" of the 4-month-old). Around 5–6 months, extensor control crosses the hips so that the legs come into alignment with the body and are no longer in a flexed posture to the side (the "frog legged" position). The infant celebrates this achievement by joyously rocking on the belly for countless hours. At approximately 7 months of age, the infant has conquered gravity in the prone position and displays controlled extension throughout the body (see Figure 3.1b).

Concurrent with the development of extension, the infant is acquiring control of flexion. As noted in Figure 3.2, it can best be seen when the child is in the supine-lying position (i.e., lying on the back). In this position, the 2-month-old assumes an asymmetrical posture, with the head usually to one side. During the next month, the infant learns to maintain the head in the body's midline due to developing coordination of the flexor muscles of the neck. This emerging flexor control becomes dramatically expressed in the symmetrical, midline-oriented play of the 4-month-old child. The child enjoys bringing the arms together in order to pluck on clothing, mouth objects, or touch the bottle or breast during feeding. All of these activities contribute to sensory, cognitive, and emotional development and rely on the infant's expanding flexor skills. By 5 months of age, the infant engages in more body-oriented play by bringing the hands to the knees and lifting the head off the mat to look at the body. Greater control of flexion in the trunk (torso) and legs allows the infant of 6–7 months to grasp the feet, suck the toes, and rock with delight in this flexed posture (Figure 3.2b). The child has now mastered gravity in the supine position and has an enhanced sensorimotor foundation for exploring the world.

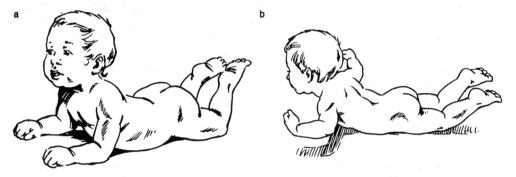

Figure 3.1. Developing control of extension: a) Propping on forearms at 4 months, and b) extension throughout the body in the prone position at 7 months.

Figure 3.2. Developing control of flexion: a) Midline-oriented play at 4 months, and b) exploration of the feet at 7 months.

When movements of extension and flexion are counterbalanced (i.e., the motions of straightening and bending are equally functional), lateral control appears (Figure 3.3a). Around 4 months, the infant begins to right the head laterally in space when the body is tilted to one side during caregiving activities such as bathing or dressing. At this time, the child has sufficient lateral control of the trunk to play in a side-lying position without falling onto the abdomen or back. During the next few months, the infant learns to shift weight from side to side when propped on the forearms or with arms extended in the prone position. This ability to shift weight laterally allows the child to free one hand to reach for objects. It also facilitates social interaction because the infant can attend more directly to the surroundings. By 7 months of age, the infant has sufficient control of lateral movements to pivot on the belly in a circle during play (Figure 3.3b).

Controlled rotation of the head, trunk, and extremities is founded on the development of extension, flexion, and lateral movement (Figure 3.4a). It is therefore the most difficult movement pattern for the infant to coordinate. Rotation (i.e., twisting and turning motions) is usually associated in the early months with reaching or kicking. As the infant reaches for an object, the upper trunk tends to twist in order to support the movement of the arm. Likewise, kicking the legs often elicits rotation in the lower trunk. These activities generally introduce early rolling. The infant reaches out in the prone position,

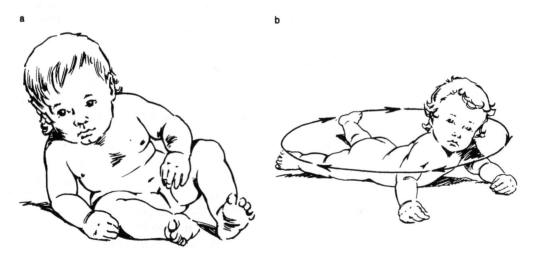

Figure 3.3. Developing lateral control: a) "Righting" the head when tilted to the side at 4 months, and b) prone pivoting in a circle at 7 months.

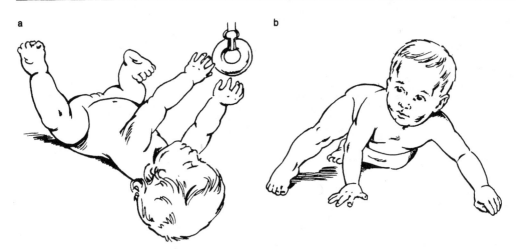

Figure 3.4. Developing control of rotation: a) Reaching across the body causing the upper trunk to rotate at 4 months, and b) coming into a sitting position at 7 months.

loses balance, and flips over onto the back. With practice, the child learns to roll with controlled rotation—the head turns, the shoulders follow, then the trunk, and finally the pelvis.

In large part, it is trunk rotation that enables an infant to assume such new positions as sitting, crawling, or standing, and to move with balance from one position to another (Figure 3.4b). In every new position, the infant must learn to coordinate extension, flexion, lateral movement, and rotation in order to become mobile in that position (e.g., reciprocal crawling, walking). The acquisition of motor skills is based on the infant's ability to organize the movements available at birth into increasingly sophisticated adaptive movement strategies.

Atypical Motor Development

Many infants with developmental delays or disabilities have difficulty organizing their sensory and motor systems in a way that allows for successful interaction with objects and people. This vulnerability strongly influences their coping efforts. Frequently, they are born with low muscle tone and may have difficulty with sensory processing. As a result, their development of functional movement becomes blocked. Generally, these infants start to develop extension but fail to counterbalance it with adequate control of flexion. As a consequence, the more sophisticated lateral movements and rotation do not develop fully (Scherzer & Tscharnuter, 1990; Williamson, 1987). Therefore, they become limited in the movement patterns available for exploration, learning, and interpersonal engagement.

An infant with low muscle tone characteristically develops a predominance of extensor movement. The result may be a tendency to pull the head and shoulders back with too much force. At the same time, the opposing flexor movements, such as reaching forward with the arms, are slow to develop. With repetition, the atypical patterns of extension tend to become habitual and hinder further development. These extensor movements make it difficult for the infant to acquire head control, to suck appropriately on a nipple, to assume a good prone-on-elbows position, or to play with the hands together in sitting. Because balanced control of extension and flexion is not attained, lateral movements and rotation often fail to develop properly. Postural control and coordination may thus be insufficient for the achievement of motor milestones. In addition, this clinical picture may interfere with the infant's capacity to elicit attention, nurturance, and care from the parents. As a result, parent–child interaction may be strained, placing at risk the ability to establish a positive attachment and sense of relatedness.

Infants with an athetotic type of cerebral palsy may serve as an illustration. These infants are initially "floppy" and demonstrate increasingly erratic movement patterns over time. To compensate for the low muscle tone and disorganization, they learn to stiffen (i.e., tense) their muscles in order to achieve some level of control. For example, they may elevate the shoulder girdle to stabilize the head (i.e., "shrug" the shoulders up), arch the trunk into extension, or stiffen the arms and legs. Because these infants are typically more involved on one side of the body than the other, the head tends to turn asymmetrically to a preferred side. Consequently, they may turn and pull away from the parents when being held. Their attempts to coordinate movement result in general stiffening, which prevents them from molding to the adult's body and being cuddled in the arms. Parents may interpret such postural responses as rejection by the infant and feel incompetent in their care-giving skills.

Interactions are further hampered by the following problems, which may make the child's behavior difficult to interpret: 1) marked fluctuations in attention and arousal, 2) facial expressions that vary from a flat affect to grimacing due to altering muscle tone, 3) difficulty in maintaining eye contact—a problem that is related to the positioning of the head, 4) incoordinated vocalizations, and 5) deficits in the use of manual gestures (e.g., giving and showing actions, pointing). Because of missed or misread signals, an interactive mismatch or breakdown in communication may ensue. In essence, therefore, it is the child's motor difficulties that undermine the effectiveness of parent–child coping transactions.

In this discussion, the focus has been on motor control and its reciprocal impact on coping. A similar analysis could be made of the other developmental domains. Coping integrates these skills functionally into the context of daily activities. The following overview of development during the first 3 years further examines the important interrelationship between coping and development.

Integrated Coping-Related Development

0–3 Months   At birth, the infant adapts to the new surroundings in the following ways: by initiating acts (e.g., crying) to secure an environmental response to internal signals of pain, discomfort, or hunger; by regulating body functions, such as breathing, heart beat, digestion, and elimination; and by maintaining a balance between sleeping and waking states. These abilities are not under the conscious and direct control of the infant but are reflexive in nature (i.e., at birth the infant does not have the capacity to understand or voluntarily control the basic regulatory processes that provide a foundation for later coping competence).

Developmentally, this is a time for the stabilization of body functions and the organization of behaviors for transactions with the environment. It is a time of global emotional reactivity; events are appraised as being either pleasurable or unpleasurable. In this sense, emotions can be considered the infant's language.

The early infant period is one of immense biological vulnerability and one in which a successful outcome depends on appropriate adaptive reactions on the part of the baby and the caregiver. Among the internal tensions that may harm, threaten, or challenge the young infant are hunger, discomfort, fatigue, and growth (or the lack of it). External stressors may be temperature change, physical handling, or variations in sensory stimulation. The baby appraises these tensions through the filter of an emerging belief system that provides a sense of personal efficacy.

If an experience is perceived as stressful, the baby uses available behaviors to make a coping effort. The actions the infants may use include signaling with facial expressions, crying, withdrawal of the limbs, rhythmic movement, jerking, or gaze aversion. In times of real distress, the coping effort is directed to getting help. However, in times of mild discomfort the infant may merely turn away, adjust body posture, fuss, or begin self-comforting behaviors. In this developmental period, the achievement of smooth organic functioning and efficient feeding patterns are the most obvious manifestations of the effective coping efforts necessary for future growth and development.

Murphy and Moriarty (1976) describe three important aspects of stimulus management, which is a basic coping task of the early months. First, the infant elicits an adequate amount and type of stimulation to meet social-emotional needs and to support the development of perceptual-motor and related cognitive functions. Second, the infant protects against excessive or painful stimulation. Third, the infant selects stimuli in a way that assists the regulation of alertness, the gradual familiarization with the environment, and the exercise of emerging skills. Thus, sensory self-regulation is critical for the achievement of homeostasis and early coping effectiveness.

The baby is dependent on external resources to have his or her needs met. The caregiver must be able to interpret the global coping effort. Effectiveness of outcome, as at all ages, is strongly influenced by available resources.

4–6 Months By 4 months, coping behaviors are most obvious in a child's adjustment to the daily routine of the home and in response to caregiving and interaction with adults. At this time, coping behaviors related to sensorimotor organization, reactivity, and self-initiation can readily be observed in the infant (see discussion of coping later in this chapter). For example, a 4-month-old infant may demonstrate satisfaction when successfully accomplishing activities, by showing pleasure following a satiating feeding, or after swiping a toy. Self-initiated behaviors are observable in attempts to act on the environment, explore body movement, and engage caregivers in interaction.

By 6 months, most infants have developed mobility in the environment through rolling and crawling on their bellies. Reaching and grasping are more controlled and directed in play and in the exploration of objects. These motor capabilities contribute to increasing self-mastery in acting on the environment and an expansion of observable self-initiated behaviors—as in more independent and varied play with objects. As communicative intent becomes more evident, the infant also shows self-initiated behaviors by using sounds, gestures (e.g., gross pointing), or body movements to indicate a desire to be picked up or held or to request help to reach objects. A broader repertoire of skills can be used to react to others and the physical surroundings. Curiosity and persistence in play are also frequently evident. Developing cognitive skills, such as awareness of simple cause–effect relations and object permanence, provide the infant with an increasing number of strategies that can be used in both a reactive and a self-initiated manner.

7–12 Months At this stage, the central nervous system undergoes major maturation and the infant moves to obviously meaningful and purposeful play. For example, an infant who previously banged a toy telephone now holds the receiver to his or her ear as if to hear. The infant can now sit independently and securely, recognize his or her own name when spoken to, watch how objects act when dropped, demonstrate self-help skills by drinking from a cup and eating with a spoon, demonstrate more mature visual and auditory systems by expressing wariness of strangers, and indicate rejection by refusing an unwanted object.

As with each stage of the developmental process, the 7- to 9-month period presents the child with new challenges that require effective coping. Expanded mobility skills (e.g., rolling, crawling, moving in and out of sitting) increase the child's repertoire of reactive and self-initiated behaviors. Emergence of these new motor abilities require the child to negotiate obstacles in the environment. The child also has to manage frustrations experienced in the practice of skills as well as the normal stress that accompanies achieving a balance between dependence and independence. A strong attachment to the caregiver, usually seen toward the end of the first year, results in increased wariness of strangers and new situations. Over time, the infant who learns to cope effectively will maintain this strong attachment to the caregiver in a way that fosters independence as well as a positive orientation to others and to the environment.

12–24 Months   By 12 months the infant produces such sounds as "ma-ma" and "da-da," which adults assume to be learned words. Most children can stand with support, play games such as "pat-a-cake," and make desires known by pointing or using sounds or words to indicate wants. A 12-month-old is independently mobile in some fashion (e.g., crawling, walking) and actively explores the environment. The child manipulates objects in numerous ways and in the process gains a continually expanding knowledge of the world and of how objects respond to his or her actions. In this period, the child moves toward increasing self-control, purposeful play, and peer interaction.

24–36 Months   By 2 years of age most children can walk and run, unscrew small tops such as those on toothpaste tubes, find their own shoes, identify their own toys, attempt to do things by themselves, assert strong independence, generate self-play and play with other children, speak in two-word sentences, and modify their activities to meet the demands of the environment.

During the third year of life, the number of strategies the child has available for coping is significantly expanded in comparison to the first 2 years. In any given situation the child has a variety of affective, social, cognitive, communicative, and motor skills that can be applied as strategies in an effort to cope. As the child develops, many behaviors are discontinued or restructured. *Transformation* is a basic characteristic of development. In the transformation process, each new skill is built on an old skill. Thus, in each developmental period one can observe sensorimotor schemes that were originally reflexive, but that have been transformed by experience into behaviors more directly under the control of the child. For example, whereas the infant exhibits smiles from birth, over time the smile becomes a response to the presence of the caregiver and is under the control of the infant. While skills and specific behaviors change, there is a continuity of self and of coping style as they evolve.

THE COPING PROCESS IN YOUNG CHILDREN

For children, as for adults, coping is a process in which internal and external resources are used to meet personal needs and manage the demands of the environment. The personal needs of the young child include fulfillment of basic requirements for nutrition, security, and a balance of activity and rest, as well as opportunities to demonstrate interest, motivation, and achievement. The demands of the environment require the child to negotiate the physical surroundings, interact with objects and people, and adapt to social expectations.

Some people may have difficulty envisioning very young children as having to cope with stress. Yet, theorists as different as Freud and Skinner have recognized that stress is inherent in development and learning. From birth it is an integral part of life. The newborn copes with pain and discomfort by adjusting body posture, employing self-comforting behaviors, and crying. Stress is a component in the development of attachment and later separation, in the temporary disorganization experienced during transitional periods of reflex maturation, and in the socialization process itself (Lipsitt, 1983). Even the normal interaction between the baby and caregiver can be a source of stress. Such stress can arise from many causes—mistimed emotional signals, misread signals, and overloading or underloading of stimulation. An optimal level of stress, different for each child at varying stages of development, is generative and growth producing. Too much can interfere with learning, as can too little. The key issue is for stress to be developmentally appropriate.

The model of the coping process presented in Chapter 2 is relevant to the entire human life span. However, because the initial 3 years of life constitute such a formative period, it is important to understand how it applies to the very young child. The model is therefore reintroduced here in relation to this age group. As illustrated in Figure 3.5, the basics of the coping process for children are the same as for adults. The primary differences relate to operational complexity.

Step 1: Determine the Meaning of the Event

In the initial step of the coping process, the young child appraises the tension-generating event, which is usually related to the gratification of immediate needs. Aspects of the cognitive domain predominantly involved in this appraisal are perception, memory, and imagery (Piaget, 1952). Perception can be regarded as the basic intake and processing of sensory information. In the case of the young child, emotions are the visually observable indicators of the perception of the event (Sameroff & Emde, 1989). Memory has to do with storage capabilities and to some extent with the quality of the child's representations be-

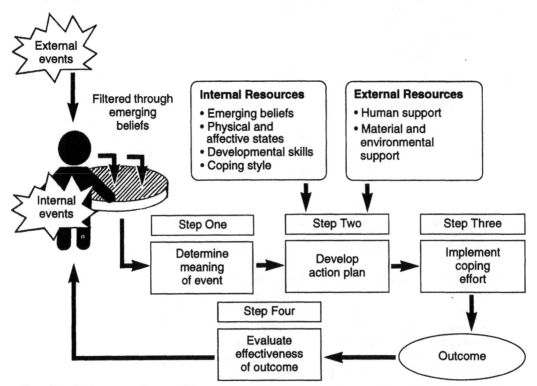

Figure 3.5. Coping process of young children.

cause they are influenced by long-term and short-term capacities. Imagery has to do with the quality of representations, which in the preverbal child are assumed to be pictorial.

As is appropriate to their level of cognitive development, the determination of meaning by infants is primarily emotionally based. Emotions that influence appraisal become more complex and differentiated over time. For example, the 3-month-old may be able to demonstrate distress, delight, and excitement. By 12 months, the child can manifest such additional emotions as fear, disgust, anger, elation, and affection. Figure 3.6 presents an adaptation by Lewis and Michalson (1983) of a theoretical framework by Bridges (1932) that charts the differentiation of emotions in the first 2 years.

As children grow older, emotions continue to be important, but a cognitive component is increasingly observable. (When having difficulty coping, however, children may regress in their adaptive strategies and demonstrate a predominantly affective reaction.) Thus, cognitive and emotional processes are at work in the appraisal of events as they are filtered through the child's belief system. The young child's beliefs emerge over time through experience. They are rudimentary and global (e.g., an evolving sense of personal agency that influences whether an event is perceived as a threat or challenge).

Step 2: Develop an Action Plan

The decision-making skills necessary to develop an action plan are limited in the young child. The decision is based on whether the event has generated a positive or negative emotion, the internal resources the child can draw on to manage the situation, and the external resources available to facilitate the coping effort. Each child has a unique and often changing pool of coping resources. With time, the child progresses from primarily applying internal resources to engage the support of significant others to being able to apply resources directly to manage events. A more detailed discussion of internal and external resources is provided later in this chapter.

Step 3: Implement the Coping Effort

The next step is to implement the action plan through the employment of coping strategies. A coping strategy is a behavioral sequence, however simple or complex, used to deal

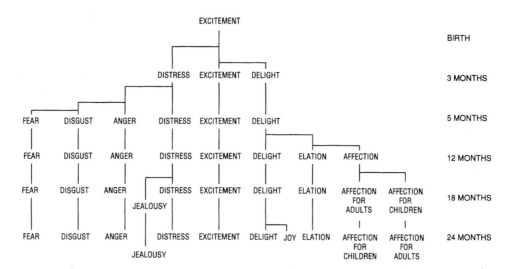

Figure 3.6. Differentiation of emotions in the initial 24 months. (From Lewis, M., & Michalson, L. [1983]. *Children's emotions and moods: Developmental theory and measurement*, p. 108. New York: Plenum; reprinted by permission.)

with a specific event. Obviously, no single coping strategy (or set of strategies) is consistently best for all types of events. The action most likely to be effective will vary with the nature of the stress generated and the circumstances surrounding the event. Strategies that are successful tend to be repeated. However, when the old strategy does not work in the new situation the child needs to use personal resources to devise a new type of adaptation. The young child's coping effort (or strategy) may be action-oriented, may be directed to managing the related affect, or may attempt to modify the physical tension; usually it is a combination of all three.

Action-Oriented Coping Efforts   Very young infants have limited means to take direct action to manage the stressor. For example, they can signal the caregiver by crying and by body movements such as flailing their arms or legs. The caregiver then has to interpret the meaning of this global effort. As children develop skills, they can cope more autonomously by acting directly on the stressor. For example, the toddler whose toy has disappeared under the couch can search for it; when hungry, the child can verbalize the need for food, point to it, or sometimes obtain it independently.

Managing the Affect   Coping efforts are directed to helping the child feel better. At times, children can achieve this on their own. When they are stressed, they can self-comfort by sucking their thumb or cuddling a special toy. Often, however, they are dependent on the caregiver for help. Some infants respond to a soothing voice or crooning; others need to be rocked. Some children have extreme difficulty managing their feelings and go through a whole range of tantrums or other acting-out behaviors. Others, such as the institutionalized infants described by Spitz (1945), seem to manage their feelings by not having any.

Modifying the Physical Tension   Some of the strategies used to manage the affect associated with stress (e.g., vigorous banging on a table top, gross rocking of the body) are also used to modify the physical tension generated by the stress. Children may get very active to discharge their physical tension, which helps them organize themselves and modulate their level of arousal.

Step 4: Evaluate the Effectiveness of the Outcome

The fourth step in the coping process involves evaluating the outcome of the coping effort. Evaluation can be from a number of perspectives: from the child's personal orientation or from the observations of an adult, and with regard to a single coping effort or to numerous efforts over time. In addition, one can address the short- or long-term impact of such efforts.

For the child, the outcome of the coping effort may have many meanings and the adult can only conjecture, on the basis of the infant's behavior and affect, what the child is feeling. It is important to appreciate that many of the coping experiences of children occur during intrinsically motivated exploration and play. The child is in command and can flexibly shift goals and expectations. Under these conditions, criteria for success and gratification are self-determined. The child's point of view can be surmised only by observing the expression: curiosity, interest, playfulness, wonder. One must be cautious not to assume that the adult's standards are necessarily those of the child.

Given the critical significance of adaptive functioning, adults tend to make subjective judgments of the child's coping behaviors. There are three criteria of effectiveness: 1) the behavior is appropriate for the situation, 2) the behavior is appropriate for the child's developmental age, and 3) the behavior enables the child to achieve his or her objectives. Application of these criteria can be confounded by complex issues. For example, the major adaptational outcome of any coping-related transaction often depends on a complicated trade-off of costs and benefits or divergent values about what is positive or negative, important or unimportant. To illustrate, an infant may habitually cope with environmental stimulation by "shutting down" to reduce the stress of the moment. This strategy, however, may interfere with the child's ability to learn, and the action may be a source of frustration for the caregiver.

In addition to looking at specific coping behaviors, it is also possible to take a broader perspective and view the child's overall coping competence. Evaluation is then described in more global terms and reflects perception of the child over time. Evaluation takes the form of defining how children feel about themselves and their situation in life. It is usually associated with a relatively enduring overall affect, leading adults to make such comments as "Carmella is such a happy little girl," or "Omar seems to be a frustrated child."

For adults, the factors commonly associated with well-being are the ability to work well, play well, love well, and expect well (Grinker, 1968). These factors can be translated into terms that apply to young children as they manage the demands of daily living.

1. The child works well when:
   - He or she demonstrates openness to learning by using self-initiated behaviors.
   - He or she appraises events more often as a challenge than as a threat (i.e., a motivating belief system that says "I can").
   - He or she evidences mastery of developmental tasks.
2. The child plays well when he or she interacts with people in the environment in ways that are pleasurable.
3. The child loves well when there is a good attachment to caregivers and other significant individuals—when emotional warmth and responsiveness are observed in the child's transactions.
4. The child expects well when there is a match between personal expectations and the reality of situations.

These four criteria may be used to evaluate a child's overall coping capability and level of well-being.

COPING RESOURCES

As noted previously, coping resources are a critical component of the coping process model (see Figure 3.5).

Internal Resources

The internal resources of the child are emerging beliefs, physical and affective states, developmental skills, and coping style.

Emerging Beliefs   The guiding role of beliefs and values in adult coping has been well documented, but very little is known about their importance in childhood. Although young children have not yet acquired personal values, their emerging beliefs are influenced by the values of the significant people in their lives. Children's beliefs develop from their interpretation of their transactions with the environment (Greenspan & Greenspan, 1989; Stern, 1985).

For young children, beliefs relevant for coping are related to beliefs about personal efficacy (i.e., ability to master new learning, control events, and trust others to meet personal needs). There are two categories of belief:

1. General belief, which is a disposition the individual brings to all situations (e.g., the world is a place in which one can be trusting). (The child's emerging concept of self constitutes a general belief.)

2. Belief in a specific context (e.g., when my diaper irritates me and I cry, someone will change it)

In the early stages of development, beliefs play a lesser role because of the child's restricted experience, limited memory, and lack of integration. As the child becomes self-regulated and learns that personal actions have an impact on events, one can observe the increased role of past experience on present functioning. Beliefs may serve as a motivator for initiating action or as a motivator to avoid action.

Physical and Affective States   *Physical state* refers to general health and physiological condition, such as endurance and wellness. It influences the child's level of arousal, which is important for achieving and maintaining the awake-alert status necessary for optimal interaction. For an infant who generally enjoys good health, this robust state is an important resource. Should the child catch a cold, this indisposition will influence coping (e.g., it may cause lethargy), but only temporarily. Conversely, a child with a chronic illness such as asthma may be consistently debilitated by the physical consequences of the condition. Physical appearance, especially at the extremes of attractiveness or unattractiveness may also constitute a resource or a vulnerability.

Affective state refers to the child's moods and feelings (e.g., happy, sad, depressed, anxious, angry) and is reflective of the child's beliefs about self and the world. For example, a depressed child may exhibit inhibition, withdrawal, or an aimless quality of play. An angry child may be characterized by aggressive, disorganized behavior or a low frustration tolerance with frequent outbursts. A happy child may show a bright affect, be curious, and be open to learning.

Physical and affective states are interrelated. For example, a tired body more readily generates depression. Conversely, feelings of depression may deplete the body's energy supply. Both states influence the child's alertness, motivation, and feelings of general self-worth.

Developmental Skills   Developmental skills are the building blocks or foundation for the child's coping efforts. Performance in all developmental domains contributes to the child's level of coping effectiveness. The child draws from a repertoire of emerging and previously acquired developmental skills to manage any given situation. Consider, for example, a 2-year-old child who functions within developmental expectation for that age. The child sees a box of cookies on top of the refrigerator and wants it. On the basis of the child's developmental competence, several options are available for coping with this personal need. The child can use acquired verbal skills to ask the caregiver for a cookie; relying on problem-solving and motor abilities, the child can use a chair to climb up and reach the cookies independently; or the child can repeat an action that has previously resulted in eliciting attention from others (e.g., fussing, having a temper tantrum, waiting in front of the refrigerator until someone arrives to help). In a similar situation, a child with delayed acquisition of developmental skills has fewer coping options with which to meet this challenge. In fact, the only available options for obtaining a cookie may be uncoordinated gesturing until an adult becomes aware of what the child wants.

Typically, young children develop across skill areas in their own unique pattern. For example, a child may be advanced in cognitive behaviors and slow in social development. Although there are broad normative expectations for developmental attainment in relationship to chronological age, children vary considerably. However, developmental delay or minimal competence in any area of development increases the child's vulnerability. A child is also at risk if there are major differences in the rate of development in specific skill areas.

Coping Style Coping style refers to the way an individual routinely uses certain types of strategies, rather than others, to manage situations that require coping efforts. Although the term describes a characteristic way of behaving, it cannot predict the specific actions a child will use in a particular situation. The coping style of infants and toddlers can be described in terms of the unique pattern of their sensorimotor organization, reactive behaviors, and self-initiated behaviors (Zeitlin et al., 1988).

Sensorimotor organization refers to the child's regulation of psycho-physiological functions and the integration of the sensory and motor systems (e.g., response to vestibular, tactile, auditory, visual, and proprioceptive sensations). Representative behavioral characteristics in this category (referred to as *coping behaviors*) are the child's ability to self-comfort, to demonstrate visual attention, to organize information simultaneously from the different senses for a response, to maintain an appropriate activity level, and to adapt to being moved by others during caregiving.

Reactive behavior consists of the types of actions used to respond to the demands of the physical and social environments. Behavioral characteristics that typify this category are the ability to respond to vocal or gestural direction, to react to the feelings and moods of others, to bounce back after stressful situations, to adjust to daily routines, and to accommodate to changes in the surroundings.

Self-initiated behavior refers to autonomously generated actions that meet the personal need to interact with objects and people. Such coping behavior is intrinsically motivated and not directly linked to environmental cues. Sample behavioral characteristics are the child's ability to apply a previously learned behavior to new situations, to initiate interactions with others, to demonstrate persistence during activities, to anticipate events, and to explore objects independently using a variety of strategies.

External Resources

External resources include the human supports and the material and environmental supports that are available to the child.

Human Supports *Human supports* comprise the people in the child's social environment. They reflect the quantity and quality of parent–child transactions and relationships with siblings and peers, adults in the community, and all those who provide child care and intervention services to the child. Without human support, the infant and toddler cannot survive. It provides the child with direct assistance such as feeding and diaper changing, contingent feedback that helps the child achieve mastery, and emotional encouragement that makes an activity pleasurable and desirable. Human support generates the belief that the caregiver can be counted on to respond when signaled.

The quality and amount of support influences the child's attachment to primary caregivers. This attachment provides the secure base from which the child can explore the environment and is a source of comfort in times of distress. Attachment can be considered a unique emotional relationship between two people that endures over time and distance. Although it is difficult to define operationally, such behaviors as kissing, cuddling, fondling, and prolonged gazing are indications of adult–child attachment. Some specific dimensions that describe parental attachment are quality of interest, attentiveness, commitment, and protectiveness. There are, of course, cultural differences in how these dimensions are demonstrated. Supportive caregivers must be able to read the child's signals. Regardless of the characteristics that each parent and child brings to the relationship, an appropriate match between their characteristics is necessary for an emotionally rich relationship. If support is inadequate, inconsistent, or lacking in nurturance, the child is at risk for retarded or deviant development.

Material and Environmental Supports   *Material supports* of the family, such as sufficient food, clothing, shelter, and availability of medical and other services, are clearly critical to the infant's well-being. A family often wants to purchase an amazing array of furniture, equipment, and supplies to accommodate the new member of the family. Standard
items may include a crib, cradle, infant seat, high chair, and car seat. This list is complemented by volumes of consumable supplies, such as disposable diapers, baby powder and
lotion, formula, baby food, and so forth. From a child's perspective, toys and playthings
are also an important resource.

With growth and development, the material needs of the child are continually changing
with concomitant demands on the family's financial resources. Children with disabilities
may require additional specialized support, such as braces, wheelchairs, power-activated
toys, and more technologically advanced equipment (e.g., augmented communication
systems, ventilators).

Environmental supports that can influence coping in young children include size and
organization of space, quality of air, levels of noise and light, and appropriateness of temperature. Environments that are chaotic, disorganized, and either overstimulating or lacking in stimulation may have an undermining impact on the child's learning and development. In large families living in crowded conditions, for example, the infant may have
difficulty achieving self-regulation and homeostasis. It is difficult to organize oneself
when lights are on at all hours, the radio and television sets are constantly blaring, and
street noise is ongoing. To compound this situation, there may be a lack of predictable
daily routines, such as regular times for eating, sleeping, and playing.

Critical for healthy child development is an environment that is safe for exploration
and discovery. Adaptations are often necessary to "baby-proof" the home—window
guards, gates protecting stairways, electrical outlet covers, and locks on cabinets and
drawers. Indeed, parents may crawl through the house or apartment to identify potentially dangerous situations. An obvious additional environmental support for children
with special needs involves modifications to make the home and community architec-
tually accessible (e.g., curb cuts, ramps, wide doorways, handrails).

TRANSACTIONS BETWEEN CHILD AND CAREGIVER

As described previously and depicted in Figure 2.2, Chapter 2, this volume, transactions
are reciprocal coping efforts. A transaction has four components: 1) a demand, 2) a coping
effort, 3) the environment's response to the effort, and 4) the evaluation and internalization of the experience. The importance of the intimate transaction between infant and
parent is well established in the literature. Brazelton and Cramer (1990) refer to it as the
"earliest relationship," and Greenspan and Greenspan (1989) describe it as the "essential
partnership." It is the very core of attachment and emotional development (Mahler, Pine,
& Bergman, 1975; Stern, 1985). Although the young child is uniquely dependent on the
caregiver, each partner shapes and is shaped by their transactions. To appreciate the transaction from the child's perspective, each component is discussed.

Demand

Internal Demands   Young children seem to delight in self-generated sensorimotor
experiences. There is an extraordinary urge to seek stimulation, engage in exploration,
and repeat pleasurable events. This self-initiated activity appears to be motivated by internal demands. Numerous interrelated factors contribute to these demands. A basic one is
the physical and neurological maturation of the body, which enables the emergence of
increasingly complex behaviors. Another is the satisfaction of immediate physiological

needs, such as for food, sleep, and comfort. Bandura (1986) suggests self-efficacy as an-other primary need, and Murphy (1991) discusses the drive for mastery.

External Demands   Although young children have a comparatively limited range of experiences, the environment from the moment of birth provides both stimulation and stress. There are external demands both from people and from the physical surroundings. Most parents have specific expectations for their child's performance. Parental expecta-tions are influenced by many variables, the most significant being their own beliefs and values. Examples of beliefs include "he could do it if he just tried harder" and "my child is above average for her age." Other factors contributing to parental expectations include the parents' knowledge of child development, parenting skills, coping styles, and social pres-sures from the extended family and the community.

External demands change over time with the evolving needs of the child and family. For example, as the infant begins to develop greater inner organization, caregivers expect the child to fit into the family routine. Demands are made for the child to eat and sleep on a regular schedule and to be responsive to family interactions.

In addition to interpersonal situations, the physical environment places demands on the child. For effective adaptation, coping efforts must accommodate to the properties of the inanimate world: arrangement of space, size of furniture, texture of objects, intensity of surrounding noise, and so forth.

The Child's Coping Effort

The child's efforts to meet demands are based on available developmental skills and other coping resources, including the beliefs acquired through past experience. Types of coping strategies were presented earlier in this chapter.

The Adult's Response to the Child's Coping Effort

The adult's response provides feedback about the child's coping effort. One type of feed-back is for the adult to assist the child physically or verbally. For example, when the child's coping effort is directed toward reaching a toy, the caregiver can help by pushing it closer. Feedback is also evaluative, providing information regarding the quality, success, and per-ceived value of the child's efforts. In addition, the feedback can take the form of a new demand. For instance, when the child has successfully placed a piece in the puzzle, the adult may hand the child another piece.

The Child's Reaction to the Response

The child's reaction to the adult's response is internalized and helps to shape emerging beliefs about self and the world. When the response from the significant other is support-ive of the child's behavior, the child is validated; the behavior is reinforced and mutually positive feelings of satisfaction are engendered. When the response is negative, feelings of frustration and inadequacy are reinforced.

These four components of a transaction are intimately related and cyclical in nature. Transactions occur naturally in daily life and may range from single encounters to more complex interactional sequences.

SUMMARY

This chapter emphasizes the special relationship of coping and development in the first 3 years and reviews the coping process from the perspective of the young child. From that viewpoint, coping resources are reexamined, as well as transactions between the child and caregiver.

CHAPTER 4

The Family System

A coping-related approach to early intervention recognizes the complexity and diversity of families. The use of family systems theory facilitates an understanding of the many factors influencing family life. As discussed earlier in this book, the birth of any child has a significant impact on the family. There are changes in the family's daily routines, in the roles of family members, and in the plans the family makes for their future. When a child has special needs, these changes may be even more substantial. A knowledge of family systems helps the practitioner to be responsive to family dynamics, to the ways in which members interact with one another and with the community.

The idea that the family could be viewed as an interacting system stems from the work of biologist Ludwig von Bertalanffy (1968). He pioneered the idea of general systems theory based on his work in the natural sciences. Social scientists took the principles of general systems theory and applied them to the transactions of the family. In this perspective, the family is considered a set of interdependent parts. A change in any one part of the system affects other parts. Each part, like the entire system, has basic needs for survival, adaptation, and maintenance. The family system has its own structure, rules, and problem-solving strategies. Additionally, it is controlled by principles of communication and feedback.

An important part of systems theory is the concept of *homeostasis*, which is defined as a relatively stable balance. Systems and their parts strive to attain a balance that supports harmonious functioning. Change in any part of the system upsets the balance. Once upset, the goal of the system and its parts is to reestablish homeostasis or create a new balance. Each developmental phase of the family life cycle represents a new threat to the balance, as do most changes. Mastering these challenges and their attendant demands in an adaptive way is a basic striving of the family system. Each change can be viewed as a demand, and each part of the system must respond to cope with that demand.

This chapter first describes critical factors that affect the family system—its structure, cultural diversity, functions, life cycle, and subsystems. Then there is consideration of the impact of a child with special needs on the family system.

FACTORS INFLUENCING FAMILY LIFE

Family Structure

Family structure refers to the composition and associated roles of family members. The American family has experienced many changes during the past 4 decades. Television, a mirror of society, reflects these trends. Old favorites of the 1950s and 1960s depicted the traditional two-parent nuclear family. In "Ozzie and Harriet" and "Leave It to Beaver," the father was the breadwinner and the mother the homemaker. In the 1970s, programs began to present different family structures. "The Brady Bunch" represented a blended structure in which a mother and her daughters joined with a father and his sons. Ideas were introduced related to remarriage, step-parenting, and half-siblings. Programs such as "Alice" showed a single working parent raising her child. Multigenerational families were illustrated by "All in the Family" and "Maude."

Since the 1980s, prime time series have shown increasingly diverse family structures. For example, "Kate and Ali" portrayed two single women and their children residing in the same household. "My Two Dads" depicted two men raising a teen-age daughter.

In the early 1990s, the most watched series was "The Cosby Show," which portrayed a black middle-class family headed by two professional working parents. The program emphasized family values, togetherness, and family pride. In "Murphy Brown," another popular show, Ms. Brown elected to have a child whom she would raise without the father. These trends in television reflect the changing demographics of contemporary society, and all of them recognize the importance of parenting and family life.

The traditional nuclear family of "Ozzie and Harriet" is now a minority. The U.S. divorce rate, although apparently stabilizing, is close to 50% of all marriages—one of the highest rates in the world (Hoffman, 1992). The majority of children born after 1980 may spend some time in a single-parent family before reaching 18 years of age. The percentage of blended families—families where remarriage has resulted in combining children from previous marriages—is also common. Remarriages presently account for 30%–40% of all marriages each year (Hoffman, 1992). Remarriage not only results in a complex web of step relationships for children, parents, grandparents, aunts, uncles, and cousins; it also introduces the possibility of future family dissolution. Approximately 40% of white children and 60% of African-American children in blended families will experience the breakup of that marriage as well (Children's Defense Fund, 1990).

Marriage, separation, and divorce are not the only factors that influence the contemporary family. The increased number of women in the work force has also had a major influence on family roles and functions. In 1988, 51% of all women with children under 6 years of age worked outside the home—up from 29% in 1970 (Children's Defense Fund, 1990).

The increased number of working mothers raises the need for more child care. In the past, child care was a function often shared by the extended family, such as aunts or grandparents, usually living in close proximity to the family. Today it is less common. The number of infants who spend 6–8 hours daily in care outside the home is increasing. Likewise, latchkey children—children who spend time alone and unsupervised after school—have become a national phenomenon.

Teenage pregnancy is also becoming more frequent. In 1989, 8.6% of all infants were born to teenage parents (Center for the Study of Social Policy, 1992). This trend is ironically juxtaposed against other data revealing that women in general are marrying and having children at an older age than previously. Another significant trend is the number of American families living in poverty. In 1988, 23.3% of families with children under 3 years of age had incomes below the poverty level (Children's Defense Fund, 1990). In particular, families headed by women are much more likely to be poorer than traditional families. More than half of the children in these single-parent families are living in poverty.

The above data indicate that family structure is quite diverse and continuing to change. As a consequence, many families may experience more stress and less stability in their lives.

Cultural Diversity

Ethnicity plays a major role in developing group identity and shaping family beliefs and values. In *Ethnicity and Family Therapy* (McGoldrick, Pearce, & Giordano, 1982), practitioners from different cultures present information about their ethnic groups. Three cultures described in this book are highlighted as examples of cultural diversity—Mexican-American, African-American, and Asian-American families.

Falicov (1982) describes the Mexican-American nuclear family as being embedded in an extended family network that includes godparents and close friends. The values of family proximity, cohesiveness, and respect for parental authority are present throughout an individual's lifetime. Autonomy and personal achievement are not particularly emphasized. As a consequence, parents tend to have a rather relaxed attitude toward their children's achievement of developmental milestones. In contrast, the preservation of dignity is a fundamental value. While there are marked differences of behavior across socio-economic strata, the male is generally dominant and the female submissive. Questions are often addressed first to the father and then to the mother. In this culture, physical distance from strangers is typically preferred.

A disability, particularly one evidenced at birth, is more likely to be perceived and accepted as an "act of God" with initial efforts for help through family or church. Extended family, especially godparents, can usually be counted on as a supportive resource. When therapy is sought, the initial interaction is likely to be formal, with the therapist of either sex viewed as an authority. When relationships are established and a comfort level achieved, there may be spontaneous hugging and touching. The therapist may then be treated like extended family (Seligman & Darling 1989).

According to Hines and Boyd-Franklin (1982), African-American families also tend to have an extended kinship system. In these families, relatives expect and accept reliance on one another in times of need and often live in close proximity. There is frequent interchanging of roles, tasks, and functions. For example, an aunt or grandmother may share the responsibility for child care. In some cases, a child is informally adopted and reared by extended family members who have resources not available to the child's parents. African-American women have historically worked outside the home and have often been the sole wage earners in times of high unemployment. It is not uncommon for the family to be matriarchal, with fathers having less active involvement in daily family matters. The church traditionally plays a key supportive role for many families, with women tending to be more active in their religion.

Particularly in low income families, parents are more likely to accept a young child with a disability as just another family member. The many pressures of survival may reduce the degree of priority given to active intervention efforts on behalf of the child. Prior experiences of the family with racism and working with agencies, especially those with white personnel, may also influence their involvement in early intervention.

According to Shon and Ja (1982), Asian-American families may have a philosophical approach to life that stems from such traditional systems as Confucianism and Buddhism. These systems emphasize that family needs supersede those of the individual. Rules of behavior and conduct are formalized to a greater extent than in most other cultures. Sons tend to be more highly valued than daughters, with different expectations for the two sexes. The most important offspring is the oldest son. The father is the leader of the family and his authority is unquestioned. The wife generally has the traditional role of nurturer, taking care of both her husband and her children. Shame and loss of face are traditional mechanisms that help to reinforce societal expectations for proper behavior. Patterns of communication are highly structured because harmonious interpersonal relationships are so highly valued. Communication tends to be indirect, with talking around an issue used to avoid confrontation.

Some Asian family members may feel that nothing can be done to change their fate when a child has a disability. Parents may attribute a birth defect or disabling condition to their own behavior during pregnancy and may feel very guilty. Birth order and gender might also influence the parents' reaction to the child's disability. Shame may be attached to seeking help.

The general characteristics of these three cultures are given to highlight the importance of being aware of beliefs. These beliefs influence the family's expectations for daily living, attitudes toward having a child with special needs, and participation in an early intervention program. These general statements are reflective of each group. However, it cannot be assumed that they describe a specific individual or family with that cultural background.

Service providers also come from families of diverse cultures, which influences their perception of the people with whom they interact. A close fit between the cultural background of the family and staff can increase initial comfort and facilitate entry into an early intervention program. When this option is not available, it is particularly important for practitioners to be aware of the family's cultural values (Lynch & Hanson, 1992). It is equally important for them to recognize the pitfalls of stereotyping any individual or group of individuals.

Family Functions

Each family engages in many different activities to meet the complex and changing needs of its members. A family's needs can be classified into seven functional categories: economic, domestic/health care, recreation, socialization, self-definition, affection, and educational/vocational (Barber, Turnbull, Behr, & Kerns, 1988). Table 4.1 presents sample tasks associated with each function. Often an activity serves several functions. For example, family dinner time not only addresses daily care, it also provides an opportunity to socialize, share affection, and acquire new knowledge. This interrelationship also means that one family function can influence others. When economic pressures, for instance, require both parents to work, time may be limited for recreation, daily care, and socialization. It is important to be aware of these functions to be able to help families balance their multiple needs and avoid over-involvement in any one function at the expense of others.

Family Life Cycle

Similar to individuals, families with children go through a developmental process. Each phase has specific issues and challenges that have to be faced. Numerous models have been created to conceptualize and describe the family life cycle (Carter & McGoldrick, 1989; Walsh, 1982). Commonly, eight phases are used to depict family life over time: the beginning, infancy, preschool, school age, adolescence, young adulthood, empty nest, and elderly years. The initial four phases are most pertinent to this discussion of families with young children. Although these phases are representative of traditional intact families, they can also be useful in understanding families with more diverse structures.

In the beginning phase, which can include courtship and early marriage, the major challenges revolve around boundary issues. New relationships need to be established, refined, and negotiated with the partner, in-laws, parents, and siblings, as a new family is forged separate from the family of origin. Rules for family life are established, roles are defined, and communication patterns are crafted. This time of change, coupling, and growth can be complicated by the early birth of a child.

Table 4.1. Tasks associated with family functions

Economic	Domestic/health care	Recreation
Generating income Paying bills and banking Handling investments Overseeing insurance benefit programs Earning allowance Dispensing allowance	Food purchasing and food preparation Clothes purchasing and preparation Health care and maintenance Safety and protection Transportation Home maintenance	Individual and family-oriented Setting aside demands Developing and enjoying hobbies
Socialization	**Self-definition**	**Affection**
Interpersonal relationships Developing social skills Engaging in social activities	Establishing self-identity and self-image Recognizing strengths and weaknesses Sense of belonging	Nurturing and love Companionship Intimacy Expressing emotions
	Educational/vocational	
	Continuing education for parents School work Homework Cultural appreciation Career choice Development of work ethic Support of career interests and problems	

From Turnbull, A.P., & Turnbull, H.R. (1986). *Families, professionals, and exceptionality: A special partnership* (p. 68). Columbus, OH: Charles E. Merrill; reprinted by permission.

The second phase usually begins with pregnancy or the birth of the first child. Critical issues revolve around a dyad becoming a triad, which involves changing roles and child-care responsibilities. The birth of a child generates many challenges—some expected, others unexpected. For example, the decision may be for the mother to continue working; yet, the problem of the mother having to work in spite of a chronic sleep deficit may not be contemplated. While child care is considered, parents rarely envisage the trials of getting a screaming infant to or from the childcare center in rush-hour traffic.

The stress of this stage is potentially extreme, with conflict and crisis common. Demands and adjustments are particularly increased when the child is born to a teenager, a single mother, a mother who is at a relatively late stage in her own life cycle, or when the child is born with a disability. Adjustments must then occur not only within the family, but also in the family's interactions with the world. The behavioral patterns established, often with great effort, are tested and may need to be changed.

The third phase is characterized by two events—family expansion and preschool. Often, these two events occur close together. For some families, preparing the child to enter a childcare or preschool program may be quite stressful. For example, toilet training becomes more important when the child's entry into the program depends on it. The birth of a second child poses additional demands; the only child must become an older brother or sister and learn to share the parents. Parents need to care for their new baby and their semi-independent preschool child while still maintaining their adult relationships.

The fourth stage is characterized by the full-time school attendance of the children who are having to cope with the demands of the school and their peers. Parents face sharing responsibilities and possibly the renegotiation of roles. This is a time when children are becoming more involved in community activities, which place time pressures on the family and may tax communication. Many women choose this stage to start work outside the home or to shift from part-time to full-time employment. For those who have worked all along, career decisions and moves are often contemplated. In many cases, parents have to face new questions concerning the balance between home and family and their roles outside the home.

These first four phases of the family's life cycle highlight the ever-changing roles and needs of individuals and family units. While this developmental model largely reflects a traditional view of the American family, it provides a framework for understanding the complex challenges of family life. This complexity is compounded when, for example, there is remarriage resulting in a blended family or a new baby added to a family with adolescent children. In these cases, the family has to manage two different stages in its life cycle simultaneously.

Family Subsystems

Families are structured into a number of subsystems (Minuchin, 1974), each being a functional unit with organized sets of relationships and specific, although unwritten, rules. Each subsystem carries out particular functions important to the overall family system. Each member of the family is a part of more than one subsystem and may play a very different role in each one. Subsystems have, or should have, clearly defined boundaries, and at times subsystem coalitions are formed to carry out various family functions.

In most families there are three subsystems: the spousal subsystem, the parental subsystem, and the sibling subsystem. The *spousal subsystem* is most basic to the family—its membership is limited to two people who form a couple. The spousal subsystem provides a key model for the establishment of rules, resolution of conflicts, and determination of the kinds of transactions that represent the family's values. Divorce is a major threat to this subsystem. In the case of a single parent there is no spousal subsystem. The parent may look toward other adults for some of the attributes and support generally found within the spousal relationship.

The *parental subsystem* performs the basic child-rearing functions for the family and is composed of the primary caregivers with the children. This subsystem provides guidance and nurturance to the young. In some families it may include grandparents, stepparents, older siblings, or even paid caregivers.

The third category, *the sibling subsystem*, comprises offspring of the spousal relationship as well as other children living in the home. This system is the child's first peer group.

Families are most effective when subsystem membership and rules are clearly defined by boundaries (i.e., delineations between systems). When boundaries, rules, and membership of subsystems are either too rigid or too diffuse, problems and confusion can develop. Primary relationships within the family, often called *alliances*, optimally occur within subsystems rather than across subsystems.

The identity and influence of family subsystems can be quite complex. Consider the example of a teenage mother who has no contact with her baby's biological father, lives in her parents' house, and has younger brothers and sisters. To which subsystem does she belong? How does the baby fit in? Who constitutes the spousal subsystem? Who constitutes the parental subsystem? What are the implications for early intervention?

IMPACT OF THE CHILD WITH SPECIAL NEEDS ON THE FAMILY SYSTEM

Although the professional literature has been helpful in increasing awareness of the influence of the child with special needs on the family, for the most part it emphasizes negative aspects. Focus is on the emotional reactions to a child's diagnosis and the disruptions in routine family life. Case studies tend to describe pathological responses of families. The literature rarely recognizes that most families do not become immobilized by anger, sorrow, or depression. Somehow within the family, strengths and resources are mobilized—allowing meals to be prepared, beds to be made, babies dressed, and children sent to school each day.

The birth of a child with special needs presents families with physical and emotional demands that may increase their levels of stress. This stress may influence each aspect of the family system in both positive and negative ways. Although problems may be generated, opportunities are also created for mobilizing positive forces. The usually unanticipated event of having a child with special needs may cause changes in the family system.

The impact of disability on the family structure is often complex and multifaceted. Certain family structures, such as those with incomes at the poverty level and those with teenage or older mothers, have a higher incidence of children with special needs. The presence of a child with a disability may also influence decisions regarding employment. For example, some mothers may want to seek employment due to extra financial demands, whereas others may choose not to work because of the increased parenting responsibilities. Likewise, economic pressure may require some fathers to take a second job, which limits their time at home. Also, in some families, the likelihood of divorce may increase and the potential for remarriage decrease. Divorce is more likely in situations where the marital relationship was vulnerable before the birth of the child. With the high demands of caregiving, extended family members, such as grandparents or aunts and uncles, may share these responsibilities with the nuclear family.

Families are most effective when there is an opportunity to address in their daily lives all of the previously described functions. The presence of a child with special needs may interfere with this happening (Barber et al., 1988). Some children, due to the nature of their disability or its severity, place added demands on specific functions, making some more stressful and limiting the time and resources available for others. For example, when the child requires complex daily care, the family has less opportunity for recreation and homemaking activities.

A less tangible impact is on the more emotionally based functions of socialization, self-definition, and affection. Some parents of children with special needs describe experiences that lead to feelings of social isolation. Ventures into the community are sometimes uncomfortable because of the behavior of others who may stare at them, make insensitive comments, or ask intrusive questions. One mother shared her feelings of anger when a photographer at the shopping mall told her that children more than 6 months of age were required to sit in a regular chair, an impossible task for her toddler with cerebral palsy.

Friends and relatives sometimes do not know what to do or say and consequently may feel inadequate and awkward. These feelings may cause them to withdraw from intimate involvement with the family or to develop a habit of giving unsolicited, inappropriate advice. In contrast, other families describe how their relationships deepened with relatives and friends, and how their social network expanded as a result of meeting other parents who have children with special needs.

Within the family, the development and expression of affection may also be influenced by the child's disability. When a baby is not responsive to caregiving, parents may become upset, withdrawn, or ambivalent, and, therefore, less likely to give sensitive caregiving. This interaction pattern with its reciprocal negative reinforcement strains the development of attachment and diminishes feelings of efficacy for both parent and child. However, the child's special requirements may generate an outpouring of love and caring that substantially increases the cohesiveness of the family.

A child with a disability may add to the demands families have to cope with at specific stages of the life cycle. The family with a young child faces the challenges of obtaining a diagnosis, informing siblings and relatives, acquiring needed services, and deriving personal meaning from the experience. Subsequent periods of the life cycle may be delayed because of the child's developmental pattern and increased dependency. Family expansion is sometimes postponed or rejected due to the extra economic and caregiving demands or the fear of having a second child with a disability. Returning to work can be complicated by problems related to securing adequate day care and intervention services. A pervading issue that influences all stages in the life cycle is the degree of functional independence the child can be expected to achieve.

Like other dimensions of family dynamics, the boundaries, rules, and membership of the subsystems are also influenced. Much has been written about the positive and negative impact on the spousal relationship (Gallagher et al., 1983; Garland, 1993; Turnbull & Turnbull, 1990). A similar range of reaction and fluctuation is also evidenced by siblings who have a brother or sister with a disability. At times, these children may experience great satisfaction from the achievements of the exceptional sibling. At other times, they may feel too much attention is paid to this family member.

SUMMARY

This chapter discusses many facets of family systems that need to be considered in professional practice—structure, cultural diversity, functions, life cycle, and subsystems. Whereas having a child with special needs has an impact on the family system, one cannot make generalizations or assumptions about what the impact is for a particular family without information about their characteristics, priorities, and coping resources.

CHAPTER 5

Planning Coping-Related Services

The first four chapters of this book presented information about coping and families. The purpose of this chapter is to start to apply that information to the development of early intervention programs that reflect the coping perspective. In this chapter, the coping-related program goals of these authors are restated and linked to their beliefs about the nature of intervention and the helping relationship. These beliefs—drawn from theory, research, and practice—provide the foundation for planning, implementing, and evaluating services. The personalized decision-making model is also introduced. This model provides a structure that facilitates ongoing, flexible decision making that helps ensure effective services over time. Finally, various methods are presented for collecting and sharing information.

FOUNDATIONS FOR SERVICE DELIVERY

Early Intervention Goals

Families in early intervention programs vary greatly in their composition, concerns, and resources. Programs also vary in their purpose, philosophy, resources, and staff. To be optimally effective, however, there has to be a good fit between family requirements and program capability.

Each early intervention program needs to have a philosophy that provides principles for guiding its practical affairs. This philosophy is often reflected in a mission statement that delineates the program's goals for intervention. These goals identify the desired outcomes the program wishes to achieve, which in turn form the basis for evaluating the program's effectiveness. Program operations are assessed to see how they influence achievement of the goals. As a consequence, the first question an early intervention program has to consider is: Within the constraints of law, policy, and available resources, what outcomes does the program seek to achieve? Stated another way: What has to happen for the program to be considered successful?

Different practitioners and programs may have varied responses. The following list is a sampling of expected outcomes culled from discussions with hundreds of staff members in programs throughout the country.

> To increase children's ability to reach their fullest potential
> To teach family members how to help their children
> To assist parents to come to terms with their child's disability

To reduce family stress
To enhance parent–child interactions
To foster the emotional adjustment of siblings
To support the relationship between family members and the community at large
To empower families so that they can be lifelong advocates for their children
To strengthen the independence and interdependence of each family member

As stated earlier, the two major goals for intervention with a coping frame of reference are:

1. To enhance the life outcomes of young children with special needs by increasing their developmental and coping capability
2. To enhance the coping resources of families of children with special needs

Implementation of services to achieve these goals are strongly influenced by beliefs about intervention and the helping relationship.

Beliefs About Intervention

Intervention that incorporates the coping perspective is based upon the following beliefs. They are instrumental in the planning and provision of services.

1. All early intervention services need to have a clearly identified purpose and expectation of outcome for the designated activities.
2. Intervention that focuses on building coping resources prepares children and their families to meet present and future demands.
3. A collaborative relationship is a key to providing services that are responsive to family priorities.
4. The development and implementation of services must reflect an awareness and respect for the family's culture, values, privacy, and style of decision making. These factors influence the manner and mode in which the family functions and the child learns.
5. Families change over time, so a component of service provision is the ongoing clarification of the family's concerns, priorities, and resources. The sharing of this and other pertinent information is an evolving process that continuously shapes and alters the service plan.
6. Adults in children's lives behave differently with each child, not only because each child is unique but also because the transactions for each interactive pair are unique.
7. Children strive for mastery of their own private inner world as well as for mastery of the world outside them. These two worlds are interrelated, and the child needs understanding and support to operate in both.
8. Teaching and learning are interactive processes that are the mutual responsibility of the teacher (e.g., parent, practitioner) and the child. This mutual responsibility applies to learning specific skills, their application for functional outcomes, and their generalization to other areas. The adult, however, takes responsibility for managing the process.
9. A role of the professional is to support the parents' efforts to achieve their desired outcomes.

Beliefs and the Helping Relationship

The need to establish a collaborative relationship with parents challenges staff members to think carefully about their roles. Practitioners in early intervention programs often believe that their job is to help others. Helping becomes both their personal style and a core activity that gives meaning and purpose to their lives. Help, however, is not always perceived by the recipient as being useful in leading to greater satisfaction or a better situation.

Practitioners may offer help for a variety of motives. They may wish to improve another's performance, reduce their own feelings of guilt, obtain gratitude, make someone happy, or give meaning to their own lives. A person may want to demonstrate superior skill or knowledge, induce indebtedness, control others, establish dependency, or simply meet what is believed to be a job requirement. These conscious or partially conscious motivations may be so intermingled in any act of helping that it is often difficult for the helper or the recipient to sort them out.

Depending on the way the recipient sees the motives of the helper, his or her reactions may range from feelings of gratitude to those of resentment and hostility. The recipient may feel helpless and dependent or may feel jealous of the helper having the strength or resources to be in the helper role. The person may feel genuinely indebted or may simply feel pressured to conform to the perceived demands or beliefs of the helper.

As a consequence of being helped, the recipient may become more helpless and dependent, less able to make decisions or initiate actions, less self-sufficient, more apathetic and passive, and less willing to take risks. Alternatively, the recipient may become more creative, less dependent on helpers, more willing to risk making decisions, more highly motivated to tackle tough problems, and more effective at working independently or interdependently.

Table 5.1 presents six orientations described by Pfeifer and Jones (1972) that influence the helping relationship. One set of conditions maximizes help; a parallel set minimizes help. Early intervention practitioners need to consider the personal and programmatic impact of each of these orientations. When does the helping relationship promote collaboration and individual coping efforts, and when does it hinder them?

Reciprocal Trust versus Distrust   When a relationship is characterized by mutual acceptance and trust, offers of help are more likely to be appreciated, listened to, seen as potentially helpful, and acted upon. Help tends to be rejected when it is seen as being offered as a means to control, correct, or gain power. When there are feelings of distrust, even well-intended help may be resisted, resented, or seen as unhelpful. It may be perceived that help is being offered to place the recipient in a dependent position, to elicit expressions of gratitude, or to assert superiority.

Cooperative Learning versus Training, Advice Giving, and Indoctrinating   When there is a cooperative quest for learning, people are helpful to each other and generate an

Table 5.1. The helping relationship

Orientations that help	Orientations that hinder
1. Reciprocal trust (confidence, warmth, acceptance)	1. Distrust (fear, defensiveness)
2. Cooperative learning (inquiry, exploration, quest)	2. Training, advice giving, and indoctrinating
3. Mutual growth	3. Evaluating (fixing, providing a remedy)
4. Reciprocal feedback	4. Planning for
5. Shared problem solving (defining, producing alternatives, testing)	5. Steering and controlling
6. Experimenting (play, innovation, provisional trying)	6. Patterning (standard, static, fixed)

Adapted from Pfeifer & Jones (1972).

atmosphere of joint inquiry and exploration. Help is reciprocal in that the roles of helper and helpee are interchangeable. Each can learn from the other and from the common task. When one tries to train, advise, persuade, or indoctrinate the other, or is perceived as wanting to do so, the possibilities for learning are reduced on both sides. Each person has to accept personal responsibility for learning.

Mutual Growth versus Evaluating   The most significant evidence of help in a relationship is continual growth by both parties. Growth is often hindered when one seeks to appraise or remedy the problems of the other. Help is most effective when it is seen as a force moving toward growth rather than an effort to fill gaps, remedy defects, or bring another person up to standard criterion.

Reciprocal Feedback versus Planning For   An important condition for effective learning is the opportunity to give and receive feedback, to know how the other feels and sees things. Consequently, the helping process is most effective when one plans with another, not for another. It is not helpful when there is no feedback and a person is maneuvered into taking some action that is not understood. Feedback is essential in acquiring skills, knowledge, and attitudes (see chap. 14, this volume, for a discussion of how to provide feedback).

Shared Problem Solving versus Steering and Controlling   Problem solving involves a joint determination of the problem, continual redefinition of the problem as successive insights are gained, a joint focus on possible alternative solutions, a joint exploration of the data, and continual reality testing of the alternatives. Each person shares his or her expertise and resources. When there is one-way steering or controlling, the recipient of help is encouraged to be dependent on the helper and, therefore, does not develop confidence in personal skills.

Experimenting versus Patterning   Important characteristics of a productive, helping relationship are innovative experimentation and a tentativeness in the search for solutions. This is evidenced by a sense of play, excitement, and fun in the collaborative effort to find ways to resolve problems. Help is limited when the process is approached as an effort to meet a prescribed standard, meet criteria, or reach a rigid, predetermined goal.

In summary, "help" is not always helpful. It has meaning when both the helper and the recipient can grow and learn in a spirit of trust, joint inquiry, openness, and interdependence. Early intervention practitioners need to examine their perception of what it means to be in a "helping profession" and how their personal view of helping influences their relationship with families.

Collaboration

Collaboration between the parent and the professional is at the core of effective intervention. How, then, can a collaborative relationship be fostered best? Collaboration may be a new and sometimes uncomfortable role for both partners. Most professionals are discipline-trained and feel pride in their ability to know what to do without having to consult those whom they consider to be "untrained." Parents may lack confidence in their knowledge or simply may not know what they believe to be best for their child. The following are some guidelines that can facilitate collaboration.

Parental efforts to share information and become involved in the program need to be encouraged and received nonjudgmentally by professionals. It is important that parents be a part of the early intervention team. Communication that is characterized by listening, empathy, and mutual feedback enhances trust and respect between parent–professional partners. Sensitivity to the feelings of parents decreases the likelihood that they will feel threatened or judged by professionals and helps to support parental feelings of confidence in caregiving.

A collaborative partnership involves mutual decision making based on shared knowledge. A partnership implies a "doing with," not a "doing for" or a "doing to." Information, including medical and technical information, has to be communicated in clear and understandable language in a format that fosters understanding. This type of communication encourages informed decision making.

A parent–professional partnership provides mutual support for each other's efforts. Support to parents can include reassurance, positive feedback, knowledge sharing, and mutual problem solving, as well as the provision of specific services in response to family priorities. The partners work together toward mutually established outcomes for the child and family. The child's development and the family's well-being are the major concerns of the partnership.

There is no single "right way" to collaborate with parents. Each family has a unique set of resources and vulnerabilities that influence their priorities, coping effectiveness, and preferred style of interacting with others. Though families may have many common issues, no two families are exactly alike; thus, interactions with a family need to be personalized. Basic to collaboration is an atmosphere of acceptance of differences in skills, acceptance of differences in approach, willingness not to try to know everything, an ability to call on others for assistance and ongoing knowledge, and nonthreatening opportunities for discussion in these areas (Johnson, McGonigel, & Kaufmann, 1992). The following is a list of questions that practitioners can ask themselves to help facilitate the development of a collaborative relationship.

Do I really understand how family members perceive their concerns? Did I check it out?

Do I know the depth of feeling they have about their concerns?

Did I take over the family's concerns? Did I try to solve them for the family? Did I ignore any concern?

Did I really listen?

Was I able to help identify resources available to solve the problem?

Do I understand how family members feel as a result of the information I provided?

Of the questions that I asked, which ones were particularly helpful?

What can I do to become better at collaboration?

THE PERSONALIZED DECISION-MAKING MODEL

Basic to planning, implementation, and modification of the individualized family service plan (IFSP) is the ongoing need for decision making. The personalized decision-making model is an effective tool that facilitates such collaborative efforts. The model has three steps that guide planning for change. Decision-making questions help to work through each step in the process and then to integrate the parts into a whole. Implementation and evaluation of the service plan generates the need over time to repeat the decision-making process.

Use of the model facilitates the development of IFSPs that are practical, personalized, and integrated. A step-by-step response to the decision-making questions helps to design plans that build from the child's present functioning and the family's concerns, priorities, and resources. These plans include services and activities offered by the early intervention program as well as the community. The model provides a structure for communication and collaboration among parents and practitioners who may have varying points of view. This decision-making process is appropriate for use with diverse families and can be used in a variety of service delivery environments. Chapters 10 and 11, this volume, present the decision-making questions that guide the process of developing an IFSP. Actually, the model can be used whenever change is planned. Following are the three steps of the personalized decision-making model:

Step 1: Information Collecting and Sharing   In the first step, the information that is needed to achieve a specific purpose is identified, collected, and summarized. (Information collection from a coping perspective is discussed in greater detail later in this chapter.)

Step 2: Information Analysis and Long-Term Functional Outcome Planning   In this second step, the summarized information is analyzed and the factors that are likely to facilitate or to interfere with achievement of the desired outcome are determined. The interfering factors are studied to identify those that can be changed and those that cannot (at least for the present). Among the factors that can be changed, priorities are established. Priorities are those factors whose change would make the most difference in moving toward achieving the desired outcome. That decision establishes the long-range functional outcomes toward which planning is directed. These goals or outcome statements become the basis for an implementation plan to achieve them.

Step 3: Development of the Implementation Plan   The purpose of this step is to identify the short-term goals and objectives to achieve the identified long-range functional goals. In Step 3, services, strategies, and activities are planned for reaching the desired outcomes.

INFORMATION SHARING

Information sharing is the first step toward developing a collaborative relationship between parents and professionals. Information is a powerful tool, not a neutral commodity. Individuals perceive the information they acquire in a subjective and personal way. The emotional impact of this information can neither be overlooked nor taken for granted. In addition, every opportunity to gather, provide, or share information is also an opportunity for feedback and the clarification of intentions and perceptions. Without feedback, misunderstandings may be generated or existing ones may become magnified. Information sharing is beneficial for everyone involved, as it facilitates the recognition of feelings and of changing demands or priorities. It also provides feedback regarding different perceptions of what is or is not happening.

In early intervention, there tends to be a focus on intensive initial assessment to develop the first IFSP. There is increasing recognition, however, that learning about children and their families is a continuously evolving process rather than an activity that can be initiated and completed at a single point in time. There has to be a delicate balance between: 1) collecting and sharing the information needed to develop service plans collaboratively, and 2) allowing families time to develop the trust that is necessary for sharing.

It is important to draw a distinction between information that is needed for effective service delivery and information that places excessive demands on the family and staff or that crosses the boundaries of a family's rights to privacy. Each early intervention program must carefully determine the purposes for which information is needed and the sequence in which it is needed. In general, there are five key reasons for collecting and sharing information: 1) to determine eligibility for services, 2) to get started in a program, 3) to develop a service plan, 4) to implement intervention activities, and 5) to evaluate and modify activities on an ongoing basis. In reality, information sharing is integral to all aspects of intervention.

The two-way process involved in information sharing recognizes that families want information about the early intervention program. To get started, they want to know about the program's philosophy, activities, procedures, and staff. A glossary of terms may also be useful for a new family.

Orientation to early intervention may take many forms. Some programs run periodic meetings for new families. Others provide tours prior to screening or evaluation; some use a variety of brochures and handouts; and still others use videotapes to introduce the program. The purpose, rather than the format, is the critical issue. There are three reasons for orienting families: 1) to provide family members with basic information about the program; 2) to begin to establish a relationship based on trust and mutual collaboration; and 3) to clarify roles, expectations, and responsibilities.

Providing the family with initial information about early intervention services is an activity that requires thoughtful preparation by program staff. They have to be careful not to limit a family's vision of early intervention by the way in which they describe existing services. Instead, the staff can describe a range of services and activities in the program and community that may be supportive of the child and family.

Methods for Collecting and Sharing Information

There are numerous methods for learning about children and their families. These include the use of structured interviews, informal interactions, observation, and various types of instruments. The clinical judgment of the professional is an essential tool for collecting critical information. In selecting methods, care is taken to consider the experience of the staff, the need for standardized or specialized procedures and staff training, the specific population for which the method is intended, and its usefulness for intervention. Basic to all information gathering is: 1) that families feel free to share what they choose without prejudice to the availability of desired services, and 2) that information about children stems from more than one source. Specific tools for information collection are described in Chapter 6, this volume.

Structured Interviews   The use of planned questions in an interview format provides a consistent structure for the collection of relevant information. An advantage of this approach is that it is flexible: Additional questions can be asked when indicated, or questioning can be stopped if there is discomfort. Responses can also be made to nonverbal communication. The structure helps give confidence to practitioners who have minimal experience working with families by providing them with appropriate questions or guidelines. Structured interviews are particularly useful for the initial meeting with the family as well as when additional information is being gathered about their coping resources.

During an interview, staff or a family member may feel uncomfortable with certain topics. A statement, such as "If you are feeling uncomfortable, we can drop the question" or "If you prefer, we don't have to discuss that right now" will help allay the fears of either party. In many cases, a natural conversation can substitute for an interview, and it is preferred. Information is shared in a free flow, conversational dialogue.

Informal Interactions   Additional information about the child's capabilities and coping behaviors, as well as the family's interests, priorities, and coping resources, is often gained during informal interactions with family members over time. There are numerous opportunities for these exchanges: the intake process, the initial evaluation of the child, home visits, casual contact in the hallways, and intervention sessions. Staff have to be flexible as they work with the child so they can also be responsive to the parent's need to talk—even if planned activities have to be postponed.

One should be alert to parental behaviors that frequently indicate worry or undue stress. The following behaviors require attention: When one topic is continually pursued regardless of its appropriateness to the situation; when extremely unrealistic expectations are voiced; when a parent's interpretation of an event is very different from that of others; when there is evidence in body posture or facial expression of anger, anxiety, or confusion; when voice tone is too loud or too soft; or when any behaviors appear unusual.

One also has to be alert to atypical behavior in the child; for example, when a usually easy-to-handle child becomes difficult, when a usually happy child cries excessively, or when a child is very cranky or lethargic. Although one needs to be very cautious in interpreting these impressions, they should not be overlooked or quickly dismissed without considering their possible meaning.

Observations   Observation is an important tool for learning how the child and family behave in a variety of planned or unplanned situations. Observations can be made either randomly or in a structured, preplanned manner. Methods range from the systematic counting and recording of predetermined behaviors in a uniquely designed environment to anecdotal recording of behavior in a more natural and functional context. The method selected is determined by the information sought. For example, frequency counts of a child's behavior in response to specific environmental events may be needed when assessing a targeted maladaptive behavior, particularly when a behavior modification approach is indicated. More informal methods are appropriate when the purpose of observation is to know more about coping style and other coping resources. Chapter 6, this volume, provides a format for the systematic observation of transactions.

Anecdotal observations of the child in a variety of situations are very useful. They provide the descriptive information from which judgments can be made. It is often hard for practitioners who are trained to make quick judgments from the observation of actions to set aside the judging temporarily and just record what they see. But it is important because there can be more than one interpretation of most observed situations. Once a judgment is written, what actually happened is lost and the meaning of the event cannot be reconstructed. For example, here are two versions of the same event:

John is having a difficult time stacking the little boxes. (Judgment)

John puts his hand on top of the first box with his fingers barely reaching the edges. He raises the box an inch or two in the air and it drops out of his hand. John pauses and looks around, then he picks up another box using two hands and places the box, somewhat askew, on top of the one that is lying on the floor. (Description)

Norm- and Criterion-Referenced Instruments   When selecting instruments, their validity and reliability should be examined. Instruments that focus on the identification of pathology are to be avoided for general usage, as are instruments that are so broad in scope that they touch on issues beyond the concern of early intervention programs.

Many of the developmental instruments generally used with children provide results that are difficult to translate into program planning. They also do not consider how the child learns new information or applies previously learned skills. A number of child-related factors can also limit the validity of an assessment. These factors include effects of medication on the arousal state of the child, physical limitations and sensory impairments, general variability in behavior, unique individual differences, and culturally related influences on development (Simeonsson, Huntington, & Parse, 1980). The validity of the information collected is enhanced by assessing the child over time using a variety of instruments and procedures.

In norm-referenced instruments, the child's performance is compared to the performance of a specified population. Standardized procedures are required for administering the instrument. Frequently these procedures cannot be followed with young children who have a disability. Likewise, many of these instruments do not have a disabled group in their norming sample. Little consideration is given to the variabilities that may occur in a child's developmental progress because of a specific disability. These factors must be attended to in using normative instruments.

In criterion-referenced instruments, items are rated according to specifically stated standards of mastery. The child is assessed according to these criteria, as opposed to a comparison group. This approach focuses on the child's repertoire of available skills and facilitates personalized intervention planning.

Self-Reporting Instruments Self-reporting instruments can be used by family members to identify or clarify their concerns, priorities, and resources as well as to choose desired activities and services. When many families respond to the same set of questions, there is greater consistency in the type of information collected. As a consequence, similarities and differences within the group of parents in a program are easier to appreciate and plan for. These instruments can be completed by the parents at their convenience, either at the center or at home. This approach allows time for reflection and an opportunity for parents to decide what information they wish to share.

Practitioners need to be aware that family members may sometimes give replies that they think professionals want to receive rather than revealing how they see themselves. The use of self-reporting instruments protects against professional bias in recording information. For families that are less familiar with the English language or may not be comfortable with a paper-and-pencil activity, the questions from the instrument can be presented in an interview format and the replies shared as feedback—"I think this is what you said"—not as interpretations. Such feedback facilitates the discussion of information that might otherwise be difficult to introduce. Self-reporting instruments can also be completed in a group and may be used to stimulate group discussion.

The use of a checklist enables practitioners to plan services that meet the identified concerns of the family. Parents and siblings can check off their preferences for program participation (e.g., special topical meetings, services during the day or evening, support groups, respite care, social events).

In summary, no one method for gathering and sharing information is best. Each technique has value when used appropriately. It is generally preferred to use more than one method for information gathering and to select procedures that are relevant to intervention activities. Choices about which method to use also depend on the characteristics and experiences of the family, their educational and cultural background, the structure of the program, and the experience of the staff.

SUMMARY

In this chapter, initial steps are taken to translate coping-related theory and information into practical application for intervention. The importance of program goals is presented and related to beliefs about intervention and the helping relationship. A personalized decision-making model is introduced to provide a structure for collaborative planning. Methods for information collection and sharing, a component of the process, are also discussed.

CHAPTER 6

Assessment from a Coping Perspective

Effective intervention builds from information about the coping resources and transactions of the child and family. This chapter focuses on methods of learning about the coping resources of the child. The family is considered the child's most critical external resource—human support. A method is also provided for observing and analyzing coping transactions. (Chap. 9, this volume, expands the discussion of the family's resources.)

Initially, each of the child's resources is discussed separately. External resources are described within the context of the family and community. In the actual process of information collection, however, many interrelated resources are assessed simultaneously.

THE CHILD'S COPING STYLE

Coping style refers to the child's characteristic way of behaving in situations viewed as harmful, threatening, or challenging to the child's sense of well-being. It includes the repertoire of behavioral attributes that a child draws on to manage the opportunities, demands, and frustrations encountered in daily living. It is most effectively assessed through observation of the child in a variety of situations. Observations can be conducted informally or through the use of an instrument. Generally, available assessment tools tend to address only certain aspects of coping, such as temperament, locus of control, social skills, and personality attributes. In response to the need for an integrated, clinically applicable assessment tool, these authors developed two observation instruments that specifically assess the coping style of children—the Early Coping Inventory for infants and toddlers (Zeitlin, Williamson, & Szczepanski, 1988) and the Coping Inventory for children and youth ages 3–16 (Zeitlin, 1985).

The Early Coping Inventory is designed for children 4–36 months of age or for older children with special needs who function within this developmental age range. The Coping Inventory is intended for an older group of children 3–16 years of age. Each item to be rated in the instruments specifies a behavioral characteristic documented in the research literature, or identified by expert clinical judgment, as important to coping in children. Because coping is an integrated process, items to be evaluated in the inventories tap a range of domains—temperament, sensory processing, motor control, psychological functions, and socioemotional factors.

The instruments do not assess specific coping efforts (i.e., strategies used in a particular situation) but instead the broader behaviors, attributes, or competencies of the child that serve as a resource to support coping efforts. These behavioral characteristics or coping behaviors represent such attributes as flexibility, independent problem solving, generalization of learning, and expression of emotional range. Any item depicting a coping behavior can be demonstrated by a variety of discrete actions. For example, "the ability to initiate action to communicate a need" is an item in the Early Coping Inventory that is representative of a coping behavior common to all ages. However, the actual coping efforts used to implement this coping behavior are influenced by the child's developmental age: a 6-month-old infant may initiate actions to get needs met by crying or changing body posture, a 12-month-old infant may indicate a desire for an object by pointing, and a 2-year-old toddler may indicate needs or preferences by speaking. Thus, coping style reflects how the child functionally applies general capabilities to the generation of purposeful, effortful responses to the multiple demands of daily living.

Early Coping Inventory for Infants and Toddlers

Because this book focuses on the adaptive functioning of infants and toddlers, the Early Coping Inventory is emphasized. This criterion-referenced observation instrument is primarily designed to be rated by professionals in their educational and therapeutic practice; however, it may also be used by parents to help increase their understanding of their child's behavior. Psychometric validation of the inventory is based on a series of studies that establishes its construct and content validity as well as interrater and test–retest reliability. Validity is concerned with the appropriateness, usefulness, and meaning that can be drawn from scores on an assessment instrument. Reliability refers to the accuracy of test scores; that is, how free scores are from errors of measurement (American Psychological Association, 1985). Interrater reliability coefficients for the instrument's different categories range from .80 to .94.

Information used to rate the Early Coping Inventory is collected by an individual who observes the child in a variety of situations over a period of time. The amount of time spent observing is determined by the rater's previous knowledge of the child and the type of activities taking place during observations. For example, a rater who is familiar with the child may evaluate from personal knowledge and prior experience; a rater who is unfamiliar with the child will need to utilize planned and systematic observation. After the observation phase, the actual rating and scoring of the instrument takes approximately 30 minutes. The inventory has an accompanying manual that provides comprehensive instruction for its administration and the interpretation of findings.

The Early Coping Inventory consists of 48 items divided equally into the three categories of coping style described in Chapter 3, this volume—sensorimotor organization, reactive behavior, and self-initiated behavior. The three categories are not mutually exclusive, but they are used to group coping behaviors to foster systematic observation and description of the child.

As previously discussed, *sensorimotor organization* refers to behaviors used to regulate psycho-physiological functions and to integrate sensory and motor processes. It includes self-regulation, adaptive responses to a variety of sensory stimuli, and the organized use of the sensory and motor systems. *Reactive behaviors* are actions used to respond to demands of the physical and social environments. In general, this type of behavior is elicited by external events. *Self-initiated behaviors* are autonomously generated, self-directed actions used to meet personal needs and to interact with objects and people. Whereas reactive behaviors are contingent on environmental cues, self-initiated behaviors are more sponta-neous and intrinsically motivated.

The Early Coping Inventory yields three different types of clinically relevant informa-tion: 1) an Adaptive Behavior Index, 2) a Coping Profile, and 3) a listing of the Most and Least Adaptive Coping Behaviors. (See Figure 6.1 for an example of an adaptive behavior summary.)

The Adaptive Behavior Index is an average of the child's scores on the three categories of the instrument and serves as an overall measure of the child's coping competence. The index indicates whether the child's coping style is an effective resource or an area of con-cern requiring intervention.

The Coping Profile graphically depicts the child's unique behavioral patterns. It shows the relationships among the three categories of sensorimotor organization, reactive behavior, and self-initiated behavior. The range of scores indicates whether the child's be-havior is consistent across these coping categories or if there are idiosyncratic patterns of strengths and vulnerabilites.

In addition, a listing of the Most and Least Adaptive Coping Behaviors is generated that reflects the items with the highest and lowest ratings respectively. The list of Least Adaptive Coping Behaviors indicates the behavioral characteristics that need to be ad-dressed in the IFSP. Intervention goals and objectives are targeted to remediate deficits in these coping behaviors. The list of Most Adaptive Coping Behaviors can be used to develop intervention strategies for enhancing the less adaptive behaviors and to expand the child's general coping effectiveness. Thus, intervention builds upon the child's coping strengths.

Coping Effectiveness

	Effectiveness Score
Sensorimotor Organization (SM)	2.6
Reactive Behavior (R)	1.4
Self-Initiated Behavior (SI)	2.7
Adaptive Behavior Index	2.2

Coping Profile

Most and Least Adaptive Coping Behaviors

Most adaptive			Least adaptive		
Category	Rating	Behavior	Category	Rating	Behavior
SM	3	Adequate level of energy in free play situations	R	1	Does not follow directions
SM	3	Maintains visual attention to objects but not people	R	1	Frustrates easily
SI	3	Demonstrates persistence when playing alone	R	1	Fails to accept help when necessary
SI	3	Enters new situations ap-propriately depending on the setting	R	1	Does not adapt to changes in the environment

Figure 6.1. Paul's adaptive behavior summary from the Early Coping Inventory for infants and toddlers. (Copyright © 1988 by Shirley Zeitlin and G. Gordon Williamson. Reprinted by permission of Scholastic Testing Service, Inc. From: Early Coping Inventory.)

Using the Rating Scale   A discussion of the rating scale is provided not only as an introduction to the Early Coping Inventory, but also to explain its clinical relevance when observing children. This scale can be used when rating the instrument or during informal observation of coping transactions.

The rating scale assesses coping effectiveness—"effectiveness" means the coping behavior is: 1) appropriate for situations, 2) appropriate for the child's developmental age, and 3) successfully used by the child. In determining behavioral appropriateness and success, it is important to consider the cultural environment of the child. Thus, coping behaviors are evaluated in a way that is sensitive to cultural diversity and reflects the best judgment of the observer. Ratings are assigned following observation of the child in a variety of circumstances to ensure a representative assessment of the child's coping style (e.g., in the presence and absence of caregivers, in familiar and novel environments, in one-to-one and small-group situations).

Each item on the inventory is rated on a 5-point scale. The rating scale is designed to reflect coping effectiveness ranging from ineffective coping (1) to consistently effective coping across situations (5). This scale is used to determine effectiveness scores in each of the three coping categories and in the Adaptive Behavior Index, as well as being used in the rating of specific items on the instrument. Table 6.1 provides sample items with the accompanying scale as they appear in the Early Coping Inventory for infants and toddlers. Table 6.2 depicts the five levels of coping effectiveness.

A Rating of 1   If the behavior is *not effective,* a rating of 1 is given. Either the child is not able to perform the behavior, for whatever reason, or the behavior that the child tries does not work.

A rating of 1 indicates that the behavior is not available as a resource for coping or that the behavior is unsuccessful in meeting functional needs. In the case of a child with a disability, a rating of 1 is given when the condition markedly interferes with the ability to demonstrate the behavioral characteristic. For example, a child who is blind would receive a rating of 1 on the items that require vision. For this child, seeing is not a coping-related attribute that is available for managing the world.

Table 6.1.   Sample items from the Early Coping Inventory

Sensorimotor Organization

Child adapts to a range of intensity of touch (e.g., from light to firm touch during handling).	1	2	3	4	5
Child organizes information from the different senses simultaneously for a response (e.g., combines looking, listening, and touching in exploring a toy).	1	2	3	4	5
Child varies activity level according to the situation.	1	2	3	4	5

Reactive Behavior

Child accepts help when necessary.	1	2	3	4	5
Child finds a way of handling a new or difficult situation.	1	2	3	4	5
Child uses self-protective behaviors to control the impact of the environment (e.g., withdraws from or stops the activity when over stimulated, fusses when tired).	1	2	3	4	5

Self-Initiated Behavior

Child initiates interactions with others.	1	2	3	4	5
Child tries new behavior on own.	1	2	3	4	5
Child enters new situations easily or cautiously as the occasion demands.	1	2	3	4	5

Table 6.2.   Scale for rating coping behavior

Rating	Functional level
1	Not effective
2	Minimally effective
3	Situationally effective
4	Effective more often than not
5	Consistently effective across situations

It is clinically useful to note the specific ineffective strategies that are used by the child. Knowledge of the child's maladaptive responses is critical for designing intervention. For example, intervention is quite different for a child who demonstrates ineffective behavior by incessant crying in novel situations as contrasted to the ineffective child who "shuts down" (e.g., demonstrates total passivity and lack of involvement).

A Rating of 2   If the behavior is *minimally effective,* a rating of 2 is given. The child's behavior is inconsistent, or is rigidly repetitious, or generates negative outcomes over time. That is, the child's behavior tends to be erratic and unpredictable, or the child repeats the same type of behavior regardless of the circumstances, or the child uses behavior that reduces the stress of the moment but impedes effective adaptation and interferes with learning.

The first minimally effective behavioral pattern is inconsistency. The child with inconsistent behavior has an erratic, trial-and-error quality to managing daily demands regardless of past experiences in the situation. For example, each time Rasheeda goes to her early intervention center, she reacts differently despite a highly structured routine. She may wander aimlessly, cling to her parent, aggressively push another child, or appropriately adhere to the routine.

The second minimally effective behavioral pattern is rigidity. The rigidly repetitious child has a limited repertoire of coping strategies that tends to be used repeatedly in an inflexible manner. The child may perseverate in a behavior even though it does not achieve desired results. For example, a typical illustration of Theresa's coping is to tug on the toe of a shoe until completely frustrated, trying to pull it off, and never attempting alternative strategies.

The third minimally effective behavioral pattern is one that assists the child to avoid stress or gain control in the immediate situation, but limits growth over time. An example is the behavior of Ahmed, a physically attractive child who frequently misbehaves. When confronted by his caregiver, Ahmed distracts the adult from reprimands by giving hugs and kisses. This seductive behavior interferes with his learning to accept responsibility for the consequences of his behavior and helps to establish the belief that he can manipulate others by such coy actions.

In summary, the practitioner needs to distinguish in the assessment whether the reason a child is minimally effective is due to inconsistency, rigidity, or a behavioral pattern with negative outcomes over time.

A Rating of 3   If the behavior is *situationally effective,* a rating of 3 is given. Behavior that is used effectively in one type of situation is not generalized to other types of situations.

Variables that influence the effectiveness of the child's behavior may include the place or environment in which the behavior occurs, the presence or absence of the caregiver or familiar adult, the presence or absence of other children or strangers, the level of familiarity with objects, the degree of structure and adult encouragement, and the use of proper physical positioning and adaptive equipment. For example, a child who responds appropriately and effectively to vocal or gestural directions from parents, but does not follow similar vocal and gestural direction from other familiar persons, would receive a rating of 3. Another illustration is the child who asks appropriately for dinner, but often yells furiously when requesting help getting dressed.

A rating of 3 is given when the child's behavior varies in appropriateness to the situation (i.e., appropriate in some types of situations but not in others), in appropriateness for developmental age, or in the level of success (i.e., the behavior is successful only under certain circumstances). When assigning a rating of 3 for a coping behavior, the practitioner needs to note the specific situations in which the child is effective and ineffective. Because performance may vary on the basis of environmental circumstances, the professional should note the context and condition under which the child is successful (e.g., when positioned in adapted furniture, in structured or unstructured environments, when prompted or guided to perform).

A Rating of 4   If the behavior is *effective more often than not,* a rating of 4 is given. A rating of 4 indicates that the child is able to generalize effective behavior to a variety of situations. The behavior is competent in various circumstances and conditions; however, there is still not the consistency that would earn a rating of 5.

A Rating of 5   If the behavior is *consistently effective across situations,* a rating of 5 is given. A rating of 5 indicates that the behavior is consistently appropriate and successful for the child's developmental age. To obtain a rating of 5, the child has to be effective most of the time, but not necessarily all of the time—no child copes effectively under all circumstances.

Ratings of 4 and 5 are in the range of effective functional coping. The following examples demonstrate the difference between 4 and 5 ratings on specific coping behaviors. In observing the effectiveness of how a child adapts to being moved by others during physical handling and caregiving, a child rated 4 accepts being moved by others more often than not. This child may fuss with sudden or new movement experiences, but then adjusts. A child rated 5 consistently accepts being moved by adults across a variety of situations involving physical handling and caregiving.

Another example involves how effectively a child adapts to daily routines and limits set by the caregivers. A child rated 4 cooperates with established routines (e.g., taking a bath) more often than not, usually demonstrates anticipation of regular activities, and participates as developmentally appropriate. Occasional resistance to routine activities appears to be related to fatigue. The child complies to limits set by the caregiver, but occasionally persists in the activity or behavior to receive additional attention. A child rated 5 consistently cooperates with a wide variety of daily routines established by the caregiver. The child adapts to changes in a routine, such as using a cup instead of a bottle during mealtime or playing independently when left alone for a longer time than usual. The child generally responds effectively to structure and limit setting. Occasionally the child requires some repetition and guidance when new limits are established.

As indicated earlier, it is important when observing a child to note the specific actions or strategies that the child uses to cope. This information is particularly relevant for those coping behaviors with which the child is having difficulty. Although a child's level of effectiveness is indicated by the rating, the specific way in which the child demonstrates the behavioral characteristic is documented for purposes of planning intervention.

Interpreting the Instrument: Case Examples   Two case examples, those of Paul and Janet, are provided to illustrate interpretation of the Early Coping Inventory. In the sample

Adaptive Behavior Summary shown in Figure 6.1, Paul's Adaptive Behavior Index is 2.2, which indicates that he is minimally effective in his overall coping. Review of his Coping Profile reveals that the categories of sensorimotor organization (scored at 2.6) and self-initiated behavior (scored at 2.7) are relative strengths when compared to the category of reactive behavior (scored at 1.4). Paul's most adaptive coping behaviors received a rating of 3 because he is effective only in situations that do not require social interaction. He demonstrates adequate energy, persistence, and visual attention when he is playing alone, but appears listless in group situations. His least adaptive coping behaviors are all in the reactive category and received a rating of 1. The behaviors that make Paul most vulnerable are his inability to follow directions, accept help when necessary, adapt to changes in the environment, and manage frustration. Goals and objectives for intervention would focus on changing these coping behaviors that significantly interfere with Paul's adaptive functioning.

Janet's Adaptive Behavior Summary is presented in Figure 6.2. Her coping competence is considered situationally effective, as her Adaptive Behavior Index is 3.2. She is able to manage routine and familiar environments, but she has great difficulty handling change and new situations. Her scores are very similar on all three categories of the inventory, which is illustrated in her Coping Profile. Janet's relative strengths and vulnerabilities

Coping Effectiveness

	Effectiveness Score
Sensorimotor Organization (SM)	3.2
Reactive Behavior (R)	3.0
Self-Initiated Behavior (SI)	3.3

Adaptive Behavior Index   3.2

Coping Profile

```
                        1     2     3     4     5
Sensorimotor Organization |___|___|__●__|___|___|
Reactive Behavior         |___|___|_/_|___|___|
Self-Initiated Behavior   |___|___|●_|___|___|
```

Most and Least Adaptive Coping Behaviors

Most adaptive			Least adaptive		
Category	Rating	Behavior	Category	Rating	Behavior
SI	5	Initiates action to communicate a need	R	1	Does not bounce back after stressful situations
SM	4	Demonstrates pleasure in self-initiated body movement and sensory exploration	R	2	Minimally able to accept substitute people or objects when necessary
R	4	Demonstrates an awareness that own behavior has an effect on people and objects	SI	2	Minimally able to enter new situations easily or cautiously as the occasion demands
SI	4	Initiates exploration of own body or objects using a variety of strategies	SI	2	Minimally able to balance independent behavior with necessary dependence on adults

Figure 6.2. Janet's adaptive behavior summary from the Early Coping Inventory for infants and toddlers. (Copyright © 1988 by Shirley Zeitlin and G. Gordon Williamson. Reprinted by permission of Scholastic Testing Service, Inc. From: Early Coping Inventory.)

in coping become evident only by reviewing ratings on the individual items of the instrument and by identifying the most and least adaptive behaviors in each category.

Janet's specific strengths include an ability to communicate her needs, demonstration of pleasure in self-initiated body movement and sensory exploration, awareness that her personal behavior has an effect on people and objects, and exploration of her own body and surroundings using a variety of strategies. Janet is least effective in handling stress and bouncing back after difficult situations. She is minimally effective in accepting substitute people and objects, entering new situations, and balancing independent and dependent behaviors.

Based on these findings, intervention would focus on enhancing Janet's ability to generalize and to manage change, transitions, and novel experiences. As her capability in these areas improves, her overdependence on adults for constant comfort and support is likely to decrease. Thus, she will acquire independence more appropriate for her developmental age.

Coping Inventory for Children and Youth Ages 3–16

The coping style of children 3 years of age and older can be assessed using the Coping Inventory, which is the same in its general format and scoring system as the Early Coping Inventory. The instrument has two categories: 1) *Coping with Self,* which includes the behaviors a child uses to meet personal needs; and 2) *Coping with the Environment,* which involves the behaviors used to adapt to external demands and pressures.

In each of these categories, three bipolar dimensions are used to describe a child's coping style. The *productive-nonproductive dimension* assesses the child's capacity to be socially responsible, maintain self-esteem, and produce desired results. The *flexible-rigid dimension* evaluates the child's ability to use a variety and range of strategies, to shift plans appropriately, or to reformulate ideas currently held. The *active-passive dimension* measures the child's ability to initiate and sustain mental or physical action when managing daily events. Table 6.3 presents sample coping-related characteristics that reflect items in the Coping Inventory.

In summary, the Early Coping Inventory for infants and toddlers and the Coping Inventory for children and youth provide a structured, systematic approach to assessing a child's unique coping style. These instruments can also be used to measure change in a child's coping ability over time. Additional information can be acquired through interviewing the parents. Questions to guide an interview may include: Are there any situations that are particularly stressful for your child? What does your child do in these situations? How does your child respond to change? Does your child like to explore and try new things? How does your child play with adults and other children?

Whether assessment of the child's coping style is conducted formally or informally, several issues need to be considered.

Table 6.3. Sample characteristics assessed by the Coping Inventory

Coping with Self	Coping with the Environment
Confidence	Curiosity
Task persistence	Awareness of feelings of others
Generalization of learning	Resiliency following disappointment
Creativity and originality	Ability to follow instructions
Sense of self-worth	Awareness of and response to social expectations
Expression of personal needs	Acceptance of warmth and support from others

1. To what extent does the child engage in self-initiated behaviors? Are these coping behaviors productive?
2. Is the child able to use coping strategies flexibly across a variety of situations?
3. Is there a difference between the ability of the child to cope with self in contrast to coping with environmental demands?
4. How does the child seem to evaluate the effectiveness of coping efforts? The nature of this evaluation strongly influences the development of the child's self-esteem.

THE CHILD'S DEVELOPMENTAL SKILLS

A second coping resource that needs to be assessed is the child's developmental status. It is beyond the intent of this book to provide a comprehensive discussion of developmental assessment. The reader is referred to the literature for descriptions of assessment formats and available instruments that are currently used in clinical practice (see Bagnato, Neisworth, & Munson, 1989; Bricker & Cripe, 1992; Gibbs & Teti, 1990). The important issue from a coping perspective is to interrelate the developmental and coping assessments in such a way that the focus is not only on what the child can do, but also on how the child functionally applies skills as integrated coping efforts within situations. The acquisition of developmental skills does not automatically lead to effective coping. A process-oriented approach to comprehensive assessment includes identification of the circumstances in which skills are demonstrated, the degree to which the child uses skills in a self-initiated manner, the approach to and organization of structured and unstructured tasks, and the ability to solve problems. Table 6.4 provides guidelines for behavioral observation that link assessment of developmental skills to their functional significance in coping.

Play provides the opportunity to see how the child uses developmental skills in a naturalistic environment. It reflects the child's ability to integrate the cognitive, emotional, social, language, and motor domains to support self-generated, spontaneous activity. The nature of the child's play can be ascertained through direct observation or interview of the caregiver. The following sample information can be gathered through either approach: the child's favorite activities and playthings, available action schemes, preference for social involvement or solitary activities, attention span, emotional expression, problem-solving skills, and physical ability. In interpreting this information, comparisons can be made between developmentally appropriate expectations and the child's competence at play. Thus, the evaluation of play complements formal developmental assessment and contrib-

---

Table 6.4. Behavioral observations to link developmental assessment with coping competence

Under what conditions does the child demonstrate specific developmental skills? (Consider whether the skills are generalized to a variety of situations or occur only under isolated circumstances.)

Does the child use the skills spontaneously or primarily in a reactive manner?

What environmental supports are required for the child to perform particular skills or tasks? (Consider such factors as the need for visual or verbal cues, special physical handling or positioning, or adult encouragement.)

What compensatory strategies does the child use, or attempt to use, to perform a requested task?

Are there ineffective behaviors that interfere with the acquisition of particular developmental skills?

Is there a characteristic pattern for learning new skills? (Consider such factors as the speed of learning, preferred sensory modalities, degree of required practice, and types of materials that evoke optimal responses.)

Is there a discrepancy in developmental levels that influences the child's adaptive functioning? (Consider significant differences between specific areas of development.)

utes to a more functional, coping-related perspective (e.g., the quality of the child's sensorimotor organization, reactivity, and self-initiation). Fewell and Kaminski (1988) and Linder (1993) describe clinically sound methods for observing and assessing play.

THE CHILD'S EMERGING BELIEFS

Inferences about the emerging beliefs of an infant or toddler can be assessed indirectly through observation of the child in various contexts, such as free play, social interaction, and goal-directed activities. This coping resource influences the meaning a child gives to events (e.g., threat, harm, challenge) and helps to determine the nature and type of coping efforts to be initiated. Beliefs are initially very primitive, global, and emotionally grounded. They are probably less of an influence in an infant than at a later age when they become more complex and focused with a child's increasing experience and cognitive ability. Emerging beliefs are intimately related to the development of a sense of self. They involve issues related to trust, security, expectation of success or failure, and predictability of events.

Information about emerging beliefs can be inferred through observation of the child's transactions in a variety of situations. Of particular relevance to coping is the child's evolving sense of efficacy—the perceived ability to produce an effect, control events, and trust others to be responsive to needs. These critical beliefs are reflected in an "I can" or "I can't" orientation to the demands of daily living. That is, they are indicative of the child's self-esteem, motivation, persistence, and autonomy. By observing these attributes, the practitioner can develop an understanding of the child's beliefs and how they influence adaptive functioning. Assessment of the following coping-related attributes are particularly helpful in clarifying the nature of the child's emerging belief system: willingness to engage in activities and to accept or create challenges and the ability to manage feelings and to demonstrate pleasure in successful accomplishments. In typical clinical practice, information regarding beliefs is acquired sequentially over time but begins in the initial assessment of the child's development and coping style.

Another indicator of beliefs is the quality of the child's attachment to caregivers. This suggests whether the child perceives the world as safe and secure or threatening and dangerous. A child with a secure attachment pattern can separate from the significant adult to explore toys or interact with strangers in the caregiver's presence. This child can be readily comforted when distressed and then return to play. In contrast, there are at least three other types of attachment patterns: avoidant, resistant, and disorganized. Insecure attachment is reflected in these patterns. A child with an avoidant pattern voluntarily separates from the caregiver, typically avoids reunion, explores the environment, and readily interacts with strangers. This child, however, tends to have little emotional expression. A child with a resistant pattern has difficulty separating from the caregiver and later reuniting, is wary of novel situations and people, and tends to have emotional outbursts that are hard for others to manage. A child with a disorganized pattern may fluctuate erratically between behaviors (e.g., be alternately rejecting and clinging), display discordant nonverbal communication (e.g., reaching for a hug with head averted), and exhibit disoriented or self-stimulating behaviors. It is most probable that these children have a conflicted view of the world, which negatively influences their sense of self and relatedness to others. Thus, an understanding of the infant–caregiver attachment helps identify relevant beliefs that contribute to a child's coping performance (Mahler, Pine, & Bergman, 1975).

It is recognized that as a child matures, a value system is established that complements beliefs as an influential coping resource. Values reflect a child's desires or preferences. They contribute to setting personal goals and motivate commitments to their attainment. A value system eventually contributes to the child's ideas about what is important in life. Values in children are demonstrated in their behaviors related to such issues as adult approval, academic achievement, task mastery, and preferences in play and leisure.

Beliefs and values are shaped and strongly influenced by familial and social experiences as well as by cultural background. Practitioners *must* take into account what the child's culture considers normal behavior and appropriate interaction. Chapter 4, this volume, provides sample descriptions of beliefs about the child and family from the perspective of several cultures.

Clinical impressions of the infant's beliefs and their impact may be speculative or rather tentative. However, an understanding of the emerging belief system is integral to a comprehensive assessment of a child's adaptive functioning. The reader is referred to the following sources for additional information: Teti and Nakagawa (1990) regarding the assessment of attachment, Stern (1985) for an integrated perspective on the development of the self, and Foley and Hobin (1981) for an instrument that assesses the attachment-separation-individuation process.

THE CHILD'S PHYSICAL AND AFFECTIVE STATES

Relevant information regarding the child's physical and affective states can be gathered through a combination of sources, such as parent interviews, the child's medical records, contact with the primary health care providers, and direct assessment by the early intervention team. Particular issues related to the child's physical state include general health, physical appearance, endurance, alertness, past illnesses and hospitalizations, and pertinent medical conditions of the family. In some cases, a physical examination and diagnostic work-up are required in order to appreciate the child's capacity for adaptive functioning and to determine appropriate intervention practices. For example, a child with Down syndrome who has respiratory difficulties, low muscle tone, and a cardiac problem is prone to fatigue and requires special physical management.

Assessment of the child's affective state includes observation of moods, the range and expression of emotions, and responses to a variety of activities and demands. Particular attention needs to be paid to analyzing the coping transactions between the child and primary caregivers, especially the parents. Difficulty in regulation of affect may be noted in the following manifestations: irritability, poor impulse control, marked mood swings, unhappy or depressed expression, hypo- or hyperarousal, fussiness, and distractibility. These variations in affect undermine the child's ability to cope. When present, further assessment is necessary to identify contributing factors (e.g., disturbances in parent–child interaction, disorder in sensory integration). The *Test of Sensory Functions in Infants* (De-Gangi & Greenspan, 1989) is a useful tool for further evaluation of sensory processing and adaptive motor capacity.

THE CHILD'S MATERIAL AND ENVIRONMENTAL SUPPORTS

Material and environmental supports can be identified through discussions with the parents or by offering an opportunity for them to complete a needs assessment survey. The practitioner can also visit the home and child care program to gain additional information. Of particular note in the area of material supports is the availability of sufficient finances, food, shelter, clothing, transportation, and developmentally appropriate toys for the child. Environmental supports are identified through observations of the physical surroundings that influence development, comfort, and safe exploration. Relevant characteristics include organization of space, levels of noise and light, and quality and temperature of the air.

A child's needs relative to material and environmental supports vary based on age, developmental capability, and the presence of a disability. Clinical impressions are made about the availability of a variety of motivating toys and the organization and accessibility of the child's surroundings. In particular, if the child has a physical disability, the material supports required to function optimally should be carefully examined. These supports may include mobility and positioning equipment, adapted toys, communication aids, and architectural modifications.

THE CHILD'S HUMAN SUPPORTS

Much is learned about the child's human supports by becoming acquainted with the family and their coping resources. This information is best generated through a continuing dialogue between the family and the early intervention team. These exchanges address the concerns and priorities of the family, the demands they have to manage, and the availability of their personal resources. Parents and other caregivers are also observed in their transactions with the child. Such information contributes to understanding the human support available to the child and the caregivers' needs in relation to parenting. In addition, it is important for the practitioner to assess his or her relationship with the child and family, as professionals also serve as their human supports. The following discussion addresses the collection of information on family coping resources. (See chap. 14, this volume, for a discussion on staff coping.)

Gathering Information About the Family's Coping Resources

When a family enters an early intervention program, it is important to gather enough information to facilitate intervention planning and a mutually supportive relationship between the family and practitioners. Attempts to gather too much information too quickly can result in excessive demands on the parents as well as possibly generating discomfort and wariness. Practitioners need to monitor their requests for information whether they are gathering it through a conversation, questionnaire, or self-reporting survey. Professionals need to ask themselves the following questions:

1. What information do I really need to know in order to collaborate with the family in designing a meaningful IFSP?
2. When do I need to know it?
3. What is the best way to gather this information?

Preplanned questions may provide a starting point for this effort. Table 6.5 has sample questions that can be used *selectively* in an informal conversation to facilitate acquiring information about the parents' concerns, beliefs about their child and family, coping style, and human supports. Because the questions are fairly open-ended, an opportunity is provided for exploration of both information and feelings. Some families more readily discuss their problems and concerns and neglect or belittle their strengths. They may, however, demonstrate and describe strengths by way of example. The mother may say, "When Helio comes home from work, after washing up and changing his clothes, he takes over caring for the twins while I prepare supper." This comment gives the practitioner information about the mother's support system.

Table 6.5. Sample questions to facilitate a coping-related discussion

- What are your concerns?
- How long have you felt this way?
- Why do you think it is important to obtain help now?
- What influenced your decision to come here?
- Have you previously sought help for your child?
- What is your child like at home and other places?
- What gives you the most satisfaction when caring for your child?
- What is most difficult?
- What would you like to happen as a result of coming here?
- What is your family like?
- Who is available when you want help or someone to talk to or to babysit?
- What demands are placed on your family because of your child's special needs?
- Do you have concerns about how these demands are being managed?
- What special resources and strengths help your family meet these demands?
- Do extended family members share your concerns and feelings?
- Are there regular routines or a "typical" day?
- Do you have other children, and if so, how do they interact with your child with special needs?
- What things are challenging for your child? What things are rewarding?
- Is there anything else you would like us to know?

Information regarding family coping resources is gathered over time as a natural part of conversing, sharing, and interacting together. Typically, a general understanding of these resources is sufficient for the parent and professionals to develop and implement the service plan. If there is an area of particular concern, that coping resource can be addressed in greater detail. The following guidelines may be helpful for this additional exploration.

Family's Beliefs and Values   The family's beliefs and values are the most sensitive and probably the most critical resource to know about because they are the filter for perception of the meaning of events. They may also be either a support or stressor. Beliefs and values stem from personal experiences and religious, societal, and cultural affiliations. Knowledge of a family's beliefs and values enhances communication and helps identify their concerns, priorities, and resources. It is appropriate to pursue discussion of them as they relate to intervention planning. When beliefs and values reflect religious and cultural orientations, these beliefs need to be respected. In cases where beliefs stem from incorrect facts, they can be identified and sensitively addressed. For example, if a family believes that cerebral palsy is contagious and therefore keeps their child isolated, it is important to provide accurate information.

Typically, in early intervention, religion is not a topic of discussion. If a family chooses to share their feelings in this area, thoughtful listening may assist the practitioner to understand better the parents' views of their child. For some families, the birth of an infant with a disability challenges their religious beliefs.

Consideration of the following issues assists professionals to gain an understanding of a family's beliefs and values. These are *not* questions to ask families, rather they are areas for reflection. Following each question are reasons this information may be useful. This increased awareness can help practitioners become more sensitive and responsive to individual families.

Are there particular beliefs and values that provide direction to the family's life? (These help to identify what is important to the family.)

Does the family tend to maintain an optimistic or pessimistic orientation toward life events? (This influences the motivation of family members and practitioners who interact with them.)

What are the beliefs about the expected roles of each family member? (These guide how family members relate to each other, determine who makes decisions on what issues and under what conditions, and influence how each member is expected to behave.)

What are the perceptions of the parents regarding the cause of the child's disability and their roles in influencing the child's progress? (These influence the parent–child relationship and expectations regarding the child's future.)

Family's Physical and Affective States   The family's physical and affective states influence their ability to manage and enjoy child care. Gathering information about this resource is limited to what the family chooses to share and what is observed. This information can pertain to a specific event or reflect health and feelings over a period of time. For example, a feeling of depression may be due to recent bad news or exist as a chronic state. Evidence of depression may include flat affect, passivity, listlessness, and an overall lack of interaction.

The following considerations increase awareness of the physical and affective states of the family.

Do the parents have any physical conditions that they think the practitioners need to know about? (This influences an ability to manage caregiving, attend an early intervention program on a regular basis, and the possible need for medical referral.)

Are the parents emotionally available to the child? (This infers the quality and consistency of parental mood and its impact on their transactions.)

What is known about the psychological and physical status of siblings? (This provides information about family dynamics and influences family priorities.)

Family's Knowledge and Skills   The family's knowledge and skills serve as a base for coping with the complexities of daily living. Information about this resource comes from observing the transactions of family members with the child and the questions that they ask. For example, a father may demonstrate discomfort and awkwardness in bathing, feeding, and carrying his infant with poor head control, or he may ask directly for assistance in these areas of child care.

The clinician can reflect on the following issues to gain an increased appreciation of the knowledge and skills of the family relevant to early intervention programming.

Are the parents' expectations for the child consistent with the child's current functional abilities? (These convey their understanding of what needs to happen for the child to be successful.)

Do the parents demonstrate necessary skills for managing their child's behavior and special requirements? (These indicate areas of competence or the need for additional assistance.)

What is the siblings' understanding of the disability of their brother or sister? (This influences the siblings' feelings about themselves and their behavior within the family.)

Family's Coping Style   The coping style of the family and its individual members can be identified by observing how they manage demanding situations. There are two kinds of relevant information: 1) what coping behaviors are used across situations, and 2) how effectively the coping behaviors are applied to achieve desired outcomes. Information about the coping styles of adults is gained through observing their transactions (see the discussion on Understanding Coping Transactions). Parents can also rate themselves on the adult version of the Coping Inventory and share their findings if they choose. Practitioners can use items from this inventory as a basis for their observations. (See chap. 9, this volume, for a discussion of the self-rated edition of the Coping Inventory and its use by adolescents and adults.)

The following questions generate reflections that may aid the practitioner in considering this coping resource.

Is there an identifiable coping style of the family? (This indicates how the family manages stress and how practitioners can help.)

Is there a good fit between the coping styles of the parents and the child? (This suggests the nature of the reciprocal interaction of the partners and their degree of shared satisfaction.)

Family's Human Supports The family's human support comes from the network of people who are a part of their daily life and whom they can call upon for help in times of need. This network may include relatives, friends, co-workers, social and religious organizations, and professional services. The availability of the family's support system, how supportive it actually is, and how willing the family is to use this support must be considered. It helps to listen carefully and observe how the family responds to different options for meeting needs and then to use the response as a basis for further clarification. For example, "You indicate that your aunt might be able to provide transportation to get your child to therapy, but I sense that you are hesitant to ask her. Is there a particular reason why you feel this way?" This type of probe provides a basis for exploring ways of making that particular source of support a more viable option or for seeking alternative options.

The practitioner may reflect on the following issues when considering the family's human supports.

Who is available when help is wanted or someone to talk to is needed? (This indicates the family's support system and whether it is adequate to meet needs.)

Is there a sense of family cohesion and belonging? (This provides insight regarding the physical and emotional support among family members.)

How does the family view involvement of "outsiders" in their life? (This indicates the family's readiness to seek and use community services.)

Do the parents have opportunities to pursue personal activities? (This suggests the availability of respite support and the ability to address personal needs.)

Family's Material and Environmental Supports The family's material and environmental supports include the services and items that money can buy and the physical environment in which the family lives. The parents can be directly asked whether finances are a concern. A home visit by the practitioner provides an opportunity to learn about the family's physical environment. The practitioner needs to be sensitive regarding the family's comfort in having visitors to their home and respectful of their economic circumstances.

These issues can help to clarify the nature of the family's material and environmental supports.

Do the parents believe that money is a problem and, if so, is it a temporary or chronic situation? (This indicates the parent's perception of their financial status.)

Are there sources for funding and assistance if the family has a financial need? (This identifies specific community agencies and services that are available to the family.)

Are the home and child-care environments safe and do they support the child's functioning? (This determines whether the physical environment is appropriate for the child and if there is a need for any specialized equipment or modifications.)

UNDERSTANDING COPING TRANSACTIONS

During the initial assessment phase and ongoing participation in the program, there are numerous opportunities to observe the child coping with adults and other children, participating in activities, and managing the physical environment. For instance, transactions can be observed in the following situations: during caregiving, free play, instructional and small-group activities, and periods of transition. Analysis of these transactions provides useful information for planning and implementing services. It gives insights regarding stressors or demands on the child and family, the availability and use of resources, the effectiveness of coping strategies, and guidance for establishing goals and activities for intervention. It also gives practitioners an opportunity to appreciate the impact of their own behavior on reciprocal interactions.

As described earlier, coping transactions have four components, all of which contribute to the outcome of the coping process (see Figure 2.2, chap. 2, this volume). They include an internal or external demand that initiates the transaction, the coping effort the child uses to manage the demand, the environment's response to that effort, and the child's reaction to the response. This feedback influences the child's perception of the effectiveness of his or her coping effort.

When learning how to observe and analyze coping transactions, it is useful to record the information according to the four components. Of course, it is necessary to be sensitive to how and when this information is recorded. With experience, this observational approach is internalized and becomes an automatic way of observing. The following questions are used in the analysis and relate to each component of a coping transaction.

What was the demand?
What did the child do to manage the demand?
How did the adult respond to the child's action?
How did the child then react?

Recording in this fashion provides an objective picture of what happened, which can be subsequently analyzed for intervention planning.

A form is suggested for recording responses to these questions. Two examples of transactions are given to show how such a form is used. The following observation, recorded in Table 6.6, identified a characteristic coping pattern of Marissa.

➡ Marissa is a 2-year-old child with limited vision. While playing at home with a plastic milk bottle with a snap top, Marissa noticed that the bottle made a jingling sound. This sound aroused her curiosity and determination to open the bottle and discover the source of the sound. Because the top was tightly secured, Marissa demonstrated an array of coping strategies in order to remove the lid. She pulled it, turned it, flicked it, shook it, and bit it before finally requesting her father's help. He opened the bottle while saying "What's in there?" and handed it to her. Marissa dumped a small bell out of the bottle, held it close to her face, and inspected it with fascination.

Table 6.6. Observation of a transaction with Marissa

Demand	Child's coping effort	Adult's response to coping effort	Child's reaction to the adult's response
What was the demand?	*What did the child do to manage the demand?*	*How did the adult respond to the child's action?*	*How did the child then react?*
Marissa's internal interest to discover the content of the bottle.	Marissa used a variety of strategies to remove the top (i.e., pulled, turned, flicked, shook, and bit) and eventually asked her father for help.	Her father observed Marissa's exploration and responded to her request for assistance by opening the lid, asking "What's in there?", and returning it to her.	Marissa took the bottle, poured out the jingle bell, and demonstrated great interest in the object through visual, auditory, and tactile examination.

The above observation illustrates the effectiveness of Marissa's coping style. Marissa was goal directed, persistent, flexible in her use of strategies, and able to ask for help when necessary. This information was used in planning intervention to help Marissa compensate for her visual disability.

Observation of this next transaction provided important assessment information related to mother–child interaction.

➡ Jason is a 15-month-old toddler with fetal alcohol syndrome. During his first visit to the early intervention program, Jason and his mother met with the service coordinator. Jason played alone while the two adults talked. When they were finished with the interview, the mother stretched out her closed hand in front of her and said to Jason, "Come, I have something for you." Jason walked over with an expectant look and made excited sounds. Then the mother opened her hand and said, "I have nothing!" Jason sat down with a dejected, unhappy expression.

Table 6.7 describes the above transaction. This type of teasing was repeatedly observed during program sessions and home visits. Such observations raised questions about the mother's knowledge of child development and her role as a parent. It suggests that she is unaware of Jason's needs and that her behavior could be interpreted by him as rejection.

It is helpful to observe the child's coping transactions in various situations over time. Multiple observations in different contexts gives the practitioner a better sense of how each component of the transaction may facilitate or interfere with effective coping. The practitioner needs to consider the appropriateness of the demands (stressors) experienced by the child, the child's coping efforts to manage the demands, the environment's response to the child's efforts (feedback), and the child's reaction to the feedback.

Table 6.7. Observation of a transaction with Jason

Demand	Child's coping effort	Adult's response to coping effort	Child's reaction to the adult's response
What was the demand?	*What did the child do to manage the demand?*	*How did the adult respond to the child's action?*	*How did the child then react?*
Jason's mother made a demand by extending her closed hand and saying "Come, I have something for you."	Jason walked to his mother with a broad smile and actively vocalized.	Jason's mother opened her hand and said, "I have nothing."	Jason sat down, lowered his head, and looked sad.

Events that are perceived as threatening, harmful, or challenging generate a demand for a coping effort. These events predominantly stem from needs and expectations within the child, expectations of the family and other caregivers, and from specific aspects of the child's physical environment. In assessing *demands,* it is necessary to identify what they are and determine their relevance and developmental appropriateness. The internal needs and expectations of young children can only be inferred through observation of their actions. Older children may be able to express internal demands verbally. Examples of these inner demands include the child's physical and emotional needs for food, rest and comfort, personal preferences and desires, and expectations for success or failure.

Adults' demands of the child stem from their expectations for the child's social behavior, performance, and management of daily activity, as well as their own emotional needs. These expectations are derived from their personal and cultural background, their knowledge and experience as caregivers, and current demands that require their attention. Awareness of these expectations and the demands that they generate may be determined through interviewing the adult or through observing social transactions. Expectations that generate demands that are particularly relevant for children with special needs include expectations for developmental achievement, independence in self-help skills, and participation in social and community activities. In addition, the physical environment imposes a unique set of spatial and temporal demands that the child must negotiate, such as ambulating in a crowded store, reacting to a thrown ball, and obtaining toys and materials in an often inaccessible environment. Physical demands are best identified through direct observation of the child in typical surroundings.

Assessment of the *child's coping efforts* in response to demands involves considering the repertoire and flexibility of available coping strategies, the circumstances under which they are applied, and their success in managing specific stressors.

The next component of coping transactions is the *environment's response to the child's efforts.* This feedback, particularly from the primary caregivers, is critical for helping the child learn to cope and for the development of a sense of self. In assessing the nature of the feedback, it is necessary to determine how it is provided (e.g., physically, verbally), whether it gives accurate information regarding the child's performance, and whether it is offered in a timely and contingent manner.

The last transactional component to be assessed is the *child's reaction to the feedback.* The practitioner observes the child's affect and subsequent actions to infer how the child interprets the effectiveness of his or her efforts. That is, observing the child's reaction helps the practitioner to appreciate how the child internalized the meaning and quality of the transaction.

Observation and analysis of single and multiple transactions are clinically important. Analysis of a single coping transaction is useful in understanding the dynamics of a specific situation and concretely focuses on behavior that facilitates or interferes with the outcome. The following questions help to guide the analysis of a single transaction by identifying its component elements.

What was the outcome?
Did the coping effort effectively satisfy the demand?
What, if anything, facilitated the outcome?
What, if anything, interfered with an effective outcome?
Did the child have the skills and resources to manage the demand?

Analysis of multiple transactions enables the practitioner to describe the child's characteristic coping pattern as well as the coping of those who interact with the child.

The following questions assist the clinician with synthesizing and integrating information gained from observing transactions. They are particularly relevant to appreciating the reciprocal relationship between the child and the parent. The questions help to determine which components of the coping transactions may need to be addressed in intervention.

> Are the expectations evidenced in the adult's demands appropriate for the child's developmental age? If not, are they too high, too low, inconsistent, or unclear?
>
> How do the child's resources influence his or her coping efforts? (Consider emerging beliefs, physical and affective states, developmental skills, coping style, human supports, and material/environmental supports.)
>
> What are the characteristic coping strategies that the child or adult tends to use?
>
> What is the quality and nature of the adult's or physical environment's response to the child's coping efforts? Is the feedback timely, appropriate, and contingent?
>
> Does the feedback contribute to the child's perception of personal adequacy and well-being? (Consider positive and negative influences.)
>
> What changes could enhance the effectiveness of the coping transactions for the child and adult?

SUMMARY

In this chapter, various instruments and guiding questions are described that can be used to acquire information about the child's coping resources. Attention is given to the gathering of information about the family's resources and the family's critical role as the child's human support. A structure is also offered for the observation and analysis of transactions.

CHAPTER 7

Intervention Planning

The primary goals of intervention are to enhance the child's developmental capabilities and coping behaviors and to promote a good fit or congruence between the child's coping resources and environmental demands and expectations. When the child can engage in effective transactions with others in his or her environment, learning and development are fostered and the child experiences a sense of mastery and well-being. Thus, intervention options are based on the components of the transactional coping process and how they can be influenced.

Each component is amenable to change: the demands of specific situations, the child's coping resources to manage the demands, and the environment's response to those efforts. Although presented separately, the three intervention options are typically addressed simultaneously.

Option 1   Modify demands so that they are congruent with the child's capabilities to manage them.
Option 2   Enhance internal and external coping resources.
Option 3   Provide appropriate, contingent feedback to the child's coping efforts.

In this chapter, intervention strategies are discussed to implement these options. Chapter 8, this volume, describes additional methods and activities to achieve therapeutic and educational goals. In Chapters 10 and 11, the intervention options are used to help develop an individualized family service plan (IFSP) that has a coping perspective.

INTERVENTION STRATEGIES

A variety of strategies can be used to implement the three intervention options. The selection of these strategies is based on an understanding of how young children learn and of ways to influence behavioral change. Professionals representing a range of disciplines have referred to different types of strategies as instructional methods, guidance or management techniques, and therapeutic procedures. The strategies practitioners elect to use usually reflect their philosophical or theoretical orientation.

In the coping frame of reference, an intervention strategy is defined as any general tactic that can facilitate the changes required to achieve a desired outcome. A strategy can be used by the parent or professional to influence the child's behavior in varying situations. Likewise, the same strategy can be used with different children to elicit a variety of behavioral changes. Intervention strategies may be classified as indirect or direct. This conceptualization is borrowed from Hildebrand (1975) in a discussion of guidance techniques.

Indirect Intervention Strategies

Indirect intervention strategies influence the child's behavior through management of space, materials, equipment, and individuals in the surroundings. These strategies "set the stage" for learning by modifying the environment. Sample indirect strategies include: 1) adapting the size and type of play materials; 2) eliminating distractions for the impulsive child; 3) grouping children together to foster social interaction; 4) providing a predictable sequence of activities during intervention for the child who has difficulty adjusting to change; and 5) using splints, adaptive devices, or special positioning equipment for children with physical disabilities. In Figure 7.1, social interaction is facilitated by grouping children together to share materials.

Table 7.1 provides additional examples of indirect strategies that can be used to help a child cope more effectively.

Direct Intervention Strategies

Direct intervention strategies influence the child's behavior through specific interaction with the adult. Traditional teaching techniques and procedures for behavior modification exemplify direct strategies. Sample direct strategies include: 1) verbal guidance to help the child solve a task, 2) modeling desired behaviors for the child to imitate, 3) physical prompting to assist performance of an activity, and 4) providing feedback through specific reinforcement schedules. Table 7.2 offers other examples of direct intervention strategies.

An important factor to consider when using direct intervention strategies is timing. Direct strategies that are delivered too soon communicate a message of incompetence to the child and stifle self-initiated learning. Direct strategies that are applied too late allow the child to experience unnecessary frustration and may encourage use of established, maladaptive behaviors. As a result, mistrust and negative expectations are reinforced for similar encounters in the future.

Figure 7.1.   An example of playing close together with shared materials to foster socialization.

Table 7.1. Examples of indirect intervention strategies

Balance the composition of the group to encourage active involvement and interaction of the children (e.g., considerations may include developmental age, mobility, severity of disability).

Involve families in clearly defined ways that match the preferences of the parents and the needs of the children.

Develop a daily schedule or routine that paces the energy levels of the children.

Arrange the environment so there are clues as to the appropriate behavior for that space (e.g., push toys in a large area and manipulative toys on shelves near a table).

Plan rich and varied activities appropriate to the ages and experience of the children.

Design activities in interesting ways that invite participation.

Arrange materials, furniture, and playthings so children can use them safely and with minimal help.

Use adaptive equipment to foster independent functioning to the greatest degree possible.

Store materials that children are not supposed to use out of sight.

Cluster small groups of children in a defined space when trying to encourage interaction (use selectively).

Confer with parents to develop a fuller understanding of children's total experiences and to gain assistance in deciding intervention strategies.

In most cases, some combination of direct and indirect strategies is required to foster effective coping. Care needs to be taken, however, to avoid over-reliance on direct intervention strategies, because they may reinforce a reactive, dependent coping style. It is helpful to consider indirect strategies for implementation prior to the use of direct strategies. Sometimes the slightest modification of an environmental factor can result in successful coping. When a child copes ineffectively, it is important to identify the antecedent events in the environment that may have provoked or elicited the maladaptive behavior. The following questions may help to identify antecedent events.

Are there characteristic behaviors or attitudes of adults that stimulate or contribute to the child's maladaptive actions?

Table 7.2. Examples of direct intervention strategies

Use verbal guidance or cues to influence children's behavior:
  Speak to children at their eye level.
  Use short sentences.
  Give positive directions by telling children what to do rather than what not to do.
  Place the action part of directions at the beginning of statements.
  Give directions at the time and place the behavior is to occur.
  Make it clear whether the children have a choice or not.
  Give short, logical, and accurate reasons for requests.
  Praise children for tasks well done by focusing on the action rather than on approval of the children (e.g., avoid saying "good boy" when referring to a well-accomplished activity).

Reinforce successive approximations of a desired behavior.

Intensify or augment instances of naturally occurring reinforcers with additional feedback for children who have difficulty perceiving the relationship between a behavior and its consequences.

Offer additional visual cues by using pictures, materials, gestures, and modeling.

Provide assistance by physically guiding children through an action sequence.

Provide positive feedback to children for application of learning to new situations (i.e., generalization of skills).

Label children's feelings during regular events of the day (e.g., "You are tired and ready for a nap.").

Are the available toys appropriate to the child's interest level and functional ability?

Are play materials organized and presented in a way that appeals to the child's learning style and preferences, thereby inviting independent and productive use?

Is there a daily routine of active and quiet experiences that correspond to the child's biological time clock (e.g., patterns of sleep, wake, and hunger)?

Is the routine consistent from one day to the next so that the child can begin to anticipate events and apply appropriate behavior?

The following case example of Soo Ling shows how her mother used an indirect intervention strategy to increase her daughter's coping capability.

➡ Twenty-month-old Soo Ling had difficulty completing self-initiated activities and balancing independence with necessary dependence on adults. At home, Soo Ling could not be left alone because she required adult direction to choose and complete activities. Her play consisted of pulling numerous toys off the shelf in her room for brief visual inspection before throwing them on the floor in a fury to explore the next appealing object. An observation of Soo Ling's play at home indicated that she might be overwhelmed by the demand to choose a toy from too large a selection. As a result, the play environment was modified to include a more limited display of two to three toys from which to choose. With fewer options available, Soo Ling was able to select a toy and play with it independently for an age-appropriate period of time.

When environmental modifications do not result in desired behaviors, indirect intervention strategies can be augmented with the use of more direct strategies. In the case of Soo Ling, for example, her mother could further facilitate her daughter's ability to choose and play with toys more independently in the following ways: 1) model for her the selection of a single toy, saying "I want to play with the ball," and 2) verbally cue Soo Ling, saying, "Do you want the doll or the car?" Another example of combining direct and indirect intervention strategies involves the use of adapted positioning for children with physical disabilities. A modified chair, an indirect strategy, provides stability to the trunk so that the child can maintain an upright sitting posture. Prompting by the adult using hand-over-hand assistance, a direct strategy, enables the child to explore objects manually. The combination of both types of strategies enhances active participation of the child.

INTERVENTION OPTION 1

The first intervention option to facilitate effective coping involves modifying environmental demands so that they are congruent with the child's coping capability. Characteristics of both the physical and social environments place demands upon children and influence their behavior. Complexity of demands may range from those requiring a simple one-step response to a response involving a multistep action sequence. A simple demand may require the infant to attend to an adult's face, whereas a complex demand may require the infant to engage in reciprocal interaction with a variety of adults and peers. To generate new learning and reinforce feelings of competence, the demand has to be within the child's present capability. This intervention option can be implemented in at least two ways: 1) collaborative planning of achievable goals and objectives, and 2) modifying the procedure or grading task demands during implementation.

Planning Achievable Goals and Objectives

The expectations of parents and professionals determine the demands placed on the child. These demands are eventually translated into the child's intervention goals and objectives in the individualized family service plan (IFSP). For the goals and objectives to be meaningful, the expectations of the parents and practitioners (and sometimes the child) need to be actively addressed. Therefore, collaboration is a critical aspect of goal setting. Collaboration is directed toward having a shared understanding of the child's disability and developmental pattern. Also, there has to be an appreciation of the family's resources to support the child within the context of the needs of other family members. Equally important are realistic expectations by everyone concerned regarding what the early intervention program can accomplish.

When too much is expected of the child, the parent, or the program, regardless of the extent of achievement, the result is disappointment and frustration rather than valid feelings of success. If the parents' goal for early intervention is for the child to "become normal," any progress less than age-expected development may not be considered "good enough." When too little is expected, the child does not experience the developmentally appropriate stress needed to motivate efforts to learn new skills. The child may lose interest, withdraw, or become distracted. Parents and practitioners may feel disappointed with the lack of progress. In other instances, minimal expectations foster a mutually satisfying dependency between parent and child. Whereas this emotion may be momentarily gratifying, it interferes over time with development.

Consistency in expectations for behavior is most essential when trying to facilitate new learning. Children are usually quick to ascertain differences in the behavioral expectations of adults. Such mixed messages interfere with learning and often result in an increase in manipulative and other maladaptive behaviors.

In some cases, children may have to be helped to develop more appropriate expectations of their own ability to perform certain developmental skills. For example, a young child with cerebral palsy may become extremely frustrated when he cannot stand up and run after a ball with his peers. The child's internal demands to master walking and running will be more functionally appropriate if his expectations can be modified to include the supportive assistance of a walker, braces, or crutches. For example, it is helpful to introduce early the concept that functional mobility for the child with moderate to major physical limitations may best be achieved by a combination of wheelchair use and ambulation with braces. One mode of locomotion may be preferred over the other depending on the circumstances. The wheelchair may be more practical in a crowded shopping mall, whereas ambulation with crutches may be more efficient at home. By establishing realistic and shared intervention goals, parents, professionals, and eventually the child can place ambulation training in proper perspective and avoid the narrow attitude that walking is always the desired means of mobility.

For some children, the number of goals and objectives may need to be limited and worked on for longer periods of time in order to increase chances of steady and consistent progress. There is a tendency to do too much, too fast, too soon with children who have minimally effective coping styles. The result can be an increase in aggression or withdrawal. Goals and objectives need to be focused to avoid a fragmented intervention approach and the program must be carefully tailored to match the child's ability to participate. For example, the assessment of an infant with a pervasive developmental disorder may indicate the need for intensive physical, occupational, and speech-language therapies. However, due to the severity of the disability it may be difficult for the child to manage such a rigorous intervention schedule. The child may have difficulty adjusting to three different therapists and in maintaining an alert learning state during multiple therapy sessions per week.

To enhance this child's ability to cope with intervention demands, the number, variety, intensity, and duration of recommended therapies need to be changed over time. The intervention program may be designed initially to involve one practitioner who addresses the major therapeutic priorities. The child can be involved in short intervention sessions that foster low-key, pleasurable interactions.

It is also vital to balance the number of intervention objectives that target different stages of learning: acquisition, fluency, and generalization. Too often intervention objectives focus only on skill acquisition. The child does not have sufficient practice to achieve fluency and the ability to generalize the skill to various situations. The result is that the skill is not functionally available in times of stress and the child never has the opportunity to develop a sense of mastery.

As the child acquires new abilities and gains confidence, intervention demands are increased to reestablish a fit with the child's enhanced resources. The spiraling effect of the goodness of fit relationship necessitates ongoing assessment of intervention practices. As the child's coping resources develop, goals and objectives are upgraded to ensure that the child is continually exposed to demands that are developmentally stimulating and appropriate. A further discussion of developing goals and objectives is found in Chapter 11, this volume.

Modifying the Procedure and Grading the Task

The planning of appropriate goals and objectives sets the stage for intervention. However, there is a continuing need for flexibility in activities to achieve the goals and objectives. The procedures may need to be modified and the tasks may need to be graded. Both possibilities are typically used together by the parent or practitioner when interactions with the child are not generating desired outcomes.

There are a variety of procedures to implement or modify the achievement of any objective. The previously described direct and indirect intervention strategies can be used to modify existing procedures. Likewise, there are numerous tasks that can be the focus of intervention, including therapeutic and educational activities, child care practices, and the child's play. The major method of grading a task is to increase or decrease its level of complexity. A case example of modifying procedures and grading the task is the feeding regimen developed for Trishna.

➡   Trishna is a 7-month-old infant who has major oral motor incoordination. During spoon feedings, she frequently chokes and regurgitates the food. A number of strategies were designed to decrease the demands of the task and the accompanying frustration. The size and shape of the spoon were changed so that the bowl of the spoon was smaller and flatter, the texture of the food was made less coarse through finer pureeing, the schedule was altered to have shorter but more frequent feedings, and a different rhythm was introduced with bottle drinking interspersed with the spoon feeding to provide more relaxed pacing. The combination of these intervention strategies adjusted the feeding demands to a level congruent with Trishna's ability to manage them.

The case of Juanita, a 3-year-old child with developmental delays, is another example of modifying demands.

➡   Juanita stubbornly refused to participate in any self-dressing activity. The clinician worked closely with her foster mother to devise a dressing program that was personalized to foster success and motivation. Initially, it was decided to simplify the endeavor by focusing solely on managing clothes above her waist. Demands were introduced at contextually meaningful times when Juanita was motivated to accomplish the task. She enjoyed going to her early intervention program and taking a bath, but she usually resisted going to bed. Thus, putting on her shirt and coat before going out and taking off the shirt before her bath were emphasized at home. Managing pajama tops was deferred to a later date. Likewise, donning and doffing a smock were encouraged during intervention sessions when she was engaged in favorite messy activities such as finger painting.

In addition, the practitioner taught Juanita's foster mother an instructional procedure that divided the task into component parts and required Juanita to participate gradually in an increasing number of steps over time. Using a backward-chaining technique, Juanita was expected to perform only the last step, then the last two steps, then the last three steps, and so forth until the task was learned. Through these methods, demands were modified so that Juanita could acquire increased independence in dressing without eliciting resistant maladaptive behavior.

INTERVENTION OPTION 2

The second intervention option, which is directed to increasing the child's production of effective coping efforts, is the core of intervention from a coping perspective. In the first intervention option, the nature of the demand is established (i.e., the appropriateness of the antecedent condition that the child has to manage). The second intervention option focuses on enhancing coping resources—the source the child draws from to generate coping efforts. The third intervention option targets the consequences of these efforts by providing appropriate contingent feedback. The external coping resource of human supports is clearly important for all three intervention options. For clarity of the discussion, human support as a resource is addressed in the discussion related to option 3.

The practitioner helps the child develop specific coping-related skills and strategies, teaches the child how to use other existing resources more effectively, and provides the child with support. It is difficult to enhance just one coping resource in isolation because of the interrelatedness of all factors in the coping process. What is done to expand one resource affects the other resources. For example, improving the child's flexibility, a coping behavior, will have a positive effect on the child's affective state and beliefs about personal adequacy. However, each resource is considered separately in the process of intervention planning.

Intervention to Enhance Emerging Beliefs

The emerging belief system of young children may be the most critical resource to address in intervention. It is also the most challenging because it can only be influenced indirectly. In essence, everything children experience contributes to their emerging beliefs of who they are and what the world is like. The outcome of every transaction is stored in some way in memory and shapes perception. Children whose transactions with the world result in effective outcomes develop a positive belief system. They learn to view the world as a place where needs are met. Eventually, they understand that they can influence their surroundings through their personal actions. Children who are less effective in their coping transactions are more likely to develop negative beliefs. For these children, the world may be seen as a frightening, unsafe place where their needs are not met. These children begin to believe that they can have little control of their lives because past efforts resulted in unsatisfactory outcomes or had minimal impact.

Children literally define themselves by how they are treated. They internalize behaviors of others toward them and assume they are correct. If a parent handles a baby as if she is precious and endearing, that little girl will grow up feeling herself to be precious and endearing. If a parent handles a baby as if she is smelly and disgusting, that baby will grow up feeling herself to be smelly and disgusting. Therefore, service providers must be concerned about the emotional climate of the family and its impact on the parent–child relationship. When relational issues are evident, they can be respectfully addressed through various means, such as active listening to increase awareness of interfering factors, providing information and support, modeling desired interactions, and short-term counseling. If intensive services beyond the early intervention program seem necessary, referral of the family to a more specialized community mental health agency may be indicated. Valuable references that offer more in-depth discussion of this critical infant mental health issue are provided by Brazelton (1992), Fraiberg (1980), Greenspan (1992), and Sameroff and Emde (1989).

An important reason for intervening to enhance beliefs is to change the "I can't" thinker to the "I can" thinker—to change the belief that the world is threatening and "I am inadequate" to the belief that the world is exciting and "I am competent." The following strategies, which are linked to all three intervention options, can be used to enhance a child's emerging belief system:

> Provide the child with successful experiences that promote positive self-esteem.
> Teach developmental skills and coping behaviors to increase the child's repertoire for
>   use in coping efforts.
> Respond contingently to the child's actions in order to increase the child's awareness
>   of having a positive affect on the environment.

The following case example involves a child who approaches experiences with an "I can't" belief. Intervention strategies are described that can be used to influence his belief system.

➡   Archie is trying unsuccessfully to grasp a red ball that is just out of his reach on the floor. He manages the situation by some ineffective flailing movements and then crying until his mother gets it for him. To improve Archie's coping effectiveness, intervention strategies might include modifying learning demands. For example, the ball could be placed just close enough so that he is motivated to crawl the short distance. As Archie's confidence increases, the ball can be placed farther and farther away. In addition, adults can model new coping strategies, such as pulling the blanket on which the ball is resting, and they can choose not to respond to his inappropriate behaviors. Also, Archie can be taught to request assistance, such as vocalizing and pointing (see Figure 7.2). Furthermore, he can be helped to bounce back from stressful events by learning to substitute objects when necessary (e.g., redirecting his attention from an inaccessible toy to another available one). Archie's successful experience managing these types of situations may contribute toward the develop of an "I can" orientation, in which he believes in his own ability to cope.

Intervention to Enhance Developmental Skills

Because developmental skills provide a foundation for coping efforts, adaptive functioning can be facilitated by expanding the child's repertoire of available developmental capabilities. The practitioner needs to foster skills related to postural control, mobility, object manipulation, cognitive processing, communication, social-emotional development, and self-help tasks. Intervention focuses on teaching prerequisite developmental skills that prepare a child to cope. For example, an infant may have a limited ability to play with his mother. In order to expand his interactive competence, he can be taught visual skills (attending and tracking), fine motor skills (reaching and grasping), and cognitive skills (cause–effect relationships and early problem solving).

The challenge is to structure early intervention so that acquisition of developmental skills is closely linked to coping-related outcomes. Therefore, the child has the opportu-

Figure 7.2. Archie and his older brother engage in a game of handing the ball back and forth. Later, the play can be expanded by expecting Archie to "ask" for the ball and roll it between them.

nity to integrate and apply the skills within a functional coping context. It is helpful to make this linkage by writing intervention goals that use phrases such as "in order to." For example, Stacey will improve her bilateral coordination *in order to* expand her play schemes, increase her self-initiated problem solving, or communicate what she wants through gestures.

The vignette of Jack, a 2½-year-old child with very limited language and communication skills, describes how his intervention program was modified to help him reach the goal of developing communication skills to cope with the social demands of his day-care program.

➡   Jack is a shy child who frequently becomes frustrated while playing with other children. Jack's parents enrolled him in a daycare program that they believed would provide opportunities for learning play skills. It took Jack several months to adjust. He was quieter than the other children and tended to cling to the teacher. Jack had acquired most age-level skills with the exception of language. He had a vocabulary of about 10 words; however, he did not use his acquired single-word utterances to communicate. The only time the teacher heard Jack "talking" was during solitary play in the block area.

Assessment of resources revealed that Jack had negative beliefs about himself as demonstrated in his reserved demeanor and cautious, almost passive, approach during transactions with people in his environment. He coped by engaging in solitary play (a situation in which he felt safe and could be successful) to avoid interacting with his peers.

Jack needed to learn additional communication skills and their use for managing transactions with people. Because he was a slow-to-warm-up child, intervention was conducted by his teacher, with whom he felt comfortable and seemed to prefer as a playmate. At the initiation of intervention, a developmentally appropriate goal for Jack was to use his 10 acquired vocabulary words during a nonstructured parallel play situation with his teacher. Use of Jack's known words plus a few new single word utterances were modeled for him during one-to-one play with his teacher in the block area. When Jack consistently initiated use of these words to express his needs and ideas to his teacher, learning demands were upgraded to match his developing resources. Then, another child was invited to join the play. The teacher continued to model and encourage Jack's use of learned communication skills to interact with this one peer. Slowly, but surely, Jack began to converse and actively participate in other play activities with a small group of children. He became more independent and relied less on the teacher for social support.

Due to significant disabilities, some children may not be able to master certain developmental skills. In these instances, adults need to make adaptations to compensate for the limitation. For example, a floor seat and a power-operated toy may allow a child with a physical disability to play independently. Chapter 8, this volume, provides activities and strategies to expand developmental skills.

Intervention to Enhance Physical and Affective States

It is important to be aware of the child's physical and affective states and whether any difficulties are temporary or chronic. When a chronic health condition exists, guidance from a physician is necessary in order to plan appropriately for daily activities and emergency situations. For children with a fragile medical status, such as a severe respiratory or cardiac condition, home programming may be suggested. If the child has a temporary health problem, brief suspension of services or modifying the program may be necessary. When the child has a cold or other contagious condition, parents need to realize the importance of keeping the child away from other children.

Allergies to particular foods and elements in the environment must be monitored, and exposure must be limited. Children with chronic conditions (e.g., asthma, epilepsy) may require prophylactic or emergency medication. Practitioners should know the side effects of the medication and proper procedures for handling associated problems. For some children, medical and dietary management is a high priority. For example, urinary tract infection (cystitis) is common in young children with spina bifida. When an infection occurs, antibiotic therapy is used in combination with techniques for bladder management (e.g., the Crede Maneuver, which involves external manual pressure on the lower abdomen to assist bladder drainage). As a preventive measure, cranberry juice is often suggested, as it alters the pH of urine and helps to deter bladder stone formation.

The child's physical status may require that the daily schedule be adapted to prevent fatigue. The routine of the day or intervention session may need to balance active and quiet activities. Consistency in the routine may initially be important so that the child can achieve internal organization. For the child with low energy, the pace of activities needs to be modified and graded to build physical endurance.

Young children, especially infants, have relatively short ready or alert states—the time in which optimal learning can occur. Participation in the early intervention program should be scheduled at a time that is compatible with the child's sleep-wake cycles. Learning demands are best presented when the child is in an alert state. A temporary disruption of mood, such as crying, irritability, or fear, becomes the priority for intervention before learning can take place. Parents and practitioners need to share strategies for helping the child achieve self-control and emotional stability.

Of course, a smiling, attentive child is easier to interact with than a tired, crying, tense child. It is important to differentiate whether a child's difficult behavior reflects temperament, reaction to temporary stress, or a more chronic emotional disorder. In the latter case, the active involvement of mental health professionals is critical. Greenspan (1992) provides therapeutic guidelines for working with young children who have interactive disorders, regulatory disorders, and multisymptom disorders.

Areas of increasing concern are the physical and affective states of children who are prenatally exposed to drugs or born HIV-positive. Intervention with these children and their families has unique aspects. For intervention to be successful, the parents who are substance abusing must address the issue of their drug use. If the early intervention program is not specialized in drug rehabilitation, referral for supplementary services is often necessary. When actively using drugs, it is difficult for these parents to have the energy and consistent emotional availability to interact meaningfully with their children and develop secure attachments. There are a number of characteristics of children exposed to drugs that influence their affective state. These characteristics commonly include poor self-regulation, limited attending and tracking, hypersensitivity or lethargy, and low muscle tone. These factors must be considered when planning intervention (see chap. 8, this volume, for therapeutic strategies and activities). Children with HIV infection often have similar problems. In addition, the practitioner has to consider the progressive nature of the condition of the child and mother, as well as the need for universal precautions for infection control. As with all children, however, their growth and quality of life are intervention priorities.

Intervention to Enhance Coping Style

Intervention planning can focus on the overall effectiveness of the child's coping style or on the child's least effective coping behaviors. (Chap. 8, this volume, presents activities to foster specific coping behaviors.) The level of effectiveness of a child's coping style influences the selection of intervention strategies and the intensity of the program. Three levels of coping effectiveness, adapted from the rating scale of the Early Coping Inventory, are used to describe a child's coping style: minimally effective coping (an Adaptive Behavior Index of 1 or 2), situationally effective coping (index of 3), and effective coping (index of 4 or 5). The following discussion provides guidelines for addressing the unique needs of children with coping styles at the three levels of effectiveness.

Minimally Effective Coping   A child with a minimally effective coping style requires intensive intervention consisting of direct teaching of developmental skills and coping behaviors. This child's coping efforts are inconsistent; rigidly repetitious, or reduce the stress of the moment but generate negative outcomes over time (e.g., habitual withdrawal or temper tantrums). It appears that a child continues to use ineffective coping behaviors either to avoid or gain control over stressful situations or due to a very restricted repertoire of alternative coping strategies (Schaffer & Schaffer, 1982). The minimally effective child usually has limited developmental, behavioral, and/or environmental resources to draw on for coping efforts or is unable, for whatever reason, to use available resources adaptively. Intervention focuses on expanding the child's resources while also grading environmental demands to decrease the need to use stereotypic or other ineffective behaviors.

Because successful coping requires the integrated use of developmental skills to produce functional, goal-directed coping efforts, intervention emphasizes expansion of developmental capabilities. In addition, intervention is designed to teach desired coping behaviors and to modify the physical and social environment to reduce opportunities for the reinforcement of maladaptive patterns. Consistency is necessary in the choice and presentation of activities, and practice is emphasized. Because the minimally effective child is often incapable of independently applying learned behaviors to new contexts, the clinician gradually introduces new activities in a variety of situations as the child's coping ability increases.

It is important to establish priorities for intervention because it is unrealistic to address all developmental and coping-related problems at once. Likewise, it is important to determine appropriate expectations for the child's progress. Change can be effected through a combination of direct and indirect teaching strategies. However, minimally effective children will most likely require extensive use of direct strategies to elicit behavioral change. Direct strategies (e.g., modeling of target behaviors, prompting of coping efforts, and reinforcement of gradual approximations of desired behavior) are used to teach necessary developmental skills and more successful coping behavior (see Figure 7.3). Indirect strategies are used to modify those components of the environment that trigger and reinforce the child's maladaptive responses. It would be inappropriate to expect the minimally effective child to become an effective coper after a 6-month period of intervention. Caregivers and practitioners need to maintain realistic expectations and to support one another, because disappointments and frustration may be communicated to the child who probably already has a negative belief system.

The following guidelines summarize the priorities of intervention with children who have minimally effective coping.

> Foster parent–child communication and play.
> Establish realistic priorities with parents.
> Assist parents with behavior management and the use of appropriate feedback.
> Provide support to parents and opportunities for them to share feelings of success and disappointment.
> Modify environmental demands to reduce opportunities for eliciting and reinforcing maladaptive behavior.
> Teach developmental skills and desired coping behaviors.
> Emphasize direct intervention strategies.
> Initially emphasize consistency in choice and presentation of intervention activities.
> Provide repeated opportunities for practice.

➡ Ms. Benson is an 18-year-old single mother living on public assistance in a housing project with her son Max, who was prenatally exposed to cocaine before Ms. Benson successfully completed a drug rehabilitation program. She is currently being monitored by the child welfare agency in order to maintain custody of her son. Max, who is 7 months of age, is delayed in development and inconsistent in mood and regulation of state. His coping style is minimally effective. Sometimes Ms. Benson interacts with Max as if he were very special to her. At other times, when he is temperamentally difficult, frantically crying, or ferociously eating and spitting up, she gets extremely angry with him. Ms. Benson tends to interpret his behavior as spoiled, greedy, and manipulative. In

Figure 7.3.   Direct intervention strategies to teach new skills: The therapist on the right offers manual support to help the child maintain the short-sitting position while the father provides physical guidance and an encouraging smile to assist the child's play with the toy.

these situations she will put him in his crib and let him cry or try to quiet him by use of a pacifier. The inconsistencies in mother–child transactions have generated an insecure attachment that often leaves both parties dissatisfied. Despite these difficulties, it is evident that Ms. Benson cares for Max and would like to be a good mother.

An integrated program was developed in which one practitioner came to their apartment three times a week. With the support of a supervisor, the practitioner was able to work with both mother and child. The priority was to enhance the mother–infant relationship. As Max developed a more secure attachment, he became more regulated and able to learn needed developmental skills. Intervention focused on increasing the quality of the attachment by helping Ms. Benson to reexamine her perceptions of Max and to learn to interact with him with greater consistency and responsiveness.

Intervention was organized around daily activities, such as playing, feeding, bathing, and going to the laundromat. The practitioner helped the mother to identify how Max felt, how she felt, and why she felt that way. For example, when Max cried, the mother tended to label him "spoiled rotten" and let him cry it out in his crib "to teach him a lesson." At these times, questions were asked to assist her to think about what was really happening. How do you think Max feels? What do you think Max is crying about? Do you think anything else might be happening? How does it make you feel? What was it like when you were growing up and cried? How are things different this week than last week?

This scenario was repeated innumerable times—when intensive sucking on the bottle was interpreted as "greedy" or hysteria during dressing was considered "disrespect and a nasty attitude." An emphasis of this intervention was to help Ms. Benson appreciate the impact of her own experience of being parented on her relationship with Max and how it plays out in her feelings and behavior.

Intervention structured around daily activities helped Ms. Benson establish a consistent, daily routine. It provided opportunities for identifying when things were going well between her and her child. For example, during a relaxed interaction, the practitioner said, "See how Max cools down when your voice is soft. You are special to him." Such intervention was a powerful tool for fostering their attachment. The practitioner was also able to model behaviors that aided Max to cope and learn. She then encouraged Ms. Benson to practice them. As the mother became more confident in her role and Max became easier to manage, both of their coping styles became more productive.

Situationally Effective Coping A child with a situationally effective coping style has some adaptive competence. However, coping behaviors used effectively in one type of situation are not generalized to other types of situations. Intervention is geared to helping this child learn to generalize the use of effective coping behaviors to environments and circumstances in which the child is currently less successful. Particular emphasis is placed on the use of indirect intervention strategies because they foster self-initiation.

Intervention planning needs to identify the nature of the situations and environments in which the child demonstrates effective coping. Sample contextual variables to consider may include: the presence or absence of a caregiver, the degree of structure, solitary or group environments, the time of day when demands are presented, the child's preference for certain types of sensory input, or the availability of adaptive seating for a child with a physical disability. An important indirect intervention strategy is to modify the environmental characteristics of situations in which the child copes ineffectively to resemble more closely the environmental characteristics of successful coping experiences. For instance, Shannon was active and flexible in routine settings, but she became anxious in new surroundings. The parents were taught various techniques for making novel situations more familiar and less intimidating for their daughter. These included previewing what to expect so that she could anticipate events, having her carry a tote bag that was a comforting object, and allowing time for her to warm up and acclimate. Under these conditions, Shannon was able to generalize her adaptive behaviors with growing comfort to new environments.

Indirect intervention strategies are emphasized to assist the child to learn to generalize his or her coping behaviors, and direct strategies are used to supplement them. After modifying environmental aspects of situations in which the child copes ineffectively to more closely resemble environmental components of successful coping experiences, direct strategies can be used to facilitate further generalization. In summary, the following guidelines need to be considered when working with a child who has a situationally effective coping style.

Focus on helping the child learn to generalize.

Modify the environmental characteristics of situations in which the child copes ineffectively to resemble more closely the environmental characteristics of situations in which the child copes effectively.

Reinforce gradual approximations of desired coping behaviors in new contexts.

Gradually introduce more demanding environmental circumstances while providing social support.

Emphasize indirect intervention strategies.

Expand the repertoire of developmental skills and coping strategies so that the child has choices for appropriate behavior.

The following vignette about Susie provides an example of intervention for a child with a situationally effective coping style. Susie, born with fetal alcohol syndrome, displayed very different behavior at home than she displayed at the early intervention program. Services focused on the parents and professionals working together to help Susie generalize her coping skills to the home environment.

➡   Susie was attending a young toddler group 2 days a week for nearly 6 months. At the program, Susie was a cooperative child who followed the routine and recognized limits, responded effectively to vocal and gestural directions, and participated enthusiastically in activities. At progress report time, Susie's mother, Mrs. Ford, was pleased to receive a positive report. Mrs. Ford did feel somewhat dubious, however, because Susie's behavior at home was such a source of concern for family members. She described her daughter's behavior as frequently loud and destructive. Susie was unable to play independently for an appropriate period of time.

Further discussion revealed a home routine that varied from one day to the next and a disorganized play environment. It appeared that structure, the factor that enabled Susie to cope so well with demands at the program, was missing from her home environment. Collaborative planning resulted in the use of an indirect strategy to enhance effective coping at home. A daily routine for home life was developed that was responsive to Susie's need for external structure as well as the family's needs for flexibility. The day was structured by having reasonably consistent times for meals, naps, bathing, play, and similar activities. For example, a favorite television program was scheduled when Mrs. Ford was preparing dinner. Situational routines were also emphasized. If she sat quietly in the cart at the grocery store, Susie was allowed to select one thing for Mrs. Ford to buy. An hour was set for her to go to bed and the routine included a story, prayers, a kiss, and lights out. Weather permitting, Susie and the sitter would go to the playground after lunch on days when she did not attend the toddler group. The routine involved staying within the fenced area surrounding the sandbox and playing with sand toys. To help Susie further generalize the use of effective coping behaviors at home, it was suggested that Mrs. Ford employ some direct teaching strategies. Verbal cues from supportive adults helped Susie remember to use behavior appropriate to the situation rather than experience the consequences of her inappropriate behaviors. Verbal preparation for predictable changes in the home routine facilitated Susie's adaptation to transitions in her environment.

The case example of Kwang Mee shows how expanding developmental skills enhanced the coping efforts of a situationally effective coper.

➡ Kwang Mee was a 26-month-old child diagnosed as having spina bifida. Her parents were particularly concerned that she was growing increasingly frustrated by the limitation imposed by her physical disability. Results of the developmental assessment indicated that her major strengths were her skills in cognition and communication. She understood simple sentences and used words and gestures during interactions. Kwang Mee had significant delays, however, in gross and fine motor skills. Although she could move about in the prone position by pulling with her arms, this form of locomotion required excessive energy. Efficient use of the hands for manipulative play was restricted by her lack of postural control, requiring her to use one or both arms to support her sitting position. The motor limitation appeared to be interfering with her development of self-esteem and autonomy.

Kwang Mee's coping style was situationally effective. Her motivation to explore and interact with the environment was undermined by her restricted motor skills. The effectiveness of many coping behaviors was dependent on proper physical positioning by an adult and structuring of the environment so that play materials were within reach. Kwang Mee's most effective coping behaviors were related to her social competence. She was able to accept warmth and affection, was responsive to the feelings and moods of others, engaged in reciprocal social interactions, and had a keen visual and auditory interest in her surroundings.

Her least effective coping behaviors were strongly influenced by her physical involvement. She had poor control of her posture and minimal ability to adapt movements to meet the requirements of specific situations. As a result, she frustrated easily and lacked persistence during play. Kwang Mee attempted tasks, but she tended to give up quickly if her actions failed to achieve desired results. When frustrated, she typically arched into an extensor posture. Her motor difficulties were hindering the development of independence in play. For example, play skills that she demonstrated when seated on her father's lap could not be applied successfully when she was left on her own.

A major priority for intervention was to improve Kwang Mee's postural control, mobility, and manipulation. Her coping effectiveness was enhanced substantially by decreasing the impact of her physical disability on her performance. Stress related to motor demands was reduced and graded. Kwang Mee's ability to generalize coping behaviors expanded as she developed motor skills. Gradually, she was able to persist with a task for longer periods of time and consequently experienced less frustration.

Numerous intervention strategies were employed to facilitate Kwang Mee's success in goal-directed activity during play. An adapted seat for use on the floor or in a regular chair provided the external support that she required for manipulation of toys (an indirect intervention strategy). Likewise, a small hand-propelled cart was used to allow independent mobility. At the same time, therapy focused on strengthening the muscles she needed for postural stability and ambulation with braces.

Kwang Mee was taught to change her behavior to solve a problem before getting frustrated. When initial attempts to do something resulted in failure, her parents and the therapist demonstrated alternative ways for Kwang Mee to move herself or the toy to achieve success (a direct intervention strategy). In addition, she was encouraged to use her social and communicative skills to obtain assistance rather than arching into extension. Through activities, Kwang Mee was taught to be aware of when and how to request adult help by pointing and vocalization. Kwang Mee's successful use of these coping behaviors and developmental skills reinforced emerging belief in her own competence and resulted in more independent play.

Consistently Effective Coping   A child with an effective coping style uses behaviors that are consistently appropriate. The child is able to generalize coping behaviors across a variety of situations. No child copes successfully under every circumstance, but a child with an effective coping style has sufficient resources to modify behavior and adapt to new demands. Even for effective copers it is important to monitor on an ongoing basis the balance between environmental demands and the child's coping resources. Intervention emphasizes maintaining and promoting the most adaptive behaviors. Attention is also given to preventing regression prior to and during anticipated stressful life events. Extra support is also offered during times of unanticipated excessive stress. Activities of a preventive nature can help the child and family prior to situations that are predictably very demanding, such as hospitalization, modifications in the child's current program, birth of a sibling, or changes in residence.

Prevention not only focuses on avoidance of stressful events. It also focuses on active, adaptive management so that the growth-enhancing potential of these experiences can be realized. Several factors are considered when planning preventive intervention, including the extent and quality of resources available for use by the child and family, additional familial and child stressors, and program resources. Prevention efforts may require a skillful combination of direct and indirect intervention strategies to help the child learn new behaviors. Additional family-centered support may include counseling with the caregiver, role-playing with siblings, and expanded interagency collaboration.

A disabling condition can have a different coping impact at various stages of development. For example, lack of mobility may cause more frustration for a 12-month-old infant with a physical disability who is motivated to "do" than in a 6-month-old infant. Similarly, a child with delayed speech may do well at home using gaze and gesture, but in a day care environment, the child may have difficulty making his or her needs known to others.

The following list summarizes guidelines for working with a child who has an effective coping style.

Monitor on an ongoing basis the balance between environmental demands and the child's coping resources.

Use primarily indirect intervention strategies.

Emphasize prevention to prepare for upcoming stressful situations (e.g., hospitalization, change in early intervention personnel).

Increase awareness of new events and rehearse coping strategies. Provide anticipatory guidance to the parents.

Keep in mind that a disabling condition may have a varied impact on the child's coping competence over time.

Stephanie, a 2½-year-old child with a hearing loss, is an example of an effective coper.

➡   Stephanie is well adjusted to her loss of hearing and actively participates in the various activities of a growing child. She has a good attention span and many age-appropriate developmental skills. She has a good frustration tolerance, creatively uses a variety of strategies to solve problems, and is persistent in mastering self-initiated tasks. She is a happy child who initiates social interactions with peers as well as adults.

For Stephanie, a potentially stressful event was the upcoming birth of a sibling. Up until then she was an only child. Soon she would have to adjust to the many demands a new baby brings to the existing family system (e.g., sharing Mommy and Daddy with a new person, feelings of displacement, learning to delay gratification, being more independent, taking on the new role of sister).

Through role-playing, intervention focused on helping Stephanie prepare for the new baby's arrival. Play situations gave Stephanie the opportunity to experience new feelings and to try out new coping strategies in a safe, supportive environment. When the new baby arrived, Stephanie was usually able to manage the situation. She had a repertoire of rehearsed behaviors to draw on, had some sense of what the baby's needs would be, and had an emerging understanding of her new role in the family. At times when she felt jealous or left out, she expressed her feelings through angry, aggressive play with her stuffed animals (Figure 7.4).

Intervention to Enhance Material and Environmental Supports

When families do not have the basic material and environmental resources necessary for daily living, intervention in this area becomes the priority. Families cannot focus on helping their children when they are homeless; in extremely violent circumstances; or when they have critical needs related to food, clothing, shelter, and health-related services. Their service plan would highlight linking them to appropriate governmental and community agencies and guiding them when necessary through the attendant bureaucracy.

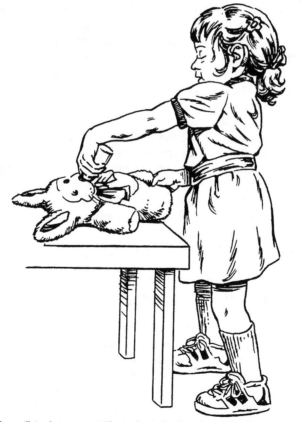

Figure 7.4. Stephanie ventilates her anger and frustration by forcing the stuffed animal to drink from the bottle; she may say "Bad baby, drink milk now!" She then burps the stuffed animal by banging it aggressively against the table.

In early intervention planning, the environment is often taken for granted with minimal awareness of its impact on behavior and feelings. It is important to view from a child's perspective the space of the home, childcare environment, or early intervention program. What would an infant or toddler see and feel in this place? Does the environment support purposeful, self-initiated behavior? From the adult's perspective, is it an easy and comfortable place to be? Is the environment structured so that adults have time to interact with the child, rather than having to use their time setting up, taking down, or managing the child's disruptive behavior?

There are many material and environmental supports that specifically contribute to the ability of young children to cope effectively in the home, the childcare center, and the early intervention program. Some important supports are described below (some of the supports are interrelated).

Child-Proof the Environment   To make the environment safe for a child, place gates in front of stairwells, cover electrical outlets, discard broken toys, install window guards, and remove appliances with electric cords that can be pulled off a table.

Ensure Quality of Light   A mixture of natural light and incandescent lighting is preferred. If fluorescent light is used, the "day light" or "warm light" fluorescent tubes are recommended for a soft quality of illumination. Fluorescent fixtures should be covered with diffusing screens to prevent glare. Exposed tubes and bare light bulbs should be covered because they cause eyestrain, especially for infants who gaze upward. In general, a diffused light is best so that all areas of the room are equally illuminated. Often, classrooms and clinic environments are too bright, resulting in visual fatigue. The degree of illumination can be controlled by a rheostat on the light fixtures and venetian blinds on the windows. The lights can be temporarily dimmed to achieve a calming influence on overly stimulated young children. Direct, glaring sunlight can be avoided by adjusting the blinds to reflect the light off the ceiling.

Ensure Quality of Heat and Ventilation   Monitor the temperature of rooms, especially at floor level. Be aware of drafts.

Monitor Degree of Environmental Stimulation   Limit clutter, distractions, and extraneous noise. Acoustic tile, drapes, area carpets, and fabric on walls can diminish sound. (Close-weave, low-nap carpeting on the floor also helps prevent slipping.) Avoid complex wallpaper or long stretches of brightly colored walls; emphasize neutral, soft colors on the walls and ceiling. It is desirable that furniture be child-height and pictures and posters be placed at the general eye level of the children. Decoration should be simple and aesthetically pleasing, with materials readily accessible.

Areas of the room need to be well defined according to functional use to enhance a sense of order. For example, specific activities are best allocated to different areas, and particular shelves should be designated to store particular toys. Children then learn where to go to become involved in certain activities and where play materials are located and should be returned after use.

Encourage Full Use of Available Space   There is a tendency for caregivers and young children to crowd together regardless of available space. Adults tend to sit together in group care settings with the infants and toddlers in close proximity. The result is major congestion with inevitable conflicts and clashing of the children. An open-center arrangement is preferred with activity centers, large permanent equipment, and adult furniture distributed around the perimeter of the room. In this way, the children and adults are spread out to allow for one-to-one and small-group interaction (1–3 children). Intimate spaces can be created by the arrangement of furniture, shelving units, and low dividers (18"–40"). This allows children to be in open view of adults, but visually separated from other action in the room. This arrangement decreases aimless wandering and over-stimulation; it helps the children organize their play and regulate their behavior.

Provide Toys and Play Materials   Developmentally appropriate toys are an important resource for children. Playthings can range from lavish store-bought toys to the pots, pans, spoons, and discarded adult clothes that intrigue young children. In addition to these commonly enjoyed playthings, parents and practitioners may select toys and materials that are responsive to the special needs of a particular infant or toddler. For example, a child with poor attending skills may need brightly colored, noise-making toys that provide multisensory experiences. Orange, red, and yellow are particularly stimulating colors, whereas black and yellow offer a sharp visual contrast. A child with tremorous movements may find lightweight toys difficult to manage; toys of greater weight are easier to handle, such as those made of heavy rubber or wood. For a child who requires arm strengthening, it is helpful to introduce hammering, play with squeeze toys, and rolling or pounding Play-Doh. A child who has independent sitting balance with good trunk control can be provided with the opportunity to play on gross motor equipment, such as rocking boats or horses, large inflatable shapes, slides, and tunnels. Such experience is also important for a child with poor trunk control, although physical support may be required for safe participation. In addition, young children enjoy climbing and playground equipment.

Provide Adapted Equipment   Young children can profit from adapted equipment that ranges from very simple to complex. Adaptations can be used to enhance functional capability in many areas. The choice of equipment should follow the principle of parsimony—use the simplest means to achieve the desired outcome. The following are examples of simple adapted devices: cut-out cups or special spoons to facilitate feeding, Velcro fastening on clothing to assist dressing, simple communication boards used by pointing to identify needs, and puzzle pieces with knobs to manage the task.

Modern technology has expanded the resources available to children with disabilities. Battery-powered toys adapted to operate with a touch pad are often the young child's first exposure to this development (see Figure 7.5). Computers and electronic equipment have introduced new opportunities for communication and mobility. Augmentative communication systems have been developed for children under 3 years of age. Mobility aids

Figure 7.5.   An example of a child using a power-activated toy. When the infant presses on the touch pad, the toy dog begins to bark and wag its tail.

range from adapted tricycles to powered wheelchairs. Braces, walkers, and strollers are also used to support mobility. In addition, adaptations can be made to assist positioning during daily activities. Sample equipment includes floor seats, tub seats for bathing, modified car seats, standing devices, and adapted chairs and tables (Scherzer & Tscharnuter, 1990; Williamson, 1987).

At first glance, interventions to address material and environmental supports may seem obvious; however, in practice one must recognize the realities of each environment and the complexities of often conflicting needs. The following vignette illustrates the challenge of knowing when, where, and how to intervene with a family receiving services in their home.

➡ Each time Jim, the special educator, went to the Hawkins' apartment to work with Ariel (age 11 months), he experienced a dilemma. There were several environmental factors that were not in Ariel's best interest. For example, the window shades were always drawn, making the apartment dark, and Ariel was routinely placed in her Jolly Jumper in front of the television.

Jim's initial impulse was to start making recommendations for change. Upon reflection, however, Jim wondered if there could be valid reasons for this situation. He told the mother, "I notice that when I come here you always have the shades down." Ms. Hawkins replied, "This is because we live on the first floor. To feel safe in this neighborhood, I keep the shades down and the TV on. When I do, people on the street can't look in. When they hear the TV, they know there is someone at home."

Jim had to consider how to address these conflicting needs. He decided to focus on Ariel's need for movement and exploration (not always being in the Jolly Jumper) and modifying the passive television watching. When he raised this issue, Ms. Hawkins said, "I hear what you are saying and I know it is important, but I don't want to put Ariel on the floor because of splinters and roaches. The other day, I was scared stiff, a rat ran through the room." Jim responded, "You have really helped me to see things in a different light. I will give a lot of thought to what we can do together to help Ariel."

The following questions may help to review the environmental factors that can foster or inhibit engagement and learning.

Is the child in a stable position that allows his or her hands to be available for manipulative activities?
Are there auditory distractions that interfere with performance, such as extraneous noise from the street or hallway?
Are there visual distractions, such as cluttered walls or work surfaces?
Are the instructional or play materials visually confusing or overly complex?
Is the lighting in the room appropriate to prevent glare?
Is there available and safe space for active movement and exploration?

INTERVENTION OPTION 3

The third intervention option based on transactions is to provide appropriate, contingent feedback to the child's coping efforts. Through feedback, children learn about the impact of their behavior on the environment. When effective coping is reinforced through timely, positive, and accurate feedback, the child experiences a sense of mastery that contributes over time to a belief regarding personal worth and autonomy.

Meaningful feedback is often subtle, but it has a clear message. It is frequently expressed affectively through smiles, frowns, looks of admiration or consternation, and appearance of delight or worry. The quality of the feedback can have positive or negative consequences. For example, appropriate feedback can reinforce desired or newly acquired coping strategies. Inappropriate feedback can perpetuate undesired, maladaptive behavior. Particularly with young children, the feedback needs to be provided in an immediate and succinct manner in order for the child to learn to cope.

Research suggests that children with special needs tend to assume passive, respondent roles rather than active, autonomous ones (Brinker & Lewis, 1982; Sullivan & Lewis, 1993; Zeitlin & Williamson, 1990). This behavioral pattern can be reinforced unintentionally by parents and professionals. When a child has a disability, parents may tend to assume a strongly dominant interactional style (Barrera & Vella, 1987; Hanzlik, 1989; Rosenberg & Robinson, 1988). Likewise, professionals may tend to implement intervention that is highly structured and adult directed, with an emphasis on eliciting responses from the child that are then reinforced by the clinician (Dunst, Cushing, & Vance, 1985). In both cases there is little opportunity for the child to learn that intrinsically motivated behavior can be used successfully to achieve personal needs.

Therefore, it is important to encourage the development of self-directed, purposeful behavior. Such an approach focuses on the adult responding contingently to the child's self-generated action. The child learns to detect, associate, and remember co-occurrences. That is, the child perceives things happening as a consequence of his or her behavior. The emphasis is on the physical and social environments supporting child-initiated activity and providing feedback that encourages the extension and elaboration of demonstrated, emerging skills. In this context, the child has the freedom to explore, problem solve, and experiment with alternative management strategies.

The following vignette is an example of an adult responding contingently to a child's self-initiated action. It occurred when the clinician was on a home visit.

➡ Rachel, the teacher, was sitting on the rug with Andrew, a 2-year-old child with cognitive delays. She had previously placed three toys on a nearby couch. Rachel remained quiet, waiting for Andrew to initiate some action. After a few moments, Andrew toddled over to the couch, surveyed the toys, and picked up the doll and brush. He brought both items back and sat down next to Rachel. Andrew smiled sheepishly at her and started to comb the doll's hair. Rachel, making eye contact, said, "You are combing the doll's hair." After a few seconds, Andrew tossed the doll and comb down. Rachel said, "What else can you do with the doll?" Andrew stared aimlessly in space, and finally picked up the doll and hugged it. Rachel responded, "You are hugging the doll. You must love her." Andrew looked up at Rachel, smiled, and climbed onto her lap and gave her a hug.

Balanced turntaking between the child and the adult provides ample opportunity for the child to lead the interaction within socially acceptable limits. Turntaking is a way of enhancing mutual responsiveness in a transaction. A turn is any verbal or nonverbal behavior produced by the adult or child during this engagement. The following five intervention strategies are described by Mahoney and his associates to facilitate effective turntaking (Mahoney, Powell, Finnegan, Fors, & Wood, 1986).

1. *Take one turn and wait.* The adult's turn should be very short and include only one simple, discrete behavior or action. Each time the adult takes a turn, there should be a waiting period (possibly as long as 10 seconds) to allow the child to respond.
2. *Imitate the child.* Children often increase their participation when the adult imitates their behavior. Even children who seemingly have little interest in social interaction

can be engaged in this way. This may include imitating such "inappropriate" behaviors as making bizarre sounds or gestures, throwing objects, or thumbsucking.

3. *Follow the child's lead.* This strategy requires that adults play with toys or engage in activities in the same manner as children even though it may mean using the toys in an atypical way and with less than optimal outcomes.

4. *Signal for turns.* Even when a child shows little or no inclination to take a turn, the adult should signal him or her to take turns. Two ways of signaling are to wait with anticipation or to point to the child or object; this depends on the desired response. Waiting with anticipation involves maintaining eye contact with a facial expression and body posture that communicates that the adult expects something from the child. Pointing is another nonverbal way of communicating expectation.

5. *Decrease requests.* Requests for involvement should be kept to a minimum. To support the child's involvement, the adult can label, comment, notice, express delight or pleasure, and provide helpful information. When a request is made it should be closely related to what the child is already doing.

The following example shows how contingent responding helped Todd become more involved in the world around him.

➡   Todd and his twin brother just turned 8 months old. The boys were born a month and a half premature. Todd, the second-born twin, was lagging developmentally behind his brother.

Todd had low muscle tone, which made development of postural control and motor skills difficult. He could not sit unsupported or roll over independently. Todd had little opportunity to control his environment through physical actions and seemed most content when lying on his back. Unfortunately, this position reinforced his passive nature because he could not bring his hand to midline for exploratory play when in this supine position. Although Todd was frequently described as a "good baby," there was concern that his passivity was being interpreted and reinforced as an easygoing temperament. Todd was, however, very responsive to adult-initiated social interaction and cuddling. Because of this behavior, the intervention team felt that Todd could learn to "control" this interaction by having significant adults respond contingently to his behavioral cues.

Observation of Todd's acquired motor skills revealed that when placed in an adapted infant seat that supported his trunk, Todd was able to raise his arms in a swinging motion that could become a more directed reach or intended gesture if reinforced contingently with a social act. Todd was placed in the infant seat, which not only gave him more postural control, but also made him available for face-to-face interaction in an upright position. His mother was asked to respond contingently by tickling his belly and vocalizing the first time that he moved his arm in an upward motion. She was instructed not to repeat the tickling until Todd raised his arm again. After several times, Todd began to understand the social game and made the association that raising his arm up had a consequence that he enjoyed.

Todd generalized his behavior of raising an arm to play with an adapted toy. Todd now raises his arm, and as it descends it presses on an adapted switch plate that activates a toy dog. The dog wags its tail and barks in a friendly way. His mother and the intervention team have begun to notice Todd initiating attempts to manipulate other play objects and to instigate social interactions.

SUMMARY

This chapter discusses the three intervention options to foster effective coping transactions, as well as direct and indirect intervention strategies for implementing these options. Whereas each option is described separately, any change in one typically influences the other two options. For example, modifying demands calls for a different coping effort that would probably change the required resources. In time, this generates the need for different contingent feedback.

CHAPTER 8

Intervention Strategies and Activities

The intervention options for developing effective transactions between a child and an adult provide a context for planning. A whole range of strategies and activities (many familiar to the reader) can be used for implementing the individualized family service plan (IFSP). There are two important considerations for their selection: the purpose for choosing a particular strategy or activity (i.e., what is the functional outcome to be achieved?) and the structure for helping the child manage the learning demand (i.e., how is the desired learning facilitated?).

The activities and strategies described in this chapter are divided into three sections and can be used to assist young children to learn to cope. Because children learn best when interventions are designed to be sensitive to their coping style, the first section of this chapter suggests ways to provide a structure for learning: personalizing sensory experiences, using physical handling and positioning procedures, and capitalizing on children's love of play. The second section focuses on facilitating functional developmental skills that form the building blocks for coping efforts. The final section addresses the additional coping-related considerations of attachment, temperament, and daily challenges.

PROVIDING A STRUCTURE FOR LEARNING

Each child has a unique approach to coping with learning. Learning is facilitated when experiences are structured in ways that make the most of the child's strengths and minimize the child's vulnerabilities. Sensory information can be graded to support the child's ability to organize attention, affect, and engagement. In addition, special physical handling and positioning techniques can be used to encourage functionally relevant movement and interaction. Furthermore, play opportunities can be provided to bolster the integration of the child's internal and external worlds.

Personalizing Sensory Experiences

Through spontaneous interaction and planned intervention, parents and practitioners have an opportunity to influence a child's sensory experience. During caregiving and play, for example, adults modulate the type, intensity, and frequency of sensory stimulation. The processing of sensory information forms the foundation for the infant's attention, self-regulation, and coping capability. Young children vary greatly in their capacity to control states of arousal, habituate to environmental events, and perform adaptive skills in response to their surroundings. Some infants and toddlers are hyporeactive and require active stimulation to become engaged. However, many children with special needs are hyperreactive and readily overload with multisensory stimulation. These children develop defensive behaviors that are exaggerated emotional responses to specific sensory stimuli—most commonly hypersensitivity to touch, movement, and/or sounds. They tend to develop either a fearful and cautious behavioral pattern or a negative and defiant one (DeGangi, 1991; DeGangi, Craft, & Castellan, 1991; Greenspan, 1992).

Tactile defensiveness is the tendency to react negatively to sensations of touch—a child is overly sensitive to tactile input that others would hardly feel. Because his or her immature central nervous system is unable to manage the sensation, this child reacts with flight (i.e., avoidance, withdrawal) or fight (i.e., anger, hostility). Certain parts of the body may be particularly hypersensitive, such as the face, mouth, hands, and feet.

Intolerance to movement in the young infant may be indicated by persistent irritability, fussing, and crying in response to being moved, and an inability to be calmed with slow, rhythmic rocking by the parent. A resistance to prone positioning may also be seen. Such behaviors not only affect the infant's course of motor development but they may influence the development of attachment and social interaction with the parents. Intervention emphasizes the introduction of slow, carefully graded movement experiences based on the infant's ability to integrate the sensory input in order to respond adaptively. Care is taken that passive and active movement is encouraged only to an extent that is within the tolerance level of the child.

A child with auditory defensiveness, especially an infant, may react to sounds with hyperirritability, distractibility, or restlessness. These children cry at unexpected or high-pitched sounds and may even cover their ears. As they grow older, this sensitivity to sound can interfere with their ability to attend to a task.

Hypersensitivity   The following intervention guidelines are helpful when working with infants and toddlers who are *hypersensitive*. An individualized sensory approach is recommended because these children vary greatly in their preferences and levels of tolerance. These guidelines are relevant when planning for young children prenatally exposed to drugs; these children often exhibit fussiness, resistance to change, poor self-regulation, and sensory disorganization.

Watch for early signs of distress. If there are signs of distress, stop the activity and provide time to recover. (Slowing the pace, rather than stopping the activity, is sufficient for some infants but not for others.)

Use a calming technique that is effective with the child and be consistent in its application (i.e., stay with a procedure and do not jump from one to another). Examples include:

- Firm pressure on the skin (Avoid a light touch that tickles and is excitatory.)
- Massage for relaxation
- Slow repetitive rocking of the infant held in a vertical position in the adult's arms or on the adult's lap over the knees (gentle patting on the infant's back can also be soothing).
- Rhythmic motion (e.g., rocking infant seat, wind-up infant swing, ride in a baby carriage or automobile)
- Swaddling (see Figure 8.1)
- Soft melodic lullabies and music boxes
- Sucking on a pacifier

Encourage the child to develop self-comforting behaviors (e.g., mouthing, cuddling a soft toy, hugging hands against chest, using transitional objects such as a blanket or teddy bear, snuggling into a quiet place such as the corner of the crib).

Figure 8.1. An example of swaddling an infant in a light blanket to promote sensory organization and behavioral control.

Consider the complexity of the sensory input during interaction. Some infants may only be able to handle one sensory modality at a time (i.e., looking, listening, feeling, or moving, but not two together). Other infants may require specific multisensory combinations.

Notice that the infant's irritability may tend to cause the adult to overreact emotionally. To avoid escalating tension, caregivers need to take breaks.

Be careful that the child's difficult behavioral pattern does not condition the adult to avoid presenting appropriate developmental challenges (e.g., avoiding textured foods or making disciplinary demands, overuse of a walker that the infant prefers).

Grade environmental stimulation (e.g., avoid overcrowding, loud noises, glaring sunlight).

Engage the child in activities of high interest; sensory tolerance increases when the child enjoys the task.

Provide a routine that is reasonably consistent, predictable, and structured.

It is important to be aware of signs that a child is becoming sensorially overloaded, such as active withdrawal (e.g., arching, running away); tuning out (e.g., staring into space, yawning); rejection (e.g., pushing away with the hands or feet); or signaling distress (e.g., crying, verbalizing). When a child is in such an emotional state, muscle tension is increased, undesired movement patterns are reinforced, and the child cannot learn. Likewise, the child's trust of the adult is undermined. The intervention challenge is to grade the choice, intensity, and variety of environmental demands based upon the child's changing ability to process sensory information and respond adaptively.

Managing the young child who is intolerant of movement illustrates this point. Intervention involves the introduction of slow, carefully monitored movement experiences. In grading the intervention, it is easiest for the child to tolerate movement while being held in a maximally supported position as the adult moves (e.g., held in the arms as the adult gently steps in various directions). The next progression is to move the child while supported on the adult's lap (e.g., shifting the child from side to side by raising and lowering the adult's legs). Motion is therefore translated through the adult's body to the child (see Figure 8.2). Over time, the child may be able to accept direct facilitation of movement on a stable surface such as the floor or a table top. For the toddler, self-initiated movements may be more readily tolerated than those superimposed by an adult's handling.

Physical Handling and Positioning

In typical development, young children spontaneously and frequently move from one position to another as they change play activities, explore their surroundings, and interact with others. In contrast, many young children with physical disabilities or motor delays tend to maintain rather static postures for prolonged periods of time (e.g., supine position

Figure 8.2.   Lateral shift of the child toward the side when the adult lowers one of her legs and raises the other.

or propped in sitting). This restricted physical activity not only limits opportunities for participation in family life but can also undermine emotional growth. For instance, a child may be unduly frightened by a loud noise because she is unable to turn to the sound to ensure that she is not being personally threatened.

For the child with a physical disability, it is essential to have a variety of alternative positions that can be provided throughout the day and that are appropriate to the task at hand. Of particular concern is the need for positions that allow the child to be involved in social interactions with the family. It is helpful to review the progression of family and caregiving routines within a typical day and then determine how the child can be physically handled and positioned for optimal participation. What are safe and appropriate positions in the kitchen, dining room, bathroom, living area, or bedroom? Are any modifications or adapted equipment required to ensure proper positioning? Are there options that enable the child to play in an independent, self-initiated manner? What are the best alternatives for fostering parent–child communication and motorically vigorous play (e.g., "rough-house")?

Various positions can be considered depending on the child's age and physical status: supine lying, prone lying, side lying, floor sitting, short sitting (the typical posture in a chair), standing, and carrying. (Refer to chap. 3, this volume, for a review of motor concepts and terminology.) Keep in mind that positioning should not be static during caregiving and intervention; instead, the child and adult move together in a dynamic fashion. When the infant is on the adult's lap, for instance, he or she should be encouraged to move between these positions (and their innumerable combinations) as they interact together. The professional literature describes in detail principles for physical handling and positioning as well as adaptations that may be required (Campbell, 1987; Kramer & Hinojosa, 1993; Scherzer & Tscharnuter, 1990; Williamson, 1987). A few positions are described for illustrative purposes.

Side Lying   The side lying position is helpful for some children who have little postural control against gravity (e.g., a young infant or older child with severe physical involvement). In side lying, the child does not have to maintain an upright posture; therefore, the child may be able to bring his or her hands together to manipulate toys and explore the lower body. It is often necessary for the head to rest on a pillow for support (see Figure 8.3). Toys are placed below the child's eye level to foster a forward orientation of the head and arms, thus discouraging a tendency to arch the body backward into extension. This toy placement encourages swiping and reaching.

Floor Sitting   Playing on the floor is a natural component of parent–child interactions and early intervention activity. The child needs to have a number of floor-sitting positions that allow for optimal functioning and social exchange. In general, postures that are symmetrical (i.e., both sides of the body are positioned the same) and provide a wide base of support are the easiest to maintain, such as ring (bow) sitting or cross-legged (tailor) sitting (see Figures 8.4 and 8.5 respectively). If necessary, external support can be provided by the adult, by having the child rest against a wall or a piece of furniture, or by using a floor seat. In this manner the child is posturally secure and able to cope more effectively.

Side sitting, the most developmentally sophisticated floor-sitting position, should be encouraged because it facilitates easy transition from one posture to another during play (e.g., progressing from lying on the floor to the crawling position). In side sitting, the child rests predominantly on one buttock with both knees facing in the same direction (see Figure 8.6). This position fosters the development of lateral control and rotation of the trunk, which are needed for mobility skills.

Figure 8.3. Side lying facilitates a midline orientation with the hands together for swiping or mouthing objects.

Figure 8.4. Infant in a ring (or bow) sitting position.

Figure 8.5. Cross-legged (or tailor) sitting position.

Short Sitting   In short sitting, the child should be well positioned in a regular chair, high chair, stroller, or wheelchair. This posture requires placing the body weight equally on both buttocks with the hips placed back into the chair. Figure 8.7 depicts a desirable and undesirable short-sitting position. With the pelvis properly placed, the trunk is usually in erect alignment and the legs are positioned to provide a wide base of support. The feet should rest firmly on the floor or on a footrest. Therefore a right-angle (90° of flexion)

Figure 8.6.   Side sitting is the most sophisticated floor sitting position.

a   b

Figure 8.7. a) Undesirable short sitting position with the pelvis dropped back in a posterior tilt causing the trunk to be rounded; b) desirable short sitting position with the pelvis in proper placement and the trunk erect.

is maintained at the hip, knee, and ankle joints. Some modifications of this position and specially adapted equipment may be required for children with low muscle tone or an imbalance of muscle action in the trunk.

Play in the Context of Intervention

Play is a critical activity for learning and self-expression. It provides an opportunity for the child to organize thoughts, feelings, and skills within the context of discovering the new and making sense of the familiar. Play integrates the child's internal and external worlds. It is a spontaneous, voluntary involvement that is initiated and regulated by the child. The acts of play are performed for their own intrinsic reward. Because the child is in command, the constraints of reality can be ignored for free expression of emotions, fantasy, and imagination (Florey, 1981).

Play can serve as a medium within professional practice for remediation of specific physical, mental, or psychosocial deficits. The practitioner can create a play milieu that encourages the acquisition of developmentally appropriate skills in an emotionally rich environment. Therapeutic and educational intervention that fails to appreciate this natural drive to play can result in distress, resistance, or boredom by the child. The incorporation of play activities as part of intervention usually involves: 1) adapting the size and type of play materials, 2) modifying the position of the child and the placement of toys, 3) adjusting handling procedures in a dynamic manner to enable the child to be engaged, and 4) controlling the nature and degree of interpersonal interaction (Anderson, Hinojosa, & Strauch, 1987).

The ability of the child to participate independently in play can vary depending upon his or her physical position. Some children may regress in their play behaviors when in more upright positions requiring greater postural control. For example, an infant with a developmental delay who has difficulty maintaining a sitting position may only be able to demonstrate primitive play schemes, such as holding, mouthing, and looking at objects in this posture, whereas the same child in the supine position may have better control of the arms for shaking, waving, and banging toys together. A baby may play best when supine lying, in an infant seat, or on an adult's lap. An older child may be most functional in supported or independent sitting.

A key to facilitating motor control and coping is for the child to be motivated through play experiences that build on emerging cognitive, social, and communicative skills. By providing activities that promote active engagement, the child can practice purposeful movement within a personally rewarding context. The following vignettes illustrate ways that play was employed to expand the motor and coping competence of specific children with physical limitations.

➡ To encourage side-to-side rolling, Mrs. Schwartz, the teacher, sang to Jacob, an 8-month-old infant with a motor delay, while he was lying on his back. When Jacob was attending to her voice and face, Mrs. Schwartz leaned in one direction, which facilitated him to turn his head and roll onto his side. She continued the singing as she leaned in the opposite direction and elicited a head turn and partial roll onto the other side. Thus, Mrs. Schwartz was building on Jacob's social and attending skills to foster his motor development.

➡ Intervention was personalized for Tara, a toddler with poor sitting balance and a rather passive coping style. In a stable floor-sitting position, Tara was encouraged to swipe overhead to pop bubbles or bat a balloon. These playful activities provided immediate contingent feedback regarding the success of Tara's reaching efforts. As a result, she demonstrated an unusual degree of persistence during the session. At the same time, the activities stimulated the combined action of the abdominal and extensor muscles of her trunk, which is necessary for an erect sitting posture.

➡ To enhance imaginary play and rotation of the trunk, Ms. Jackson, the therapist, placed Rena, a 3-year-old child with spastic diplegia, astride a bolster in the sitting position (see Figure 8.8). She initially invited Rena to reach down with both hands to pick up large stuffed animals from the floor. (Reaching bilaterally encourages rotation of the trunk rather than lateral bending, which is easier.) Rena would identify and pet each animal before placing it in the "zoo" on the other side. Ms. Jackson then commented that the animals may be hungry. This suggestion elicited a play sequence in which Rena lifted imaginary vegetables from one side and reached across her body to feed the animals on the other side. Therefore, controlled rotation of the trunk was experienced toward both directions. If Rena started to become physically tight during the session, Ms. Jackson gently rocked the bolster to decrease spasticity of the trunk and limbs.

➡ Stan, a 12-month-old boy who was prenatally exposed to drugs, disliked crawling and preferred to scoot on his buttocks. His parents were taught simple crawling games that

Figure 8.8. The child practices motor skills while engaged in imaginative play: a) picking up the teddy bear on the right side, and b) petting the bear before placing it in the "zoo" on the left side.

Stan found highly motivating. They would play hide-and-seek or "I'm going to catch you" to great squeals of delight. Thus, Stan was learning to master a challenging motor skill while expanding his reciprocal social interaction.

➡ To encourage bilateral hand use and self-initiated problem solving in Jeffrey, an infant with hemiplegia, toys were hung from his high chair on yarn strings of various lengths. Through trial-and-error, Jeffrey gradually learned to pull up on the yarn with both hands to attain the toys for play. In the process, he was expanding his coping-related ability to change strategies when necessary to achieve a goal.

➡ Finger painting with yogurt or pudding was used with a group of toddlers to foster coordination of the arms; parallel play; and integration of visual, tactile, and proprioceptive information. The play surface was adjusted over time from a horizontal plane to an incline, and later to a vertical orientation. As the play surface progressed to a more upright position, increased muscle action was required in the shoulders to maintain the arms away from the body. Simultaneously, the children were learning to cope with changes in the environment.

A disability may interfere with the development and expression of various types of play behaviors in the young child. The following discussion highlights issues that are related to body-oriented play, manual or manipulative play, symbolic or dramatic play, and social play with peers.

Body-Oriented Play   Early play behavior tends to focus on the body. The infant enjoys patting, scratching, and looking at body parts; plucking clothes; kicking the legs and rubbing them together; and eventually sucking on the toes and rocking in various positions. Often, children with physical disabilities are not able to perform this sensorimotor exploration. For instance, the movements of a child with spastic cerebral palsy may be slow, laborious, and limited in range. In the supine position, the head and shoulders may press against the mattress preventing the emergence of flexor control necessary to explore the body. The "floppy" infant (who may later develop athetosis, spasticity, or ataxia) may tend to assume a static frog-like posture when on his or her back (see Figure 8.9). In this posture, the chest appears flat; the hips are flexed, abducted, and externally rotated; and the arms are out to the side. This hypotonic infant may appear self-contained and unresponsive—staring blankly at an unfocused point in space.

The following sample activities can be provided within a pleasurable, social context to promote self-awareness and body-oriented play.

Rub the child's body with lotion, powder, or material of different textures (e.g., sponge, towel). This activity can be incorporated quite naturally in the home during bathing and diapering.

Encourage the infant to play with his or her legs in hand-to-knee, hand-to-foot, foot-to-mouth, and foot-to-foot patterns. Simple action songs with the feet can be introduced, such as "This Little Piggy Went to Market." Other songs that usually involve the arms can also be played with the legs (e.g., "Pat-a-Cake," "So Big," "The Itsy, Bitsy Spider").

Tie a ribbon and bell around the child's wrist or ankles so that movement of the limbs creates auditory and visual feedback.

Emphasize gross motor experiences, such as rolling, bouncing, and "rough-housing" within the range of the child's tolerance. Be careful to avoid disorganized responses or abnormal postures. For example, if the child is bounced while straddling the adult's lap or leg (playing "horsey"), the head and trunk should be in erect alignment so that the child experiences normal extension patterns against gravity during the bouncing movement.

Manual Play Playing noisily with objects is common among young children, particularly after 4–5 months of age. A physical disability may limit the coordinated use of the arms necessary to acquire a wide repertoire of play schemes. Therefore, intervention must facilitate not just fine motor skills but their functional application as increasingly complex strategies for use in manual play. Initially, spoons and plastic keys encourage

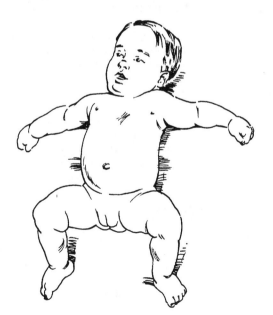

Figure 8.9. The frog-like posture of an infant with low muscle tone.

banging, hitting, and shaking. Enjoyable activities that foster more sophisticated motor actions include crumbling and tearing paper, playing with a busy box, pulling tissues from a box, and pushing toy cars. The ability to combine objects in play is promoted through putting objects into containers and emptying them out, pulling apart or putting together pop beads, stacking blocks, and stringing beads to wear as a necklace.

From an early age, the child with hemiplegia needs experiences that involve the use of both hands. Bilateral reach and grasp are provided by large toys such as balls and cuddle animals, as well as "hold-on" toys such as rocking horses, riding cars with steering wheels, and push toys (e.g., doll carriage, toy lawnmower). Likewise, many musical toys involve two hands, such as cymbals, drums, and triangles.

Symbolic Play   The development of symbolic or dramatic play is particularly crucial for children with limited physical capabilities. It provides an opportunity to manifest thoughts and emotions that are more typically expressed through gross motor activities. Symbolic play provides a natural outlet for the expression of themes related to control, fear, anxiety, dependency, aggression, and loss. Some children with disabilities tend to stay at a rather concrete level of play, such as combining common objects together (e.g., using a brush to comb the hair). Through modeling and elaboration, the practitioner or parent can extend the play content to a more representational and dramatic level. Intervention should initially emphasize helping the child pretend actions that involve the self and later pretending with a doll or the adult. With time, the child is assisted to use one object to represent another. Early symbolic play can be encouraged by playing with spoons, cups, and plates to model stirring, dishing out food, drinking, eating, or blowing on hot food. Washing and drying the dishes can also be a part of the play sequence.

Imaginative play situations may incorporate the use of stuffed animals, puppets, and miniature people with accompanying environments that represent the home, gas station, or school. Likewise, pretend play episodes may entail dressing up, going to the store, having a tea party, and playing house. The therapeutic benefit of play is demonstrated by the case of Amber, a bright 3-year-old child who was scheduled to have hip surgery, and Ikeem, a child having difficulty adjusting to his new baby sister.

➡ Amber was helped to prepare for her operation by playing "doctor and nurse" with other children in the program during the preceding weeks. They dressed up in uniforms and surgical gowns, played with a toy doctor's kit, and gave each other "pills" and physical therapy. Gradually, Amber's fears seemed to diminish as she rehearsed the coming event and practiced coping strategies.

➡ Ikeem, a child with spastic cerebral palsy, was having great difficulty adjusting to the arrival of a baby sister. His anger and resentment were demonstrated through irritability and a marked increase in muscle tone throughout his body. He was emotionally and physically "tied up in knots." Occupational therapy during this period involved procedures to reduce his physical tightness followed by opportunities to play in a doll corner. The therapist provided dynamic external support through her handling and positioning to allow Ikeem to express freely a diverse range of emotions and actions.

Ikeem's ambivalence regarding how to manage his current situation was dramatically evidenced by his play sequences. Sometimes a baby doll would be smashed by the HeMan, eaten by a monster, and left in a trash can. Other times, the doll would be hugged, comforted, and "made okay." It was very important that the therapist avoid the tendency to tell Ikeem to "be nice" to the baby. Instead she provided an opportunity for him to learn to cope with himself (i.e., his mixed emotions).

Social Play with Peers   In the typical development of social interaction with peers, the child initially tends to observe the play of others or to play in parallel fashion beside other children. Over time, the child engages in associative play in which there is talking and toy sharing, but the children have separate play agendas (e.g., they are involved in different activities in the play house). Gradually, more cooperative play emerges with the children playing together in a goal-oriented manner with a common end. This more advanced level of play evolves into the ability to participate in games with pre-established rules.

For some children with special needs, it is a challenge to progress through these various developmental stages. Problems in cognition, communication, or coordination make it difficult to keep up with the social exchange and shifting pace that should occur naturally during play sequences with peers. As a result, there is a tendency for some of these children to prefer solitary play or to assume a passive role of watching others.

A goal of intervention, therefore, is to assist children with special needs to acquire more sophisticated skills in social interactions with peers. Typically, such experiences are provided through circle time and other group activities. It is also beneficial to cluster children together in pairs or small groups during occupational, physical, and speech-language therapy sessions. Many children become more expressive and actively involved in these situations than in adult–child individual therapy. Interacting with other children is highly motivating.

In pairs or small groups, the children begin to develop an awareness of the feelings of others, they learn how to be a friend, and they learn to help each other. The adult can foster this development by labeling moods and reactions of the children and encouraging them to assist one another in completing activities. For instance, the child with restricted mobility can learn to ask a friend to retrieve a toy that has fallen from reach instead of always relying on adult assistance. Thus, the child acquires the self-initiated coping ability to balance independence with necessary dependence on others.

One intervention strategy to enhance social interaction for a child with a physical disability is to design play activities that are rather sedentary and do not have gross motor requirements. For example, a child with braces can stand at a water table with friends as they play with bubbles, fill and empty containers, or bathe dolls. Likewise, the child can be placed in an adapted chair at a table or in a floor seat to enjoy associative play with trucks, blocks, or "little people" (i.e., miniature figures).

It is also important, however, to encourage social engagement with peers during movement-oriented activities. Movement experiences can be selected in accordance with the child's ability and modified according to the disability. Obstacle courses can be created in which the children maneuver under, over, up, and through objects in the environment by rolling or crawling in the all-fours position. Circle games in the sitting position may include "Simon Says," which uses the arms to imitate different movement patterns; action songs such as "Wheels on the Bus"; and bouncing balloons or foam balls on a large sheet shaken by the children to make "popcorn." Furthermore, children who use crutches can participate in modified kick ball or soccer by hitting the rolling ball with a crutch, one leg, or both legs.

TEACHING FUNCTIONAL SKILLS

Functionally applied developmental skills are the foundation for coping efforts. Intervention strategies and activities are described in this section for helping infants and toddlers acquire and generalize skills (an example of increasing coping resources—Intervention Option 2—discussed in chap. 7, this volume). The following developmental domains are highlighted: interactive and communicative skills, cognitive skills, fine motor skills, and mobility skills. Bricker and Cripe (1992) present the following list of strategies that are particularly useful for teaching functional skills and coping behaviors.

Sample Teaching Strategies

Preview and Review   Children learn to anticipate events and to try new behaviors on their own when there is a brief preview of the steps of the task prior to beginning the activity. A similar review is performed on completion of the activity. This intervention strategy not only encourages greater understanding and participation, but it also helps the child internalize a structure for addressing other similar tasks.

Set-Up and Clean-Up   Children learn how to actively participate in a situation when they have some part in preparing for an activity and helping to clean up afterward. By having a role in an activity, children take responsibility and are not merely passive recipients; for example, a child may be asked to bring certain materials to the activity area and to return them when finished.

Novelty and Familiarity   Introduction of a new toy or activity may stimulate some children to try new behaviors. For other children, the use of a familiar toy or activity may provide the necessary security to encourage participation. The practitioner needs to moderate the degree of novelty and familiarity based on the learning style of the child.

Planned Forgetting   The adult encourages the child to seek the missing element by omitting an important action or material in a familiar activity. For example, the adult may not set out the juice at snack time or may present the child with only one glove of a pair. The child is encouraged to ask questions or seek some appropriate solution.

Omitting or Changing a Familiar Step   When an adult does not do what is expected, children are stimulated to recognize the unusual or missing action, ask the adult about it, or find some innovative solution. When using this intervention strategy with a young child, the chosen behavior may border on the absurd (e.g., putting a diaper on the foot or combing the hair with sunglasses).

Piece by Piece   The piece by piece strategy can be used when an activity has material that includes many pieces (e.g., a puzzle, food, blocks). The child is encouraged to ask for each piece as needed, thereby setting his or her own pace and taking responsibility for completing the task.

Visible but Unreachable   The placement of a desired object out of reach but within sight encourages problem solving. The child may have to retrieve it independently or learn to ask for help.

Repetition   Children acquire new skills, become fluent in performing skills, and learn to generalize skills through repetitive practice. The same activity can be repeated over time or modified to encourage adaptive problem solving.

Adult Assistance   With the use of materials or activities that require adult assistance, the child learns to ask for help when needed; for example, giving the child a toy that has a lid that is too complex to open independently.

Interactive and Communicative Skills

Infants acquire the skills necessary for the development of language through interaction with their caregivers. These early interactional behaviors expand from gazing, smiling, and vocalizing to the use of gestures and imitation. The earliest "communicative" interaction occurs between the infant and caregiver during feeding and face-to-face exchange. It is characterized by changing patterns in rhythm and responses of both partners. The rhythm patterns correspond with the infant's alert periods. Over time, the infant is able to remain alert longer and the adult learns to identify and control these periods for interaction. Likewise, the adult and infant display a broader repertoire of responses when interacting, such as facial expressions, gazing, vocalizing, and body movements. Adults often imitate a baby's actions, which in turn seems to elicit the infant's attention and desire to respond. The infant soon learns that initiation of a behavior evokes responses from the other; for example, gurgles by the infant stimulate the adult to gurgle or smile back. The infant also learns to initiate behaviors—laughing, smiling, crying, and vocalizing—to gain the adult's attention. Early development of interaction between a caregiver and an infant is the foundation for the development of communication and coping competence.

It is important, therefore, that parents have the opportunity to spend time with their infant from the beginning, even if the newborn is hospitalized due to prematurity or a physical condition. Depending on the medical status, parents may be able to hold, feed, and interact with the child, particularly during quiet alert periods. As the infant stabilizes medically, the parents learn to recognize the child's response repertoire. Play is encouraged when parents make a variety of sounds, imitate the baby's behaviors, and gently stroke the child. The parents may initially require emotional support to develop feelings of attachment to their baby and to become comfortable in handling the young infant. The following are ways to foster the child's vocal and gestural imitation, nonverbal communication, and early words.

Vocal Imitation Initially infants imitate adult sounds that are already in their repertoire. By approximately 12 months of age, they learn to imitate new sounds. Vocal imitation is an important factor for the development of an expressive vocabulary. Likewise, the turn-taking that is involved in imitative games fosters knowledge of conversational skills.

Children continue to imitate words and phrases even when they have developed an expressive vocabulary that they are using to communicate. From 18 to approximately 24 months, the child will imitate novel words and complex verbalizations such as phrases or sentences. Even though these expressions may not be meaningful to the child or may merely be deferred imitation (i.e., imitating from memory), the act of imitation assists the child in the acquisition of an expressive vocabulary.

Excellent times for vocalization to take place between the child and caregiver are during feeding and diaper changes because physical proximity to adults appears to be a crucial stimulus for increasing vocalizations by the infant. For imitation to develop, the infant and the adult must have learned to engage in reciprocal vocalizations; that is, they must have learned to play the game in which one will coo or babble to elicit the other's vocal responses. At first, the caregiver should merely imitate the sounds that are made by the infant because the infant will most readily imitate sounds that he or she can already produce. The next step is to encourage the infant to imitate novel sounds that are similar to the ones the infant can produce (e.g., if the infant can say "ba," the adult can attempt to elicit imitations of "da"). Attempts to approximate novel sounds should be reinforced.

Early sounds and words can be naturally modeled in the context of play or routine caregiving activities to promote understanding of the words. For example, the caregiver might ask if the infant wants to go "bye-bye." An early response would be a contingent, nonspecific vocalization ("ah"); at a later stage the infant might respond "ba-ba;" and yet later the infant will be able to imitate "bye-bye" accurately. All along, the simultaneous physical action of leaving one place and going to another reinforces that "bye-bye" means going away.

Gestural Imitation Imitation of gestures proceeds along the same course as vocal imitation—from imitating the familiar to imitating the novel. Infants initially produce random movements in response to an adult's movements (e.g., banging hands on the table in response to the adult shaking a rattle). Between 4 and 8 months, children will imitate simple gestures in their repertoire.

Gestures to model for imitation include clapping hands for "Pat-a-Cake," arms up for "So Big," opening and closing the hands, or other actions that accompany simple songs. Gestural imitation can progress between 8 and 12 months to novel movements that comprise familiar actions (e.g., clapping hands on knees instead of together). The pairing of vocalization and gestures can be used to develop imitative skills; for example, patting one's nose can be paired with the vocalization "beep-beep." Simple songs, such as "Roly, Poly" and "Six Little Ducks," can be used to develop gestural and vocal imitation. Children's records that involve gestures are also good facilitators of imitative skills. By 12–18 months, children can be encouraged to imitate complex, novel actions.

Nonverbal Communication   The use of expressive gestures such as pointing, giving, and showing seems to be related to the development of language. These gestural schemes appear at approximately 9–12 months of age and continue to be displayed in conjunction with the child's verbal efforts to communicate.

Pointing   Pointing is employed to call an adult's attention to objects or to request specific objects or actions. Pointing can be facilitated through modeling by the adult in specific situations in which the adult knows the child wants a particular object, such as a bottle, cookie, or favorite toy.

Giving   Giving behaviors are exhibited when the child hands an object to an adult. This action can take place for several reasons: The child may be asking the adult to perform an action on the toy that the child cannot do independently (e.g., activating a wind-up toy); the child may be initiating interactions by giving the toy (e.g., "Play with me"); or the child may simply wish to share the object with another.

Gestural and verbal cues such as an outstretched hand and saying "Give it to me" are facilitators of giving behaviors. Also, by structuring the situation in such a way that the adult must activate or retrieve a toy in order for the child to play with it, the adult can motivate the child to use this mode of nonverbal communication.

Showing   Showing objects is also a behavior used initially to gain an adult's attention. The child may use the eyes—gazing alternately at the adult and at the object—to share interest or excitement in the object. The child may also hand new or interesting toys to the adult to initiate interaction.

Showing behaviors usually occur when something unexpected or novel occurs. New toys can be presented to the child and the adult can say, "What do you have? Show me." When the child looks at the object and then the adult, or picks up the object and gazes at the adult, positive reinforcement by the adult should occur, such as smiling or nodding the head. The practitioner can also model showing behaviors to the child as they both share the excitement of the new toy or the unexpected event.

Early Words   Prelinguistic play activities are important to develop a child's knowledge of objects, actions, and their relationship, which serves as the basis for learning early words. Imitative vocal and gestural skills are just as critical for the development of future conversational abilities. Thus, for any young child experiencing language delay, prelinguistic play and interactive skills are goals of intervention that should be introduced before early words.

Intentional vocal communication (sounds or sound combinations) can occur at 9–12 months of age. By approximately 18 months of age, children use words to communicate about the here and now and to comment on their own actions. The content of their language includes the following types of meaning: existence (naming, objects); nonexistence (no, all gone, no more); recurrence (more, again); rejection (no); attribution (big/little, good/bad); possession (mine, Mommy); action (go, eat, come); and location (in, on) (Bloom & Lahey, 1978; Lahey, 1988). Another system of classifying early words identifies nine ways the child can use language: labeling, repeating, answering, requesting actions, requesting answers, calling, greeting, protesting, and practicing (Owens, 1991).

Imaginative play situations can be used to increase a child's understanding of the types of meaning in language; this expanded awareness fosters the development of specific words. For example, play with a pitcher and cup can be used to facilitate the understanding of the concept of "recurrence." In a pretending game, the adult refills the cup repeatedly for the child to receive more juice to drink. The vocabulary word "more" is verbally modeled during the activity. Thus, the child is given a specific context for learning the word "more."

Therapeutic and educational activities to encourage the development of early words should take place in a quiet environment with minimal auditory or visual distractions. Poor attending behaviors; hypersensitivity to auditory, tactile, or visual stimuli; and perceptual difficulties are factors that may hamper the child's ability to develop speech and language normally. Simple manipulative activities with few materials presented focus the child on the intent of the activity (e.g., just two cups and one teapot, rather than the entire set, can be used when working on the word "more"). The use of pictures during intervention should be carefully considered based on the abilities of the child; some children are not able to derive meaning from pictures.

Cognitive Skills

Play with objects and exploration of the environment not only contribute to the development of communication, they also enhance cognitive growth and coping. Key aspects of cognitive development that are highly relevant to adaptive functioning are described below, and intervention activities are suggested.

Visual Pursuit and the Permanence of Objects   Object permanence is the understanding that an object continues to exist even though it is out of view. At approximately 4–6 months of age, a child visually searches for an object at the point of disappearance. The infant visually follows an object falling from sight, particularly if the child was previously handling it. Likewise, the infant follows the caregiver's movements about the room and gazes at the spot where the adult just left the room. Later, the infant searches for an object partially hidden by a cloth or screen. By 8 months, the child uncovers a toy hidden under a cloth after observing the adult hide it. Over time this skill develops so that the child can locate an object after it has been hidden under a series of screens. This cognitive awareness of the permanent existence of objects is important because it contributes to the child's ability to anticipate events—a critical coping attribute for self-initiation.

To enhance this skill, one begins with tasks that promote visual fixation and tracking. Next, the adult can play modified hide-and-seek games with the infant in which visually stimulating objects are partially hidden within reach of the child in order to elicit an active retrieval. Gradually, the complexity of the activity is increased by following the previously mentioned developmental sequence. In the beginning, it is important to allow the infant to observe the hiding of the object as a cue to solicit searching.

Purposeful Problem Solving   Purposeful problem solving, another crucial coping ability, is involved when a child begins to develop simple ways to achieve a desired end. For example, the young infant will use visually directed reaching to explore an attractive mobile or toy placed in the crib. When multiple objects are involved, a child at the age of 7 months will drop one or more objects held in the hands to obtain a newly presented object.

Having the child pull a string to obtain or activate a toy is one play activity that develops means-ends or problem-solving abilities. Oscar the Grouch in a garbage can or toy dogs that make noises when moved are inviting pull-toys. The task is made easier by shortening the string or tying a plastic ring to the end of it. The child can also learn to retrieve toys that are hung from the high chair on lengths of yarn. Purposeful problem solving is further facilitated by having the infant learn to obtain an object out of immediate reach by pulling a towel on which it rests. The development of gross motor skills, such as crawling, pulling to stand, or walking, are other means for obtaining desired ends such as objects that the adult has deliberately placed out of reach.

Causality   Cause-and-effect relationships develop as an infant begins to anticipate events, which is an important coping behavior. The child acquires strategies for stimulating objects or people to create interesting sights and sounds. For example, an infant may display general body movements, such as leg kicking or arm waving, to elicit a repeat performance of the adult's caresses and kisses. Infants as early as 3 months will repeat an arm movement to keep a toy activated.

It is important for the adult to be sensitive to the infant's signals that communicate a wish for an action to be repeated. Cause-effect behaviors can be developed through many of the common activities of daily living, such as flipping on light switches, opening and closing drawers, and turning knobs.

Spatial Relationships   The term *spatial relationships* refers to the infant's ability to appreciate the orientation of objects and sounds in space and their relation to the infant and to each other. A young infant develops the ability to look for and localize sound; for example, the infant learns to locate the caregiver's voice through visual gaze when the adult is in close proximity and then at greater distances across the room.

Brightly colored, noise-making toys can be used to facilitate visual and auditory attention. As the infant begins to reach for objects and hold them, a variety of rattles and toys can be provided. The infant is encouraged to turn objects around to look at all sides. A toy with a mirror on one side stimulates the child to turn it over for exploration. Further activities to foster spatial relations include placing objects in containers and dumping out the contents, building towers with blocks, and rolling toys down various inclines.

With increased mobility in the environment, awareness of the body in space is enhanced through having the child move around and between furniture. Placing obstacles in the child's way encourages the solving of spatial problems—the infant learns to take a detour around the obstacles to obtain a desired object.

Fine Motor Skills

Competence in fine motor tasks is founded on the following major skills: postural stability, ocular-motor control, visual perception, tactile and proprioceptive discrimination, cognition, and muscular strength and coordination. These areas all contribute to the development of fine motor control. In particular, the child needs to be well positioned in order to attend, feel emotionally secure, and have the arms free for activity.

In a sitting position, it is easier to reach forward or to the side than overhead or behind the body. An overhead reach requires a secure trunk to maintain balance and scapular stability to support the raised arm (firm maintenance of the shoulder blade against the rib cage). To reach behind the body, the child must rotate the head and trunk while visually directing the arm backward. Usually, body weight is shifted onto one buttock as righting reactions are elicited to prevent a fall. The abdominal muscles are particularly important to maintain the trunk control necessary for reaching with the arm.

More sophisticated reach patterns can be promoted by encouraging reaching in a developmental sequence: first forward, then sideways, and finally overhead or backward (see Figure 8.10). As the child acquires motor skills, toys can be positioned to facilitate reach in all directions and across the midline of the body.

The work surface can be graded from horizontal to an incline and later to a vertical orientation. By gradually increasing the incline of a table top, for example, the amount of support given to the child's shoulder and forearm is progressively decreased (see Figure 8.11). More muscle action is then required to maintain the arms in an antigravity position. Educational tasks can be adapted to use a large vertical mirror, felt board, easel, or paper taped to the wall. In this way, the child plays with both arms held in shoulder flexion away from the body, or one arm can prop forward against the upright play surface while the other arm is engaged in the activity.

The gross movements of the young infant become increasingly selective and voluntary as the child develops motor control. At first, motion is directed from the shoulder as

a

b

c

d

Figure 8.10. An example of an intervention sequence for promoting reach in the sitting position: a) reach forward, b) reach to the side, c) reach overhead, and d) reach backward.

a   b

Figure 8.11.   An example of grading the motoric demands of the work surface: a) an inclined table top, and b) a more difficult vertical orientation.

the infant swipes and bats. Later, the limb can accommodate innumerable positions of the joints for reach and manipulation. The following points should be considered in planning intervention to facilitate coordinated use of the arms.

- The infant initially reaches with both hands (bilateral reach) before a unilateral reach is demonstrated. Early reach patterns of the young infant are more controlled in a supine position than in a sitting position. As the child gets older, reaching across the midline of the body reinforces an integrated body scheme.
- Toys should be positioned to encourage the development of rotation in the upper limbs. In the earlier stages, the arm approaches the toy from above in a downward direction (a "top-level" reach). Gradually, the infant learns to have the arm approach the object from the side (i.e., external rotation of the shoulder with supination of the forearm).
- The infant first mouths the back of the hand because the forearm remains palm down (pronation). Over time, the infant is able to turn the hand palm up (supination), which positions it for sucking the fingers and eventually the thumb (see Figure 8.12). Mouthing objects and finger feeding provide opportunities to practice controlling the hand in this new supinated position. In a similar fashion, the infant first exhibits vertical banging of the arms before acquiring the control required for horizontal clapping (i.e., external rotation of the shoulder with forearm supination).
- Learning to grade motion at the elbow is often achieved in a prone-lying position as the infant pushes up on extended arms and bounces. The degree of elbow extension when reaching seems to be related to the infant's ability to assume and

a   b

Figure 8.12.   a) Mouthing the back of the hand because the forearm is in a pronated position. b) Mouthing the fingers because the forearm is rotated out into a supinated position.

maintain this gross motor position. Midrange control of the elbow is also fostered by playing with rattles, mobiles, pull-toys, and pop beads.

The development of isolated wrist movement facilitates the appearance of skilled hand function. In the beginning, the infant tends to grasp objects with the wrist flexed. The goal is to achieve a stable wrist in slight extension during manipulative play. Coordination of wrist motion is practiced when the infant rocks in antigravity positions while bearing weight on the hands or when the child pivots on the abdomen in a circle. Later activities—those requiring grasp, release, dumping, pouring, and hammering—refine this control. As previously discussed, grading the work surface can also be used to elicit gradation of wrist extension during activities.

Opposition of the thumb is the key to acquiring fine pinch patterns. It allows the thumb to approximate the ends of the index and middle fingers in a two- or three-point pinch. The fingers are then positioned for the discrete manipulation of objects. The type of grasp used by the child depends in large measure on the size and position of the object to be handled. For example, a young child tends to use a gross grasp to pick up a 1" block, but a neat pincer (fingertip) grasp to retrieve a small pellet. The hand accommodates to the dimensions of the object. Consequently, the practitioner should analyze which grasp and pinch patterns can be elicited by objects of varying sizes and shapes.

Fine motor activities are sequenced to expand the repertoire of grasp, release, and manipulative skills (e.g., tearing and crumpling paper, playing with a busy box or pegboard, transferring objects in and out of containers). The following sample activities can be employed to promote fine motor control.

Emptying and Filling Activities   Developmentally, a child learns to empty a container before filling it and does so with solids before liquids. In the beginning, the child often engages in these take-out and put-in activities with pegs, blocks, or beads and a bucket. Pots, pans, and utensils of different sizes are used in play with sand or water. A turkey baster is particularly effective for strengthening the hands during water play. Pouring and filling skills can also be practiced using uncooked kidney beans, a scoop, and a container.

Paper Tearing and Crumpling   Depending on the child's level of functioning, the resistance of the paper to be torn or crumpled can be graded from light tissue paper to heavy construction paper. In teaching paper tearing, the adult first initiates the tear and holds one side of the paper while the child tears it from the other end. The next step is for the child to hold the paper with two hands and tear it apart after the adult has started the tear. Finally, the child can handle the complete task independently. This intervention sequence can be followed in a climate of exploration and fun rather than didactic instruction. After tearing, the paper can be crumpled with both hands and glued to another sheet for a collage, or it can be rolled into little balls and flicked with the fingers across the table. In this game, isolated finger extension is encouraged.

Finger Painting   Finger painting stimulates gross arm motions as well as isolated movements of the fingers. Yogurt or pudding are excellent media for toddlers who tend to bring their hands to their mouths. Preschool children can use regular finger paints, shaving cream, or Crazy Foam. The work surface can be adjusted to a horizontal, inclined, or vertical plane. Playing on a large mirror adds special interest to the task.

Clay Activities   Clay, putty, or Play-Doh provide an opportunity to develop strength and coordination in the arms. Because these media are free form, they foster imaginative play and guarantee success. The activity can be graded by rolling the material into long cylinders ("hot dogs") with one or both hands pressed against the work surface. Rolling the clay into round balls requires more coordination, particularly if each hand rolls a separate ball on the table. Of greater difficulty is the use of reciprocal circular movements of the hands in front of the body to make clay balls. Strengthening is enhanced by squeezing the clay, pushing fingers through the medium to make a tunnel, or molding animals or other sculptures.

Finger Games   Books are commercially available describing finger games of varying levels of complexity. These action songs foster motor planning, gestural imitation, language, and social interaction. Gross arm movements are practiced in such games as "Pat-a-Cake" and "Little Rabbit in the Woods"; finger movements are required in "The Itsy, Bitsy Spider." For the older child, shadow figures can be made with the fingers.

Bead Stringing   A child can learn the concept of bead stringing by the use of a large rubberized board with holes. At first, the adult places the string in a hole and the child pulls it through from the other side. In the next step, the child learns to place the string in a hole with the adult pulling it through. Finally, the child can sequence both steps—push in and pull out—to execute the task independently.

After use of the board, large beads are introduced following the same instructional procedure. With the adult holding the bead, the child can learn the activity using one hand before graduating to a bilateral approach (i.e., use of two hands).

Cutting with Scissors   Depending on the child's level of functioning, three different types of scissors can be used. "EZ grip" scissors require only a squeezing motion in order to cut; the child holds the scissors with a gross grasp. Four-hole training scissors enable the adult to assist the child in hand-over-hand fashion. The regular two-hole scissors are available with either a blunt or sharp cutting edge and for right- or left-handed use.

Cutting with scissors can also be graded by varying the resistance of the paper and the degree of assistance in holding the paper. The child first learns to produce simple snipping motions and cuts very short strips. Later, continuous motion is required for cutting straight lines across a page and, eventually, cutting shapes.

Mobility Skills

Mobility facilitates the self-initiation of children and encourages their curiosity. The capacity to roll, crawl, and later walk expands children's ability to explore their physical surroundings, get needs met, control the level of personal involvement in situations, and release physical energy and psychological tension. Poor mobility skills can restrict these coping-related functions.

A therapeutic priority is to teach the child a means of functional mobility as early as possible. For example, physical therapy for many infants with spina bifida initially focuses on teaching a modified crawling pattern and the ability to scoot on the buttocks by use of the arms. Standing and ambulation with braces are then introduced at approximately 12–18 months of age (Williamson, 1987). Special equipment may be purchased or adapted to supplement these efforts. In the prone position the child may propel a scooter board by use of the arms. Tricycles may be modified with trunk supports and footstraps. In addition, various types of riding toys are available that can be activated by either the hands or the feet.

Mobility is an important factor that helps young children achieve separation and later individuation in their psychosocial development. Parents are used as a safe base from which infants and toddlers move out into the world. Through varying means of locomotion, children regulate their level of emotional comfort by grading physical proximity to their caregiver. They experiment with autonomy by practicing leave-taking and reunion.

For children with physical disabilities, this normal process may be disrupted. This young child may not have mobility skills that allow practice in controlling experiences of separation. Therefore, parents must adapt caregiving so that the motor limitation does not overly interfere with development. It is a particular challenge for parents who are highly protective or ambivalent in regard to their child's emerging independence. The acquisition of coping strategies expands the child's capacity for successful adaptation. The child can be taught compensatory behaviors such as visually "checking-in" with the parent and using transitional objects to manage periods of being alone (e.g., accepting a favorite teddy bear as a comforting substitute). The ability to play independently in the presence of the caregiver can also be emphasized. In addition, adapted equipment may provide mobility not generally available to the child (e.g., modified swings, walkers, riding toys).

The following case study illustrates how the previously described intervention activities and strategies were implemented to foster the motor control and coping of Patti, an infant with delayed motor development. An analysis of Patti's coping resources helped to determine the goals and activities of intervention that promised to make the most functional difference.

➡ Patti was a 9-month-old premature infant with a corrected age of 7 months who functioned developmentally at approximately 5 months of age. She had low muscle tone that interfered with her ability to assume and maintain positions against gravity. Her development of extension was not balanced by controlled flexion; therefore, she had little control of lateral movements and rotation (see chap. 3, this volume). As a result, her posture was insecure and the use of her arms was restricted.

In the prone position, Patti was able to push up on extended arms for very short periods of time; however, she could not maintain the position, shift her weight to one side, and reach out with one hand. She was also dominated by gravity when lying on her back. In the supine position, Patti assumed a frog-like posture (see Figure 8.9). She did not have the antigravity flexor control to bring her hands together and to engage in body-oriented play with her legs. When placed in a sitting position, she could not reach forward independently to explore toys.

Her coping style was situationally effective. She had difficulty generalizing coping strategies to different types of situations. When the environment was structured to encourage adaptive behavior, Patti was successful. If not, she tended to assume a passive respondent role. Due in part to her low muscle tone, it was hard for Patti to initiate and sustain interactions. The struggle to maintain her posture against gravity seemed to deplete her energy. In these circumstances, she would typically withdraw or cry.

To plan intervention, it was important to identify the strengths and vulnerabilities of Patti's coping style. Her most adaptive behaviors were her visual and auditory interest in the surroundings, her ability to react to the feelings and moods of others, and her ability to accept warmth and support from familiar persons. Her least adaptive coping behaviors were her minimal effectiveness in initiating exploration of her own body and objects, her difficulty in coordinating movement to be responsive to specific situations, and her passivity in trying new behaviors on her own.

Patti's family was very supportive and understood her emotional and developmental uniqueness. They were eager to adapt their caregiving in a way that fostered her development. Her parents and the early intervention staff decided that one important goal for Patti was to develop the necessary motor control to support self-initiated exploration. The following sample activities were implemented to enhance her motor and coping competence. They illustrate the use of common strategies that apply the intervention options for promoting effective transactions.

If Patti could improve her coordinated movement, she would be better able to engage in active exploration. The following intervention sequence was used to expand her control of flexion, lateral movements, and rotation respectively. The therapist facilitated her efforts by emphasizing her coping strength of visual and auditory interest in social interaction. He continuously changed his physical position to ensure that their eye contact and social exchange helped Patti to organize her movements. They first played a foot-clapping game that required Patti to maintain flexor control of the head and trunk (see Figure 8.13).

Figure 8.13.   Promoting flexion of the head and trunk with "foot-clapping."

By capitalizing on her coping strength, the therapist was able to increase the demand by progressing to a more difficult activity that required control of lateral movements. In this case, he shifted her body to the side by lowering one leg and raising the other (see Figure 8.14). She responded by laterally righting her head in order to maintain visual regard of his face. The task was repeated in the other direction so that she could experience lateral control of the head toward both sides. Patti was motorically successful because: 1) the activity was in a social context, 2) she could tolerate the weight-shifting of her body because it was smoothly translated through the therapist's lap, and 3) she held a toy that assisted her to stabilize the upper body.

Based upon this success, the therapist presented a game to encourage rotation of Patti's trunk (see Figure 8.15). Patti became intrigued by yarn that was placed on one foot and she started to play with it. She was able to reach across her body and maintain the rotation of her trunk because the therapist provided support at the shoulder. Next, she played with yarn placed on the other foot in order to experience rotation of the body in the other direction.

Variations of this intervention sequence were introduced in a naturalistic manner into caregiving activities in the home. For example, the parents were shown an easy way to diaper Patti that offered an opportunity to practice control of desired movements and to begin exploring her legs. She soon developed sufficient coordination to enjoy body-oriented play on her own.

Other intervention strategies structured the physical environment to promote self-directed activity. Her side-lying position in the crib was modified so that she could employ lateral control to maintain the posture and not arch onto her back. A pillow was placed under her head and another partially supported her back. With these adaptations she was able to bring her hands together to manipulate toys.

In addition, a special chair was used that stabilized her sitting position and guided her arms forward for reaching. A variety of toys was selected that encouraged Patti to expand her play schemes with objects. As shown in Figure 8.16, any slight lateral movement of the arms caused the balls to travel on the track. Over time she learned to bang the balls together and flip them vigorously from side to side. Thus, the physical environment assisted her motor coordination and provided contingent feedback to her self-generated efforts.

Figure 8.14. Encouraging lateral control of the head and upper trunk by shifting the body to one side by lowering one leg and raising the other.
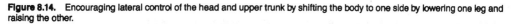

Figure 8.15. Facilitating rotation of the trunk by supporting the child's shoulders while she plays with yarn placed on her opposite foot.

Figure 8.16. Increased trunk support in a corner chair to assist forward reach of the arms.

Patti's mother was interested in finding a way to position her daughter on her lap so that Patti could be more active when they played together. Due to the child's low muscle tone, she was usually held cradled in a reclined posture. In this position she tended to be passive. The mother laughingly said that "Patti is becoming a couch potato!" One position devised to address this issue was for Patti to sit on her mother's crossed legs with slight support provided to the trunk by her mother's hand (see Figure 8.17). In this position they faced each other and Patti was able to reach independently to touch her mother's face and clothes. Thus, the position fostered social interaction, communication, and motor expression.

PROMOTING POSITIVE, CARING INTERACTIONS

In addition to providing a structure for learning and teaching functional skills, three other considerations warrant attention. First, it is important to reemphasize that promoting a positive, loving parent–child attachment is fundamental. Second, personalized caregiving means that the temperamental characteristics of the child are respected. Third, relevant

Figure 8.17. The child is sitting on her mother's crossed legs with slight support provided to the trunk by her mother's hand. This position fosters social interaction.

individualized family service plans (IFSPs) address practical daily challenges that confront parents and other family members.

Attachment

An essential concern is to support the development and maintenance of a secure attachment between the infant and parent (or other key caregivers). This support may involve helping the infant to develop self-regulation, an interest in the world, and a loving affect toward the parent. Likewise, the parents may be assisted in their efforts to engage, comfort, understand, and love their infant. Mutual attention, connection, and communication are sophisticated achievements that do not occur automatically. For example, some fussy babies cry excessively and are irritable during their early months. The parents often attend to them diligently for weeks on end without sleep or satisfaction. In some cases, this depressing and exhausting scenario leads to an unhappy outcome—by the time the infant becomes stable and organized, the parent has emotionally disengaged. An insecure attachment results, leaving both parent and infant disaffected. At other times, a loving relationship can be blocked because of the extreme focus of the parents on the child's disability. They only see "the problem" and not the child.

Some parents believe that letting the child do whatever he or she wants is an expression of their love and makes the child happy. In reality, children need the security of consistency, predictability, and self-protecting limits. Parents can be encouraged to identify boundaries for the child, to set rules that support safe practices, and to recognize their own rights and needs. A routine is useful for bringing order to each day by setting a time and sequence for activities. If parents request assistance in establishing a routine, they can be asked to record their activities for several typical days (e.g., wake-up time and bedtime, meals, bathing, napping, shopping). These daily logs can then be examined to determine areas that may be changed to reduce stress and promote family life.

Throughout this book are many strategies and activities for fostering close, secure parent–child attachments. Knowledge of parenting for most individuals comes from their own positive and negative experiences growing up. When interactional patterns are not generative, parents can be guided to discover how their current behavior may be influenced by their past experiences of being parented. By exploring how it felt then and what it means now, they can be empowered to relate to their infant without the undue influence of their personal family history.

Greenspan (1992) provides suggestions for therapeutic intervention that fosters emotional development and the parent–child relationship. Specialized psychological or related services may be indicated for some parents who are, for example, excessively anxious, intrusive, indulgent, punitive, or self-absorbed. When there is appropriately trained staff, most relational issues can be addressed within an early intervention program. The following case example describes the rather common concern of a father regarding his relationship with his son.

➡ Mr. Rodriguez shared his frustration with the social worker regarding the behavior of his son, 29-month-old Edward. The father reported, "Edward is uncooperative, stubborn, and always saying 'No.' I've heard about the terrible two's, but this is really too terrible!" He found his son's behavior very oppositional, provocative, and maddening. Mr. Rodriguez and the social worker spent numerous sessions exploring the father–son relationship and creating new ways for him to interact with Edward. They discussed the importance of this developmental phase for Edward's identity and that there were strategies other than punishment for managing his son's behavior.

Over time, Mr. Rodriguez realized that he had many rigid, developmentally inappropriate expectations for Edward that were needlessly creating confrontations. He was frequently directing, instructing, and correcting his son. Through intervention, Mr. Rodriguez discovered how his experience being parented as a child was playing out in the way he was parenting Edward. He said, "My father was mean and tough with me. I guess that's not so good for a 2-year-old."

Mr. Rodriguez learned to be more flexible and emotionally available with his son. "No's" by Edward were no longer viewed as a challenge to his authority. He discarded unimportant demands and rules that merely elicited power struggles. The boy was given more choices in everyday activities in order to increase his sense of independence and control; for example, he could choose which shirt to wear, what juice to drink, or where to play. Edward was forewarned when it was necessary to change activities and was given time to adapt to the transition. As the boy developed a greater sense of autonomy, his behavior changed. Mr. Rodriguez was delighted and said repeatedly how much he now enjoyed being with his son. The social worker reminded him how much his own changes contributed to Edward's progress.

Temperament

Effective caregiving and intervention require the adult to be sensitive to the temperamental characteristics of the child. The California State Department of Education (1990) developed a videotape with an accompanying pamphlet that provides guidelines for practitioners on how to interact with infants and toddlers with different temperaments. Children with feisty (difficult) temperaments are particularly challenging to manage. These children tend to be intense, active, moody, sensitive, distractible, and irregular. Flexibility of caregivers is necessary to avoid endless confrontations regarding their erratic patterns of napping, eating, and arousal. The practitioner and parent need to establish an orderly sequence in daily activities but then follow the schedule in a flexible manner.

Redirection is a useful technique to use when a child is having an intense reaction. An example is the feisty toddler who wants the toy of another child. The toddler may react by screaming and trying to grab the toy. Redirection begins by sympathizing with the child's desire for the toy and recognizing the anger at not being able to have it. The adult is firm, however, in setting limits and not allowing disruptive behavior. Generally, the toddler needs time to calm down before being redirected to another toy or activity.

Because children with a difficult temperament are often hypersensitive, it is beneficial to provide an environment that is relatively calm. In this way, overstimulation is avoided and the children are helped to be composed. Many of these children are resistant to change. They can be aided to handle transitions by letting them know beforehand that a change is coming. Those children who tend to be very active need opportunities for vigorous play in order to discharge their physical energy. In contrast, their quiet moments should be capitalized on for affectionate exchange and focused learning.

Children with a slow-to-warm-up (fearful) temperament tend to be cautious of new experiences. Due to their shyness, they need to be engaged slowly, allowing plenty of time for them to accommodate and for independence to unfold. The adult may need to go through a sequence of graded involvement—being with, taking to, stepping back but remaining available, and moving on. A consistent routine with a limited number of adults is especially important for the fearful child.

Children with easy (flexible) temperaments have an adaptable style that supports satisfying relationships. However, because of their agreeable ways, the feelings and needs of these children may be overlooked. More demanding children may get the majority of attention. It is essential to observe these children on a regular basis and to check in with them periodically so that they receive the individualized support and nurturance required by all children.

Daily Challenges

In the development of the individualized family service plan (IFSP), specific situations are commonly identified that are a challenge for parents or other caregivers to manage. They may voice concerns regarding how to handle stares or comments of strangers, to explain their child's condition, to cope with their child's fear of heights, or to deal with their child's attention-seeking behavior when the adult is on the telephone. These practical issues of daily living need to be addressed in the service plan. Such functionally relevant intervention enhances the coping resources of the parents and, therefore, the competence of the child. Table 8.1 lists typical coping-related concerns and circumstances that can be incorporated in the IFSP. (Schmitt [1987] provides helpful guidance for managing many of these issues.)

The following vignette is an example of intervention that focused on how to cope with a child's daily temper tantrum.

⇒ Mrs. Fisk, a foster mother, described 11-month-old Andrea in the following way: "She is a real charmer for most of the day. Andrea loves being talked to, and I sing and play with her while I do my housework and tend to the older children. But each day at five o'clock in the afternoon, she turns into a terror, and it is getting worse. I just don't know what to do. I hold her, rock her, sing to her, and try to interest her in toys. But nothing works. She just cries and cries."

Mrs. Fisk and the home visitor from the early intervention program talked about Andrea's "five o'clock crazies." They recognized that this was a common occurrence in many young children. It was a predictable time in Andrea's daily body rhythm when she was tired, disorganized, and emotionally volatile. They decided that Mrs. Fisk's attempts to soothe her were possibly over-stimulating and that Andrea needed to learn strategies to organize and comfort herself. Mrs. Fisk remembered a favorite videotape that Andrea liked that had a little angel eating a snack and saying "simply delicious." Usually Andrea got very quiet and watched the video intently. When the angel said her line, "simply delicious," Andrea would smile and clap her hands together. They agreed that the videotape had promise as an intervention.

The next day when the crying began, Mrs. Fisk turned on the video and said, "Let's watch the little angel." Sure enough, the angel amused Andrea. She smiled, calmed down, and later fell asleep on the couch for a short nap. This experience was the begin-

Table 8.1. Examples of common coping challenges for caregivers

Refuses to nap or go to bed	Hurts pets or another child
Climbs out of crib	Holds breath when angry
Wanders during the night	Uses temper tantrums often
Cries at night	Demonstrates head-banging or biting
Wakes too early or late	Resists toilet training
Jumps on furniture	Whines and clings during transitions
Stands up in the high chair	Runs away from parents in public places
Has a poor appetite	Touches objects that are off limits
Eats too fast or slow	Takes toys away from others
Resists using a car seat	Throws, but does not play with, toys
Dawdles when asked to get ready	Disrupts shopping and chores
Interrupts family conversation incessantly	

ning of a daily ritual that became very effective for helping Andrea manage the "five o'clock crazies." Over time, Andrea became increasingly active in her own regulation—giving the tape to her foster mother and climbing onto the couch with her blanket. This routine lasted for 6 months with Andrea saying the phrase, "simply delicious" by the time she was 14 months old! Mrs. Fisk would say, "Here comes the angel, what is she going to say?" and Andrea would giggle and say, "simply delicious" in the most self-satisfied manner.

SUMMARY

In this chapter a variety of intervention strategies and activities are described to increase the coping effectiveness of infants and toddlers. They can be used to implement the intervention options—modify demands, enhance coping resources, and give contingent feedback. The chapter begins with ways to structure learning (i.e., personalizing the sensory experience, providing physical handling and positioning, and using play). The focus then shifts to teaching functional developmental skills that can be applied as coping efforts. The chapter ends with a discussion of attachment, temperament, and daily coping challenges. Case examples are presented to demonstrate how interventions can be used in practice.

CHAPTER 9

Enhancing the Coping
Resources of Families

Families vary greatly in the services they need and want. Similarly, communities vary in the services they provide for families—they can be limited or far-reaching, ranging from an informal play group for children to a sophisticated network of community agencies. Optimally, a community should have a spectrum of services in order to be responsive to the priorities of different families and to provide families with options for meeting them.

This chapter briefly highlights common family needs and gives an overview of a range of community activities to support families. The discussion then focuses on a few services that have been particularly effective in assisting families to enhance their coping resources—support groups and workshops. Materials are also introduced that supplement these efforts.

The needs of families have been classified by Bailey and Simeonsson (1988) into six different categories: information needs, support needs, ability to explain needs to others, community service needs, financial needs, and family functioning needs. Families also request opportunities to express their vision for their child, to share their viewpoint, to ask questions, and to discuss how their child with a disability is influencing their lives. A challenge for practitioners is to assist families to translate their specific concerns and priorities into plans for addressing them.

A guiding principle for intervention planning is to use the naturally occurring services and activities of the community whenever possible. For example, many family priorities can be met through involvement with the community's libraries, houses of worship, recreational programs, neighborhood associations, and centers offering child care and respite care. Parent-to-parent networks and family resource groups provide opportunities to discuss with others who share common experiences. Early intervention programs may offer specialized services for siblings, grandparents, and others involved in the family's life. This is by no means a comprehensive list, but one that indicates the variety of options. It is the caregivers' choice to use the available resources in ways they believe will be most beneficial for them.

Activities suggested in this chapter are directed not only at assisting families to address their specific individual priorities, but also at enabling them to have experiences related to the broader program goals of promoting well-being and supporting the quality of family life. With these goals in mind, a question for the professional is: What do parents need to know, feel, and do to have mutually satisfying transactions with their child? A few guidelines are helpful when deciding what family-related activities an early intervention program might offer. The activities should:

> Focus on achieving identified outcomes that have a positive impact on parents and staff
>
> Build from staff strengths and not over-burden the staff's capabilities
>
> Respond to the greatest interests of most families
>
> Not duplicate what is already available elsewhere in the community

Although structured activities are important, often the most meaningful, potent intervention occurs in the informal interactions between parents and staff. This ongoing relationship provides opportunities for mutual learning, collaboration, and support. It is important for the practitioner to apply the intervention options when interacting with family members. The following vignette shows how a service coordinator helped a parent increase her coping resources.

➡ Mrs. Yates, whose identified priority was to have a more supportive extended family, talked to Alice, her service coordinator. She told Alice about her anger toward her mother-in-law, who was unwilling to stay with Jeremy, her 1-year-old child with spina bifida, so that she could do her marketing. Alice asked Mrs. Yates to tell her a little about her mother-in-law, Mrs. Jerian. Mrs. Yates said that Mrs. Jerian lived by herself, was not a very sociable person, and did not seem comfortable with Jeremy. They discussed options and decided to modify the demand by asking her mother-in-law to come shopping with her. In this way they could share the supervision of Jeremy, Mrs. Jerian could have some adult company, and they could both do their shopping. In the process Mrs. Yates could model ways to manage Jeremy and support her mother-in-law's interaction with her grandson. Through this intervention Alice helped Mrs. Yates to modify the demands she made on her mother-in-law, thereby enhancing the effectiveness of her transactions with Mrs. Jerian.

SUPPORT GROUPS

Support or discussion groups generate opportunities for learning that can influence beliefs and values, increase knowledge and skills, and enhance coping styles. Groups may include fathers, mothers, other caregivers, siblings, extended family members, or any combination of these. They may be led by professionals or function as a self-help group without a professional facilitator. They may be offered for a time limited period or be ongoing. Their purpose may be educational, therapeutic, or both. Other groups may have a more social function.

Support groups allow participants to share perceptions, skills, and feelings; solve individual and common problems; generate new learning; and give and receive support. One father described the value of participation in a group by stating:

➡ As a parent of a child with a disability, I need to be freed from my sense of isolation. I need a place where I can be myself and discuss my situation openly. I often feel the world is full of 'normal' children, except for my own. For me it is very necessary to come into contact with professionals and parents who have been there.

The following sections describe parent groups and specialized father groups. Activities and instruments are presented to facilitate discussion.

Parent Groups

Parent support groups that meet while the children are participating in the early intervention program are popular because they are convenient for parents who are already at the program site. When programs are home-based or involve parents in all activities with the children, parent groups may be scheduled in the evening or at another time that enables both parents to attend, particularly if babysitting services are provided at that time. Staff availability may also be a factor in determining the nature and scheduling of the group. Parent groups should provide the following benefits.

Peer support   Because of many commonalities in their experiences, parents can offer each other empathy and reassurance that they are not alone in their situations. They can provide mutual encouragement to examine emotions and handle demands.

Ventilation   Groups provide a safe environment to express feelings that may seem difficult or threatening to others who are not experiencing the same issues.

Vicarious Learning   Parents can learn coping skills by listening to the ways in which others manage situations and feelings similar to their own.

Mutual Help   Some parents are more comfortable giving and accepting help from one another than they are from professionals. They can better accept insight, advice, or confrontation from parents with whom they are able to identify.

Dilution of Responsibility   Parents can share responsibility and receive reinforcement regarding the appropriateness of some difficult action. For example, the parent who experiences extreme guilt when saying "no" to requests from an impulsive child may feel more comfortable about setting limits when he or she is aware that other parents are being equally strict.

The group leader (e.g., social worker, psychologist, counselor, parent) provides needed information, guides the group to problem solve, and facilitates participants to be mutually supportive. The leader may ask questions, encourage others to speak, and offer feedback. It is essential that the leader recognizes personal biases and needs in order to manage the group process appropriately. This is critical when working with individuals from various cultures.

The group can be most effective when the leader has knowledge about each participant's child and is aware of the resources, vulnerabilities, concerns, and expectations of each family and the specific outcomes they are working to achieve. The leader can then help participants achieve their priorities through involvement in the group and possibly assist them to become aware of other needs. The following case example describes how a group helped a parent to problem solve and generate effective change.

➡   Kathy, a single mother of a toddler with Down syndrome, had as one of her priorities "to learn more about the condition and what it means for the raising of my child." Kathy and her son shared a room in her parents' house. Although Kathy was employed by a major corporation in an extremely responsible position, she felt like a child at home. Prior to the birth of her son, she had "never even seen a child with Down syndrome." She told the group that enrolling her son was one of the "most difficult things I've ever done in my life." She explained that her parents refused to acknowledge that any special attention was needed beyond the love and care they would provide for any other child. She was unsure what was right, unsure how much to expect or demand of her child, and unsure how to respond to her child or her parents. Kathy appeared to the group leader and to other members as withdrawn, depressed, and overwhelmed.

Armed with knowledge of Kathy's expressed concerns, the leader used group members as resources to provide the information Kathy sought. Other parents were encouraged to share what they had learned; in the process of providing information, they also provided personal insights and reactions. The focus, then, was targeted to "what one knew" and "how one felt." Those who provided information and shared their own experiences not only felt helpful to Kathy, but they enhanced their own feelings of worth.

Kathy was able to find social support in the group—people who cared and accepted her and could relate to her concerns. The group served as a major external resource and a wellspring of information, sharing, and growth. It became a place where Kathy could examine the demands she set as well as those placed on her and on her child.

The group also helped Kathy see that some demands did not make sense. For example, Kathy seemed constantly tired. When asked about this, she told the group that she woke up every 3 hours with her child, who at the time was 2 years old. "Why?", a member asked. Kathy explained that her father got angry with her when the "baby" cried at night. To prevent this she never let him cry during the night. The group suggested to Kathy that her father's demand was unreasonable and not appropriate for Kathy or her child's growth and emotional development. Their support led Kathy to talk to her father. Reinforced with information and strategies used by others, Kathy presented a plan to help her child sleep through the night. The group felt pride in Kathy and in themselves.

The following case example shows how the strength of one group member can be drawn upon to benefit another participant.

➡ Beth was an expert in managing time and juggling busy schedules. She seemed able to manage three children, the children's assorted activities, a part-time job, a hobby, and a house. Beth's children also seemed quite able to take on their share of responsibilities. They had household chores and were, for the most part, able to respond to these demands. Beth's child with special needs was quite independent and scored well on the Early Coping Inventory, especially in the area of self-initiated coping behaviors.

Anne and Beth were in the same support group and had the same number of children. They each had a child with the same disability. These two women, however, represented quite different constellations of resources and vulnerabilities. Anne seemed unable to coordinate anything. Time, Anne said, was her enemy because she never seemed able to accomplish what she wanted. She placed few demands on her children, gave them few chores or responsibilities, and was disappointed when they could not carry out assignments. Anne's daughter with a disability was quite dependent and passive.

The group leader was well aware of the differences between Anne and Beth. Whenever Anne began to identify her difficulties or express concern as to whether her children could handle some responsibility, the leader would defer to Beth. "How would you handle that Beth?" became a standard question. Gradually Anne began to explore alternatives and recognize she could place more demands on her children. Both Beth and Anne benefited from the interactions. Beth received positive reinforcement from the group and Anne learned new strategies to manage her life more effectively.

One group's year-long experience is documented in Appendix A at the back of this book. This group met biweekly during their first year of attending an early intervention program. The group leader, a psychologist, wrote the report at the end of the year. The sessions in the report were separated into three phases: 1) getting acquainted, 2) working through beliefs and feelings about having a child with special needs, and 3) establishing a relatively stable pattern for family living. There were overriding themes that surfaced during the group process, including the need to ventilate feelings related to anger, grief, and blame; the management of issues associated with guilt and self-esteem; and dealing with specific parenting challenges.

Fathers' Nights

Planning services with fathers reflects the changing ways in which men are approaching the demands of parenting. Once thought to have a limited role in the parenting process and primarily functioning as providers, fathers are now acknowledged as being vital to family health and well-being. Fathers are often directly engaged in caregiving tasks and responsibilities. While fathering is an old game, it is now being played by new rules.

Many fathers express the wish to learn more and to share their feelings with other fathers. For many, sharing feelings is a new experience and easier to cope with in a same-sex group. The following service model is an example of how one early intervention program responded to this need.

➡ As most fathers were not available to participate in the regular center-based intervention sessions during the day, they were invited to participate with their child in a monthly Fathers' Night. The sessions were 2 hours in length. The first hour was spent with the child and the early intervention team. The second hour was spent in a discussion group with other fathers.

In the initial hour, the fathers had the opportunity to observe and engage in activities typical of their child's daytime program. This period generally involved some educational group experiences as well as individual therapy. During this time, the fathers discussed their specific concerns with a team member and, if desired, received instruction and practice in handling their child.

Over time the fathers expressed particular interest in the following areas. They wanted a better understanding of the nature of their child's early intervention program and wished to develop a better relationship with the staff. They had many questions about their child's intervention goals and how they were being achieved. Many fathers requested information regarding what they could do at home to assist their child's development. They had opportunities to practice these new skills with guidance from practitioners. Despite the hour being late, most children were responsive, and interaction between fathers and staff was active and enthusiastic.

In the second hour, the fathers met as a group with a social worker. During this time, the children were cared for by other staff members. The group was structured informally so that fathers could discuss issues of their own choice. In general, the interests of this group and the topics selected for discussion were similar to mixed-sex parent groups. However, group members emphasized the male's role in the family, their coping strategies as fathers, and issues of how to give and receive support within and outside the family. The fathers found it very meaningful to be able to discuss their concerns with other men in similar situations.

The following vignette describes what happened during the discussion period for a group of fathers who were meeting for the first time. The group was composed predominantly of young fathers employed in low-paying jobs in a large city.

➡ The fathers introduced themselves and talked about their children, their diagnoses, and how long their children had been in the early intervention program. The group leader asked how each father learned about the program. This question initiated a discussion of the problems each had experienced in seeking services. Many were extremely critical of and angry at physicians for: 1) the way in which the fathers initially were told of their child's medical condition; and 2) the lack of urgency doctors seemed to have concerning the child's diagnosis, prognosis, and treatment alternatives.

Everyone agreed that having their children in the program was a tremendous relief. Each felt he was doing the most he realistically could do. Fathers expressed satisfaction that they had the opportunity to meet with clinicians and hear firsthand what progress their children were making, what activities they could engage in at home, and how they could best help their children. The fathers explained how they usually received this information in a rushed fashion from their wives.

A discussion concerning acceptance of their children and establishing expectations for them occupied a good portion of the hour. The fathers discussed whether or not having unfulfilled goals for their children would be as upsetting as when they learned that their children had special needs. Toward the end of the hour, one father introduced the idea that perhaps they as fathers were too defensive about their children and too protective. Another father contributed that he had a brother who was blind and shared his experiences growing up as a sibling of a child with special needs. All of the fathers were actively involved in the discussion.

WORKSHOPS

The priority most commonly identified by parents in early intervention programs is obtaining information—a critical resource that helps them cope with their many demands. Workshops are an effective way to meet this need because they provide preplanned opportunities for active learning. Workshops may be scheduled for one session or take place over a period of time. Entering a program or leaving a program are particularly stressful times, when a lot of new information is required. Appendix B at the back of this book has examples of two informational workshops that were developed by these authors. One was for parents new to the early intervention program. The other was offered to parents before their children were due to leave the program and make the transition to public schools.

Particularly relevant for early intervention with a coping perspective is the provision of workshops that specifically address the topic of coping with stress. The following workshop was developed to meet this need and was validated as effective by the participants. The workshop consisted of four 2-hour sessions. It had the following educational goals:

1. To become familiar with the model of the coping process
2. To identify one's personal coping style and other resources most commonly used in managing daily living
3. To identify and manage a child-related stressor that causes personal concern
4. To evaluate the effectiveness of specific coping efforts and coping strategies

Below, an outline is presented of the learning objectives and activities for each session. They were designed to address the preceding goals. In addition, an overview is provided regarding what happened in an actual workshop in which five couples participated in four weekly sessions. These couples asked to join the workshop because of their high child-related stress levels.

Session 1: Stress, Stressors, and Resources for Coping

Objectives   Participants will:

Learn about the model of the coping process
Identify the internal resources they use to cope with stressors
Identify their external resources of human and material supports
Determine a specific child-related stressor
List skills necessary to cope with the targeted stressor

Activities

1. Introduction: Explain the purpose and format of the group.
2. Dyadic activity: Participants divide into pairs and identify their coping style to their partner, the resources they use for effective coping, and what they believe are their vulnerabilities. Partners then introduce each other to the group.
3. Distribute and discuss a copy of the model of the coping process (see Figure 2.1, chap. 2, this volume).
4. Have a group discussion to identify one or two specific child-related stressors that each participant might address during the workshop series.
5. Examine human and material supports related to their targeted stressors.
6. Homework assignment: Participants make a list of personal stressors that influence family life and identify beliefs and expectations regarding the targeted stressor that they may choose to work on.

Overview of Experience   Participants found it quite easy to describe and globally categorize themselves as either good or bad copers; yet, they found it much more difficult to describe their particular coping style. All of them identified perceived weaknesses and problems, but they had difficulty identifying specific strengths. As the discussion proceeded, group members cited situations where they did cope well.

The presence of spouses in the group was particularly useful. It allowed for direct and immediate feedback concerning coping styles. Additionally, it allowed for a discussion of the family coping style. Couples seemed amused and curious about the idea of considering their family coping style. For some, this appeared to be the first opportunity they ever had to consider the issue publicly or privately. For others, the opportunity to identify their style and receive feedback on it was somewhat threatening.

One couple described their coping style by saying that "the husband had 51% of the votes." This comment generated a strong reaction, with the women and men divided by gender over the issue. This lively and open discussion served a variety of functions: It helped the group to become cohesive, it permitted families to identify stressors and conflict areas that could be addressed in the workshop, and it provided sample illustrations that could be used for the purposes of group discussion and clarification.

The group then reviewed the model of the coping process and relevant coping-related definitions. This discussion was important because individuals were using terms such as stress, stressor, and coping in a variety of ways to identify stimuli, responses, and feelings. Clarification of basic definitions facilitated understanding and future discussion among members of the group.

Parents chose a variety of targeted stressors, many of which were child related but not always focused on the child with a disability. A number of personal, couple, and sibling problems were identified as targets. These targets included: the dinner hour and its attendant chaos, a repetitive child behavior (e.g., not listening when spoken to), the morning routine of waking a child and getting ready for school, talking about having more children, and concern about an overly attached father–daughter relationship.

The homework assignment was unexpected and a few parents commented that they might not have time to do it. This issue provided an opportunity to discuss personal responsibility and motivation as they relate to change and stress as well as group involvement. Furthermore, it reinforced the expectation that participants were to be actively involved.

Session 2: Impact of Beliefs and Expectations on Coping

Objectives   Participants will:

> Determine individual and family coping strengths and vulnerabilities
> Identify patterns of reactions to stressors
> Discuss and analyze coping transactions and their impact on a specific stressor
> Identify elements of the targeted stressor that can be changed and those that cannot
> Discuss the role of beliefs and expectations on functioning
> Develop an initial action plan aimed at the targeted stressor

Activities

1. Start with group feedback and discussion of the homework assignment.
2. Examine expectations and beliefs about the targeted stressor using a group-identified stressor as an example.
3. Distribute a copy of a coping transaction and discuss its application to managing the stressor (see Figure 2.2, chap. 2, this volume).
4. Examine factors associated with the stressor that can be changed.
5. Homework assignment: Develop an action plan for managing the targeted stressor.

Overview of Experience   The session began with a review of the homework. Three parents did not do the assignment and volunteered that they did not have time due to their busy week. Other group members gently applied pressure and confronted them, reinforcing the issue of motivation and responsibility for change.

Those members who had completed their stress list shared their observations and insights. Some believed that creating the list forced them to be more aware of previously unidentified stressors. One father discovered that he gets tense as he leaves work and anticipates the scene he will encounter at home. A mother discussed waking up in the morning feeling tense and staying that way until the children go to bed. "I wait until almost 10 P.M. for some peace and quiet and even though I'm tired, I stay up to enjoy it. It's my only time of relaxation."

Most participants had some difficulty listing in detail their beliefs and expectations concerning their targeted stressor. "I just expect that she'll listen when I tell her 'No!' I expect the house to be calm and that we can have a nice dinner like when I was a kid." Some identified what they did not expect: "I don't expect him to fight me every morning. It's the same battle day in and day out." These examples led participants to share their style of responding to specific stressors and how their coping strategies worked. Some parents noticed that their feelings of stress actually increased as a result of their coping efforts.

After much discussion, the group agreed that the dinner hour, which they labeled as the "six o'clock terror," was a common stressor for all of them. Therefore, it was selected to illustrate the process of examining beliefs and expectations and how they influenced transactions during the dinner hour.

Parents easily stated their beliefs and expectations concerning how things "should" be; they were listed on a blackboard for discussion. Parents laughed when recognizing how unrealistic some of the expectations were. The following examples are some of the expectations cited: "The children should be quietly watching TV or playing quietly in their rooms when I prepare the meal.", "The house should be calm.", "I should be able to unwind and sit peacefully.", "The phone shouldn't ring.", "We should be able to sit at the table as a family and talk about the day's happenings.", and "There should be no fighting."

Parents were asked to examine and evaluate each statement and consider if each expectation was realistic and rational. They were also asked to elaborate on why things should be as they expected versus why they should *not* be that way. The final activity related to this issue was the creation of a list of realistic expectations and some discussion as to how these reasonable expectations might be translated into action.

Session 3: Planning and Implementing Coping Efforts

Objectives   Participants will:

Identify the impact of the previous session pertaining to beliefs on current behavior related to the targeted stressor

Determine their coping styles, emphasizing the most and least adaptive coping behaviors

Identify how their coping styles influence outcomes

Apply new learning to refine the action plan for managing the targeted stressor

Activities

1. Engage in group feedback and discuss the homework assignment and how changing beliefs influence perceptions of the stressor.
2. Complete the self-rated edition of the Coping Inventory (described in next section of this chapter).
3. Discuss feelings and insights gained from rating themselves on the Coping Inventory.
4. Make the final revision of the action plan for implementation.

Overview of Experience   Participants came to the session eager to talk about how they had modified their expectations and beliefs about the "six o'clock terror." Most agreed that they noticed improvement in themselves and in the dinner hour. When pressed to identify specifically what had changed, everyone recognized that the change was in their beliefs and outlook. By modifying their expectations, the transactions and perceived stressfulness of the situation had changed.

A brainstorming and problem-solving process was used to further examine the "six o'clock terror." Participants were able to identify factors contributing to the problem and created a list of possible factors that could lead to reducing or managing the problem. The group was able to provide very specific and concrete examples. These examples included: structuring activities for the children, having them help prepare dinner, giving them a snack at 4:30 or 5:00 P.M. so they are not as hungry and distraught if delays occur, and taking the phone off the hook or using an answering machine before and during dinner. Participants were encouraged to use this problem-solving process with other identified targeted stressors.

The next portion of this session involved the completion of the self-rated Coping Inventory. Parents were instructed in how to complete the inventory and given time during the session to fill it out. Upon completion, they identified their most and least adaptive behaviors and had the opportunity to share this information if they wished. Many parents laughed as they recognized themselves in their ratings. In discussion they tended to focus on their least adaptive coping behavior. The group became aware that under stress they often reverted to least adaptive behaviors rather than using their coping strengths. This finding raised the question of how to change behavior so that they could capitalize on their strengths. The group was then asked to revise their action plans based on their new learning.

Session 4: A Model for Change

Objectives Participants will:

> Evaluate the effectiveness of the implementation of their action plan for managing the targeted stressor
> Review the model of the coping process and its relevance for handling daily stress
> Evaluate the workshop experience

Activities

1. Discuss their experiences and learning related to the implementation of their coping action plan.
2. Distribute the Stress Manager handout (see Figure 9.1) as a mechanism to summarize and review the content of the workshop.
3. Complete the evaluation form of the Coping with Stress workshop (see Figure 9.2) and discuss suggestions for future directions.

> ***Overview of Experience*** The group was aware that this was the final session and commented about how they wished they could continue for a few more weeks. One participant said, "This has turned into a pleasant night out"; others agreed. The initial portion of the meeting was dedicated to feedback and discussion of their experiences implementing their coping action plans.
> Everyone reported continued success with the "six o'clock terror." One couple discussed their experiences of getting their child out of bed without fighting. A father shared the progress he was making in allowing his child to become more independent. There was general discussion of the importance of being self-reflecting regarding beliefs, particularly those that are prefaced by "should."
> The Stress Manager handout was used to structure a review of the coping process model. Specific workshop activities were related to different components of the model. The general reaction of the group was "this brings it all together and makes things

---

Stress Manager

When confronting stressful situations or feelings, the following questions serve as a guide to determine the actions you may take.

1. Can I specifically describe the stressor? What exactly is the problem?
2. Am I experiencing the stress physically and emotionally? Is it affecting my thinking?
3. What are my beliefs and expectations about the stressor? How do I expect it "should" be?
4. Are my beliefs and expectations logical? Are they appropriate for the situation? Are they realistic?
5. What elements of the stressor can I change? What elements can I not change?
6. What coping behaviors do I usually use in stressful situations? Which ones are the most and least adaptive?
7. Am I able to change my behavior at this time? How can I go about doing it? Am I willing to take the steps needed?
8. Are there specific human and material supports that I could use to help me?
9. What action would I *like* to take? What action *needs* to be taken? Have I examined or identified all the possible alternatives?

Figure 9.1. Stress Manager.

Evaluation Form for the *Coping with Stress* Workshop

Please circle a rating from 1–5 for the first six items—1 is the lowest rating and 5 is the highest positive rating.

		Quality of presentation	Usefulness	Objective attainment
1.	Explanation of the Coping Model	1 2 3 4 5	1 2 3 4 5	1 2 3 4 5
2.	Identification of personal resources and stressors	1 2 3 4 5	1 2 3 4 5	1 2 3 4 5
3.	Identification of individual and family coping styles	1 2 3 4 5	1 2 3 4 5	1 2 3 4 5
4.	Identification of beliefs associated with specifically identified stressors	1 2 3 4 5	1 2 3 4 5	1 2 3 4 5
5.	Learning an approach to problem identification and problem solving	1 2 3 4 5	1 2 3 4 5	1 2 3 4 5
6.	Learning skills necessary to cope with specific stressors	1 2 3 4 5	1 2 3 4 5	1 2 3 4 5

7. Suggestions for improving the workshop: _____
_____
_____

8. Overall rating and satisfaction with the workshop: _____
_____
_____
_____

9. Other comments: _____
_____
_____

Figure 9.2. Evaluation form for the Coping with Stress Workshop.

clearer." The final activity of the evening was to complete the workshop evaluation form. The group found the experience extremely useful and expressed interest in more sessions.

MATERIALS FOR USE IN INDIVIDUAL AND GROUP ACTIVITIES

Materials can be used to promote individual insight or to generate a shared experience for group participants. They help to foster discussion in specific and often sensitive areas. Self-rated instruments and structured experiences that assist adults to learn more about their own coping resources are described on the following pages. It is important to recognize that the rating of any instrument is individual and personal. Adults must always know the purpose of the instrument, have the option of whether they choose to complete it, and be able to decide what results, if any, they elect to share. Time also needs to be available to discuss any item that is unclear or anxiety producing.

The Coping Inventory: Self-Rated Form

The Coping Inventory has two forms—the observation form for children 3–16 years of age described in Chapter 6, this volume, and the self-rated form for adults that is discussed here. Both forms use the same format and rating procedure to identify individual coping styles, including most and least adaptive behaviors. Similar to the observation form, the self-rated form of the Coping Inventory (Zeitlin, 1985) has two categories—Coping with Self and Coping with the Environment. Within each category, three dimensions are used to describe the coping style—productivity, activity, and flexibility. Figure 9.3 provides sample items from the instrument.

This instrument can be completed by parents as part of a group experience, completed in the privacy of the home, or rated by mutual agreement with the assistance of a practitioner. The following four steps can be followed when using the Coping Inventory as a group activity. In the first step of the process, the facilitator describes the purpose of the activity and reminds the group members that participation and sharing in this experience is optional. The purpose may vary based on the interests of the group (e.g., increase awareness of coping style, appreciate the importance of coping behavior, reflect on the similarities and differences between a parent's coping style and that of their child and other family members). Depending upon familiarity of the group to coping-related concepts, definition of terms used in the Coping Inventory are either introduced or reviewed. The participants are then given time to complete the instrument. Scoring is generally not appropriate when the instrument is being used for discussion purposes. Instead the focus is on the identification of participants' most and least adaptive coping behaviors.

The second step addresses coping strengths. Using their item ratings of 4 and 5 as a stimulus (their most adaptive coping behaviors), parents are asked to share occasions when they used the identified behaviors to cope effectively. The higher self-esteem generated by this positive reinforcement facilitates later discussion of problem areas.

The third step identifies the participants' least adaptive coping behaviors (item ratings of 1 or 2). The parents reflect on how they are currently managing certain demanding circumstances. This increased awareness helps them to start to generate new coping strategies to use in the future. For example, in terms of the ability to self-protect under stress (a

---

A rating of 1 indicates the behavior is not effective, and a rating of 5 indicates that the behavior is consistently effective across situations.

Coping with Self: Productive Dimension

1. When you are presented with a new or difficult situation, do you find a way to handle it?   1 2 3 4 5

2. Do you respond to control by others in a way that is helpful to you and/or to the situations? (For example, how do you react to rules set by others or orders given to you on the job, within the family, or in the community?)   1 2 3 4 5

Coping with Self: Active Dimension

1. When you are angry or disagree with others, do you tell them how you feel?   1 2 3 4 5

2. Do you ask for help when you feel you need it?   1 2 3 4 5

Coping with Environment: Flexible Dimension

1. Do you bounce back after disappointment or defeat?   1 2 3 4 5

2. When necessary, do you try a variety of ways to reach a goal or to solve a problem?   1 2 3 4 5

Figure 9.3. Sample items from the Coping Inventory.

frequent issue for parents), participants can discuss strategies that they use. Do they with-draw or engage in some productive activity? Do they use babysitters or family members to allow themselves time without the child? Do they retire and go to bed or stay in the situation no matter what?

Another possible topic that may surface involves coping with social interaction. The following questions may facilitate discussion. Has their coping style changed since the birth of their child with special needs? Have they dropped old friends or been dropped by them? Have they become isolated? Do they avoid social interactions because they cannot cope with the reaction and advice of others? Once parents become aware of their coping style through reflecting upon these types of questions, they can begin to evaluate the im-pact of their behaviors and consider whether they would like to modify them.

The fourth step is to explore and develop alternative coping strategies in areas where parents have difficulty managing. Strategies that are productive for some parents may or may not be effective with other parents. For example, whereas one mother may cope productively for both herself and her child by becoming more involved in the early inter-vention program as a volunteer, another mother may cope more productively by spending less time with the child and getting a part-time job and a good babysitter.

The Belief Scale and the Definition Scale

The Belief Scale and the Definition Scale are two self-rating instruments that are useful for generating discussion regarding parents' beliefs about their child with special needs. The scales can help the parents become more aware of their feelings and they permit staff members to react openly to shared information. The Belief Scale (Bristol, 1983a) measures parents' beliefs about what influences their child's improvement or recovery. The five areas of possible influence are: chance, divine influence, the parents' efforts, the profes-sionals' efforts, or the child's own efforts. Figure 9.4 provides sample items from the in-

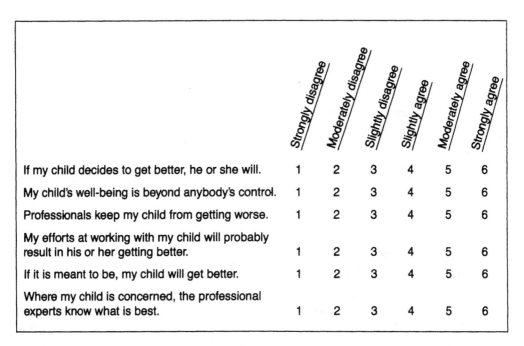

Figure 9.4. Sample items from the Belief Scale.

strument. The scale can be utilized selectively with families to help them appreciate how their beliefs are influencing their relationships and actions.

The Definition Scale (Bristol & DeVellis, 1982) identifies what parents may believe is the impact of having a child with special needs in their family. The 16 items are statements that parents have made about having a child with a disability. Figure 9.5 presents sample items from the instrument.

The Carolina Parent Support Scale

The Carolina Parent Support Scale is a self-rating instrument developed by Bristol (1983b) that assesses parents' perceptions of the support they receive in caring for their children. The scale identifies the supportive people in their lives as well as the availability of community support. The scale also identifies the relative helpfulness of the support network. Alternate forms of the scale are available for two-parent or single-parent families. Figure 9.6 has sample items from the two-parent form.

In addition to the use of these or other self-rated instruments, the parents can complete some of the child-related instruments discussed in Chapter 6, this volume. Parents can gain a better understanding of their child's coping style by completing the Early Coping Inventory. Such awareness can facilitate improved parent–child transactions and aid the development of behavior management strategies to use in the home. The parents and staff can also discuss differences in the child's behavior in different environments, such as the early intervention program, the home, and the family day-care environment. Temperament scales can also be completed by parents to achieve additional insight (e.g., the Infant Temperament Questionnaire by Carey and McDevitt [1978]). They are particularly beneficial for appreciating the characteristics of a child with a feisty, difficult temperament.

	Strongly disagree	Moderately disagree	Slightly disagree	Slightly agree	Moderately agree	Strongly agree
A child's special problems give the whole family an opportunity to become more understanding of others.	1	2	3	4	5	6
Children have problems because of something their parents have done or failed to do.	1	2	3	4	5	6
Caring for a child with special problems gives meaning and purpose to life.	1	2	3	4	5	6
Caring for a child with special needs is part of God's plan for a family.	1	2	3	4	5	6
Having a child with special problems harms other members of the family.	1	2	3	4	5	6
Caring for a child with special needs is an opportunity to learn new skills.	1	2	3	4	5	6

Figure 9.5. Sample items from the Definition Scale.

	Not applicable	Not at all helpful	Somewhat helpful	Moderately helpful	Quite helpful	Extremely helpful
Husband or wife	NA	0	1	2	3	4
My relatives	NA	0	1	2	3	4
My husband's (or wife's) relatives	NA	0	1	2	3	4
My own children	NA	0	1	2	3	4
Friends	NA	0	1	2	3	4
Other parents of children with special needs (informal)	NA	0	1	2	3	4

Figure 9.6.   Sample items from the Carolina Parent Support Scale (two-parent version).

Similar to the use of instruments, structured experiences provide participants with a common exercise that generates information for learning and discussion. Two activities are provided as examples—the family coping quiz and the family map.

The Family Coping Quiz

The following seven questions can be made into a Family Coping Quiz handout, with space left after each item for a response. If this activity is conducted in a group, each parent completes the handout independently and a group facilitator uses the questions to guide discussion.

1. Think of a demand, challenge, or predicament that your family has faced. What was the issue?
2. Did everyone define the issue in the same way?
3. What was the outcome? (How did it turn out?)
4. List some of the behaviors that different members used to handle or cope with the issue.
5. What resources were used in coping with the issue?
6. What did you or other family members learn about yourselves and the family's coping style or beliefs from the way this issue was handled?
7. How did this experience affect you and your family when facing other issues?

The Family Map

Completion of a family map may be used as the basis for many family-related discussions. It can also be used as a staff training activity to help practitioners learn more about families. Figure 9.7 shows a blank family map.

Instructions for use:

1. Display a sample family map.
2. Point to the area on the map where information should be written.
3. Have participants fill in the names of individuals living in the household; include ages of the children.

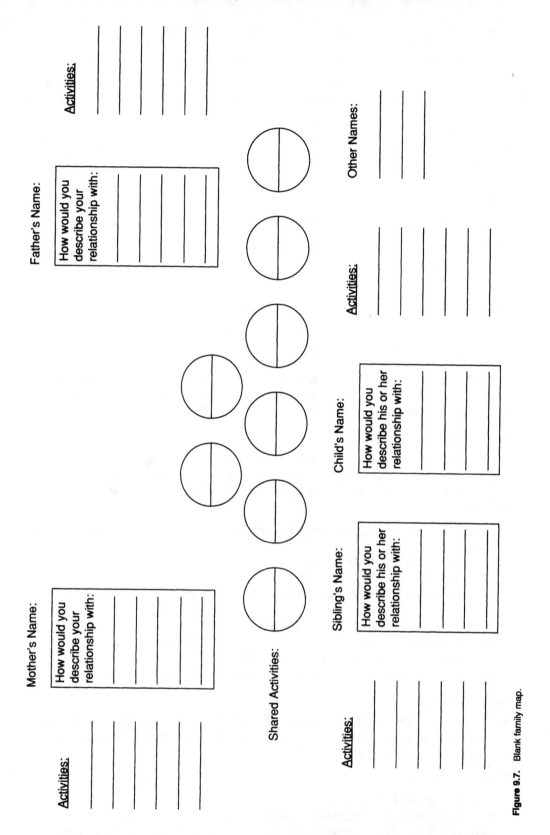

Figure 9.7. Blank family map.

4. Have participants list the names and relationships of individuals who are not living in the home, but who are "part of the family" in terms of involvement, caregiving, or sources of support (e.g., grandmother—frequent babysitter and support to mother; divorced natural father—weekly visitor and source of financial support).

After identifying the family members, parents can be asked to describe their relationship with each member (e.g., very good, good, fair, poor, very poor). These exact words do not have to be used; however, using some consistent scale helps later in discussing the data. In addition to an overall rating, parents can use other words to describe the quality of each relationship (descriptions should be limited to two to four words).

The time taken to complete the maps varies according to the number of dimensions included. The facilitator should watch the group and announce a time limit when about half of the participants have finished. Once the participants have completed their maps, the facilitator should take time to have them share and process how the experience went for them. The group can then consider what other areas they would like to include on their maps. The following are two dimensions that can be considered (see the completed map in Figure 9.8).

1. Close family supports: List individuals who interact closely with the family (or key members of the family) on a daily basis or very regularly (e.g., best friends, neighbors). Note the frequency with which these individuals interact with the family and the quality of the relationship.
2. Shared family activities: In circles on the map, note any activities that the family regularly participates in together. Even if only two family members are involved in an activity, it should be included. For example, if the mother always takes her son shopping with her, then one circle labeled "Shopping" (in the top half of the circle) should be drawn with a line from the mother and the son to that shared activity. If all family members participate (e.g., go to grandmother's for dinner on Sundays), lines should be drawn from each member to the circle labeled "Sunday Dinner at Grandmother's."

The quality of the shared activity can be recorded in the bottom half of the circle, using just one key word. For example, an activity in which all family members participate might be "Going to church on Sunday." However, when the parents are asked to describe the experience, they say that the kids hate to go and put up a fuss. This behavior frustrates the parents so much that most of the time spent in church is stressful and annoying. So even though the entire family participates, the quality may be described as poor. Yet, a simple activity performed by only the mother and the child, such as food shopping every Friday afternoon, may be a warm and positive experience for both—time alone to share a simple task. This activity would be given a high-quality rating.

SUMMARY

In this chapter a variety of activities are suggested that can be supportive of parents and provide opportunities for them to enhance their coping resources. The activities and materials selected by an early intervention program should address the priorities and interests of the families and be commensurate with the professional expertise of the staff.

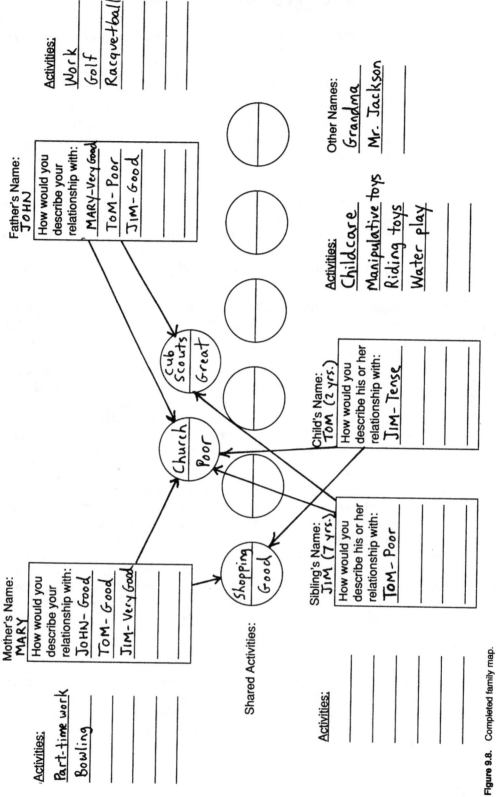

Father's Name:
JOHN

How would you describe your relationship with:

MARY—Very Good
TOM—Poor
JIM—Good

Activities:
Work
Golf
Racquetball

Mother's Name:
MARY

How would you describe your relationship with:

JOHN—Good
TOM—Good
JIM—Very Good

Activities:
Part-time work
Bowling

Child's Name:
TOM (2 yrs.)

How would you describe his or her relationship with:

JIM—Tense

Activities:
Childcare
Manipulative toys
Riding toys
Water play

Sibling's Name:
JIM (7 yrs.)

How would you describe his or her relationship with:

TOM—Poor

Activities:

Cub Scouts — Great
Church — Poor
Shopping — Good

Shared Activities:

Other Names:
Grandma
Mr. Jackson

Figure 9.8.   Completed family map.

154

Developing an IFSP
with a Coping Perspective

First Steps

There are many ways that a coping orientation can be incorporated into the philosophy and practices of an early intervention program. This chapter and the next demonstrate one method for developing an individualized family service plan (IFSP) with functional outcomes directed toward expanding the developmental capability and coping effectiveness of children and supporting families to enhance their resources.

The collaborative development of the IFSP integrates and applies the coping-related material described in previous chapters. The personalized decision-making model, introduced in Chapter 5, this volume, is used to develop an IFSP with the family. This chapter addresses the initial two steps in the process: 1) collecting and sharing information, and 2) analyzing information and setting long-range functional outcomes. The third step, developing an implementation plan, is discussed in Chapter 11, this volume.

A coping-related IFSP reflects the following key features:

Builds on a theoretical model of the coping process as translated into clinical practice

Recognizes the complexity of family life and considers the critical factors that affect the family system—its structure, cultural diversity, functions, life cycle, and subsystems

Represents parent and professional collaboration and the influence of their reciprocal interaction

Addresses the nature of the child's coping resources and transactions with significant others

Uses intervention options to achieve coping-related outcomes

Facilitates generalization of learning to achieve functional competence in daily living

Identifies parent-selected activities that support the enhancement of family resources

REQUIREMENTS OF AN IFSP

The IFSP is the document that specifies the desired services and outcomes for the child and family. Its creation, implementation, and revision are one important facet of intervention.

It is the result of a dynamic collaborative process of analysis and decision making between family and staff.

Public Law 99-457 (the Education of the Handicapped Act Amendments of 1986) directed states to introduce the IFSP as part of the comprehensive, coordinated, inter-agency program of early intervention services. The 101st Congress reauthorized this legis-lation with Public Law 101-476 and changed its name to the Individuals with Disabilities Education Act (IDEA). Section 677 of IDEA describes the IFSP. The law mandates that each infant and toddler with a disability and his or her family shall receive:

1. A multidisciplinary assessment of the child's unique strengths and needs and the identification of services appropriate to meet such needs
2. A family-directed assessment of their concerns, priorities, and resources, and the identification of the supports and services necessary to enhance the family's capacity to meet the developmental needs of their child with a disability
3. A written IFSP developed by a multidisciplinary team, including the parent or guardian

The law further states that the IFSP must be evaluated once a year and reviewed at 6-month intervals. The plan must be written within 45 days from the date of assessment; however, services may commence prior to the completion of the assessment with the par-ent's consent.

The content of the IFSP includes the following components:

1. A statement of the infant's or toddler's present levels of physical, cognitive, commu-nicative, social/emotional, and adaptive development based on acceptable objective criteria
2. A statement of the family's resources, priorities, and concerns related to enhancing the development of the child with a disability
3. A statement of the major outcomes expected to be achieved for the child and the fam-ily, and the criteria, procedures, and timelines used to determine the degree to which progress toward achieving the outcomes is being made
4. A statement of specific early intervention services necessary to meet the unique needs of the child and the family, including the frequency, intensity, and the method of de-livering services
5. A statement of the natural environments in which early intervention services shall be appropriately provided
6. The projected date for initiation of services and the anticipated duration of such services
7. The name of the service coordinator from the profession most immediately relevant to the child's or family's needs, or the name of the service coordinator who is qualified to carry out all applicable responsibilities and be responsible for the implementation of the plan and coordination with other agencies
8. The steps to be taken supporting the transition of the toddler with a disability to services provided under Part B of IDEA, to the extent that such services are considered appropriate

The final requirement for the IFSP refers to parental consent. The law states that the contents of the IFSP shall ''be fully explained'' to the parents or guardian and informed written consent shall be obtained prior to the provision of early intervention services de-scribed in the plan. To be consistent with these requirements, the following format is used in the IFSP examples given in this book:

1. A summary of the development and coping capability of the child and the concerns and priorities of the family
2. Long-range functional outcomes that will increase the child's development and coping capability and will enhance supportive family resources
3. Six-month implementation plan with short-term goals directed to achieving the long-range functional outcomes
   a. The program and community services for the child and family
   b. Short-term goals and objectives with strategies and activities to achieve them
   c. Evaluation procedures
4. Plans for update or transition

USING THE PERSONALIZED
DECISION-MAKING MODEL TO DEVELOP THE IFSP

The personalized decision-making model has three steps. In the first step, *collecting and sharing information,* the parents provide information regarding their concerns, priorities, and resources. The practitioners provide information regarding the services of the program and community. Collaboratively, they identify and summarize the child's developmental status and other coping resources. In the second step, *analyzing information and setting long-range functional outcomes,* the family and practitioners examine the summarized data to determine the fit between resources and concerns. They identify outcomes that will make the most difference in increasing the child's developmental capability and coping effectiveness and in enhancing family resources. These are the long-range functional outcomes documented in the IFSP. In the last step of the model, *developing an implementation plan,* the parents and practitioners determine the services and activities that will help the child achieve the long-range outcomes and that will respond to family priorities. Procedures are also delineated for evaluation of the plan and, if appropriate, for transition.

When the personalized decision-making model is used to develop the IFSP, the family and practitioners are engaged in a continuing interactive process. The model provides a structure for cooperative problem solving that results in a functionally oriented service plan that addresses real life concerns. The family participates in a decision-making process that is relevant and applicable to daily living. In this sense, the development of an IFSP using this model is an important intervention effort. It provides the opportunity for family members to acquire skills and other coping resources that help them face current and future challenges.

In each of the steps of the model, specific decision-making questions are addressed (see Table 10.1). Sequential responses to each question guide the development of the IFSP. For the first two steps described in this chapter, the decision-making questions are considered. The experiences of the Kelly and Gomez families are then shared as examples of how the decision-making model is applied. The Kelly family is presented in greater detail so that each aspect of the process can be discussed. A more abbreviated procedure is used for the Gomez family. These are the initial IFSPs for the families, and they cover a 6-month period of time. They were developed in a program that was responsible for working with families from referral through service delivery.

When first learning the process, it is helpful to respond concretely to each question. When the process is more familiar, it can be used as a structure for thinking through each step. Actual writing may be limited. Each early intervention program develops its own procedures when adapting the decision-making model to its environment. This model can

Table 10.1.   Questions to implement the decision-making model

Step 1.   Collecting and sharing information

     1.1.   What information is needed to write the IFSP with this family?

     1.2.   How is that information collected?

     1.3.   How is the information summarized in preparation for analysis?

Step 2.   Analyzing information and setting long-range functional outcomes

     2.1.   Of the information collected, what facilitates and what interferes with the child's development and coping and the addressing of family concerns?

     2.2.   Of the factors that interfere, what can be changed and what cannot be changed (at least in the near future)?

     2.3.   Of the interfering factors that can be changed, what changes will make the most difference?

Step 3.   Developing an implementation plan

     3.1.   What short-term goals will move the child toward achieving the long-range functional outcome and address the concerns and priorities of the family?

     3.2.   What services, strategies, and activities can help the child and family achieve these outcomes?

     3.3.   How can the plan be evaluated?

     3.4.   What procedure will be used to update the plan or to support transition from the program?

also be adapted to settings in which IFSP development occurs at a service coordination level that is distinct from the direct service level.

COLLECTING AND SHARING INFORMATION

> 1.1.   What information is needed to write the IFSP with this family?
>
> 1.2.   How is that information collected?
>
> 1.3.   How is the information summarized in preparation for analysis?

1.1.   What Information Is Needed to Write the IFSP with this Family?

To write an IFSP, information is needed to describe the child's present status and to identify family concerns, priorities, and resources. In general, this information is acquired by considering relevant family characteristics and background history, the family's priorities, the child's coping resources, and observations of the child's transactions. Likewise, family members need enough information about the early intervention program so they can begin to collaborate with staff in the decision-making process. Although there needs to be some consistency in these broad areas of information, the amount and type gathered at this time should be guided by the specific concerns and issues raised by the family and the staff's perception of the child's disability. It is not essential, possible, or even desirable to collect extensive data at the start of the family's participation in the early intervention program.

Identification of the specific issues of a family is an ongoing process that starts at the first transaction between the staff and family, whether it is over the phone or in person. For example, there would be a different focus for a family with a young infant just discharged from a neonatal intensive care unit than for a family who is anxious about their toddler's behaviors but coping with their feelings by denying the importance of their observations. The family with the infant may come with comprehensive medical records. Through help from the social worker in the intensive care unit, they may have developed clear priorities for the family's participation in the early intervention program. For the toddler, a more complex initial assessment may be needed to clarify the child's present status. The parents may also require much more information about the program and its value to their child.

Transactions that occur at the first meeting set the stage and direction for information collection. At that time there is an opportunity for talking, listening, providing support, and giving feedback. The reciprocal interactions that occur between practitioners and family influence mutual perceptions. The staff develops beliefs about the family and the family develops beliefs about the staff and program.

As information collection is an ongoing process intimately intertwined with intervention, the data needed for the first IFSP must be adequate to generate agreement about the initial directions for intervention, but not so cumbersome that it becomes an end in itself. With some families, agreement comes early; with others, there may be a more active process of compromise and modification of goals. It is always important to remember that services to families are not contingent upon the collection of "required" information and that families reserve the right to withhold information.

1.2.   How Is that Information Collected?

There are many options for gathering and sharing information between the staff and family (see chap. 6, this volume). In some programs, information collection occurs in stages over time: 1) to determine program eligibility, 2) to get started in the program, and 3) to write the first IFSP. All these stages contribute to IFSP development. Other programs may consolidate the process and collaborate with the family to develop IFSP goals in one session. They may vary in child assessment procedures (formal instruments, informal methods), staff composition (different combination of professional disciplines), and team process (interdisciplinary, transdisciplinary). Detailed information regarding staffing patterns and practices is available in the literature (Garland & Linder, 1988; Linder, 1993; Woodruff & McGonigel, 1988).

The initial meeting with the family may take place either in the home or at the program. The selection of the meeting place is contingent upon the program's policy and resources as well as the family's preferences. In some circumstances, when transportation, babysitting, or similar issues are factors, it may be particularly appropriate to conduct the session in the home. The following vignette is an example of one parent's experience during the initial visit to an early intervention program. Ms. Williams was a single mother who believed her toddler was developing typically.

➡   When Ms. Williams took her daughter, Tammy, to the medical clinic for her 2-year check-up, she expected the doctor to say that everything was fine. She was shocked when he told her of his concern about how little Tammy was speaking. When he recommended that Ms. Williams take Tammy to an early intervention center for an evaluation, she became very upset. After much discussion with her family, Ms. Williams called a program that had been recommended and brought Tammy for an initial meeting. Ms. Williams told staff that she felt apprehensive walking into the center because she did not know anything about early intervention. She saw other children there who looked much needier than her child. Some were in wheelchairs; some walked with crutches; some wore helmets on their heads. Ms. Williams did not know about these other children, but she felt sure that this was not the place for Tammy. At this first meeting, the staff felt that giving Ms. Williams information about assessment and intervention had to precede asking her for much information about Tammy. It was critical for Ms. Williams to feel that Tammy could be different than the other children and yet benefit from the services offered.

Children and their families vary in how readily and easily their needs can be identified. It is critical not to make premature or hasty decisions. Because families generally participate in an early intervention program over time, a thoughtful pace is often indicated.

1.3. How Is the Information Summarized in Preparation for Analysis?

It is a challenge to organize and summarize diverse information so that it can be examined in ways that give as complete a picture of the child and family as possible. This is important because looking at a piece of information out of context allows for misinterpretation of its meaning for a particular child. For example, 18-month-old Tiffany had a situationally effective coping style (Adaptive Behavior Index of 3.2). Her coping behavior was a strength because she had very limited developmental skills but she was able to harness them quite successfully to function in certain environments. She made the most of her assets. In contrast, 18-month-old Ivan was developmentally at age level but also had a situationally effective coping style (Adaptive Behavior Index of 3.2). Ivan did not use his assets to his best advantage—he could only cope when he was in familiar environments with familiar people.

There are a number of ways that information can be summarized. A suggested way is for the team to create a matrix that includes each area for consideration. (See Table 10.2 for a suggested form and categories of information.) Examples of this procedure are given in the cases that follow. At this point, some programs may use the summary to write the first section of the IFSP that includes the child's present status and family concerns and priorities. It is often helpful, however, to wait until there has been some analysis of the summarized information. During that process the need for more or different information may be identified.

Case Examples   The Kelly and Gomez families were in the same early intervention program, although they entered at different times. Their children were at different stages of development at the time of entry, and the families varied in their personal circumstances.

The Kelly Family   Mrs. Kelly called the early intervention program and said she had a 13-month-old daughter, Marie, with a severe skin condition and many other difficulties. Marie's dermatologist told Mrs. Kelly about the program and Mrs. Kelly asked if she could make an appointment. The secretary who answered the call took basic information and set up an appointment for Mrs. Kelly to meet with a social worker. The secretary asked if she wanted to bring her daughter, but Mrs. Kelly stated that her preference was to come alone. Furthermore, Marie's father would come later if Marie were to enter the program.

When Mrs. Kelly came for her appointment she seemed nervous but reserved. She tended not to initiate conversation nor to ask many questions. However, when asked a question, she made eye contact, seemed to listen carefully, and responded in a friendly manner. The social worker gave her a brochure describing the program and took her on a tour of the facility. As she showed Mrs. Kelly each room, she described some of the activities that took place in them. She also shared with Mrs. Kelly information about the staff, children, and families that participated in the program.

The following discussion took place between Mrs. Kelly and the social worker at the conclusion of the tour.

Social worker: *What are your concerns?*
Mrs. Kelly: What will the future be for Marie? Will she be like other children? Will she be able to play, learn, have friends, join the Brownies? What do we need to do as a family to help her? Are we doing the right things? Do we protect her too much?

Table 10.2. Information matrix

	Emerging beliefs	Physical and affective states	Developmental skills	Coping style	Human supports	Material and environmental supports
Family concerns						

How long have you felt this way?

Since she was born and we found out about the skin condition. Her skin is sensitive, raw, and peeling. Sometimes she has blisters that ooze. The doctor said that the condition is hereditary.

Why do you think it is important to obtain help now?

We see that she is not doing the things she should be doing. At first it wasn't too bad, although she always cried and was irritable, especially when she was touched. But after her cousin was born, we began to see how slowly she was doing things—sitting, crawling, things like that. People began to notice how different she was. It was even hard to find out what to do or where to take her. The pediatrician was no help at all. Finally, a dermatologist told us about early intervention and we called.

What influenced your decision to come here?

We want her to walk and the program has a physical therapist. We feel that if she gets therapy she will be able to walk.

Have you previously sought help for Marie?

We didn't know where to get help or if there was any help like this. We took her to several doctors for physical things—lots of ear infections—but nothing like this.

What is Marie like at home and other places?

Marie is really good when no one is around. She is irritable, but who wouldn't be with her condition? She loves to look at things and listen to music. She gets very shy, cranky, and afraid when people are around. She tries to play with children, but they are too rough and mean to her. Marie likes to be with us.

What gives you the most satisfaction when caring for her?

When she doesn't cry.

What is most difficult?

I have to apply creams two times a day and give her baths. She really hates it and gets so upset she practically faints from crying.

What would you like to have happen as a result of coming here?

We'd like Marie to be like other children. We want her to go to school and not be so afraid of everything. Sometimes it seems she could do a lot, but she is afraid.

What is your family like?

Marie does not have any brothers or sisters. We wanted to have a big family; that's why we bought a house with four bedrooms. But you know, Marie's disease is genetic. We found out when she was tested, so we have decided not to have more children.

My family is very supportive, but my mother is not well so we don't see her too much. My husband's family lives near us—he has lots of brothers and sisters. I thought it would be nice living so close and all, but it sometimes makes me uncomfortable. Without understanding Marie's problems, they tend to think that we spoil her.

Who is available to turn to when you want help or someone to talk to?

I really don't talk to people much. I used to have a close friend, but we lost touch, and I don't have any sisters. I guess Bob [Mr. Kelly] and I talk to each other.

What special demands are there on your family because of Marie's special needs?

Marie sleeps very poorly and has trouble breathing at night. Sometimes she cries all night. It seems as if she needs care 24 hours a day. It is exhausting for us. She won't stay with babysitters, so we never go out. When we are at home she gets upset with company.

Do you have concerns about how these demands are being managed?
Yes, but what can we do? We hate to have her cry and get upset. She is in enough pain already.

What special resources and strengths help your family meet these demands?
I sometimes wonder if we have any. I get so down in the dumps. I guess our greatest strength is each other and how much we want to be there for Marie.

Do extended family members share your concerns and feelings?
My family sometimes understands. I don't really know how his family truly feels.

Are there regular routines or a "typical" day?
I am a very structured person and I like to follow a routine, but it all depends on Marie's mood. Usually I wait to see how she is, then I plan what I can do around her.

If there are other children around, how do they interact with Marie?
Cousins who live close by tend to ignore her.

What is challenging for Marie? What is rewarding?
I don't really know. She acts fearful of new things and just cries. Sometimes if I hold her she will look and watch. Marie smiles when she is able to do something she loves—songs, rhymes, and finger plays. She would like to play with other children, but usually she can't.

Is there anything else you would like us to know?
I'm sure there is, but I can't think of anything now.

The discussion provided enough information to indicate that Marie would probably be eligible for the program. At the same time, much was learned about the family and their concerns and resources. The social worker could see that Mrs. Kelly was feeling quite anxious and somewhat deprived. Mr. Kelly seemed to be her major support and vice versa. Marie is a first and only child. Mrs. Kelly did not appear to be very knowledgeable about developmental expectations, which contributed to an uncertainty and fear about Marie's present and potential developmental status. Mrs. Kelly's description of her home gave an impression of adequate financial resources. Management of Marie seemed difficult and demanding with no respite available.

Mrs. Kelly described Marie as a very vulnerable child who was difficult to handle physically and was often unhappy. She was probably in discomfort a great deal of the time. She indicated that Marie enjoyed and benefited most from watching people and objects. Mrs. Kelly gave the impression that she wanted to do whatever was possible to help Marie no matter what the personal cost.

The social worker, by her careful listening and interest in what Mrs. Kelly was saying, generated a feeling of support and encouragement. She told Mrs. Kelly that she thought Marie could benefit from the program and that Mr. and Mrs. Kelly would also find it helpful. Mrs. Kelly brightened and showed enthusiasm when the social worker set an appointment for Mr. and Mrs. Kelly to bring Marie for an initial evaluation. There was discussion of who would be there and generally what would happen. Mrs. Kelly was told that several people would be interested in observing Marie: an occupational therapist, a speech-language therapist, a physical therapist, and a special educator. The interviewer, a social worker, would be there also. (The evaluation team was large due to the complexity of Marie's condition.) Because Marie did not like to be touched, her direct interaction with the practitioners would need to be limited. The purpose of the next meeting was to confirm Marie's eligibility for early intervention services and to get enough information to start her in the program. They also discussed some of the special services available for parents. Mrs. Kelly was asked to sign a release giving the program authority to obtain Marie's medical report.

In preparation for the evaluation, the staff discussed what had happened at the initial meeting. The information was used to identify what needed to be known about the Kelly family to write the first IFSP. A major concern for Mrs. Kelly was whether Marie would ever be like other children; therefore, information was needed about Marie's present developmental status, her coping behaviors, and how she interacts with children. As none of the staff had knowledge of the specific skin disorder, they had to learn enough about the condition to understand its impact on Marie's behavior and development. They also needed to know how it affected physical handling and how to manage the attendant problems. It was also important to be aware of how the parents interacted with Marie and their resources for managing their own life. Further discussion was needed to learn more about how Marie's condition shaped their daily routine and influenced their beliefs about themselves and the significant people in their lives.

It was agreed that the assessment would be conducted through observation and parental report due to Marie's intolerance of touch. Because of the child's difficulties related to physical handling and hypersensitivity, the occupational therapist was identified as the temporary service coordinator during the evaluation process. The occupational therapist would be the examiner interacting with Marie through her parents, and the other professionals would be observing and giving input from the side. The social worker would support the involvement of the Kellys in the process and interpret for them what was happening.

The following is a description of the information learned about Marie during the evaluation.

➡   Marie demonstrated aversive reactions to touch all over her body and did not tolerate handling by the examiner. She tolerated being held and carried only by her parents. As soon as her clothing is removed, Marie scratches her body. Her parents reported that she experiences much discomfort during bathtime as a result of being in the water, having her body dried with a towel, and having lotion applied to her skin. They stated that when she "forgets" about herself and what she is feeling, she tolerates more and will attempt increased movement and play. This was also observed during the evaluation session when Marie would become interested in a toy and reach out for it.

Upon entering the room, Marie was placed in a sitting position on a mat on the floor. She appeared cautious and motioned for her mother to come closer. Marie seemed apprehensive and responded best when approached in a one-to-one encounter. Once comfortable with the situation, she handed toys to the examiner and appeared to enjoy interaction that did not include imposed handling or touch. Marie used gestures (pointing) and vocalization (screeching) to request objects as an alternative to reaching for them. She shook her head from side to side to express displeasure. Mr. and Mrs. Kelly reported that Marie responds to "no" and is able to calm herself when held by one of them, given raisins to eat, redirected by toys, or brought to another room. They also reported that she enjoys social games, such as rolling a ball and playing "peek-a-boo."

Marie avoided sensory contact with surfaces and as a result demonstrated limited self-initiated exploration of her environment and the toys around her. She was selective of the objects she chose and primarily preferred those with smooth surfaces (e.g., one-inch cubes, plastic balls). Marie refused to touch textured objects, such as soft stuffed animals or puppets, and cried when they were imposed upon her. With encouragement, she held two cubes and lightly brought them together. Marie took one ring off of a stack and with assistance placed it back on. She enjoyed looking at a picture book, and she could independently turn the pages.

Posture and Mobility

Marie could maintain a prone position (on her abdomen), a supine position (on her back), and a sitting position. However, she did not demonstrate any transitions into or out of these positions. Marie indicated when she wanted to be moved by crying or reaching out toward her parents. They reported that when playing at home she rolls from supine to sidelying and back to supine; however, rolling was not observed. No other transitions were noted at home.

Joint range of motion and muscle tone were not assessed due to Marie's resistance to handling. Assessment in these areas was recommended for a later date. During play and dressing, Marie presented with full range of motion in both arms in all planes. Marie's posture and mobility skills were assessed in the following positions. It should be noted, however, that Marie tended to fuss in all positions except for sitting.

Supine: In the supine position, Marie turned her head to both sides to look at toys or her parents. Her legs were positioned with approximately 90 degrees of hip flexion with her feet in the air. Her parents reported that she does bring her legs down to the surface when playing at home.

Prone: Marie was placed on her abdomen at the end of the evaluation and did not tolerate this position. She placed her head down on the mat and occasionally lifted it up to look around while propping on extended arms with weight bearing on the base of her palms. She did not have contact on the total surface of her palms and fingers.

Sitting: Marie sat in a ring sitting position with a wide base and her arms in a high guard posture. Minimal trunk rotation and weight shifting were noted. Marie rarely reached for objects; instead she waited for them to be given to her. Although Marie usually maintained her arms in a high guard position, she was able to come out of this position to pop bubbles or to hold a toy. Marie utilized mature grasp patterns in both hands, using fingertips to avoid contact of objects with the palm of her hand.

Standing: When placed in standing, Marie maintained this position by leaning forward with her chest against a stable surface. She did not use her hands for support.

Oral Motor Development and Feeding

Observation of the oral mechanism indicated all structures to be intact for speech production. Marie had active, functional eating patterns with finger foods. She independently could bring food to her mouth and chew; however, attempts to present foods on a spoon were unsuccessful. Liquid intake was hampered by her inability to hold a bottle or cup for extended periods of time.

An audiological screening was not performed at this time. Marie was observed to respond consistently to speech and environmental sounds, suggesting speech reception thresholds to be within normal limits.

Cognitive Processing

The Uzgiris-Hunt Ordinal Scales of Infant Psychological Development (1975) were used as a frame of reference to assess prelinguistic skills. Marie initiated or attempted minimal manipulative behaviors due to intolerance of sensory input; however, precursor cognitive skills appeared to be approximately within normal limits. This was observed by her intense visual observation and affective changes when the examiner performed a task. She understood the premise of object permanence with several screens, performed goal-directed behaviors through her parents, and appeared to understand spatial relationships between objects. Her specific interaction with objects was significantly limited due to her inability to derive pleasure from these activities. She did not exhibit specific learning strategies except through parental modeling and observation.

Shortly after the initial evaluation, a home visit was conducted by Antoinette, the special educator. The purpose of her visit was to:

Establish further rapport with Mr. and Mrs. Kelly.
Confirm Marie's intervention schedule and starting date.
Observe Marie's play and activities in the home.
Provide support and encouragement to the parents.

Throughout the home visit, Marie appeared very happy and playful. She reached for and picked up small toys such as blocks, small people, and animals. Marie rolled a ball to her parents and seemed to enjoy such turn-taking activities. She fed herself raisins and cheerios from a bowl, although she did not attempt to hold a cup. During this home visit, Mrs. Kelly continued to share some of her feelings and it was clear that her sense of isolation was not unfounded. Since Marie's birth, the child's irritability and constant demands for comfort had resulted in a marked decrease in social contacts for the family. According to Mrs. Kelly:

➡   Since Marie's birth our whole life has changed. It has made us feel distant and removed.
     One of Bob's sisters had a baby girl, too, shortly after Marie was born. At first it wasn't
     too bad, but now it is tough. They don't understand a thing about Marie's skin condi-
     tion, and I wouldn't begin to tell them that there might be other things wrong. They
     know that she is slow, but they really think it is because we spoil her. The worst is that
     when they, or anyone else for that matter, come into the house, Marie becomes more
     and more upset and unmanageable until I or her father have to take her to her room.
     The thought of having people over, even just family, is too much.

The home visit provided another opportunity to talk with Mr. Kelly. Because he is a salesman for a large communications company, he was able to manage his time to be at home for the visit. His major concern focused more on his wife's unhappiness about caring for Marie than on Marie's disability. He said he had done some research on her condition, but he "did not really see too much wrong with Marie. She just needed a little help and then she would be just fine."

Mr. Kelly reported that his concerns would come later when Marie had to go to school on her own and he could not be there to help her. He did not see that the extended family "put pressure" on Mrs. Kelly. He felt that they were like all families; he could not sympathize with his wife's discomfort regarding their criticism of Marie.

When asked specifically to identify his priorities for Marie and how he would want the program to help, he agreed with his wife that he wanted all the information possible, especially about how children manage this skin condition when they get older. He was absolutely convinced that the condition was not causing a delay in Marie's development. However, he wanted the program staff to compare her developmental gains with the norms for her age and report those results to him regularly. He said that would assist him to understand Marie's problems "if there were any."

The home visit was successful in establishing a rapport between the Kellys and the special educator. Antoinette observed that Marie could initiate activities that involved touching when she was motivated. Mrs. Kelly was again able to ventilate and expand on her feelings of separation. Although Mr. Kelly conveyed a mixed message of concern and skepticism, it was clear that they both loved their daughter very much, but felt lonely and frustrated. They seemed to be searching for help regarding how to be available for Marie and how to have a satisfying life as a family.

Shortly after the home visit, with the active involvement of Mr. and Mrs. Kelly, Marie was placed in an early intervention toddler group. This placement allowed her to receive services immediately and to determine her tolerance for group activities. It also gave the staff the opportunity to collect additional information for IFSP development. The group of eight children was chosen because they ranged in age from 12 to 18 months and had mild to moderate disabilities. The children had some degree of mobility and interaction. As a consequence, there was a potential for Marie to learn through observation. The group met for 2 hours once a week. Three practitioners worked with the children individually and collectively. For the first hour, the parents were active participants in the room; during the second hour, the parents had the option to attend a parent discussion group.

In the first weeks of Marie's enrollment in the program, the team had opportunities to observe and analyze transactions during planned activities and in more spontaneous interactions. In Table 10.3, a planned transaction between Marie and Gloria, her occupational therapist, is described. The initial purpose of the transaction was to provide a sensory experience that would assist Marie to explore different textures.

Marie was sitting unsupported on a smooth plastic mat on the floor. Gloria was sitting opposite her and there was a plastic bucket filled with rice on the floor between them. Mrs. Kelly was sitting next to Marie.

The following questions helped to analyze this transaction:

What was the outcome? Marie did not have to touch the rice.

Did her coping effort effectively satisfy the demand? No, Marie did not explore or touch the new material.

What, if anything, facilitated the outcome? Mrs. Kelly supported Marie in disengaging from the activity.

What interfered with an effective outcome? The particular sensory experience chosen (tactile exploration of rice) seemed to be too uncomfortable and frightening for Marie to deal with at that time.

Did Marie have the skills and resources to manage the demand? She could not tolerate the demand to play with the rice; however, she had strategies for avoiding an unpleasant sensory experience. She communicated her distress by crying and moved to her mother for comfort.

After observing Marie in many different transactions, the staff summarized and analyzed their observations by responding to the following questions.

What behavioral patterns were observed across the transactions? Marie's primary strategy for managing demands is to reject them and to cry frequently. In transactions with staff, Marie is generally apprehensive and says, "No," or shakes her head in response to proposed activities. In new situations or when pressed to move and

Table 10.3. Observation of a transaction: Marie

Demand (*What was the demand?*)	Child's coping effort (*What did the child do to manage the demand?*)	Adult's response to coping effort (*How did the adult respond to the child's action?*)	Child's reaction to the adult's response (*How did the child then react?*)
Gloria asked Marie to touch rice in the plastic container by demonstration, making a verbal request, and physical guidance.	Marie watched as Gloria scooped up the rice and poured it on her own hand; Gloria reached for Marie's hand and poured rice on it. Marie grimaced pulled her hand away, started to cry, and began to crawl toward her mother.	Gloria stayed quietly in place. With Marie's response to the feel of the rice, Mrs. Kelly reclined on the mat so that Marie could reach her. Mrs. Kelly took Marie in her arms and said, "It's okay, it is only rice."	Marie cried briefly on her mother's lap and looked with an expression of annoyance.

explore through touch, she usually becomes very upset—she virtually "shuts down" and becomes unavailable for further activity.

What seems to be the impact of these behaviors on Marie's emerging beliefs? She seems to be developing the following belief: "When I avoid experiences that are unpleasant, I will be comforted by Mom and Dad. Being with them is the only safe place."

What needs of the adults were observed? Mr. and Mrs. Kelly want to keep Marie happy and comfortable at all costs. They set up the environment in a way that Marie can have successful experiences. They ask Marie what she wants and then perform the requested action (e.g., activate the toy, carry her to desired locations); in general, they do most of the interaction for her. Marie smiles and provides positive feedback to her parents for their help.

What are the implications for intervention? Initial demands on Marie must be such that she can meet them through her own efforts. Her coping resources should be strengthened so that she can be more active and self-reliant. Mr. and Mrs. Kelly need to learn to be supportive of Marie without doing everything for her.

During this initial period, the staff were able to sufficiently observe Marie to complete an Early Coping Inventory (see Figure 10.1). It was difficult to determine an accurate developmental profile for Marie. Although many of her behaviors were below age expectation, her potential was unclear due to limitations imposed by her skin condition. The Hawaii Early Learning Profile (Furuno et al., 1979) was administered to achieve an approximation of her developmental status. Marie demonstrated a scattering of skills in the following areas of development. (Marie's developmental age range for each area is listed.)

Gross Motor	7–11 months
Fine Motor	8–10 months
Social	7–10 months
Self-Help	7–10 months
Cognitive	8–13 months
Language	7–10 months

The next challenge was to examine all of the collected information and develop a summary matrix that had the most salient information. In preparation for an IFSP conference the staff met, discussed the accumulated information, and completed the matrix. (See Table 10.4.)

The Gomez Family Nelson Gomez displayed problems from birth and was diagnosed as having microcephaly. Initially, he was not referred to the early intervention program due to his medically fragile status and seizure activity. At 3 months of age he became medically stable. At this time, Mrs. Gomez contacted the program and made an appointment for an initial meeting. Mrs. Gomez said she would bring Nelson, but Mr. Gomez would not be able to attend.

A social worker and therapist met with the Gomez family. As planned, Mrs. Gomez came with Nelson, but she also brought two older children, Olga, 2 years old, and Martin, 3 years old. She held Nelson in her arms and the two siblings played close by. In an informal discussion, she shared that also living at home were Nelson Sr., the father, and his two sons by a first marriage—Manuel, 20 years old, and Aaron, 22 years old. Mr. Gomez's first wife was deceased. Mrs. Gomez was in her late twenties and her husband was about 45 years old. He was a long distance truck driver and Mrs. Gomez said that she was about to begin a mail order business in her home.

Effectiveness Score	
Sensorimotor Organization (SM)	1.4
Reactive Behavior (R)	2.9
Self-Initiated Behavior (SI)	2.3

Adaptive Behavior Index 2.2

Coping Profile

	1	2	3	4	5
Sensorimotor Organization					
Reactive Behavior					
Self-Initiated Behavior					

Most Adaptive			Least Adaptive		
Category	Rating	Behavior	Category	Rating	Behavior
SM	4	Maintains visual attention	SM	1	Does not tolerate being in a variety of positions
R	4	Demonstrates pleasure in her success	SM	1	Unable to comfort self
R	4	Uses self-protecting behaviors to control impact	SM	1	Minimal energy
SI	4	Anticipates events	SM	1	Does not vary activity level according to the situation
R	3	Accepts warmth and support from her parents but is cautious with others	SI	1	Does not initiate exploration of own body or objects

Figure 10.1. Marie's adaptive behavior summary at 14 months of age.

Mrs. Gomez seemed very anxious and shared her concerns readily. She came to the program because she believed that it would provide therapy and help her baby. She said, "What can the family do for him?" and "Are we doing the right things?" Mrs. Gomez also expressed concerns about the two older boys. Both have had legal and other difficulties related to drug abuse. Mrs. Gomez and her husband do not agree about how their problems should be handled.

As Mrs. Gomez talked, it became apparent that she had a need to express her concerns, anger, and frustration. She discussed her dissatisfaction with the medical commu-

Table 10.4. Information matrix: Marie Kelly at 14 months of age.

Emerging beliefs	Physical and affective states	Developmental skills	Coping style	Human supports	Material and environmental supports
The world is not a safe place (apprehensive, fearful behavior). Interactions result in painful or unpleasant feelings. Parents will protect and take care of her needs without self-initiated efforts.	Genetic skin disorder (itchy, peeling skin) Overly sensitive to touch and movement (tactilely defensive) Normal vision and hearing Low energy level Cries easily Happy when no demands are made Secure with parents Low self-esteem	Relative strength in cognition and receptive language, but limited expressive language (verbal and gestural) Indicates preferences by head shaking and pointing Appreciates object permanence and spatial relationships between objects Understands simple directions and social games Visual learner Motor skills limited by fear of touch and pain Crawls with difficulty Maintains sitting position and supported standing Socially interactive with parents but not others Independent finger feeding	Upset by change Avoids interaction Passive with limited self-initiation Has some self-protective behaviors Unable to self-comfort Minimally effective coping style Demonstrates pleasure when successful Accepts help, warmth, and support from parents Anticipates events Maintains verbal and auditory attention	Parents are responsive to her every whim. Parents value family life and believe support of Marie to be their highest priority Parents believe Marie's well-being is their responsibility, and Marie is different from other children Parents have good health and education with minimal experience in child rearing Father's family lives close by, but does not understand Marie's special needs Maternal grandmother is supportive.	Spacious, comfortable home Middle-class neighborhood Appropriate toys and equipment Creams and lotions to medicate for skin condition

Family concerns

How can the parents learn more about Marie's skin condition?
Will Marie ever be like other children?
Will Marie ever walk unassisted?
How can they better manage the demands of caregiving so they do not feel continually tired, anxious, and lonely?
How can they explain Marie's condition to other people?

nity and what seemed to be an unclear diagnosis and prognosis for Nelson. In talking about her worries regarding his development, Mrs. Gomez said, "If Nelson would only smile at me I would feel better." She expressed an interest in more free time. She also needed to find a nursery school for Martin, the 3-year-old son. She said her own appearance and weight gain after childbirth were a source of stress and personal dissatisfaction.

Mrs. Gomez said that her parents were on an extended trip and her sister lived in the southern part of the state. She said she was emotionally close to her sister, but Mrs. Gomez did not share other information about family or friends. Mrs. Gomez had a car available and could drive. In the course of the first visit to the early intervention program, she offered to drive another mother who did not have transportation, expressing her interest in being responsive and useful. She said she "liked to help out" and that it would be no trouble to pick her up.

Mrs. Gomez's intense concern regarding what was wrong with Nelson was expressed many times. She said that if he is "retarded," she wants to know so that she can do something. Mrs. Gomez said that her desire to work from her home was her way of caring for the children while contributing economically to the family. During the session she had a very matter-of-fact manner and did not get frustrated by the children running around, spitting cookies into her hand, and exhibiting other typical child-like behaviors.

While Mrs. Gomez and the social worker were talking, the therapist had a dual role of managing the siblings and observing Nelson and his interactions with his mother. Nelson appeared to be small for his age, with a disproportionately small head. He cried often with a weak high-pitched sound. Mrs. Gomez would offer him a bottle and he would make great efforts to suck and then give up. Mrs. Gomez would try rocking him back and forth in her arms, while continuing her conversation and visually focusing on the social worker. At the conclusion of the meeting, Mrs. Gomez signed a release giving permission to get Nelson's medical records. The social worker made an appointment for the following week to plan Nelson's entry into the program. General information about the program was also shared with Mrs. Gomez.

After the family left, the social worker and therapist discussed what they had learned from this initial meeting. They recognized that the Gomez family had many stages of family life to cope with—a relatively new marriage, two young children other than Nelson, and two adult children with problems. Mrs. Gomez indicated that she had a minimal support system, financial pressures, and conflicts with her husband about some family issues. She seemed to have many strengths as evidenced by the relaxed, comfortable manner in which she managed her young children. However, she was not satisfied with her appearance and how hectic her life was at that time. Although she evidenced feelings of confidence in raising her other two children, she was less confident in how to manage Nelson.

At the next staff meeting, the social worker and therapist reported that Nelson was clearly eligible for services. As he was so young and frail and had developmental delays, the staff felt that he and his family would benefit by being involved in a program as quickly as possible.

Mrs. Gomez came with Nelson to the second meeting and met with the social worker, the occupational therapist, and the speech-language pathologist. The social worker confirmed Nelson's eligibility for services. The purpose of the meeting was to agree on how they would get started.

The staff and Mrs. Gomez discussed the best placement for Nelson. Because Nelson was so frail and had two young siblings, a home-based program was chosen. Mrs. Gomez said that Martin would soon be attending part-time nursery school and that Olga would be easier to handle if her older brother was not present. Mrs. Gomez hoped that she and her husband could occasionally attend some of the parent programs at the early intervention center. Due to the comfortable rapport between Mrs. Gomez and the social worker, it was decided that the social worker would be the service coordinator at this time.

During the discussion, Mrs. Gomez reiterated her great concern that Nelson never smiled at her. The speech-language therapist picked up on this comment and used it as an entry point for further information collection and intervention planning. After Mrs. Gomez gave permission, the therapist repositioned Nelson on his mother's lap so that he could see her. The therapist then suggested a way for Mrs. Gomez to touch his cheek lightly. As a result Nelson looked at his mother and made a fleeting smile. Mrs. Gomez was visibly pleased. She said, "I never had to work at getting Martin and Olga to smile. I guess Nelson just needs more attention." She was excited, saying, "I will have to work a little harder to get Nelson to smile, but I am so glad he did it. I need to help him to do what the other children did."

Soon after this session, Mrs. Gomez brought Nelson to the center for a comprehensive evaluation. The following findings also include observations and discussions from earlier meetings.

➡ *Pertinent History*

Nelson was born at a community hospital by cesarean section following an uncomplicated, full-term pregnancy. His birth weight was 6 lbs. and 14 oz. Within 30 minutes after birth, Nelson developed seizures and was transferred to the neonatal intensive care unit. The seizures were partially controlled with the use of phenobarbital. He was discharged from the hospital at 12 days of age and continued to receive phenobarbital. At 5 weeks of age, Nelson was admitted to another hospital for a battery of tests. Results were all found to be negative except for a skull X-ray, which indicated a small anterior fontanelle. Additional neurological assessments at approximately 10 weeks of age revealed both head circumference and weight to be below the fifth percentile for age. Phenobarbital was gradually discontinued at approximately 3 months of age as seizure activity was no longer observed. Reportedly, no seizure activity has occurred since that time.

Coping Style and Behavior

Nelson was able to establish eye contact momentarily. It was difficult to calm him when he was crying. His mother reported that when Nelson cries unconsolably she takes him to a quiet room and tries various strategies to comfort him, including a pacifier, a bottle, talking to him, and rocking him. These episodes last anywhere from 15 minutes to an hour.

Nelson demonstrated a minimally effective coping style. He was generally passive in his behavior; however, he did initiate some actions by undifferentiated crying when he was tired or hungry. Nelson had difficulty regulating his physical state. He was unable to self-comfort and it was hard to soothe him when he was upset. Nelson became quite fussy in response to a noisy environment. He would push the bottle away when he had enough or was fatigued from the sucking effort. Mrs. Gomez reported that Nelson had been slow to gain weight. She also said that Nelson sleeps through the night and prefers to be on his abdomen when sleeping and awake.

Functional Skill Development

Nelson lifted his head and maintained it above 45 degrees for short periods when on his abdomen. He was able to find his hand to suck when his head was turned toward either side and when he was cradled in his mother's arms. Nelson did not like being placed on his back and cried whenever this was attempted. Upon being pulled to sit, there was a head lag until he was halfway up into sitting.

Supported sitting was tolerated by Nelson for short periods. He could bring his hands together, but he could not swipe at suspended toys. Nelson made only momentary eye contact at faces and had a fleeting visual focus on objects.

Oral Motor and Feeding Skills

Observation of the oral peripheral speech mechanism revealed structures that were essentially symmetrical. Evaluations were made of Nelson's rooting and sucking reflexes. Although these were elicited, the strength of the reflexes was diminished.

Mrs. Gomez reported that Nelson would not breastfeed and was a slow feeder. Nelson drank a bottle of 4–6 oz. of formula in 45 minutes. Due to slow weight gain, he was put on strained baby food at 5–6 weeks of age at the recommendation of his pediatrician. During bottle feeding, he used a weak suckle-swallow pattern and exhibited poor endurance.

Cognition and Communication

Selected items from the Uzgiris-Hunt Ordinal Scales of Infant Psychological Development (1975) were used to assess skills in cognition and communication. Nelson was credited with the following 1-month skills: grasping the examiner's finger and responding to a familiar voice. Nelson was observed to use an undifferentiated cry for various needs (e.g., hunger, discomfort). He also frequently demonstrated distress without crying, as evidenced by facial grimacing and turning red. He produced pharyngeal vocalizations of low intensity described by his mother as "sounding like he's constantly clearing his throat." No other vocalizations were reported or observed.

Summary

Nelson had developmental delays in all areas. He lacked eye contact and a social smile. He had frequent periods of irritability and he had limitations in visual fixation and tracking. Primitive reflexes were still apparent. There was low muscle tone with some stiffening upon passive range of motion. Nelson displayed inconsistent responses to auditory, visual, and tactile stimuli although he responded well to physical handling techniques. Swiping activities were not observed, and Nelson was unable to grasp and shake a toy.

Some developmental strengths were noted. Nelson was able to sleep 10–12 hours at night. He was able to bring his hands to his mouth. He also demonstrated the ability to recognize his mother's voice. Nelson reacted well when physically handled (e.g., firm pressure and slow movement). Other intervention that appeared to be beneficial included vestibular input (bouncing), proprioceptive input (deep pressure), and the use of a quiet environment with minimal auditory distractions.

The preceding information was gained with the active collaboration of Mrs. Gomez. She also participated in developing a summary matrix in preparation for an IFSP meeting. Table 10.5 presents the completed matrix.

ANALYZING INFORMATION AND SETTING LONG-RANGE FUNCTIONAL OUTCOMES

In Step 2 of the personalized decision-making model, parents and practitioners continue to work collaboratively to translate what is learned from the collected information into meaningful long-range outcomes for intervention. This step involves analyzing the information and determining functional outcomes. As the family and staff summarize and share information, they continue to develop trust and feel more comfortable with one another. For some families, this rapport may occur quickly, whereas for others the development of a mutually trusting relationship may take longer or not occur at all.

Table 10.5. Information matrix: Nelson Gomez at 4 months of age

Emerging beliefs	Physical and affective states	Developmental skills	Coping style	Human supports	Material and environmental support
Life is difficult and not very satisfying.	Small and frail (fifth percentile height and weight) Microcephaly History of seizures Tense body Milk allergy Fussy, cries often Sleeps through the night	Developmental delay in all areas (skills around a 1-month level) Difficulty moving Fleeting visual focus on people or objects Turns to mother's voice Brings hands together and sucks fingers Cries to be fed Lifts head for short periods Sits supported with head erect for short periods Makes grunting sounds	Minimally effective coping style Passive Difficult to comfort Becomes fussy in response to noisy environment Cries when placed on back Pushes bottle and pacifier away when finished Undifferentiated crying to indicate needs	Parents are actively involved with providing for Nelson. Brother and sister (ages 2 and 3) are playful and engaging. Mother has easy-going nature and commitment to family. Parents have many other responsibilities (family and work). Mother's sister is sometimes available to babysit.	Comfortable at home with age-appropriate toys and baby furniture Some economic pressures

Family concerns

What is Nelson's disability?
What is his future?
How can his parents help him?
Why doesn't he smile?
How can the parents manage the problems of the father's adult children?

174

> 2.1.   Of the information collected, what facilitates and what interferes with the child's development and coping and the addressing of family concerns?
> 2.2.   Of the factors that interfere, what can be changed and what cannot be changed (at least in the near future)?
> 2.3.   Of the interfering factors that can be changed, what changes will make the most difference?

2.1.   Of the Information Collected, What Facilitates and What Interferes with the Child's Development and Coping and the Addressing of Family Concerns?

When the collected information is summarized and analyzed, as depicted in Tables 10.4 and 10.5, patterns frequently emerge. For example, in examining a child's developmental achievement, one may find fairly consistent performance across developmental domains, variability in levels of performance from one developmental domain to another, or variability both within and across developmental domains (i.e., scattering within a developmental area and between areas).

Analysis may also identify information that appears to be contradictory. In young children, these inconsistencies may be due to differences among the assessment instruments used, differences in the style and knowledge of persons conducting the assessment, and differences in the environments and times in which the assessment or observations took place. The conflicting data may also result from, and realistically reflect, the variability typical of many children with special needs. Teams, including parents, need to discuss any divergent data.

To determine what needs to be changed, the summarized information is studied to understand what is interfering with the child's progress. The expressed concerns of the parents are given high priority in this consideration. For example, if the parents' greatest concern is that their child is not talking, factors relating to talking are considered in depth. When analyzing information, all too often the focus is on problems, whereas strengths are not given equal attention. Identification of facilitating factors is important because they are used to develop the activities and strategies that will promote change.

Identifying Facilitating and Interfering Factors   Each child has a unique combination of resources and vulnerabilities. In identifying factors that influence development and coping, care must be taken that they are personalized for a particular child. For example, attending skills can be interpreted as either a facilitating factor or an interfering factor depending on the child's behavior. An attention span of 40 seconds might be considered an interfering factor in an 18-month-old child whose lack of focus limits play activities and task completion. In a young infant with multiple problems, the ability to attend visually for this length of time might be considered an asset or a factor that has the potential to facilitate new learning. Table 10.6 has examples of factors that can influence development in young children in either a positive or negative manner.

The specific factors influencing learning may not always be readily apparent. The child who demonstrates little variability in an overall profile of developmental skills is a typical case in which factors may be difficult to identify. For example, a child may demonstrate consistent delays across developmental domains, and the level of coping effectiveness may be relatively stable across different coping behaviors.

When the developmental profile is fairly even, that is, when there are no outstanding skills facilitating or inhibiting learning, the behaviors observed during the child's assess-

Table 10.6.   Examples of factors that facilitate or interfere with development

Developmental domain	Facilitating factors	Interfering factors
Sensory integration	Age-appropriate response to visual, auditory, and movement stimuli	Hypersensitive to touch Intolerant of handling and movement in daily care
Postural control	Normal muscle tone that provides a basis for adaptive movement. Adequate righting and equilibrium reactions to support development of gross motor skills	Atypical muscle tone Abnormal reflexes Poor head and trunk control limiting upright positions
Mobility	Use of acquired mobility skills in purposeful goal-directed activity Coordinated use of movement patterns of extension, flexion, lateral control, and rotation	Absence of independent mobility skills such as rolling, crawling, coming to sitting, and walking Limited joint range of motion interferes with trunk and limb movement
Manipulation	Presence of a variety of reach and grasp patterns Application of age-appropriate manipulative skills in play with objects.	Incoordination that interferes with functional reach and grasp Inability to adjust and grade grasp patterns according to different sizes and shapes Hemiparesis that limits ability to engage in bilateral body or toy play Limited repertoire of manipulative strategies to use with objects
Cognitive processing	Age-appropriate sensorimotor foundations for interacting with people and objects Solves simple problems encountered in the environment	Unable to generalize emerging cognitive skills to new situations (requires excessive structure and repetition for learning) Limited cognitive strategies used in a perseverative manner
Communication	Responsive to adult-initiated interaction Communicates needs through sounds, facial expression, and body movement	Limited means for making needs known Aversion of gaze when approached by an adult Hearing impairment that limits development of receptive language

ment are used to guide identification of the factors influencing learning. For example, one might observe that a child participates best in activities when seated on his or her parent's lap. In this case, the physical presence and encouragement of the parent may be a primary factor facilitating learning. Another illustration is the child who prefers visual exploration of the environment. This child's visual interest and willingness to observe might also be considered facilitative.

An example demonstrating interfering factors comes from the following observation of adult–child transactions.

➡   Jeremy's foster father hated to see and hear him cry. As a result, he was so cued into the boy that in interacting with him he was able to predict and respond to Jeremy's needs automatically and immediately. He provided almost total support and assistance. Consequently, Jeremy seemed unable to tolerate the foster father's absence or calm himself without assistance. The foster father expressed some discontent that he could never leave the boy with anyone else and take a day or night off. His negative feelings about Jeremy's crying set off a chain reaction of interfering factors (e.g., impatient, hurried caregiving; guilty feelings about his occasional display of temper).

Brainstorming techniques can be useful in stimulating the team process required to delineate factors influencing learning. In a brainstorming session, the team can list the developmental domains and the resources of the child that have been assessed (e.g., postural control, mobility, coping attributes). For each specific domain, the team considers aspects of the child's behavior that are assets for continued learning and those that appear to have a negative impact on learning. For example, after summarizing assessment data on postural control and mobility, the team may find that a child has adequate postural responses, balance, and mobility skills for his age. However, team members note that in spite of this the child does not spontaneously move about his surroundings. Two factors influencing learning emerge from these observations. First, the child demonstrates appropriate foundational skills, a factor that can be used to facilitate the refinement of motor control. Second, the child has little motivation to move; this lack of self-initiation limits interactions with the environment and is likely to interfere with learning.

The following are some general guidelines to consider when identifying factors influencing development and coping.

Goodness of fit is considered between: 1) the environmental demands and the child's capabilities, 2) the child's internal coping resources and how they are applied to coping efforts, and 3) environmental supports and the feedback regarding the child's performance.

When analyzing coping style, the child's effectiveness in using coping behaviors in specific situations is the prime determinant of whether or not the behavior facilitates or interferes with learning. Most and least adaptive coping behaviors are discussed by the team for their relevance to the child's daily living. Analysis of the child's adaptive functioning assists the team to set priorities for intervention and to identify how, when, and where intervention is conducted.

In analyzing the child's external resources, the type, quantity, quality, and availability of the resources are considered to determine whether or not they help or hinder the learning process. An example of human support that facilitates the child's learning might be the presence of an older sibling who plays with the child in a nurturing way. For another child, overstimulation resulting from a sibling presenting too many toys at one time may be a factor interfering with purposeful play.

Do the demands and expectations of caregivers and practitioners match the child's capabilities? Expectations that are too high, too low, or inconsistent in relation to the child may potentially interfere with learning.

Is the temperamental style of the child a factor facilitating or inhibiting learning? The match between the child's temperament and the demands of the environment, as well as the match between parent and child temperamental styles, are factors that influence how effectively the child copes.

Information is best analyzed when actively engaging family members in the process. Meeting with them provides the opportunity to validate and expand the summarized information as well as to analyze it. The staff can directly share the matrix form with the family or use the information to guide the discussion. In talking about the collected information, the service coordinator may use phrases such as "This is what we believe you said," or "This is what we all observed regarding . . ." Parents and practitioners may choose to complete a form that lists the factors facilitating and interfering with effective coping and development. For each factor listed, behavioral observations are given. Sample forms for the Kelly and Gomez families are provided in Tables 10.7 and 10.8.

Table 10.7. Facilitating and interfering factors: Marie Kelly at 14 months of age

Factors facilitating effective transactions		Factors interfering with effective transactions	
Factor	Behavior observed	Factor	Behavior observed
Relative strength in receptive language and cognitive skills	Understands simple directions Demonstrates object permanence Engages in turn-taking with parents	Genetic skin disorder	Scratching of itchy, peeling skin Hypersensitive to touch Appears to have limited energy
Some comparatively effective coping behaviors	Maintains visual and auditory attention Accepts help and support from parents Demonstrates pleasure when successful Uses self-protective behaviors effectively in low stress situations Enjoys observing children play (watches, smiles)	Minimally effective coping behaviors	Poor self-comforting ability Irritable and cries easily Limited self-initiation Self-protective behaviors ineffective in moderate and high stress situations Difficulty with transitions
Relative comfort in familiar home environment	Experiences some happy moments during family routine Plays for short period of time with selected toys	General developmental delay and scattering of skills	Minimal mobility Limited expressive language Avoids many fine motor activities
Some self-help skills	Uses fingers to feed self independently	Interfering beliefs: 1) world is not a safe place, and 2) parents will take care of her needs without self-initiated efforts	Interactions result in painful or unpleasant feelings Parents anticipate or react to her needs without requiring her to make any attempts on her own.
Interventions available to reduce impact of skin condition	Applying creams and lotions can decrease pain and itching Some textures and surfaces more comfortable than others		

178

Table 10.8. Facilitating and interfering factors: Nelson Gomez at 4 months of age

Factors facilitating effective transactions		Factors interfering with effective transactions	
Factor	Behavior observed	Factor	Behavior observed
Brings hands together	Occasionally able to self-comfort by sucking hands	Overall developmental delay	Developmental skills significantly below age expectations
Recognizes mother's voice	Consistently turns in mother's direction	Irritable and fussy	Cries excessively and stiffens body
			Does not like being held or cuddled
Emerging head control	Briefly lifts head in prone and holds head erect in supported sitting		Limited availability for interaction
Makes sounds	Grunting, throaty sounds	Very limited eye contact	Visual attention fleeting and occurs only occasionally
Uses some self-protective behaviors	Turns away from noise	Small and frail	Fifth percentile for height and weight
	Pushes bottle out of his mouth when feeling too stressed or tired		Head circumference less than second percentile
Signals distress by crying	Others are aware of his distress.	Passive	Little spontaneous behavior
Family committed to helping Nelson	Mother repeatedly expresses desire to take active role in helping Nelson.		
	Younger siblings try to interact with him.		

179

In some cases, sharing the summarized and/or analyzed information can be a stressful time for family and staff. It can be overwhelming for the parent if too many people are involved or if too much technical, complicated, or medical jargon is used (e.g., pincer grasp, tactile defensiveness, weight-bearing). The parents may feel very vulnerable when addressing the reality of what is being shared; some parents may react defensively. Staff members can also be quite uncomfortable when they see themselves as bearers of "bad news."

Some parents need to be encouraged to contribute and ask questions. When approached, one parent responded to the evaluation by asking, "I know it sounds stupid, but what is occupational therapy? My child is only 7 months old!" Another began by asking about children and activities she saw just before the evaluation: "Can I ask you why those children were racing in the hall lying on skateboards with just diapers on?" One parent asked quite candidly, "When and how could a diagnosis of mental retardation be made?" Those questions allowed the parent and professional to support each other. During the analysis of facilitating and interfering factors, a need for additional information may be recognized.

2.2. Of the Factors that Interfere, What Can Be Changed and What Cannot Be Changed (at Least in the Near Future)?

This question helps to identify priorities for intervention. Sometimes the response to this question is quite obvious, and other times the question may reveal previously unexamined beliefs. (See the discussion of the Kelly family later in this chapter as an illustration.)

Families are assisted to identify what they believe can be changed through supportive discussions that provide information and validate their feelings. The combination of information and validation of feelings requires that the service coordinator balances a conscientious respect for family concerns with expertise and knowledge of disabling conditions. IFSP outcomes have to be family-driven in order to be achievable. The service coordinator's role is to support the family in reaching decisions.

The response to this decision-making question can realistically narrow choices of what the child is most capable of learning and how intervention can be most successful. Interfering factors are examined to identify those behaviors that cannot be changed due to physical reasons, lack of knowledge or experience of how to change them, limited time and resources, or any other conditions outside the control of those involved. Environmental factors are also examined for their potential for change in the immediate future.

There are benefits to recognizing factors that realistically cannot be changed by early intervention services. These include developing goals that have a good potential for achievement and preventing the development of unrealistic expectations and burnout by both the family and staff. When factors cannot be changed, the intervention plan is designed to minimize the impact of these interfering factors and their related stress. In other words, the child and family are assisted to cope as effectively as possible with circumstances that cannot be changed.

In a case of recent hip surgery, for example, a child may be casted in a position that temporarily interferes with the development of independent mobility skills. Such an interfering factor cannot be altered at that time. To minimize the impact of the immobility on current development, the child can be provided with an alternate means of mobility, such as a scooter board or a hand-driven cart. In addition, age-appropriate, self-initiated behavior can be fostered in other developmental domains during the post-surgical recovery period.

2.3. Of the Interfering Factors that Can Be
Changed, What Changes Will Make the Most Difference?

This critical question establishes the long-range functional outcomes that become the major focus for intervention planning. Short-term goals (e.g., during a 6-month period) and day-to-day activities are the steps to achieve the long-range outcomes. Functional outcomes by their very meaning reflect a coping perspective. They are achieved by behavioral changes, acquisition of skills, and expansion of other resources that help the child and family live more adaptively. Functional outcomes are often facilitated when a link between family well-being and child outcomes has been established.

The interfering factors are studied to identify what will make the most difference in improving coping competence. Often, a pattern emerges among the interfering factors; for example, there may be a domino effect as one attribute triggers another behavior that in turn triggers another in a sequential chain of behaviors. Tactile hypersensitivity in a child may lead to a hypervigilant state and an excessive activity level, which in turn may lead to aggressive behaviors toward others that result in transactions that undermine meaningful relationships. In this instance, the functional outcome that would make the most difference for the child is to increase the effectiveness of interpersonal transactions. To achieve this outcome, the practitioner needs to address through short-term goals the initial interfering factor of tactile hypersensitivity that triggers this behavioral sequence (the domino effect).

Another pattern occurs when a number of interfering factors contribute to a particular problem. For example, poor independent problem solving may be due to a child's lack of skills, beliefs about self and others, the types of available support, or some combination of the three factors. Achievement of the desired functional outcome of independent problem solving would require modifying or changing these factors.

At the end of Step 2 in the personalized decision-making model, there is enough information to complete the initial two parts of the IFSP, the summary, and the long-range outcomes. The following examples of the Kelly and Gomez families describe their involvement in addressing the decision-making questions of Step 2 and include the first parts of their IFSPs.

The Kelly Family   As requested by the Kellys, the staff analyzed the information in their summary matrix and Gloria, the service coordinator, completed a form that identified the facilitating and interfering factors to Marie's development and coping (see Table 10.7). This information was shared by Gloria and the social worker at a conference with Mr. and Mrs. Kelly to develop the initial IFSP.

The meeting began by discussing the summary matrix (see Table 10.4) and the form identifying the facilitating and interfering factors. It was emphasized that these were worksheets to help organize the collected information and provide a basis for discussion. The purpose of the conference was to continue to analyze the information, to identify priorities for intervention, and to develop a plan to achieve them.

After the information about the facilitating and interfering factors was discussed with the Kelly family, the service coordinator asked them what could be changed. Looking at Gloria, the parents said quite clearly, "Why, none of those things can change." This was a moment many professionals fear when trying to establish an "equal partnership and open collaboration"— the family did not say what they wanted to hear. They did not see the opportunity for change that the team considered possible. (At this point, how does the staff validate the family's feelings and respect their position without negating the staff's own clinical judgment about the possibilities for change?)

Gloria responded to Mr. and Mrs. Kelly with another question: "If you could change something, what would it be? What, if changed, would make the most difference?" This question had a powerful effect. With their answer, the parents were able to express what they would like to have happen based on concrete information. Through further discussion, the staff and family decided the only factor that could not be changed was Marie's genetic skin condition. The factor that would make the most difference was Marie's beliefs about herself and her world. Mr. and Mrs. Kelly were encouraged to explore the meaning of these statements. They began to see the link between their well-being and Marie's behavior, which had not been evident to them before.

They looked at Marie's scores on the Early Coping Inventory. Everyone agreed that limited self-initiation was the most critical interfering factor in Marie's coping style. Through the discussion of Marie's behavior, Mr. and Mrs. Kelly had an insight as to what they could change and what would make the most difference for Marie and themselves. They said, "Marie is not like other children. She is fearful, shy, not engaging, and not willing to play. We want her to be like other children. If she is to be like other children, she must do things on her own. That would make us feel better."

The parents became aware of their belief that in order to keep Marie happy and comfortable, they had to do everything for her. They interpreted her smallest glance as a need and the slightest grimace as a command to "Do this for me"; "Get this away from me"; or "Tell these people not to touch, talk, or come near me." At one point in the discussion, Mr. Kelly said, "Wow, here we are doing everything for Marie, but thinking we are helping her. Maybe we are not giving her a chance to try to do things for herself. If Marie did more for herself, she would be like other children." Mr. and Mrs. Kelly and the staff went on to examine ways that Marie could do more. They agreed that encouraging exploration and independent play would assist her to be more age-appropriate. It would also be a step toward helping her to have more experiences that she could initiate.

The long-range outcome statement came from the parents' insights and priorities. The family and staff agreed that the following functional outcome would make the most difference to Marie and others in her life: "Marie will learn effective ways to manage the demands created by her skin condition so that she can actively interact with people and objects." If this outcome is achieved, it will enhance Marie's positive beliefs about herself and her world.

The meeting continued as they all worked on the development of the implementation plan, which is described in Chapter 11, this volume. At this point the initial two parts of the Kelly's IFSP were ready to be written. Even though they are not actually written until the end of the meeting, they are presented now to provide closure for Step 2 of the decision-making process. It is important that the IFSP is written in language that is readily understood by the family.

➡️   I.   *A summary of the development and coping capability of the child and the concerns and priorities of the family (Marie's current status at 14 months of age).* Marie has a skin disorder that causes her skin to be hot, itchy, full of blisters, and constantly peeling. She is often low in energy. Marie has difficulty breathing because of the build-up of dry skin in her nose and air passages. Her vision and hearing are normal.

Marie has difficulty doing things with her hands because touching and being touched are painful. When placed in the position by an adult, she can sit alone or stand by leaning on a chair or small table. Marie tries with difficulty to crawl short distances. She is more tolerant of touch and movement when involved with her parents in play. Although she enjoys being with other children, Marie tends to interact with them by watching.

Although Marie has delays in her development, she has relative strengths in her cognitive ability and understanding of conversation and simple directions. She communicates her wants by using limited gestures and a few sounds and words. She has her own version of "yes" and "no." When people and objects are named, Marie will look at them. Overall, her minimally effective coping behaviors limit Marie's ability to participate in activities and feel good about herself. She rarely does things on her own and is generally passive. Marie is happiest when she is doing things with her parents. In general, she tends to be fearful, withdrawn, and lacking in confidence when expected to interact with adults and children.

Family concerns and priorities: Mr. and Mrs. Kelly are concerned about how Marie compares to children of her age. They are uncertain what to expect from Marie and what her future abilities may be. Mr. and Mrs. Kelly want her to do things that other children do. A major priority is to acquire more strategies for managing her behavior and skin condition. They also want her to be able to walk independently.

II. Long-range functional outcome: Marie will learn effective ways to manage the demands created by her skin condition so that she can actively interact with people and objects.

The Gomez Family   After Nelson had been in the program for a month, Mr. and Mrs. Gomez met with the staff to develop the initial IFSP. The staff and Mrs. Gomez shared the information that they had summarized in the matrix with the father, who previously had limited opportunity to be involved (see Table 10.5). Mrs. Gomez said she understood and agreed with the information; she had been active in the evaluation process. Together, they analyzed the information and discussed the factors facilitating and interfering with Nelson's development and coping (see Table 10.8).

Through the discussion of these factors it was clear that Nelson was a child with a significant disability. However, when they talked about the interfering factors that could be changed, Mrs. Gomez optimistically stated her belief that the only factor that could not be changed was Nelson's physical condition. She added that even his physical problems may be diminished if they knew more specifically what caused them. Although the staff had some concerns about these expectations, they respected the importance of maintaining a sense of optimism regarding his potential for development.

As they continued to address the decision-making questions, they all agreed about what would make the most immediate difference for helping Nelson. Because he had limited internal resources, intervention needed to emphasize the acquisition of functionally relevant skills. To achieve this desired outcome, they generated the following long-range outcome: Nelson will acquire basic motor, social, and communication skills that support more effective transactions with his environment. Another priority for Mr. and Mrs. Gomez was to stabilize their family life. They wanted to learn how to meet Nelson's special needs without making him the primary focus of the family. They also recognized that unless they agreed on a strategy for managing the problems of Mr. Gomez's older sons, the tensions would be disruptive to their relationship as well as the well-being of the younger children.

The remainder of the meeting focused on the development of the implementation plan, which is described in Chapter 11, this volume. Following are the initial two parts of Nelson's IFSP. They reflect the first two steps in the decision-making process.

➡   *I. A summary of the development and coping capability of the child and the concerns and priorities of the family (Nelson's current status at 4 months of age):* Nelson had seizures shortly after birth that were eventually controlled by phenobarbital. The medication was discontinued at 3 months of age. Physically, Nelson is small and frail. His head circumference, less than the second percentile, can be described as microcephalic. He tends to be irritable and difficult to comfort. Nelson has milk allergies that cause colic and gastrointestinal problems. His muscle tone is low, which results in poor head control and weak feeding abilities. Usually he tires before feeding is completed due to the great effort required to suck and swallow.

Nelson is delayed in all developmental areas. He lifts his head very briefly while lying on his abdomen and when held in a supported sitting position. He fleetingly focuses on objects and people. He does not smile, but brightens when he makes visual contact, especially with his mother. He seems to recognize her voice and occasionally makes sounds in response to her. Nelson demonstrates low tolerance for stimulating sounds and light. He frequently becomes upset, arches his body, and cries unconsolably.

Family concerns and priorities: Mr. and Mrs. Gomez are feeling stress because of Nelson's multiple problems. Medical consultations to date have resulted in conflicting information without yielding a specific diagnosis. They want to gain a better understanding of the nature and cause of Nelson's condition and what it means for his future. They are concerned that the caregiving requirements for Nelson are very demanding and take a disproportionate amount of attention away from their other children. They are also concerned about his weak sucking and whether he is receiving adequate nutrition. In additon, Mr. and Mrs. Gomez would like to achieve a mutually acceptable approach for coping with their two older sons.

II. *Long-range functional outcome:* Nelson will acquire the basic motor, social, and communication skills needed to have more effective transactions with his environment.

SUMMARY

In this chapter, the IFSP is introduced, as well as a personalized decision-making model for developing service plans from a coping perspective. The decision-making questions from the first two steps of the process are discussed with examples from two families.

CHAPTER 11

Completing the IFSP

Developing the 6-Month Implementation Plan

The development of an IFSP from a coping perspective is a three-step process. Chapter 10 described the first two steps: 1) collecting and sharing information, and 2) analyzing information and setting long-range functional outcomes. These two steps generate an understanding of the development and coping capability of the child, identify the concerns and priorities of the family, and determine one or more long-range functional outcomes for intervention. Achievement of this long-range outcome will make the most difference in the child being optimally adaptive over time. The challenge in the third step is to translate this information into a 6-month implementation plan.

In this chapter, the IFSP is completed by responding to the decision-making questions in Step 3. The examples of the Kelly and Gomez families are continued from Chapter 10. In addition, the Kellys' subsequent IFSPs are presented to show how Marie progressed over time toward achieving her long-range functional outcome. Her last IFSP includes the procedure for her transition to a preschool program.

DEVELOPING AN IMPLEMENTATION PLAN

> 3.1. What short-term goals will move the child toward achieving the long-range functional outcome and address the concerns and priorities of the family?
>
> 3.2. What services, strategies, and activities can help the child and family achieve these outcomes?
>
> 3.3. How can the plan be evaluated?
>
> 3.4. What procedures will be used to update the plan or to support transition from the program?

Implementation plans are developed within the context of an early intervention system and existing community resources. As documented in Public Law 101-476 (Individuals with Disabilities Education Act of 1990), early intervention services must be provided to the maximum extent appropriate in natural environments in which children without disabilities participate. Available sites generally include, but are not limited to, center-based programs, the home, and daycare environments.

Early intervention programs vary widely in the variety of choices they offer. Programs that have a full complement of educational, therapeutic, psychosocial, and health-related services may be able to meet most of the special requirements of the child and family. Others may depend substantially on services and practitioners within the community. There may be a need for social services, such as food assistance (Women, Infants, and Children Supplemental Food Program [WIC]), income assistance (Supplemental Security Income [SSI]), medical support (Medicaid), and community-based activities sponsored by religious and other organizations. When indicated, the service coordinator helps to identify and integrate the needed support. Recognition of the range of program and community resources establishes a context for addressing the questions in Step 3.

3.1.   What Short-Term Goals Will Move the Child Toward Achieving the Long-Range Functional Outcome and Address the Concerns and Priorities of the Family?

Short-term goals, usually written for a 6-month period, focus on modifying or eliminating interfering factors and acquiring new behaviors that move the child closer to achieving the long-range functional outcome. Short-term outcomes for the family are dictated by their concerns and priorities directly related to caring for their child or that indirectly influence caregiving because of their impact on family function.

The planning of short-term goals starts with examination of the child's interfering factors. In Step 2, the interfering factors were identified, analyzed, and their potential for change considered. This process of analysis led to the determination of the long-range functional outcome. In Step 3, the interfering factors are re-examined to plan short-term goals for change. The three intervention options (modify demands, enhance coping resources, and provide appropriate feedback) serve as the basic structure for planning (see chap. 7, this volume).

Long-range functional outcomes are usually expressed in broad, integrated statements, such as "to be flexible in stressful situations" or "to engage in developmentally appropriate social interactions." These broad statements have to be translated into short-term goals and objectives that identify the specific skills to be learned. To do this, it is necessary to analyze the task (the long-range outcome) and determine what behaviors are used to accomplish it. These required behaviors are compared to what the child is presently able to do and what still needs to be learned. Task analysis and behavior analysis help to identify what specifically has to be addressed in the short-term goals and objectives.

Task analysis is the process of breaking down a task into smaller, more achievable component skills. It has two parts: 1) identifying the prerequisite skills needed to perform the desired task, and 2) identifying the steps for learning the task from the easiest to the most difficult. After the components and requirements of learning the task have been analyzed, behavior analysis is used to determine the child's ability to perform the prerequisite skills.

Behavior analysis involves systematic observation of how the child presently behaves in the targeted area. Observation includes identifying antecedents and consequences of the behavior as well as the circumstances in which the child performs best. Antecedents include any circumstances occurring immediately before the behavior is demonstrated. Consequences reflect the results of the behavior and indicate the possible meaning and value of the behavior for the child. This information comes from observation of the child's coping transactions. Task and behavior analyses are important for generating short-term goals that address any of the three intervention options.

Modifying demands, the first intervention option, involves writing short-term goals that provide the child with developmentally appropriate stress. Demands and expectations are slightly beyond the child's immediate ability, but are within reach. In this way, intervention starts at the child's present developmental level and gradually progresses the child to the next level of functioning. The child is therefore motivated and fueled by success.

Short-term goals can also be written to *enhance coping resources,* the second intervention option (i.e., emerging beliefs, physical and affective states, developmental skills, coping style, human support, material and environmental support). It is helpful to think of intervention in this area as short-term goals that are designed to: 1) acquire developmental skills that are linked to functional application, 2) increase the effectiveness of particular coping behaviors, and 3) manage specific pragmatic situations of daily living.

A criterion for selecting developmental skills for intervention is answering the question: "How will this skill be a meaningful contribution to the child's ability to cope with self and the environment?" If the answer is not clear or is too vague, the skill is probably not pertinent to the life demands of the child. Deriving goals directly from developmental scales may lead to artificial and superficial intervention. The example of Norman demonstrates the importance of achieving a developmental skill as a vehicle to enhance coping capability. It was essential for Norman to acquire the developmental skill of "being able to walk while carrying an object" because he was emotionally conflicted about becoming more independent. He tended to be very demanding and clinging with his mother. Acquiring this motor skill assisted Norman to learn to balance independent with dependent behavior (e.g., being able to help his mother with household chores such as dusting furniture) and increased his feelings of security (e.g., holding a comforting blanket during the day when his mother was busy).

It is often critical to have short-term goals that address the child's ineffective coping behaviors. The Early Coping Inventory is useful in identifying the coping behaviors most critical for adaptive functioning. However, the items in this instrument are presented in general terms and do not describe a child's unique behavioral characteristics. Therefore, the items as written should not be used directly as short-term goal statements. "The child actively participates in situations" is an item from the inventory that exemplifies this point. This broad statement does not describe how the child participates (e.g., what the child does, in what situation, and how effectively). Translation of this coping behavior for a particular child may be "Dottie will participate in action songs during circle time." Objectives would describe the steps to achieve this goal and provide desired standards for performance.

As indicated earlier, the child's developmental capabilities are always taken into account in goal setting. That is, consideration is given to whether or not the child has prerequisite developmental skills to implement coping efforts. For example, an intervention team determines that a goal for two different children, Tim and Juan, should focus on their ability "to initiate action to communicate a need." Tim is currently inconsistent in using any behaviors to communicate (minimally effective). In order for Tim to demonstrate achievement of this coping goal, he will first have to learn to use gaze, swiping movements, head movements, or some other action that can be applied communicatively in coping efforts. Juan, however, already uses several gestures to communicate. He has acquired some skills, but they are only used in some situations for coping (situationally effective). For Juan, a desired outcome of intervention might be generalization of previously acquired gestures in a variety of situations. Tim's short-term goal may be written as: "Tim will make eye contact with an adult when positioned with head in midline and called by name." Juan's short-term goal may be stated as: "Juan will use differentiated gestures (manual signs) to communicate his need for food or drink."

Just as short-term goals can be based on modifying demands and enhancing coping resources, they can also reflect the third intervention option of *providing appropriate, contingent feedback* to the child's coping efforts. The goal is typically related to enhancing parent-child transactions. The focus is on helping the parent to provide appropriate feedback based on an expanded awareness of the child's behavioral patterns and cues. An example is the experience of Mr. Simmons and his 13-month-old daughter, Hattie Sue, who has a number of different babbling sounds depending on her mood.

➡ Hattie Sue vocalizes differently when she is excited, sad, frustrated, or playful. Each of these emotions is accompanied by different body movements and facial expressions. These signals are generally not recognized by the father. Mr. Simmons responds to Hattie Sue the same way regardless of her mood. Her seemingly inconsistent reactions to him are confusing, and he has commented that "I can't wait for Hattie Sue to be able to talk and tell me what she wants." A short-term goal was developed with Mr. Simmons for Hattie Sue's IFSP. He wanted to better recognize the range of Hattie Sue's behavioral expressions in order to respond appropriately. (See chap. 7, this volume, for further discussion of Intervention Option 3.)

For some families, it is important for the well-being of the child and the entire family that certain pragmatic situations related to daily living be managed more satisfactorily. In this case, short-term goals can be written to manage these specific situations. For example, when Lizzie cries hysterically during bathtime, the entire family suffers. The negative energy Lizzie puts into this routine task particularly interferes with mutually gratifying parent–child interaction. The challenge is for the parent to modify the routine in some way that Lizzie can better cope with the situation. An initial objective may be: "Lizzie will engage in water play for 5 minutes without crying." To achieve this objective, the parent may initially have to separate getting Lizzie clean (i.e., by use of a sponge bath) from time spent in the water.

Another example relates to the bedtime routine. Mrs. Jenkins wants Sylvester, an only child, to be asleep by 7 P.M. because her husband looks forward to a quiet dinner with his wife when he returns home at 7:30 P.M. Sylvester tends to fuss and resist going to bed. The development of a short-term goal to manage this situation more effectively would have to be a collaborative effort with the parents to determine if they want to modify the adults' routine, the child's routine, or some combination of both. For example, the parents may want assistance with how to regulate Sylvester's afternoon nap so that he will be ready for a 7 P.M. bedtime. Another possibility would involve creating a transition routine to prepare Sylvester for bed and avoid overstimulation. As another option, the parents may wish to participate in a series of meetings to explore how they can be mutually responsive to the new demands of having a child in the family. The appropriate translation of long-range functional outcomes into short-term goals and objectives is critical to the development of a meaningful IFSP.

3.2.   What Services, Strategies, and Activities
Can Help the Child and Family Achieve These Outcomes?

The parents and practitioners plan together the types of services that can best meet the child's short-term goals and assist the family to address their priorities. Services may involve various activities within an early intervention program and the community. For instance, the child may receive individual or group educational and therapeutic experiences at a community center, special program, childcare site, or home. The child may need the services of a particular specialist within the community for diagnosis, consultation, or intervention. Family members may be interested in becoming active in parent-to-parent networks. The service coordinator works with the family to identify resources and facilitate their integration into the IFSP. Once the required services are decided, the next consideration is to determine what strategies and activities can be used to adapt the programs and services to be most responsive to the child and family. These interventions are generated from identified strengths; that is, factors that facilitate effective coping. The list of facilitating factors is studied to match specific strengths with an objective. For example, one objective for Marie Kelly is that she indicates verbally when she wants to stop an activity before losing her emotional composure. Two of her strengths can be used to achieve this objective—she can say her version of "yes" and "no" and she can understand simple directions. A promising strategy is to use questioning to help her to self-regulate. For example, when Marie starts to look upset, she can be asked "Do you want to stop?" When she verbally responds, she can be reinforced with praise.

Another illustration of using a facilitating factor to develop an intervention strategy is the case of an infant who was only visually attentive to sound-producing objects. Therefore, toys such as rattles, chiming bells, and musical mobiles were used to expand his cognitive and motor skills. Similar toys were employed to engage him at the beginning of intervention sessions or parent–child play encounters. They served to harness his interest and establish rapport before new activities were introduced. The strategy was to use familiar, motivating objects to capture the child's visual and auditory attention. Intervention strategies and activities are discussed in detail in Chapters 7 and 8, this volume.

The plan to achieve the short-term goals and objectives has to be clear and concrete so that everyone involved knows what to do. The process of implementation has to be flexible enough so the plan can be modified as the child or situation changes. The responsibility for addressing some short-term goals may be delegated to one practitioner or the parents. More frequently, however, parents and staff share in implementing the strategies and activities. When they are designed for use by the parents, it is important that they are compatible with the family's interactional style, schedule, and home environment. There is a range of possible strategies and activities that can foster achievement of any goal and objective. The best choices are based on the unique strengths of the child, family, and practitioner.

3.3. How Can the Plan Be Evaluated?

An IFSP is only as good as the results it generates; therefore, the plan has to include methods and criteria to evaluate change. Both formative and summative evaluation is involved in this process.

In most early intervention programs, formative evaluation occurs on an ongoing informal basis. It provides feedback about how and what the child is learning and guides ongoing modification of the child's implementation plan. Methods used for formative evaluation include keeping records, making observational notes, using checklists, holding case conferences, and testing small units of behavior. Formative evaluation can take place daily, weekly, at the completion of a specific activity, or during routine team meetings or conferences. All interested parties participate in the formative evaluation with major contributions from family members. In an ongoing fashion the following questions need to be asked: "Is this working? Is it helpful?"

Summative evaluation is usually conducted at the end of a fixed time period, such as at 6-month intervals. This type of evaluation involves gathering information needed to make judgments about the child's progress and the effectiveness of the implementation plan. Typical evaluation methods include comparison of the child's behavior against established criteria (attainment of goals and objectives), using formal assessment instruments to evaluate progress, clinical observation, and parent reports. The completed IFSPs in this chapter show how evaluation statements are included after each short-term goal.

3.4. What Procedures Will Be Used to Update the Plan or to Support Transition from the Program?

Depending on the age of the child at the end of the 6-month period, a new plan is needed to update the existing one or to address how transition will be accomplished from the present program. The IFSP includes the necessary procedures.

Updating the Plan   Updating is based on evaluation of the existing IFSP and the identification of any additional concerns the family or staff may have. If the short-term goals and objectives were met, and before new ones are developed, it is important to consider whether their achievement actually made a functional difference in the child's coping ability. The following guides are useful for evaluating the relevance of the objective and its contribution to the child's functional competence. Such an analysis helps parents and professionals to target their efforts in increasingly meaningful ways.

1. In retrospect, the objective is not relevant for expanding the child's functional competence and facilitating learning.
2. Accomplishment of the objective is somewhat relevant to learning and functional competence.
3. Accomplishment of the objective has a high degree of relevance to function and contributes significantly to the child's learning.

If a short-term goal or objective is not achieved or only partially achieved, it is valuable to understand why. Lack of achievement may be related to child factors, program factors, or the appropriateness of the goals and objectives as originally perceived. The following list offers the major reasons for the lack of achievement.

The goal or objective is too advanced for the child.
The time period for expected achievement is not realistic.
The child made relevant progress in the skill area, but it is not reflected by the objective statement.
The objective as written is not a teachable behavior.
The objective's behavior is teachable, but there was minimal response to the intervention.
There was limited opportunity for reinforcement of the objective.
Additional strategies and teaching techniques are needed to achieve the objective.
The objective's behavior is determined to be unchangeable at this time.
Poor attendance by the child limited the opportunity to learn the desired behavior.
The services needed to facilitate objective attainment were deferred until a later time.

Identifying the reasons for inadequate achievement of goals and objectives facilitates the development of new ones that are more responsive to the child's status. The personalized decision-making model is again used to translate this new information into an updated IFSP. The case examples later in this chapter illustrate the plan for updating the IFSP when the child is going to continue in the program.

Making a Transition Plan   Family and staff need to plan for transition long before the child reaches the age when he or she is no longer eligible for early intervention services. Transition planning often evokes a range of emotions for the parents. If the child is to be placed in an inclusive environment, the parents may feel happy that their child has become more like other children but anxious as to whether the child can cope with this new set of demands. If the child is being considered for a special placement, the parents may reconfront the meaning of the child's disability in their present and future life. Related emotions may be felt by the practitioners regarding their perception of the success or failure of their early intervention efforts and their expectations for the child. During the transition process, the practitioners need to be aware of these diverse emotional issues.

The Zero to Three/National Center for Clinical Infant Programs convened a meeting of parents from 15 states to discuss transition planning. They created a pamphlet that includes the following recommendations for supporting families (National Center for Clinical Infant Programs, 1989).

1. Inform parents of all the choices currently available to them in their community (e.g., private preschool education, Head Start, integrated preschool). Also inform them of their parental rights and responsibilities.
2. Provide this information up to a year before transitioning to a new program. Some programs have extended waiting lists and early application is required for acceptance. Agencies are encouraged to target and refer to a variety of preschool settings to ensure appropriate placements for children.
3. Arrange oportunities for parents to visit potential sites, if they choose.
4. Arrange opportunities for parents to meet parents of children enrolled in the potential sites, if they choose.
5. Assist parents in evaluating programs for appropriate placement.
6. Assist parents in completing forms, applications, compiling records, etc., at the parent's request.
7. Assist the family in gaining access to the new program (e.g., securing transportation, funding).
8. Accompany parents to case conference meetings, Individualized Education Plan meetings or other intake meetings, upon the family's request.
9. Provide consultation (e.g., physical, occupational and speech therapies as needed) to the new program provider during the transition period.
10. Arrange for coordination of follow-up services from other community agencies currently involved.
11. Assist the family in advocating for the most appropriate program and services for the child.
12. Remain as a resource for the family should any future need arise. This should include periodic follow-up with the family.

In the IFSP, activities are identified for facilitating the child's transition to another service delivery system. A sample workshop for parents on transition planning that responds to many of the preceding recommendations is outlined in Appendix B at the end of this book. In addition, the last IFSP for Marie Kelly includes her transition plan.

At the completion of this third step in the IFSP process, all necessary information and decisions will have been made to conclude the writing of the service plan. It will then be ready for signature by parents and practitioners.

In summary, the IFSP is designed to expand the developmental and coping effectiveness of the child and to enhance the resources of the family as they pertain to the child's development. It attempts to achieve a thoughtful match between identified priorities and resources. The IFSP process provides opportunities for mutual collaboration, learning, and development of trust. Coping with this process may be stressful because it can be interpreted as both a threat and a challenge. The varied transactions involved in decision-making provide experiences that are intrinsic components of intervention. They can help prepare parents to cope with other decision-making situations encountered in daily living.

INITIAL IFSP FOR MARIE KELLY

At the time her IFSP was developed, Marie Kelly was already involved in a 2-hour weekly early intervention group. This initial placement allowed for sequential assessment over time during the step of collecting and sharing information. In the first part of the IFSP meeting described in Chapter 10 (this volume), the information was analyzed and a long-range functional outcome was identified—Marie will learn effective ways to manage the demands created by her skin condition so that she can actively interact with people and objects.

During the short period of time preceding this meeting, the Kellys and the staff had observed Marie's passivity; therefore, they pursued an initial plan to foster self-initiated exploration by having her do more tasks on her own. The rationale for this approach was the shared belief that she had the capability to be more independent, but that she did not want to. It was decided that if adults would not help her, she would eventually become more independent. Although this strategy works for some children, it did not take into consideration the problems generated by Marie's skin condition.

During the first few sessions, Marie was allowed to cry and fuss; no assistance was offered and her behavior was ignored. The result of implementing this strategy to improve self-initiation was increased negative behavior and an even less motivated child. Mrs. Kelly was becoming depressed about the program and working with Marie; Mr. Kelly was becoming angry. The parents and staff soon recognized that this intervention strategy would not be effective. As the IFSP meeting continued, Mr. and Mrs. Kelly, Gloria (the occupational therapist), and the social worker examined what the demand for self-initiation meant to Marie in light of the other demands she routinely faced. They also looked at the demands the parents had to cope with on a daily basis. Then they considered what resources the family had available to manage these demands. Next they examined how staff, family, friends, and strangers reacted to Marie's behavior and efforts. What emerged was enlightening and a vital breakthrough in working together.

As they considered the nature of the demand—to do things alone—they realized that there were significant factors interfering with Marie's ability to manage demands. At least one of these factors, the presence of a skin condition, could not be changed, but could be managed. Also not known was the degree to which Marie's skin condition made tactile experiences intolerable for her. They explored the inherent life demand of having to touch and be touched as well as the resources available to meet this demand. Each intervention option was considered. The demand could be modified—she could possibly interact in some situations by looking (a strength) rather than touching. Developmental skills and other coping resources could be built upon. For instance, she could use her communication skills, as limited as they were, to help control her experiences. In addition, a contingent adult response could support Marie's efforts to do things on her own. The parents and practitioners decided that if Marie could better communicate her feelings she would have more control over managing threatening demands. Versions of "yes" and "no" were within her vocabulary, and appropriate use of these words coupled with contingent adult responses would give Marie a new sense of control. Through using existing skills Marie could significantly change her coping behaviors.

These deductions led to the establishment of the first short-term goal: Marie will learn that she can control her interactions with the environment by communicating her needs in an effective manner. To achieve this goal, objectives had to build upon existing behaviors and intervention strategies had to be generated from her strengths. The following display, which is used in the IFSP document, shows the relationship among objectives, strengths, and strategies.

Objectives	Strengths	Strategies
1. Marie will ask for help or express fears using an appropriate word or gesture.	Anticipates events Understands simple cause and effect Uses several words Enjoys being with other children	Tell Marie what is going to happen next. Use other children to model for Marie. Ask, "Do you need help?" Respond appropriately.
2. Marie will verbally indicate that she wants to stop an activity.	Says her version of "yes" and "no" Understands simple directions	Observe Marie and note her cues (looking away, whimpering, pulling back). Ask, "Do you want to stop?" or "Have you finished?" Do this before she becomes visibly distressed.

The second short-term goal was designed to help Marie interact with the environment in less painful ways. It was stated as follows: Marie will interact with persons and objects in ways that cause minimal or no discomfort. The first objective to meet this goal capitalized on her visual strength by learning to be involved with other children without touching. This objective stated that: Marie will participate in group activities that do not involve direct physical contact with other children (onlooker role). The second objective, to increase her adaptive ability to play in different places, was written as: Marie will increase her tolerance for new surfaces by playing on three different types of floors. The behavioral strengths and intervention strategies to implement these objectives are found in Marie's completed IFSP that follows this section.

Because Mr. and Mrs. Kelly were concerned that Marie did not walk independently, the third short-term goal pertained to transitional movement and walking. It read as follows: Marie will use self-initiated movement (transition into standing and walking) to play on her own or near other children. Two objectives were identified to achieve this short-term goal: 1) Marie will move from lying to sitting and to standing by herself, and 2) Marie will walk short distances when she is supported by another person or a push toy.

In addition, Marie's parents wanted more information about her skin condition and effective ways to manage it. To assist them to achieve this outcome, the following statement was written in the IFSP: Mr. and Mrs. Kelly want to know how to help Marie be more comfortable and easier to manage. This issue would involve acquiring information about Marie's skin condition and its impact on her behavior, developmentally appropriate activities for Marie, and management strategies to handle her skin care and related activities.

The weekly early intervention group that Marie was attending was deemed appropriate for Marie and her mother. Marie was motivated by the other children and liked being with them. Mrs. Kelly was interested in participating in the concurrent parent support group because she felt isolated from other adults. Due to his heavy work schedule, including evening hours, Mr. Kelly indicated that he would attend periodic conferences related to Marie's needs and progress. Both Mr. and Mrs. Kelly wanted to attend the child development workshop offered by the program.

Due to the severity of Marie's condition, everyone agreed on the need for additional therapeutic services; it was believed that this need would be best met by one practitioner functioning in a transdisciplinary manner. Gloria, Marie's occupational therapist and service coordinator, was chosen because of her expertise and increasing rapport with Marie and the Kellys. Individual occupational therapy services were scheduled twice a week.

Each short-term goal included a method for evaluating its achievement. For Marie's plan, the methods of choice were predominantly observation and parent report. Because Marie was expected to continue in the early intervention program, the IFSP included a plan for updates. Marie's completed initial IFSP is included on the following pages. The cover sheet outlines the four sections of the plan and includes a place for the signatures of everyone involved.

Individualized Family Service Plan

Child's Name: ___Marie___   Parent's Names: __Mr. and Mrs. Kelly__
Date of Birth: _____   Address: _____
Chronological Age: ___14 months___   _____
Date of Referral: _____   _____
Service Coordinator: ___Gloria___   Home Phone: _____
                                           Work Phone: _____

This plan includes:
   I. A summary of the development and coping capability of the child and the concerns and priorities of the family.
  II. Long-range functional outcomes that will increase the child's development and coping capability and enhance supportive family resources.
 III. A 6-month implementation plan with short-term goals directed to achieving the long-range functional outcomes.
     • The program and community services for the child and family.
     • Short-term goals and objectives with strategies and activities to achieve them.
     • Evaluation procedures.
 IV. Plan for update or transition.

Signatures

_____   _____   _____   _____
Parent/Guardian   Date   Service Coordinator   Date

_____   _____   _____   _____
                               Date   Date

_____   _____   _____   _____
                               Date   Date

I. A Summary of the Development and Coping Capability of the Child and the Concerns and Priorities of the Family

Marie's present status (age 14 months): Marie has a skin disorder that causes her skin to be hot, itchy, full of blisters, and constantly peeling. She is often low in energy. Marie has difficulty breathing because of the build-up of dry skin in her nose and air passages. Her vision and hearing are normal.

    Marie has difficulty doing things with her hands because touching and being touched are painful. When placed in the position by an adult, she can sit alone or stand by leaning on a chair or small table. Marie tries with difficulty to crawl short distances. She is more tolerant of touch and movement when involved with her parents in play. Although she enjoys being with other children, Marie tends to interact with them by watching.

    Although Marie has delays in her development, she has relative strengths in her cognitive ability and understanding of conversation and simple directions. She communicates her wants by using limited gestures and a few sounds and words. She has her own version of "yes" and "no." When people and objects are named, Marie will look at them. Overall, her minimally effective coping behaviors limit Marie's ability to participate in activities and feel good about herself. She rarely does things on her own and is generally passive. Marie is happiest when she is doing things with her parents. In general, she tends to be fearful, withdrawn, and lacking in confidence when expected to interact with adults and children.

Family concerns and priorities: Mr. and Mrs. Kelly are concerned about how Marie compares to children of her age. They are uncertain about what to expect from Marie and what her future abilities may be. Mr. and Mrs. Kelly want her to do things that other children do. A major priority is to acquire more strategies for managing her behavior and skin condition. They also want her to be able to walk independently.

II. Long-Range Functional Outcome

Marie will learn effective ways to manage the demands created by her skin condition so that she can actively interact with people and objects.

III. 6-Month Implementation Plan

- *Program and community services for the child and family*
  1. Enrollment in the early intervention group on a weekly basis
  2. One hour of individual occupational therapy two times a week
- *Short-term goals and objectives*

Short-Term Goal 1: Marie will learn that she can control her interactions with the environment by communicating her needs in an effective manner.

Objectives	Strengths	Strategies
1. Marie will ask for help or express fears using an appropriate word or gesture.	Anticipates events Understands simple cause and effect Uses several words Enjoys being with other children	Tell Marie what is going to happen next. Use other children to model for Marie. Ask, "Do you need help?" Respond appropriately.
2. Marie will verbally indicate that she wants to stop an activity.	Says her version of "yes" and "no" Understands simple directions	Observe Marie and note her cues (looking away, whimpering, pulling back). Ask, "Do you want to stop?" or "Have you finished?" Do this before she becomes visibly distressed.

Evaluation: Developmental assessment and report by parents and staff

Short-Term Goal 2: Marie will interact with persons and objects in ways that cause minimal or no discomfort.

Objectives	Strengths	Strategies
1. Marie will participate in group activities that do not involve direct physical contact with other children (onlooker role).	Engages socially by smiling Visual attention to persons and objects Enjoys watching other children	Seat Marie in the group where she can be socially involved but not feel physically threatened. Emphasize verbal and musical activities that she can participate in as an equal. Encourage interaction with specific children whom she considers her "best friends."
2. Marie will increase her tolerance for new surfaces by playing on three different types of floors.	Tolerance level improves when engaged in play Will sit where placed	Determine Marie's tolerance to different floor surfaces according to their physical properties (e.g., prefers smooth, cool surfaces such as vinyl flooring). Grade exposure to different surfaces (e.g., experience "rougher" surfaces such as rugs when well rested and wearing clothes that cover most of the skin; grade time spent on new surfaces). Have Marie choose her play space and preferred toys. Introduce lively activities on moveable surfaces according to comfort level (e.g., vestibular board, large therapy ball).

Evaluation: Observation and report by parent and staff

Short-Term Goal 3: Marie will use self-initiated movement (transition into standing and walking) to play on her own or near other children.

Objectives	Strengths	Strategies
1. Marie will move from lying to sitting and to standing by herself.	Visual attention to persons and things Can maintain a sitting position	Use favorite toys to encourage movement. Use praise to reinforce efforts.
2. Marie will walk short distances when she is supported by another person or push toy.	Can stand when leaning on a chair or table Enjoys being involved with other children	Demonstrate desired activities with other children, giving Marie a chance to observe. Present toys and activities that require large movements in the play area (e.g., pull toys, push toys, tunnels, suspended balloons).

Evaluation: Developmental assessment.

Short-Term Goal 4:   Mr. and Mrs. Kelly want to know how to help Marie be more comfortable and easier to manage.

Priorities	Preferred activities
Mr. and Mrs. Kelly want to: 1) acquire more information about Marie's skin condition and its impact on her behavior, 2) learn about developmentally appropriate activities for Marie, and 3) learn additional caregiving strategies to manage Marie's skin condition	Work with staff to secure information about Marie's diagnosis and its ramifications.
	Attend child development workshop.
	Participate in parent support group.
	Collaborate with staff to determine management strategies for Marie's behavior and skin care.

Evaluation: Parent feedback

IV. Plan for Update

Activity	Persons responsible	When
1. Evaluate outcome of plan and determine Marie's present status.	Mr. and Mrs. Kelly and staff	Six months from initial IFSP
2. Review Marie's progress, identify ongoing or new family priorities, and analyze facilitating and interfering factors.	Mr. and Mrs. Kelly and service coordinator	Six months from initial IFSP
3. Develop new IFSP.	Service cordinator, staff, and family	Six months from initial IFSP

INITIAL IFSP FOR NELSON GOMEZ

At the IFSP meeting discussed in Chapter 10, this volume, the following long-range out-come was determined for Nelson Gomez: Nelson will acquire the basic motor, social, and communication skills needed to have more effective transactions with his environment. The next step in this meeting was to develop the short-term goals and objectives that would move him toward achieving this desired outcome. The early intervention staff worked with Mr. and Mrs. Gomez to identify short-term goals that would be most meaningful.

Nelson was a medically fragile infant with very poor sensorimotor organization. He had little ability to regulate his psycho-physiological functions and to integrate his sensory and motor systems. Of particular concern was his irritability, hyperreactivity to sensory input, and limited motor control. As a consequence, he could not develop even minimally effective coping skills and achieve a level of homeostasis that allowed him to attend and learn. A major priority, therefore, was to help him develop the organization necessary for self-regulation. Everyone agreed that the first short-term goal would be: Nelson will in-crease his ability to self-regulate with adult assistance and the support of adapted positioning.

Conversation turned next to identifying what Nelson would need to be able to do to interact more successfully. Mrs. Gomez mentioned that Nelson was beginning to lift his head and look around. He would turn his head toward her voice and occasionally make sounds. It was important to her that Nelson recognize and smile at her. This led to a second short-term goal: Nelson will interact with people and objects through sustained looking, smiling, and vocalizing.

Limited motor skills also restricted Nelson's ability to engage, interact, and explore. It was clear that expanding his motor control was critical for adaptive functioning. Mrs. Gomez said, "If Nelson were able to be more active, he would come alive and wouldn't be such an unhappy baby." As a consequence, the third short-term goal was written: Nelson will begin to use movement as a way to explore his body and connect to the world around him.

It was agreed that the supported sitting position in an infant seat or on an adult's lap and the prone-on-elbows position on a small, cushioned roll would be emphasized. These positions encouraged the desired movements of the head and trunk that could be har-nessed for purposeful use. In the infant seat, for instance, he could start to develop the midline-oriented play typically seen in 4-month-old infants (e.g., bringing hands together and to the mouth, plucking on clothes, resting hands on the bottle while nursing). Like-wise, objects such as rattles and squeeze toys could foster development of early play schemes (e.g., banging, shaking, squeezing, swiping).

Feeding was also a major concern. Nelson's difficulty sucking generated frustration in both the child and the parents. The enormous effort required for Nelson to suck often caused him to fatigue and stop feeding before he was satiated; therefore, the boy was chronically hungry and irritable. The amount of time spent trying to nourish Nelson de-prived Mrs. Gomez of the time she greatly needed to attend to personal and other family needs. A feeding program in close collaboration with the pediatrician was reflected in the fourth short-term goal: Nelson will increase his nutritional intake. Up to this point, Nelson's short-term goals focused on helping him to be organized, interactive, purpose-fully engaged, and well fed.

Mr. Gomez explained during the meeting that because he was a long distance truck driver and spent long hours on the road, he could not participate as actively as he would like in raising Nelson. Mrs. Gomez had major responsibility for Nelson's daily care as well as most other family activities. Therefore, attention was placed on adapting the environment for Nelson and easing the demands of caregiving. This priority was reflected in the fifth short-term goal of the IFSP as: Mr. and Mrs. Gomez want to learn ways to manage Nelson and still be responsive to the needs of the rest of the family. This issue was addressed in several ways. The Gomezes believed that they still did not have adequate information regarding the specific nature of Nelson's problem despite visits to several physicians. As a result, they worried a lot about him and his future. It was decided during the IFSP meeting that a referral was needed to a specialized pediatric neurologist to confirm a medical diagnosis.

It was also agreed that early intervention services should focus on assisting Mrs. Gomez to manage Nelson's daily care with greater ease and time efficiency. They decided that one practitioner would go to the Gomez residence for one hour twice a week for 2 months. The sessions would be very practical—caring for Nelson (e.g., feeding, dressing, positioning, bathing) and developing a daily routine that balanced the needs of all family members. The practitioner would function in a transdisciplinary manner with the active monitoring and support of the entire team. After this period, the parents and staff would decide if Nelson could tolerate more intensive intervention with additonal clinicians.

The complex demands associated with managing several different stages in a blended family left little time for Mrs. Gomez to take care of personal needs. Therefore, it was decided to arrange for respite care services so that she could have more flexibility in her schedule and some free time. In addition, a source of stress that permeated interactions between Mr. and Mrs. Gomez was their inability to agree on how to manage the problems related to Mr. Gomez's two older sons from a previous marriage. Both parents expressed a desire to address this difficult issue through short-term, problem-focused counseling. A copy of Nelson's initial IFSP follows.

Individualized Family Service Plan

Child's Name: ___Nelson___   Parent's Names: ___Mr. and Mrs. Gomez___
Date of Birth: _____   Address: _____
Chronological Age: ___4 months___   _____
Date of Referral: _____   _____
Service Coordinator: ___Janine___   Home Phone: _____
                                      Work Phone: _____

This plan includes:

I.   A summary of the development and coping capability of the child and the concerns and priorities of the family.

II. Long-range functional outcomes that will increase the child's development and coping capability and enhance supportive family resources.

III. A 6-month implementation plan with short-term goals directed to achieving the long-range functional outcomes.
- The program and community services for the child and family.
- Short-term goals and objectives with strategies and activities to achieve them.
- Evaluation procedures.

IV. Plan for update or transition.

Signatures

_____   _____   _____   _____
Parent/Guardian   Date   Service Coordinator   Date

_____   _____   _____   _____
                                Date   Date

_____   _____   _____   _____
                                Date   Date

I. A Summary of the Development and Coping Capability of the Child and the Concerns and Priorities of the Family

Nelson's present status (age 4 months): Nelson had seizures shortly after birth that were eventually controlled by phenobarbital. The medication was discontinued at 3 months of age. Physically, Nelson is small and frail. His head circumference, less than the second percentile, can be described as microcephalic. He tends to be irritable and difficult to comfort. Nelson has milk allergies that cause colic and gastrointestinal problems. His muscle tone is low, resulting in poor head control and weak feeding abilities. Usually he tires before feeding is completed due to the great effort required to suck and swallow.

Nelson is delayed in all developmental areas. He lifts his head very briefly while lying on his abdomen and when held in supported sitting. He fleetingly focuses on objects and people. He does not smile, but he brightens when he makes visual contact, especially with his mother. He seems to recognize her voice and occasionally makes sounds in response to her. Nelson demonstrates low tolerance for stimulating sounds and light. He frequently becomes upset, arches his body, and cries unconsolably.

Family concerns and priorities: Mr. and Mrs. Gomez are feeling stress because of Nelson's multiple problems. Medical consultations to date have resulted in conflicting information without yielding a specific diagnosis. They want to gain a better understanding of the nature and cause of his condition and what it means for Nelson's future. They are concerned that the caregiving requirements for Nelson are very demanding and take a disproportionate amount of attention away from the other children. They are also concerned about his weak sucking and whether he is receiving adequate nutrition. In addition, Mr. and Mrs. Gomez would like to achieve a mutually acceptable approach for coping with their two older sons.

II. Long-Range Functional Outcome

Nelson will acquire the basic motor, social, and communication skills needed to have more effective transactions with his environment.

III. 6-Month Implementation Plan

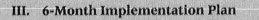

- *Program and community services for the child and family*
    1. Home-based services by an early intervention practitioner for one hour twice a week; reassess intensity and type of service after 2 months.
    2. Evaluation by a pediatric neurologist
- *Short-term goals and objectives* (listed on the following pages)

Short-Term Goal 1: Nelson will increase his ability to self-regulate with adult assistance and the support of adapted positioning.

Objectives	Strengths	Strategies
1. Nelson will be able to calm with adult assistance after stressful situations.	The Gomezs are supportive of Nelson and motivated to help him. They are patient when he is irritable.	All adults will learn procedures for helping Nelson to become organized (e.g., handling techniques, swaddling, use of automated swing).
		Teach Nelson strategies for self-comforting (e.g., sucking thumb or pacifier, mouthing objects).
2. Nelson will be positioned appropriately in a variety of situations.		Determine best positions and needed adaptations for holding, carrying, and general placement (e.g., supine and prone positions, side lying, sitting).
		Provide appropriate adapted equipment (e.g., modified infant seat, car seat).

Evaluation: Observation and report by parents and staff

Short-Term Goal 2: Nelson will interact with people and objects through sustained looking, smiling, and vocalizing.

Objectives	Strengths	Strategies
1. Nelson will visually attend to people and objects	Emerging head control in different positions Consistently turns to mother's voice Brightens when he sees others Occasionally makes responsive sounds	Determine appropriate positioning in prone, supine, and supported sitting positions when encouraging visual attending and tracking. Use toys that are visually attractive (e.g., grade color, contrast, and complexity of visual stimulation). Place toys, mobiles, and other objects at a distance to encourage visual scanning. Adults will use their own face to increase Nelson's visual skills (e.g., adult's use of voice, facial expressions, and head movements to stimulate his tracking in different planes).
2. Nelson will respond with vocalizing and smiling when interacting with others.		Use eye contact, sounds, and gentle touch to achieve initial engagement. Give immediate, positive feedback for all attempts to interact (e.g., hugs and kisses for a smile, imitate his sounds). Use action songs and play-type movements to foster reciprocal interaction (e.g., swinging and bouncing when held by an adult and accompanied by singing). Encourage young siblings to play with Nelson under supervision.

Evaluation: Document change in frequency of visual attention and social interaction.

Short-Term Goal 3: Nelson will begin to use movement as a way to explore his body and connect to the world around him.

Objectives	Strengths	Strategies
1. Nelson will increase control of his head and trunk in the supported sitting and in the prone-on-elbows positions.	Beginning head control Can tolerate supported sitting for short periods of time Responds well to physical handling procedures	Use therapeutic handling procedures to facilitate extensor, flexor, and lateral movements of the head and trunk (e.g., weight-shifting the child in various positions to elicit righting reactions of the head, deep pressure to activate the extensor and abdominal muscles of the trunk). Introduce a small roll under the chest in the prone-on-elbows position to provide stability and foster lifting of the head. Supported sitting can be achieved in an infant seat or on an adult's lap.
2. Nelson will develop body-oriented play in the midline of his body.		Through prompting, physical guidance, and reinforcement, encourage such midline-oriented play as bringing the hands together, plucking on his clothes, and resting his hands on the bottle when nursing. Use therapeutic techniques to facilitate flexor control of the head and shoulders.
3. Nelson will develop early play schemes (e.g., shaking, banging, squeezing, swiping).		Encourage swiping in various positions and activities (e.g., use of mobile and rolling toys, splashing during bathing).

(continued)

Short-Term Goal 3   (*continued*)

Objectives	Strengths	Strategies
		Place rattle and squeeze toys in his hand to elicit desired movements.
		Use powered toys activated by pressure pad switch to foster self-initiation.

Evaluation: Developmental assessment

Short-Term Goal 4:   Nelson will increase his nutritional intake.

Objectives	Strengths	Strategies
1. Nelson will drink more effectively from a bottle (e.g., increased liquid intake in shorter periods of time with less fatigue).	Nonallergenic formula identified Emerging head control	Determine best positions for feeding. Determine most therapeutic type and size of bottle and nipple. Use oral-motor facilitative techniques before or during the feedings as indicated. Implement most appropriate feeding schedule (e.g., time and frequency of feedings). Record intake for sharing with the pediatrician.
2. Nelson will learn to manage increasingly solid foods as they are introduced.		Consult with pediatrician on an ongoing basis regarding the feeding regime. Grade type and consistency of foods from soft toward more solid textures. Introduce teething biscuits for self-feeding when Nelson is ready.

Evaluation: Document changes in feeding schedule and chart intake

> *Short-Term Goal 5:* Mr. and Mrs. Gomez want to learn ways to manage Nelson and still be responsive to the needs of the rest of the family.

Priorities	Preferred activities
Mr. and Mrs. Gomez want:	
1. A confirmed medical diagnosis for Nelson	Refer to a specialized pediatric neurologist for a differential diagnosis.
2. Strategies for managing Nelson's daily care	Organize 1-hour weekly home visits by the clinician to problem-solve with Mrs. Gomez about ways to manage caregiving activities, such as bathing, dressing, and playing. Practice these skills in a naturalistic context.
3. To develop a daily routine that balances the needs of all family members.	The clinician and Mrs. Gomez will chart Mrs. Gomez's activities through the course of the day. They will also develop a 3-day behavioral record of Nelson (e.g., feeding, napping, fussing). Based on this information, they will find ways to reorganize the routine.
	Include the younger sister in Nelson's caregiving activities so that she can share her mother's attention.
4. Respite care services	Referral by service coordinator to the respite care program sponsored by the Developmental Disabilities Council.
5. Help to solve issues related to Mr. Gomez's two older sons	The Gomezes will participate in short-term, problem-focused counseling.

Evaluation: Parent feedback

IV. Plan for Update

Activity	Persons responsible	When
1. After 2 months, determine if the frequency of intervention and number of practitioners needs to change to achieve the desired goals. Revise IFSP accordingly.	Mr. and Mrs. Gomez and staff	Two months from initial IFSP
2. After 6 months, evaluate outcome of plan and determine Nelson's present status.	The Gomezes and staff	Six months from initial IFSP
3. Meet to review Nelson's progress, identify ongoing or new family priorities, and analyze facilitating and interfering factors.	The Gomezes and service coordinator	Six months from initial IFSP
4. Develop new IFSP.	Mr. and Mrs. Gomez and staff	Six months from initial IFSP

SUBSEQUENT IFSPs FOR MARIE KELLY

Each new IFSP reflects the results of intervention as well as the changes resulting from the passage of time. Subsequent IFSPs typically become more focused as knowledge and trust develop between family members and practitioners. Marie's following two IFSP's are provided to show how each one, with its modified short-term goals, moves closer to the achievement of the long-range functional outcome. Marie's long-range functional outcome remained the same throughout her stay in the early intervention program. (In other cases, long-range outcomes are revised due to changing circumstances of the child or family.)

Marie's IFSPs also demonstrate how she was able to move into more integrated community-based activities. As Marie showed progress, Mr. and Mrs. Kelly had a resurgence of hope that they could have a better life. This changing belief generated an interest in exploring the possibility of having more children. Likewise, relations improved with their extended family.

Second IFSP for Marie Kelly

I. A Summary of the Development and Coping Capability of the Child and the Concerns and Priorities of the Family

Marie's present status (age 20 months): Marie has made progress in the past 6 months toward achievement of her short-term goals. She has increased her gross motor skills, social interaction, and ability to communicate. She is able to stand up from the floor and walk with assistance a few steps. She is using more words in her speech; however, she is not very successful in expressing her needs during demanding situations and managing transitions from one activity to the next. She tends to become nervous if other children and adults become physically close.

She participates in simple motor games, such as crawling through a tunnel and swatting balloons. Her balance and coordination are labored but adequate. She says simple words and occassionally asks for help when necessary. She is beginning to demonstrate more independent skills in self-feeding, assisting with dressing and undressing, and warding off unpleasant stimulation. She continues to enjoy being with other children as an observer in the group.

Marie's condition goes into remission for brief periods and then flares again with the skin becoming red, flaking, and dry. The small ulcers that form on her fingertips, elbows, and feet also reappear periodically. The creams and lotions alleviate the itching and irritation; however, Marie is very resistant to their application and also cries when it is time to take a bath.

Family concerns and priorities: Mrs. Kelly did not find the parent discussion group very helpful and has decided not to continue. Mr. and Mrs. Kelly request more frequent feedback from the staff regarding Marie's progress and activities. They are interested in having Marie be more physically active with other children and less fearful of being touched. They also would like information on coping with stress and additional strategies for helping Marie to manage routine and new situations.

II. Long-Range Functional Outcome

Marie will learn effective ways to manage the demands created by her skin condition so that she can actively interact with people and objects.

III. 6-Month Implementation Plan

- *Program and community services for the child and family*
  1. Continued enrollment in the early intervention group on a weekly basis
  2. One-hour individual occupational therapy once a week
  3. Connect with a parent-to-parent network
- *Short-term goals and objectives*

Short-Term Goal 1: Marie will initiate communication to express her needs, particularly in demanding situations such as transitions in daily routine and new activities.

Objectives	Strengths	Strategies
1. Marie will shift between words and gestures when she is not understood.	Demonstrates persistence Demonstrates pleasure at success Says "yes," "no," "stop," "done," "more," "cookie," and "juice" Looks at or away from object or person to demonstrate her preferences	Continue asking, "Do you need help?", "Do you want to stop?" Help Marie try alternate communication strategies (e.g., "Show and tell me what you want.").
2. Marie will go from one activity to another without withdrawing or crying.	Anticipates events Maintains visual attention Understands simple directions Greater flexibility in predictable circumstances	Before the change in activity, tell Marie what is going to happen and suggest that she ask for help if she needs it.

Evaluation: Observation and parent report

Short-Term Goal 2:   Marie will learn to share some responsibility for her daily skin care. (Tolerance is increased when she controls the nature and intensity of the sensory experience.)

Objectives	Strengths	Strategies
1. Marie will participate more actively in her bath routine.	Maintains visual attention Able to say "yes" and "no" Improved motor control and sensory tolerance More playful attitude in some situations	Grade Marie's involvement in bathing activities (e.g., she selects bath toys, tests temperature and depth of water, states preference for bubble bath). Be alert for cues that Marie has been in bath as long as she can tolerate.
2. Marie will help apply skin lotion twice a day.	Understands simple directions Accepts support from mother and father	After demonstration, have Marie practice application of lotion on a doll. Then have Marie apply cream to herself on a small area of a preferred body part. Gradually expand as acceptable.

Evaluation: Parent report

Short-Term Goal 3: Marie will be physically active with other children in the early intervention program and at home.

Objectives	Strengths	Strategies
1. Marie will be physically involved in group activities of the early intervention program. 2. Marie will play with neighborhood children on a regular basis.	Expresses likes and dislikes Enjoys other children Enjoys success Lives close to extended family and an active YWCA center	Involve Marie physically in group activities such as action songs, puppet play, see-saw, and housekeeping corner. Mrs. Kelly will schedule play dates with Marie's cousins once a week and will investigate the play group at the local YWCA.

Evaluation: Parent and staff report

Short-Term Goal 4:   Mr. and Mrs. Kelly want their extended family to be more understanding of Marie's special needs.

Priorities	Preferred activities
Mr. and Mrs. Kelly want to: 1. Share their newly acquired information about Marie's condition with other family members 2. Address their concerns about the reactions and feelings of relatives toward Marie	Problem solve with the social worker to find helpful strategies for relating with the extended family. Through a parent-to-parent network, the service coordinator will introduce the Kellys to a family with similar issues.

Evaluation: Parent report

Short-Term Goal 5: Mr. and Mrs. Kelly want more personalized involvement in the early intervention program.

Priorities	Preferred activities
Mr. and Mrs. Kelly want to:	
1. Have more individual communication with the staff	Bimonthly home visits by the service coordinator
2. Learn more about coping concepts	Biweekly meeting with a staff member during the second hour of Marie's group
	Participation in the coping with stress workshop

Evaluation: Parent report

IV. Plan for Update

Activity	Persons responsible	When
1. Evaluate outcome of plan and determine Marie's present status.	Mr. and Mrs. Kelly and staff	Six months from start of this plan
2. Meet to review Marie's progress, identify ongoing or new family priorities, and analyze facilitating and interfering factors.	Mr. and Mrs. Kelly and service coordinator	Six months from start of this plan
3. Develop new IFSP.	Family, staff, and service coordinator	Six months from start of this plan

Third IFSP for Marie Kelly

> **I. A Summary of the Development and Coping Capability of the Child and the Concerns and Priorities of the Family**

Marie's present status (age 28 months): Marie has made important developmental gains. She is essentially functioning at an age-appropriate level in communication, cognition, fine motor, and self-help skills. Marie's walking is slow and her balance is rather precarious. Social skills are inconsistent and her coping style is situationally effective. These difficulties may be attributed to her continued sensitivity to touching and being touched.

Marie understands complex directions and responds with appropriate answers to requests from parents, staff, and other children. She is quite effective in warding off unpleasant or other stimulation that she does not wish to engage by simply saying, "No," "Stop," or "I do not want to . . ." At home she is able to play with cousins who are her age and no longer becomes distressed at visitors entering the house. Mrs. Kelly and Marie have joined a play group at the local YWCA with another family from the early intervention program. Mrs. Kelly has been very pleased with participation in that group. In general, Marie is initiating conversations, asking questions, exploring new objects, and being inquisitive about other children.

Family concerns and priorities: Mr. and Mrs. Kelly are concerned about Marie's transition to preschool. They wonder if she will be accepted by the new children because of her physical appearance, small size, and tactile defensiveness. They are concerned about playground activities, gym class, and other situations that involve physical contact.

Marie's overall improvement and the increased understanding by the extended family have made Mr. and Mrs. Kelly's lives more manageable. They feel able to talk about her condition with family members, especially the grandparents. The Kellys joined a support group of families of children with skin conditions and receive a monthly newsletter. They attended a regional conference sponsored by the organization and met several parents of older children who have the same diagnosis.

With the easing of demands related to Marie's condition and her upcoming transition to preschool, Mr. and Mrs. Kelly have asked for assistance in finding a genetic counselor.

> **II. Long-Range Functional Outcome**

Marie will learn effective ways to manage the demands created by her skin condition so that she can actively interact with people and objects.

> **III. 6-Month Implementation Plan**

- *Program and community services for the child and family*
  1. Continued enrollment in the early intervention group that meets once a week for 2 hours
  2. Placement in a community child-care program 2 days a week with consultation and direct service provided by the special educator and occupational therapist on a weekly basis
  3. Genetic counseling
- *Short-term goals and objectives*

Short-Term Goal 1: Marie will cope effectively in a regular childcare program in the community.

Objectives	Strengths	Strategies
1. Marie will make a smooth transition into the new childcare program.	Many developmental skills are essentially age-appropriate Ability to communicate Anticipates events Understands complex directions Ability to observe and model other children	The Kellys and the service coordinator will plan the transition with the childcare staff. Marie will attend the program in increasing blocks of time with Mrs. Kelly gradually decreasing her presence. The childcare staff will consult with the special educator and occupational therapist when they make their weekly visits.
2. Marie will use developmentally appropriate behavior in following the routine of her childcare placement.	Walks independently for short distances More flexible in following routines Has successfully played with other children at the YWCA	Monitor and limit the number of tactile stressors Marie will come in contact with in daily activities. Describe to Marie what will happen next and allow her to choose her mode of participation. If Marie shows regressive behavior, modify demands to reduce stress.

Evaluation: Observation and report by parents and child-care staff.

Short-Term Goal 2: Marie will increase her ability to interact with other children in a developmentally appropriate way.

Objectives	Strengths	Strategies
1. Marie will increase her expressive vocabulary to continue building a sense of being in control and an ability to self-initiate.	Good expressive language skills Motivated to interact with peers Inquisitive about her surroundings	Implement in the early intervention and child-care programs. Use picture books to stimulate conversation and descriptive language skills. Encourage verbal expression of feelings.
2. Marie will respond to requests from others to participate in activities.	More social awareness Expresses likes and dislikes Usually makes needs known	When asking Marie to participate, describe the activity, model involvement when necessary, and initially accept her level of engagement. When appropriate, suggest but do not insist on participation at the next developmental level of involvement.

Evaluation: Developmental assessment and report by parents, early intervention staff, and childcare staff

Short-Term Goal 3:   Mr. and Mrs. Kelly want to be actively involved in planning and implementing Marie's transition to a preschool.

Priorities	Preferred activities
The Kellys are interested in learning about the transition process and available preschool programs.	Attend the Coping with Transition workshop given periodically at the early intervention program

Evaluation: Parent report

Short-Term Goal 4:   Mr. and Mrs. Kelly want to explore genetic counseling.

Priorities	Preferred activities
The Kellys want to know the likelihood of other offspring having a skin condition and want assistance in examining the possible impact of siblings on Marie.	Refer for genetic counseling. Organize time-limited counseling with the staff psychologist of the early intervention program.

Evaluation: Parent report

V. Transition Plan		
Activity	Persons responsible	When
1. Prepare a summary report for meeting with the preschool Child Study Team from the local school district.	Service coordinator, intervention team, childcare staff, and Mr. and Mrs. Kelly	February
2. Schedule meeting with preschool Child Study Team to explore placement options.	Service coordinator	March
3. Meet with Child Study Team. Identify factors that will facilitate and interfere with successful transition. Consider preschool options (visits may be scheduled if requested). Identify appropriate preschool placement, initial goals, and suggested strategies for new setting.	Mr. and Mrs. Kelly, service coordinator, and the Child Study Team	April
4. Visit preschool placement.	The Kellys and service coordinator	May

MARIE'S TRANSITION

Marie had a final evaluation before leaving the early intervention program. Mr. and Mrs. Kelly said that they and their daughter had learned many ways to cope more successfully with the demands of daily living. Observation showed that Marie seemed to believe that most of the time she could now safely be involved with people and objects. Her parents believed that they had more knowledge and skills to manage Marie's skin condition and behavior. As a consequence, they were able to interact more comfortably with others and thus were provided with a more active support system. With Marie enrolled part time in a child-care program, Mrs. Kelly had time to manage other aspects of her life. The optimism generated by Marie's progress helped change Mr. and Mrs. Kelly's beliefs about family life and the possibility of having more children.

Not only was Marie's long-range functional outcome met, but her developmental skills were generally age-appropriate except for her gross motor ability. Her coping competence had progressed from minimally effective to situationally effective. The Kellys had expanded their coping resources and were therefore better able to manage their lives.

Marie was classified by the school district as eligible for special services due to her chronic health condition. She was placed in a regular preschool class within her neighborhood school. She received physical therapy on a weekly basis and an occupational therapist provided consultative services to the teacher. The school nurse monitored her skin condition.

The following summer, after a year in preschool, Marie was enrolled in a summer recreational program sponsored by the medical center. Although Gloria was aware that Marie was receiving this service, she was no longer directly involved with the family. One day during that summer they had a serendipitous meeting.

➡ Gloria was going down a flight of stairs at the medical center. A line of children, 4 and 5 years of age, were assembled at the bottom of the stairway ready to climb to the second floor after an outdoor session of the "Movin' and Groovin' " summer program. As they ascended one child stood behind, watching as the other children formed a single line and moved up. She was considerably smaller in stature than the other children and her skin appeared quite red, as if she had a harsh sunburn. It was Marie. Looking up to the front of the line of children, which had now reached the top of the stairs, Marie said, "I need help, would someone help me come up the stairs?" The other children stopped and one said, "Marie needs help!" The teacher quickly moved down and lightly supported Marie from behind, helping her to move on to the first step, and begin her slow climb. Marie climbed each step with effort. The children were then asked to get a partner. Marie said to the child next to her, "I'll hold your hand," and delicately took hold of the child's hand.

Gloria was fascinated by Marie's development and followed the children. They went to a classroom where small groups formed. Marie watched as the others began to play. The teacher asked for assistance with snack time and Marie said, "I'll help." She placed cups, napkins, and cookies at their proper places at the snack table and began to gather the children. When they were seated, Marie began a conversation with the teacher about tomorrow's snack. She said that she hoped it would be ice cream, and that she especially liked vanilla. She asked her table partner if he liked vanilla and what was his "best" snack.

According to her teacher, Marie was a "regular little chatterbox." She initiated conversations with the teacher, other children, and other parents. She related stories of family outings and events at home and described the play of the other children using vivid descriptive language. Marie had developed her communication skills in a way that allowed her to consistently interact with others. This capacity provided a sense of control as well as enhanced her self-esteem. She was able to control the impact of the environment through setting limits for others regarding their physical interaction with her, as well as asking for assistance when necessary. Clearly, Marie was more effective in her interactions with others and her environment.

When the session was over, Marie's mother was waiting for her and was pleasantly surprised to see Gloria. She said to Marie, "Tell Gloria our news." Marie said with a smile, "I'm going to be a sister!" Mrs. Kelly said that she was expecting and her baby was due in 6 months. With Marie 4 years old, the Kellys believed they could now add to the family. Mrs. Kelly was happy, and Marie seemed equally delighted.

SUMMARY

In this chapter, the third step of the decision-making process used to complete the IFSP is described in detail. The IFSPs for the Kelly and Gomez families provide examples of plans that reflect a coping perspective. This coping frame of reference and its decision-making questions can be adapted and modified to address the requirements of different early intervention programs and settings. As discussed in Chapter 1, this volume, the specific format for developing and writing the IFSP must be responsive to federal, state, and local conditions.

CHAPTER 12

The COPING Project

Our Learning Experience

Change is a slow and challenging process. Every new learning experience opens the door to more learning, and, sometimes, difficulties offer more opportunities for growth than successes. Nothing exemplifies this better than the challenges we faced during the development of the COPING Project. This chapter describes some of the changes during the 3-year period of the project's pilot program. It discusses the evolution of our work and provides illustrations of the project's developmental process. Evaluation data are shared that document the effectiveness of the coping frame of reference with children, families, and practitioners. In addition, lessons that we learned are identified to assist other early intervention programs in their progress toward state-of-the-art practices.

BACKGROUND

The impetus for initiating the COPING Project came from the evolving trends in the early intervention field (see chap. 1, Table 1.1) and the desire that our existing program in the Pediatric Rehabilitation Department of the John F. Kennedy Medical Center reflect these best practices. We conducted a series of evaluation and quality assurance studies to determine the current status of the early intervention program and priorities for change. This comprehensive examination included interviews with families being served, follow-up questionnaires and phone contacts with parents of previously enrolled children, content analysis of IFSPs, evaluation of child progress data, a survey of staff satisfaction with the existing program, and a cost effectiveness study of service delivery.

The early intervention program in operation at that time served 100 families with diverse socioeconomic and cultural backgrounds. The children enrolled in the program were infants and toddlers with developmental delays and disabilities such as cerebral palsy, spina bifida, Down syndrome, pervasive developmental disorder, failure to thrive, and general delays in one or more areas of development. At the time, the early intervention program was generally perceived as being one of the best in the state.

The program was primarily center based with some services provided in the home. The families were served in groups of six to eight children based on a variety of criteria including age, functional status, family preferences, and staff availability (e.g., matching bilingual practitioners with appropriate families). Each group was staffed by an inter-disciplinary team. Typically, this team consisted of three to four members drawn from the professions most responsive to the needs of the families (e.g., special education, physical therapy, occupational therapy, speech-language pathology, nursing, social work, psychology). Families also had access to medical consultation services.

Usually an intervention group met for a 2-hour session on a weekly basis with additional individual therapy when appropriate. During the session, the parents spent one hour of their time with the children in therapeutic and educational activities. The other hour was spent in a support group led by a social worker or psychologist. The only established family-focused services were the parent support groups and some crisis counseling. Occasionally evening lectures were offered on specific topics. The degree of involvement of parents during the intervention hour they were with their child varied with the comfort and style of the parents and professionals.

PILOT PROGRAM

The previously mentioned comprehensive evaluation of the program identified many strengths but also two primary concerns.

1. The acquisition of developmental skills in the children did not necessarily lead to a change in their adaptive, functional competence. Many of the children were unable to integrate, apply, and generalize their learning to meet the challenges of daily living.
2. The program was not adequately sensitive to the issues of individual families. There was a need to focus on enhancing resources in order to support present and future coping efforts related to raising their child.

The COPING Project was a model demonstration initiative to address these concerns. It was designed to refine and apply a theoretically sound intervention frame of reference that emphasized resilience of the children and well-being of the families. Funding was received for a 3-year effort from the U.S. Department of Education (Office of Special Education Programs). The project was to pilot and evaluate an intervention approach for fostering the coping resources of young children with special needs and for supporting their families. Findings of the program demonstration period would then be disseminated. Grant funding supported, on an essentially part-time basis, the two directors and an inter-disciplinary COPING Project staff of two professionals. This COPING staff worked with the early intervention staff of the Pediatric Rehabilitation Department to implement direct service activities with the families.

There were many positive factors that facilitated getting started and several difficulties that had not been anticipated. The positive factors included: 1) an established early intervention program that could serve as the site for the pilot activities; 2) an intervention staff whose members had quality experience in their specialty areas; 3) a structure in the Pediatric Rehabilitation Department that included time for individual supervision and regular inservice training; and 4) project directors who had experience in the development of coping-related intervention, with one serving as head of the department. The project benefited from the broad expertise of the directors in psychology, occupational therapy, and special education.

Two difficulties surfaced early. It was a major challenge to translate the theoretical framework into practical clinical procedures. We also underestimated the initial resistance that the early intervention staff members would have to changes in the program. We had assumed that their participation in the previously mentioned program evaluation activities would be adequately motivating. (See chap. 14, this volume, for a discussion of staff coping with change.)

The initial 6 months of the COPING Project were spent in intensive planning and model development. Questions addressed included how to: operationalize the coping concepts, collect information about the coping resources of the children and families, involve families in the collaborative process, develop and implement functionally oriented coping goals for the children, support families in the context of their selected service options, and train early intervention staff in this coping perspective.

The COPING staff spent time planning each component of the pilot program with the assistance of consultants, parents, and the early intervention staff. Detailed literature reviews were conducted on topics such as early child development, stress, coping, and parent–child interaction. As a result of these efforts, preliminary protocols and procedures were developed for testing and revision over the subsequent course of the grant period.

A fundamental inquiry throughout the program demonstration phase was the definition of key concepts and the refinement of the theoretical base for the coping frame of reference. As discussed in Chapter 2, the two basic concepts of coping and stress are defined in many different ways in the professional and lay literature. They are often discussed in a negative context of managing adversity and not appreciated for their motivating, generative aspects. In reality, coping is often related to challenge, novelty, curiosity, and excitement. Through rich interdisciplinary debate, we recognized the importance of *developmentally appropriate stress* and later tended to use the term *demands and expectations* to represent the concept of stress. It was critical for the project to have definitions that reflected its positive orientation of personal growth and empowerment. Attention was on adaptation, not pathology.

Discussion also focused on refining the model of the coping process and the internal and external resources that contribute to coping efforts. The identification of coping resources was particularly demanding. At some level one can say that everything that happens, in some way, contributes to coping. Such a global, indiscriminate view is not clinically useful. In the beginning, the model was entirely too complex to link research effectively to practice. Over time, the number of resources was consolidated. The literature review and our professional experience helped us to identify the resources that seemed most salient.

This creative process involved interdisciplinary discourse that was intellectually stimulating and at times emotionally draining. A heated debate, for instance, was conducted over whether to designate "beliefs" as an internal coping resource in young children. (In older children and adults there was agreement of its importance.) The dialogue targeted such issues as the interplay of cognition, affect, and temperament on infant behavior. Eventually the literature related to development of the self complemented our clinical impressions to support the inclusion of emerging beliefs as an essential coping resource— prelinguistic, emotionally based, and instrumental. The coping concepts described in Chapters 2 and 3 are the result of such thinking, testing out, and modification during the 3 years of model development.

After 6 months of laying the groundwork, a pilot program was initiated within the existing early intervention program of the medical center's Pediatric Rehabilitation Department. Twenty-one children were selected to participate. According to plan, these were infants and toddlers with mild to severe developmental delays or disabilities and they reflected a range of socioeconomic and ethnic backgrounds. (Subsequently, the coping frame of reference was also applied with children who were environmentally at risk.) Each family was advised of the pilot nature of the project. All agreed to give feedback about their ongoing experiences. The parents seemed pleased that their family was to be involved.

The children were divided into three groups according to criteria such as age, functional level, and concerns of the parents. Each group of seven children and their families was staffed primarily by personnel from the early intervention program and to a lesser degree by the COPING staff. In general, the staffing pattern and structure of the groups were typical of the regular early intervention program described previously in this chapter. The differences were: 1) the focus on enhancing coping resources to achieve functional outcomes, 2) intervention that emphasized the process of adaptation during daily living, 3) expanded concern for parent–child transactions, and 4) active engagement of families in collaboration and team participation.

These innovations were significant because they required the early intervention staff to acquire new knowledge, skills, and attitudes. They needed to be able to understand transactions, know how to nurture relationships, and be flexible in modifying intervention. Because change is most manageable when it builds from the familiar, the pilot program was a variation of the existing early intervention program. Thus, staff members were relatively comfortable dealing with the new innovations. In addition, it was important for the structure of the pilot program to be fairly representative of formats found in the early intervention field. Therefore, insights gained in the pilot program could be generalized to other programs.

Initial activities had two focuses: 1) to develop and implement coping-related goals for the children, and 2) to work with the families to identify their coping resources and priorities. Training was essential for intervention staff members to learn more about the coping frame of reference, ways to identify coping resources, and how to write coping-related goals with the parents. Their training and supervision were mostly managed by the coordinator of the COPING Project who formerly had been a supervisor in the regular intervention program. As a consequence, she was familiar with the staff and the departmental routine.

Change at times was arduous. For example, writing coping goals initially required much time and effort. For some practitioners, working toward functional outcomes was a natural part of their professional repertoire of skills. For others, extensive supervisory support was necessary. As the staff became more knowledgeable over time, the percentage of coping-related goals in the IFSPs increased substantially.

There was also change during the demonstration period in how to identify and address the concerns, priorities, and resources of families. At the start of the project there was a rather structured approach with heavy use of self-rated instruments. Through collaboration with parents, this approach was altered to be more conversational, interactive, and personalized. An overview of this evolution is provided to illustrate the process of program development.

CHANGE DURING PROGRAM DEVELOPMENT

The COPING staff initially focused on finding ways to acquire information about the concerns and coping resources of the 21 families. After exploration and discussion with parents and early intervention staff, the decision was made to use established self-rated instruments. With the understanding and approval of the pilot families, a number of self-rated instruments were identified and given to each family. Parents were assured that they always had a choice about completing an instrument and that all results would be shared with them in a meeting with their service coordinator. The information was used by parents to clarify their concerns, establish priorities, and determine desired services within the early intervention program and community.

An interest survey was included in the battery of instruments. Table 12.1 lists the types of activities and services requested by the majority of the parents. The instruments chosen to identify the family's coping resources and stressors are provided in Table 12.2. (Knowledge and skills were not included as a coping resource until later in the refinement of the model.) The instruments were given to the families during a number of weeks. Parents (or guardians) completed them during their time at the program or at home. The total amount of time to complete the battery was approximately 1½ hours.

Analysis of the collected data indicated that as a group the families were at or near the mean for the comparison groups used to standardize the measures (Zeitlin, Williamson, & Rosenblatt, 1987). This finding indicated that the parents as a group were not extremely stressed, dissatisfied, or lacking in resources. However, analysis of individual family data revealed wide variability among the families. Some families were quite effective in their coping efforts and had excellent resources for managing the demands of their lives. Other families were less adaptive. Indeed, a few families were quite troubled. They cited numerous vulnerabilities, many of which predated the birth of their child with special needs.

Examples of the Johnson and Acquino families are provided to illustrate how this component of IFSP development was used by the COPING Project in its early stages.

The Johnson Family

Mr. and Mrs. Johnson are parents of twins. Both girls have cerebral palsy, with one child notably more disabled than the other. A summary follows of the information the staff gleaned from the self-rated instruments completed by the parents.

Beliefs and Values   The Johnsons reported positive feelings about their family and highly valued the importance of their children in their lives. They felt a strong responsibility as parents and expressed some guilt regarding the disabilities of the twins. Mr. and Mrs. Johnson recorded firm beliefs that professionals needed to work closely with them in order for their children to make significant progress.

Coping Style   Both parents reported that they were effective in their coping and perceived themselves as being self-directed, sensitive, and responsive to the feelings of others. They viewed their energy level as lower than desired and stated that they tended to become easily frustrated. They differed in the perception of their ability to mobilize during stressful situations. Mrs. Johnson felt that she had difficulty, whereas her husband felt competent in managing stressful situations.

Table 12.1.   Most frequently requested services and activities by the pilot families

Requested services and activities	Percentage of requests
Receive information on community resources	80%
Observe child's intervention activities	75
Discuss child's progress on a regular basis	75
Participate actively in development of the child's intervention goals	65
Participate actively in child's intervention activities	65
Participate in a parent support group	65
Attend a workshop on child growth and development	60
Attend a workshop on psychological, social, and emotional issues	55
Attend a workshop on stress management	50
Attend a workshop on legal rights and responsibilities	50
Attend a workshop on diagnostic and evaluative procedures	50

Table 12.2. Self-reporting instruments used to assess coping resources and stressors during the pilot phase

Beliefs and values	Coping style	Physical and affective states	Human supports	Material supports	Stressors
Belief Scale assesses beliefs concerning attribution and locus of control (Bristol, 1983a). Definition Scale assesses perceived impact of having a child with special needs (Bristol & De Vellis, 1982). Family Inventory of Resources for Management (FIRM) has two scales to assess family strengths and one scale to assess desirability of family membership (McCubbin, Comeau, & Harkins, 1979).	Coping Inventory measures behavioral attributes most related to coping (Zeitlin, 1985).	Symptoms Checklist 90 (SCL-90R) utilizes nine scales to assess physical and psychological health (Derogatis, Lipman, & Covi, 1975).	Carolina Parent Support Scale provides a qualitative assessment of social supports (Bristol, 1983b). FIRM Extended Family Social Support Scale assesses mutual help and support from relatives.	FIRM Financial Well Being Scale assesses the family's perceived financial status. FIRM Sources of Financial Support Scale assesses stability and esteem associated with income.	Family Inventory of Life Events and Changes (FILE) assesses life events experienced by a family. Nine scales identify recent and past changes (e.g., intrafamily, marital, child-bearing, and work strains) (McCubbin, Wilson, & Patterson, 1979).

Both parents identified themselves as having positive orientations toward life. Mrs. Johnson considered herself warm and stimulating to others. Mr. Johnson reported feeling successful and flexible in new situations and enjoyed such experiences. They both stated that they were liked and accepted by others.

Mrs. Johnson cited trouble maintaining her own independence and felt rather dependent at times. She had difficulty completing tasks and considered herself impulsive. Mr. Johnson reported that he had a problem asking for help and accepting changes in an existing plan or arrangement.

Physical and Affective States   Mr. and Mrs. Johnson reported good general health and no physical limitations.

Human Supports   Both parents indicated strong social support from their family and friends.

Material and Environmental Supports   The Johnsons perceived themselves as having average financial resources. They lived in a garden apartment that was wheelchair accessible.

Stressors   The parents expressed some differences in the number of stressors in their lives. Mr. Johnson reported that he had the average stress of daily living, whereas Mrs. Johnson perceived a greater number of stressors related to raising young twins.

Summary of the Family Conference   The service coordinator met with Mr. and Mrs. Johnson at their home to discuss the results of the self-rated instruments that they had completed. The intent of this process was to assist the Johnsons to look at their concerns, priorities, and resources in a way that aided IFSP development. The information was summarized verbally in an informal manner that facilitated discussion.

The Johnsons felt that the instruments accurately described their coping resources and the opportunity to discuss them was helpful. They reflected on their many supportive resources and commented on the compatibility of their opinions. Mrs. Johnson talked about her difficulty in managing stress and her concern that she was "too emotional." Thoughtful probing of this issue clarified that it was less a case of "emotion" and more a case of decreased energy related to her heavy parenting responsibilities. She was at home full time with two young toddlers. Fatigue influenced her frustration tolerance and ability to complete tasks.

After a lively discussion, the parents decided that they wanted to focus on ways to relieve some of the childcare responsibilities carried by Mrs. Johnson. They also wanted more information on the development of their children and opportunities for social contact with adults who had cerebral palsy. They wished to learn from the life experiences of adults with disabilities in order to have a better sense of what to expect in the future. The Johnsons chose the following means to achieve their desired outcomes.

Enroll the children three mornings a week in the Mom's Day Out Program sponsored by the Women's Club. The early intervention staff would serve as consultants to enable the twins to be integrated successfully in the program.

Expand respite care opportunities by having the intervention staff train selected babysitters, friends, and relatives to manage the girls.

Meet adults with cerebral palsy through contacts made with the local affiliate of the United Cerebral Palsy Association.

Receive information about cerebral palsy and child development through written materials and participation in workshops at the early intervention program.

Appendix C at the back of this book has reflections written by Mrs. Johnson at the time the family was leaving the program to relocate to another state. She shares her feelings and experiences about the preceding 3 years.

The Acquino Family

Mr. and Mrs. Acquino emigrated from the Philippines when they were young adults. At the time of referral, they had a 6-year-old son, Pedro, and an infant daughter, Nina, who was premature and small-for-gestational-age. The following information was taken from their completed self-rated instruments.

Beliefs and Values   Mr. and Mrs. Acquino reported similar attitudes about Nina's condition. They both maintained that she provided significant meaning to their lives because she was a special child. They placed moderate importance on the role parents and professionals played in Nina's progress, believing much to be fate. Neither parent viewed her as a burden but rather as a gift.

Coping Style   The Acquinos reported that they were keenly sensitive to the complexities of their surroundings and tried hard to understand and respond to the views and moods of others. They tended to keep their feelings and concerns private. Socializing with others was not a priority.

Mrs. Acquino portrayed herself as a reserved individual who sometimes questioned her ability to cope with daily demands. She was less sure than her husband about her adaptive skills but worked hard at making her life productive. Mr. Acquino indicated that he was somewhat withdrawn and cautious. However, he had basically positive feelings about himself that helped him to handle personal and family issues. Mr. Acquino felt that he was inconsistent in being able to mobilize his energies for action, perceiving himself as rather inflexible.

Human Supports   The Acquinos stated that they primarily used each other and extended family for support. Mrs. Acquino's parents lived with them and were available for physical and emotional assistance.

Physical and Affective States   The parents indicated that they were in good health. Mrs. Acquino reported that she occasionally experienced emotional distress; in particular, she became anxious in crowds. Her tendency to keep feelings to herself sometimes exacerbated this anxiety and made her behavior rigid.

Material and Environmental Supports   The Acquinos stated that they had more than adequate financial resources to handle their personal needs and Nina's requirements. This view was especially evident in Mr. Acquino's responses.

Stressors   The parents indicated that there were few stressors in their lives. Nina's well-being was their major concern.

Summary of the Family Conference   The service coordinator went to the Acquinos' home to discuss their self-reported information and to continue IFSP development. The Acquinos were extremely cordial, cooperative, and pleasant. Mrs. Acquino, who was typically quiet and reserved at the early intervention program, displayed far more affect, spontaneity, and energy when in her own home. She generously offered snacks, interacted adeptly, and spoke at length about the virtues of the program. This was a side of Mrs. Acquino not previously observed.

Mr. Acquino was very engaging—he talked of his close relationship with Nina and he discussed future financial security for his daughter. He mentioned being somewhat anxious about having a staff member in his home and commented on the difficulty they were having as Pilipinos in American society. Recognition of this tension by the intervention staff was critical because it directly influenced the way the Acquinos had completed the self-rated instruments. Both parents stated that their responses were relevant to how they coped in the American culture. They would have responded quite differently if they were answering these questions in the context of their Pilipino culture and friendships.

As a result, Mr. and Mrs. Acquino politely disagreed with some of the service coordinator's statements that were based on their self-rated instruments. For example, on these measures Mr. Acquino had reported that he was shy and withdrawn—often feeling socially inadequate. In the meeting, he corrected this impression by saying that he was actually very outgoing and always the life of any Pilipino party. In fact, he was the lead singer in a band that played Pilipino music at weddings and other special occasions. He said, "You don't know me from those papers." Similarly, Mrs. Acquino, who had reported a number of vulnerabilities in her coping skills, maintained that she never felt that way with her "friends."

This discussion was very informative. A vastly different picture of the Acquinos was gained in this meeting. The instruments had provided an incomplete and at times faulty perspective. Within their community, Mr. and Mrs. Acquino had strong interpersonal skills; they were able to provide emotional support and accept affection from others. In fact, they had an extensive array of friends and relatives. Their church affiliation was a source of additional comfort. Helping professionals were used less frequently for support.

Likewise, there was a misleading perception of the stressors in their lives. The Acquinos were experiencing far greater stress than they had reported. They were trying to manage demanding responsibilities in a strange and perplexing culture. Many previously unreported concerns surfaced during the conversation. Nina required more consistent medical monitoring than the episodic care provided at the local health clinic. Pedro was making bad grades in school and they did not know what to do about it. In addition, Mr. Acquino had purposely left the wrong impression about their financial status. He had recently lost his regular day job and was finding few opportunities for employment.

It was clear to the service coordinator that the battery of instruments did not address cultural differences. The Acquinos felt split between two cultures and were situationally effective in their coping efforts. Within the Pilipino community they were comfortable and confident; within the mainstreamed culture they felt vulnerable and insecure. Through collaborative decision making, the Acquinos decided that the early intervention program could be most useful by assisting them to manage bureaucratic systems. The program could help them to cope with their most immediate concerns through the following actions:

Identify a physician with expertise in infants with special needs who could provide ongoing medical supervision. A Pilipino nurse on staff at the medical center would accompany them to appointments until a trusting relationship was established.

Encourage the Acquinos to have relatives and friends come to early intervention sessions so that the parents could feel supported and more relaxed.

Clarify the nature of Pedro's school failure by helping the parents to communicate with his teacher and determine next steps in solving his academic difficulties.

Refer Mr. Acquino to the county agency responsible for providing free vocational counseling and job placement.

The parents in the pilot program were asked for feedback regarding how they felt about rating the various instruments. They gave a mixed review. Some families made positive comments: "It was a good experience and I learned a lot," and "It helped my wife and I talk together about difficult issues." Other families had negative thoughts about the process: "I thought it was an invasion of privacy, but was uncomfortable saying so." The staff considered the instruments useful for identifying coping resources, but they thought that most instruments insufficiently addressed concerns relevant to families with young children with special needs. In addition, much of the information could be obtained more directly by asking questions during an informal interview or discussion. Instruments could be better used as part of intervention to address specific issues. (See chap. 9, this volume, regarding the use of self-rated instruments.)

The Johnson and Acquino families were representative of the project's divergent experiences in identifying the concerns, priorities, and resources of individual families. It was evident from the feedback that use of a battery of self-rated instruments had many limitations. Although this approach initially seemed sound from a research perspective, it was not useful as a general procedure in practice.

This insight led to a shift in information collection to a more conversational style based on informal interaction. Information about the family's coping resources needed to be collected over time through mutual exchange. There was no necessity to gain a comprehensive understanding of their resources early in the intake protocol. A general screening of their resources through thoughtful dialogue was sufficient. If issues surfaced, they could then be pursued in greater depth. As a result of the parental feedback, the interactive process discussed in Chapters 10 and 11 was adopted by the project for IFSP development.

Conclusions About Self-Rated Instruments

Through collaboration with families, we came to the following conclusions regarding the role of self-rated instruments in early intervention.

1. Instruments should be used very selectively. When employed, they are best utilized during intervention as a means to promote awareness. They can help some parents gain knowledge about their resources and better understand the vulnerabilities that interfere with their adaptive functioning. Parents have a choice regarding what they wish to share with early intervention staff. By the very nature of self-reporting, the instruments can raise important but sensitive issues that practitioners may consider too intrusive or delicate to address on their own.
2. Many instruments in the field are developed for research purposes and are inappropriate for clinical application. They are often global in their inquiry and not targeted to the realities of families in early intervention programs. For example, the Family Inventory of Resources for Management (FIRM) and the Family Inventory of Life Events and Changes (FILE) proved to be too general in their focus to provide useful information for program planning. Likewise, the Symptoms Checklist 90 was too directed toward identifying pathology to be an accurate indicator of physical and affective states. In addition, there can be significant cultural bias, with many families finding the instruments irrelevant or invasive. Pen-and-paper tasks are inappropriate for some parents who cannot manage the language requirements. Families may also view them as measures that judge their personal adequacy as parents or feel pressure to complete the instruments despite assurances of free choice.

Results of Change

The experience with the self-rated instruments was typical of the changes made by the COPING Project during the pilot program. During the 3 years of grant support, we initiated new practices, evaluated their outcome, and revised accordingly. Change was not dramatic but came from regular staff meetings and individual supervision. As one issue was resolved, new ones were identified. From the initial focus on refining the project's theoretical base and model of the coping process, attention shifted to the development and psychometric validation of the Early Coping Inventory. It became evident that the field needed a systematic way of assessing a child's coping style. The personalized decision-making model was then refined to assist writing IFSPs. It served as a vehicle for linking theory to practice and assessment to intervention.

Numerous efforts were made to establish some type of "coping curriculum" for the children. The various attempts inevitably seemed simplistic and too rigid. The cookbook approach did not capture the range of possibilities for assisting children to increase their coping capability. The breakthrough in our thinking came with further examination of coping as a transactional process. Extensive videotaping was conducted of infants, toddlers, and their parents coping with everyday challenges. These videotapes were studied in detail.

When the transactions were diagramed, it was recognized that they could be analyzed in a clinically meaningful manner. Change could be generated at each step of the transactions. These intervention options provided a structure for personalizing therapy and connecting it with moment-to-moment living: modifying demands, enhancing coping resources, and providing contingent feedback. Common intervention strategies and activities could then be applied within this structure to achieve functional results (see chaps. 7 and 8, this volume).

Concurrent with implementation of the pilot program, the COPING staff shared their findings at seminars and conferences as part of their grant commitment. Training focused on helping others adapt or replicate some of the new directions. Discussion and feedback from these experiences further refined the intervention frame of reference. Furthermore, a subsequent federal grant for outreach training allowed the COPING Project to disseminate its work on a national basis.

EVALUATION OF THE PILOT PROGRAM AND OUTREACH TRAINING

Effectiveness of the Pilot Program

As part of its evaluation plan during the program demonstration period, the COPING Project collected data on the children and families as well as the staff who received training to implement the models. There was also a follow-up study of families 3 years after they left the pilot program. Data indicated that the COPING approach was effective for serving young children with special needs and their families, and that its models could be disseminated through staff training and technical assistance. Specifically, the evaluation data supported five effectiveness statements.

The COPING models provided the necessary structure to develop functionally oriented individualized family service plans. As a result of involvement in the COPING Project, all 21 children in the initial pilot program had goals and intervention activities that focused on facilitating their adaptive behavior. During a 30-month period, 118 coping-related objectives were targeted for the children. In addition, 72 outcomes were written that addressed specific coping-related priorities of family members. Currently, in the early intervention and preschool programs at the John F. Kennedy Medical Center, service plans routinely address coping concerns that are identified by the families.

Children in the pilot program enhanced their coping effectiveness and applied their learning to subsequent experiences. The children were examined in depth during the pilot period. A comparison of the group's pre- and post-coping behaviors documented a significant shift ($p < .001$) toward more effective ratings on all items in the Early Coping Inventory. In addition to group-based analyses, individual profiles were examined to assess change in the coping ability of each child over time. An examination of these coping profiles indicated that 46% of the children made statistically significant shifts toward more effective coping. More than 33% of the other children demonstrated functionally important improvement in their adaptive functioning but were just short of statistical significance. Figure 12.1 illustrates sample coping profiles of six of these children.

A 3-year follow-up study used a structured interview format to collect information from these families. The purpose of the study was to ascertain their present status and the ripple effect of their participation in the program. The collected data were subjected to a Q sort and cluster analysis.

The results indicated that gains in coping competence were either maintained or enhanced as suggested by the following three indicators.

1. The majority of the children were placed in regular educational environments.
2. Children who were initially noted as minimally effective showed the greatest improvement in coping effectiveness during and after participation in the pilot program.
3. In follow-up interviews, 82% of the families stated that their child was coping better and credited the early intervention program for establishing the essential foundation for such performance. In their comments they used words such as "happy," "well-adjusted," "sociable," and "independent."

Families enhanced their coping resources, reduced their stressors, and were able to maintain these gains over time. During the pilot program, the majority of the parents achieved the coping-related outcomes that they chose as critical for their personal well-being. Most of these concerns (87%) were directed toward reducing specific stressors, expanding coping strategies, or improving their psychological status. In the follow-up study, 91% of the families stated that they were coping more successfully as a result of knowledge and skills acquired in the program.

Parents were satisfied with their own and their children's involvement with the COPING Project and its subsequent impact on their lives. As evidenced by parental feedback, all 21 families in the initial pilot program indicated satisfaction with the breadth, quality, and usefulness of services received. All families interviewed in the follow-up study identified specific experiences that were most helpful. They mentioned the value of the support groups, the child development services, and having experiences targeted to expanding their coping resources. Parents identified that subsequent to leaving the early intervention program they were able to cope successfully with many life events, such as the birth of another child, relocation, hospitalization, a return to work, and the child's transitions to preschool and elementary school.

Staff members increased their effectiveness in working with children and families through the use of COPING models; this programming was cost effective. Staff provided positive feedback regarding the efficacy of the COPING approach. All agreed that they had developed an important understanding of the coping styles of the children. Approximately 90% had an expanded awareness of the coping resources and stressors of the families, which increased their sensitivity and comfort in working cooperatively with them. In addition, studies involving cost-benefit analysis demonstrated that coping-related programming was fiscally efficient. Cost control resulted from various innovations (e.g., a consolidated delivery of services, increased use of community resources, more effective service coordination).

Effectiveness of Outreach Training

After the 3-year program demonstration period, the COPINC Project received federal funding to disseminate its intervention approach through training activities and technical assistance. Both the demand for training and its quality validated clinical usefulness of the

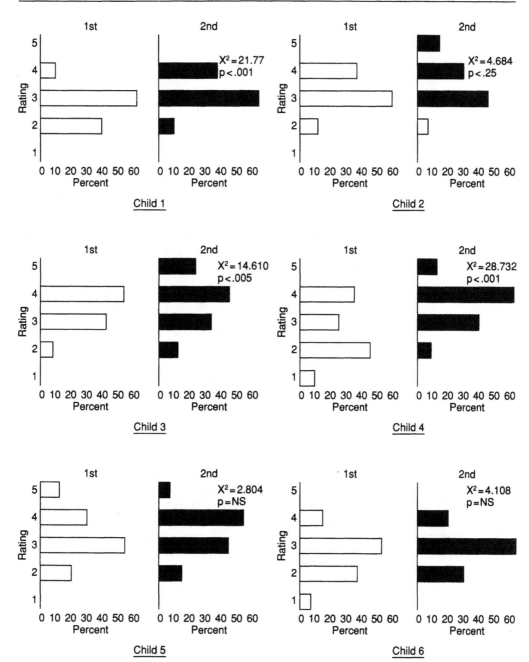

Figure 12.1. Sample profiles of changes in coping effectiveness as measured by the Early Coping Inventory.

coping frame of reference. During the following several years, the COPING Project provided training in 29 states. It included presentations at 16 national and 22 state conferences; 15 seminars at colleges and universities; and 20 staff training workshops at early intervention, preschool, and Head Start programs.

Each training activity offered by the COPING Project had an evaluation component that focused on conceptual content, clinical application, and specific training components.

Table 12.3. Evaluation summary of training effectiveness

Evaluation categories	Percentage of total ratings[a]					Mean rating
	1	2	3	4	5	
Participant understands the models	.00	.05	.14	.38	.44	4.21
Practical application to intervention	.00	.02	.08	.36	.55	4.44
Presentation effectiveness	.00	.03	.14	.44	.40	4.20
Quality of instructional materials	.00	.00	.09	.21	.70	4.61
Overall reaction	.00	.02	.11	.41	.47	4.33
Overall percentage per rating	.00	.02	.11	.36	.51	

[a]A rating of "1" = most negative; a rating of "5" = most positive

Table 12.3 provides a summary of evaluation findings from a broad sample of the training activities. These data are representative of the positive responses consistently received.

In order to evaluate the impact of training over time, a follow-up study was implemented. Structured telephone interviews were conducted with the administrators of 20 early childhood sites approximately 6 months after training. The key question was whether coping-related training had changed the program's approach to service provision. The sites reported that they were able to apply the learning in concrete and facilitative ways. A consistent response was that training helped them to shift their program's philosophy and operation toward a more family-centered approach that emphasized the expansion of coping resources to support functional outcomes.

The following specific changes were reported: 20 programs had coping-related goals in their service plans, 18 programs regularly used the Coping Inventories with children, 18 programs were employing new intervention strategies to increase the children's adaptive functioning, and 16 programs applied the personalized decision-making process to support collaboration with families. A sample of parents who were also interviewed perceived these changes as meaningful. They were particularly pleased with their increased decision making in the development of their child's IFSP or IEP and their child's greater adaptive competence in the home and community (e.g., decreased temper tantrums and sibling rivalry; better behavior in community, church, and childcare programs; increased flexibility and participation in family activities). Thus, there was a ripple effect of the project from the training experienced by practitioners and administrators to improvements in program operations to changes in the lives of children and families.

LESSONS LEARNED

Much was learned through the COPING Project during its program demonstration and outreach training phases, and much is still to be learned and perhaps relearned. The following lessons made a particular contribution to our understanding. They reflect two levels of application of the coping perspective: 1) a frame of reference for intervention with individual children and their families, and 2) guidelines for program development and change.

> The need to adapt is inherent in daily living and involves being responsive to self-generated demands and expectations and the demands and expectations of others in the environment.
> Intervention that emphasizes expanding child and family coping resources not only enhances a family's present functioning, but also prepares them to manage future challenges.

Optimal intervention outcomes are generated when there is a good fit between critical components—the child's needs, expectations of the family and staff, and available resources to achieve the desired change.

Because transactions are the core of moment-to-moment daily living, they are the basis for the intervention options.

Intervention is personalized within the common structure of the intervention options and the decision-making process.

Intervention needs to highlight the development of coping competence and address all three categories of coping style—sensorimotor organization, reactivity, and self-initiation.

Intervention activities and strategies are tailored to the child; there is no set curriculum that is applicable to all children for facilitating their coping.

For learning to take place, there must be some degree of effectiveness in the transactions between the child and the adult.

Intervention planning for children with minimally effective coping behaviors needs to reflect contributing factors (e.g., type and degree of disability, family circumstances) and the nature of the child's coping style (e.g., rigidly repetitious, erratic).

Children whose coping behaviors are situationally effective need help to generalize their coping efforts to a variety of circumstances and conditions.

Even children with effective coping styles may need extra support to deal with new or especially difficult demands.

Services need to be family centered in order for the child to make optimal progress.

Intervention services build from the collaborative involvement of parents and staff as decision makers.

One cannot assume that a family's perceptions of a situation or an experience matches those of practitioners; there is a need to check out the assumptions of all involved.

Change is an ever-present demand that is often difficult for individuals and programs to manage.

Change is facilitated when the steps toward the goals are small and participants are actively involved in the planning and revision of the goals.

SUMMARY

In this chapter, the background and sample experiences of the COPING Project are shared. Results of the program evaluation are provided, including the outcome of the 3-year follow-up study. These data document the effectiveness of the coping frame of reference. Specific lessons learned from the project are shared in order to support other early intervention programs in their journey toward best practices.

CHAPTER 13

Experiences of Four Families

This chapter describes the experiences of four of the families who participated in the initial pilot program of the COPING Project. Different aspects of their involvement are highlighted as they progressed from entry into the program to a follow-up study when the children were school age. These families had children who demonstrated problems in their adaptive behavior and resilience. With two families, important insights were gained as a result of the staff's professional misjudgments. Collaborative sharing with these families over the years was most generative in the development of the coping intervention approach.

Two of the families were selected for this chapter because their children were developmentally delayed and they were involved in early intervention services at a very young age. These families, however, had very different coping resources that influenced their adaptive capabilities. The third family consisted of an only child and a single mother. There was a long, stressful period before the cause of this child's developmental delays were accurately diagnosed. The fourth family had the challenge of raising a child with cerebral palsy who had severe disabilities. Although both parents were health professionals and had effective coping resources, they had difficulty managing their special circumstances.

ELAINE MERINO

Elaine was born full-term to a 39-year-old mother and a 42-year-old father. The mother had an uncomplicated pregnancy and delivery. However, at birth the infant was small for gestational age and had a low Apgar score, which were causes for shared concern. By 6 weeks of age it became evident that Elaine had low muscle tone, atypical reflex activity, and a developmental delay. In addition to Elaine, the Merinos had 4- and 10-year-old sons and a 7-year-old daughter. The father was the manager of the dairy department at a local supermarket and the mother was a full-time homemaker.

First Year in the Program

When Elaine entered the program at 2 months of age, she was alert, visually attentive, and able to tolerate physical handling. She produced open vowel cooing sounds in response to adult stimulation and showed an occasional social smile. She had generalized hypotonia and limited head control.

The initial IFSP focused on helping Elaine acquire developmental skills that would support her interactions with the environment. Particular attention was placed on increasing her head control and developing midline-oriented play skills (the flexor control described in chap. 3, this volume). The parents wanted to learn more about her developmental capabilities and activities to implement at home to foster her growth. Consequently, intervention emphasized showing Mrs. Merino ways to play and care for Elaine that were developmentally beneficial. The mother also chose to participate in a parent discussion group at the center as a part of Elaine's weekly program. In addition, a therapist conducted a home visit once a month in the evening to meet personally with the father. Elaine made slow but steady progress over time. Her primary delays were in expressive language and gross motor skills. An emerging concern was her minimally effective coping style (Adaptive Behavior Index of 2.1 on the Early Coping Inventory). Elaine had some coping strengths such as sensory responsiveness and an ability to accept warmth and support from others. However, she was very passive and generated little self-initiated behavior. Although Elaine was gradually developing mobility skills, she was not using them to explore.

This passivity seemed to be reinforced unintentionally by Mrs. Merino in her efforts "to help" her child. For instance, when the teacher was working with Elaine, the mother wanted to hold her daughter on her lap. Initially this seemed desirable as it assisted Mrs. Merino to learn adaptive positioning and provided Elaine with physical and emotional support. However, when Elaine no longer needed such support, it was difficult for the mother to give up that role.

As trust developed between Mrs. Merino and the staff, she began to share many worries during conversations. She talked about conflicts with Mr. Merino and tensions with her mother-in-law, who was critical of Mrs. Merino's handling of Elaine. The mother-in-law always seemed to "know a better way." Mrs. Merino also had complaints about her husband. It was evident that many family problems predated Elaine's birth.

Mr. and Mrs. Merino were aware that the tensions were undermining their family life and gradually turned to the early intervention program for support. Over time the staff helped them to clarify their concerns, priorities, and resources through informal interactions and the selected use of self-rated instruments. The Merinos's perceptions of their coping resources are summarized.

Beliefs and Values   The Merinos reported a shared belief that they had limited resources for coping effectively with their present situation. Their differing views and beliefs on a variety of issues contributed to disagreement and conflict. They differed in their view of how desirable it was to be in their family. They identified difficulties related to communication, collaborative decision making, mutual assistance, and the sharing of feelings. The Merinos reported that they were not entirely in control of family events due to these vulnerabilities. Mrs. Merino felt Elaine was having a negative impact on the family. She indicated that her outlook was somewhat fatalistic and that she often felt helpless.

Coping Style   The Merinos considered their coping behaviors to be effective in certain situations. They recognized that because they had a limited repertoire of strategies, difficult situations were very stressful and resulted in general unhappiness.

Mrs. Merino stated her coping strengths were her curiosity and ability to understand and follow directions. She also described herself as passive, easily frustrated, and quickly fatigued due to a low level of energy. She felt that she was not very stimulating to others and reported having limited confidence in her ability to solve problems.

Mr. Merino saw himself as quite able to accept support and warmth from others, but also as having difficulty communicating his feelings, responding to the control of others, and shifting plans when necessary to solve a problem.

Physical and Affective States   Both parents were generally in good physical health, but they reported somatic and stress-related complaints. Mrs. Merino mentioned depression and anxiety. Mr. Merino stated he had a negative self-image and generally felt unhappy.

Human Supports   The Merinos believed they had some support from family and friends. They differed, however, in their view of the degree and value of that support. Mrs. Merino indicated that extended family, particularly her mother-in-law, could be more understanding and helpful to her.

Material Supports   The parents differed in their assessment of their financial resources. Mr. Merino reported that material resources were quite adequate to meet family needs. His wife did not agree and stated that her husband had changed jobs several times in the last few years.

The Merinos felt that the gradual process of clarifying their coping resources was instrumental in assisting them to understand their family situation. They took the opportunity to apply this new insight when they developed their second IFSP approximately 6 months after the initial plan. The Merinos decided that their primary issue was divergent beliefs and their difficulty communicating given such differences. They would often view a situation from different perspectives and fail to check out their assumptions with each other. The resulting breakdown in communication would typically lead to fighting or hurt feelings.

Both parents described situations illustrating this critical point. Their examples ranged from mundane daily incidents to their differing views on religion and God. Mr. Merino expressed confusion and concern over his beliefs and explained how Elaine's birth had seriously shaken them. Mrs. Merino said that she was not experiencing the same religious turmoil; however, her ambivalent beliefs about Elaine were seen in other ways. She stated, for instance, that she was very protective of Elaine—"Almost like I don't want to let her go." Yet, she seldom implemented any of the home program activities that she repeatedly requested from the staff.

Through the IFSP decision-making process, Mr. and Mrs. Merino wanted to increase the effectiveness of their family's functioning by learning to communicate their differing views and beliefs to each other and by learning to provide mutual support and assistance. They chose to participate in the following activities to achieve these outcomes: time limited, problem-focused couple counseling; attendance at a coping with stress workshop; and continued participation by Mrs. Merino in the parent support group.

During the rest of the first year, both parents were actively involved in their selected activities. Attention was placed on fostering a more reciprocal mother–child relationship. During intervention sessions, the practitioners would identify the emotional and communicative cues that Mrs. Merino and Elaine were giving to each other and assist each partner to interact in ways that were mutually rewarding. One goal was to increase Mrs. Merino's comfort level with her daughter and decrease Elaine's passivity.

Second Year in the Program

As part of Elaine's reevaluation during her second year in the early intervention program, the Merinos and the staff identified the following factors as facilitating and interfering with her learning and coping.

The factors facilitating learning were:

Visual and auditory alertness
Movement skills used functionally for mobility

Manipulation of objects using familiar actions
Emerging imitative skills
Social responsiveness

The factors interfering with learning included:

Minimal tolerance to structure (e.g., crawls away from activities presented by an
    adult, fusses when physically handled, unable to sit in one spot to stay on task)
Short attention span (e.g., easily distracted both visually and auditorily, does not stay
    on task when activity is altered in some way, feedback sometimes diverts atten-
    tion from task)
Withdrawal to mother to avoid a task or another adult
Passivity (e.g., takes little initiative, prefers watching to participating, depends on ex-
    ternal cues to perform)
Independence not expected or reinforced by family (e.g., dependence reinforced by
    doing everything for the child, such as getting her toys when she throws them)
Few vocalizations and limited means for making needs known

The parents and staff felt that most of the interfering factors could be changed, so they
developed intervention strategies to address the factors that were most undermining
Elaine's daily functioning. For example, in the next IFSP they wrote a goal to increase
Elaine's attending behavior in order to enhance her impulse control and help her to stay
with tasks to completion. An objective was written to encourage her to attend to one activity independently for 10 minutes while sitting on the floor. She tended to flee quickly
from tasks and look aimlessly around the room whether at home or the program. Intervention strategies involved structuring the environment to reduce distractions and gradually decreasing physical boundaries—progressing from sitting in a cube chair at a table to
playing independently on the floor.

Another goal for Elaine was to learn to sign a few key words. In addition to developing her delayed verbal skills, it would help her communicate her needs, thereby giving her
more control in managing her world. The parents requested the initial signs to be "more"
and "finished."

A critical goal was to expand Elaine's purposeful self-initiation. Numerous strategies
were involved to contribute to this outcome. For example, an objective was developed to
encourage her to engage in independent exploration by crawling distances of approximately 6 feet to play with toys. Initially, familiar toys were presented at short distances and
then novel toys at increasingly farther distances. Eventually Elaine progressed to making
choices between toys and crawling or toddling to the desired one.

As Mrs. Merino tended to react very quickly with physical support or verbal direction, strategies were offered to help her respond to Elaine in ways that promoted the
child's self-initiated actions. She learned "to be there" for her daughter without being constantly attentive, and to provide more subtle, distant feedback (e.g., smiles, nods, nonverbal facial expressions) to keep Elaine engaged.

The intervention program continued to provide guidance and socialization for the
parents, especially for Mrs. Merino. The support group was a challenge for Mrs. Merino
because she had difficulty relating other people's experiences to her own circumstances.
For example, during a group session Mrs. Merino shared her concern about telling people
about Elaine's condition when she is shopping and in the community. She asked how she
should react, particularly at that point when her daughter was approaching her second
birthday and her developmental delay was becoming more obvious.

The group was responsive and offered practical suggestions on ways they had coped with similar situations. Although Mrs. Merino seemed to benefit from the ventilation of her feelings of frustration and depression, she had reasons why each of the suggestions could not be implemented. Finally, she said, "Perhaps I've not accepted it yet. Anything less than perfectly right is not good enough." It was clear that she was still viewing her life through negative beliefs.

Third Year in the Program

During the last year in the program, intervention services continued similarly to the first 2 years; activities were geared to facilitate Elaine's development and adaptive competence. By the time of her transition from the program, many of her coping behaviors had progressed from minimally to situationally effective. Services for the Merinos focused on helping them to expand their coping resources so they could function with greater satisfaction as a couple and as parents. There was a special emphasis on assisting them to understand the needs of their three older children, who were starting to misbehave to gain attention.

Follow-Up

When Elaine left the early intervention program, she entered a special education preschool class in the neighborhood school. She continued to receive occupational and physical therapy at the medical center and to be involved in summer programs there. At 4 years of age she was enrolled in a special activity program. At the end of the summer the following information was shared with the Merinos by the staff.

➡   Elaine was interested in most activities that were presented during the group sessions. However, her behavior limited participation. She preferred to observe group activities from a distance and required adult assistance to become more active. When an adult would physically bring her to the other children and help her to engage in an activity, Elaine was able to interact appropriately and generally enjoyed herself. Toward the end of the summer, more self-initiated involvement in activities was observed.

As part of a 3-year follow-up study conducted by the COPING Project, Mr. and Mrs. Merino were interviewed in their home. The interviewer was an external consultant to the Project who was also the parent of a young child with a disability. At the time, Elaine was 6 years of age. The following are some questions and responses from the interview.

How would you describe Elaine now?   The Merinos described Elaine as a relatively happy child with the range of emotions one would typically expect of a child—at various times up, down, happy, mad, and sad. Mrs. Merino felt her biggest problems with Elaine were behavioral. Elaine did not interact well with other children. She had little social life outside of school except with her siblings. She was a very stubborn child who seemed to pick up bad behaviors from other children more quickly than she picked up academic material. According to Mrs. Merino, these behavioral problems had limited Elaine's potential for inclusion into regular education at that time.

Elaine had relatively little motor impairment. Her father believed that her physical ability had surpassed her intellectual development. Academically, Elaine's parents believed she was not doing poorly, but she had done less well than they had hoped.

What important things have happened since the early intervention program?   Elaine was placed in a "basic skills" self-contained class in her local school system. In general, the Merinos were satisfied with this placement. They felt better able to advocate for their daughter due to skills learned at the workshop on coping with transition that was provided by the early intervention program. The only other major event since leaving had been the many job changes by Mr. Merino, which had caused great stress in the family.

How has Elaine influenced the rest of the family? Mr. Merino felt that Elaine's older brothers and sister generally treated her as a typical younger sister. They were aware of her differences but did not dwell on them. They did tend, however, to be rather protective of Elaine. Mrs. Merino was not sure whether this behavior was because Elaine was the little sister or because she had special needs.

Mr. Merino believed that Elaine had been a positive influence on her siblings. They seemed to be more aware and tolerant of people who are different or who have disabilities. Mrs. Merino disagreed somewhat; she said that they were occasionally jealous of the extra attention given to Elaine.

Do you believe that Elaine made progress while in the early intervention program? Mr. and Mrs. Merino stated that Elaine had definitely made progress in the program and that the gains in development and adaptive functioning were due to therapy she received.

Was there a connection between your involvement and this progress? The Merinos said they would like to think that their involvement helped Elaine to progress. However, both agreed they would never feel as though they had done enough unless Elaine eventually functioned like a "normal" child. They had a secret hope that Elaine would be placed in a regular class. Mrs. Merino felt that the parents who pushed their children the hardest seemed to get successful results. Yet, whenever she tried to push Elaine, the child would just shut down or go to sleep. Her slow rate of development had caused them much frustration, but they were now more resigned to this reality.

Reflections

It was very challenging for the practitioners to work with the Merino family. The parents identified numerous coping difficulties, many of which were present before Elaine was born. It was a continuing issue for them to deal with the fact that Elaine would always have special needs despite their efforts. Mrs. Merino was particularly active in the support group, counseling, and educational workshops. However, all involvement was filtered through negative beliefs about her situation and a reticence to accept as success any outcome other than Elaine becoming "normal." Mr. Merino shared this view but was less vocal about it. Despite encouragement by the staff, the Merinos never openly discussed Elaine's disability with their three older children.

The Merinos had a tendency to interpret events as threats rather than challenges. Therefore, intervention was often directed to assisting them to reframe their perspective so that they could cope with daily demands and periodic crises. It was also partially successful in improving communication between them.

Despite their many problems, the Merinos were able to remain intact and function as a family. At the time of the follow-up study, they had sufficient coping resources to manage daily living in an adequate, although stressful, manner. They gave credit during the interview to the early intervention program for helping them acquire critical skills that had increased their coping effectiveness.

ARETHA HARMON

Aretha was the second child in the Harmon family. Her mother had a part-time job as a waitress, and her father was an automobile mechanic. Their son, Roy, was 3 years of age. Aretha was born full-term with a weight of 7 pounds, 12 ounces. The only complication during pregnancy was some bleeding during Mrs. Harmon's last trimester. Aretha was diagnosed as having Down syndrome at birth with confirmation shortly after by chromosomal studies. She was healthy but showed evidence of mild hypotonia. Within a month the parents enrolled her in the early intervention program at the medical center.

First Year in the Program

At the initial evaluation, Aretha was described as an alert, attentive infant who responded to her parents with eye gaze, smiling, and vocalization. Her response to sound consisted of changes in body movement or sucking patterns. Her reaction to toys consisted of looking and visually tracking them horizontally. Initial intervention goals were directed to generating more active engagement by supporting parent–child interaction, facilitating head and upper trunk control, stimulating her visual abilities, and encouraging early play schemes such as swiping, holding, and mouthing objects.

From the start, Mrs. Harmon participated with interest during intervention sessions and followed through on suggested activities to do in the home. She generally brought Roy with her to the program. He played in the room and occasionally interacted with Aretha in an enthusiastic manner. Mr. Harmon also came to many sessions.

Aretha's first scores on the Early Coping Inventory showed her as situationally effective in her coping style (an Adaptive Behavior Index of 3.0). Some of her most adaptive characteristics included a positive orientation to life (i.e., an apparent expectation that her needs would be met), social responsiveness, and the ability to react successfully to sensory input. She was also able to accept substitutes when necessary (e.g., being held by Roy or the father when she wanted her mother). Aretha's least adaptive behaviors were her tendency to be hypoactive and to frustrate easily.

During informal conversations in their early months in the program, the Harmons talked about their concerns and resources. The following is a summary of this self-reported information that was discussed but not documented as a report.

Beliefs and Values   Mr. and Mrs. Harmon were in agreement about how to raise Aretha. Both parents felt a sense of control over their family affairs and shared a common bond of mutual cooperation, togetherness, and emotional support. Additionally, they shared an optimistic life perspective. There was a mutual confidence in their problem-solving ability, and each partner viewed Aretha's presence in the family as an opportunity for individual and family growth.

Coping Style   The Harmons reported that they were generally effective in coping with a variety of situations. In specific high-stress situations, however, there was some difficulty galvanizing themselves for action and tolerating frustration.

Mrs. Harmon reported that she had positive self-esteem and described herself as resilient and able to communicate her feelings. She was less secure in her ability to handle anxiety and had some trouble balancing dependence and independence. She identified a tendency to be rigid in her beliefs and in her approach to daily activities.

Mr. Harmon believed he was effective in applying his life experience to problem solving new situations. He did, however, state that he had difficulty asking for help and expressing personal needs, often choosing to shoulder responsibilities himself. Mr. Harmon did not share his wife's zest for life. He had a serious nature and a tendency to take charge and carry responsibility. He spoke freely about the burden associated with this style.

Physical and Affective States   Both parents were in good physical and emotional health. Mrs. Harmon described herself as having a high energy level.

Human Supports   The Harmons felt they had strong social support, especially within the extended family. A network of family and friends were seen as actively involved.

Material Supports The Harmons agreed that their financial resources were strained. They were proud that they had recently purchased a house, affectionately referred to as a "lop-sided, handy-man special."

During the process of updating the IFSP, the Harmons found it very helpful to look in a self-directed manner at their coping resources in order to identify issues they wished to address. They said that it gave them a better perspective and direction for decision making. Mr. Harmon felt pressured by his time limitations, which had an impact on his involvement with his children. He wanted to gain information first-hand from the clinicians and be actively involved in Aretha's program. Both parents requested more information about what governmental and community supports were available to them. Likewise, each partner wished to expand specific coping-related skills that they believed would enrich their family life.

As a result of this process, the IFSP was modified to target the following desired outcomes. The Harmons wanted to learn time-management strategies and how to identify local and state resources. To enhance their coping effectiveness, Mrs. Harmon wished to be more flexible and able to use a broader range of problem-solving procedures, whereas Mr. Harmon wanted to learn how to ask for help and share responsibility when appropriate.

Sample strategies to promotes these outcomes included:

1. The provision of materials related to community services and public programs that could be utilized immediately or could be available for the future
2. Attendance at an educational workshop for parents related to time management, with personalized follow-up to assist implementation of learned strategies
3. Home-based services on a regular basis to support Mr. and Mrs. Harmon in addressing their individual coping-related concerns

Second Year in the Program

At 18 months of age, Aretha's developmental skills ranged from 8 to 15 months. She was described as a very outgoing child who liked to play with other children, particularly her brother. Her coping skills had increased to an Adaptive Behavior Index of 3.4. A summary of her coping status at 18 months is presented in Figure 13.1.

When Aretha was 20 months, Mrs. Harmon told her support group that she was pregnant. She shared her pleasure and anxieties with the group. When, late in her pregnancy, Mr. Harmon had to go on a business-related trip, she told the group how upset she was about it. Mrs. Harmon said she was afraid to be alone in the house with the children. This led to the question on everyone's mind: Was she worried about the health and status of her unborn child? Mrs. Harmon denied any anxiety. She and her husband had chosen not to have amniocentesis testing because they both felt any child would be desired and welcomed.

At a session a month before her due date, the group expressed concern that Mrs. Harmon looked tired and upset. Mrs. Harmon explained that she had just had a sonogram that showed the baby was developmentally ready to be born—4 weeks early. She seemed scared and anxious. The group facilitator asked her if, in fact, she was scared. She admitted she was and defiantly said that she would "accept whatever I get." The facilitator said that she probably wanted a baby who did not have special needs. Mrs. Harmon cried openly and admitted that she had been obsessively worried that the baby may have a disability. She felt guilty that her desire for a child without problems seemed to diminish her love for Aretha. The group was respectful of her conflict and supportive in helping her to manage it.

Coping Effectiveness

	Effectiveness Scores
Sensorimotor Organization (SM)	3.8
Reactive Behavior (R)	3.1
Self-Initiated Behavior (SI)	3.3
Adaptive Behavior Index	3.4

Coping Profile

	1	2	3	4	5
Sensorimotor Organization					
Reactive Behavior					
Self-Initiated Behavior					

Most and Least Adaptive Coping Behaviors

Most adaptive			Least adaptive		
Category	Rating	Behavior	Category	Rating	Behavior
SM	5	Reacts effectively to different types of touch	R	2	Difficulty adapting to changes in the environment
SM	5	Adapts successfully to a range of sensory input	R	2	Resists limits set by caregivers
SM	5	Consistently demonstrates pleasure in self-initiated body movement and sensory exploration	R	2	Low frustration tolerance
SI	5	Gives warmth and support to others	R	2	Inflexible in shifting behavior and accepting substitutes

Figure 13.1. Aretha Harmon's adaptive behavior summary (18 months of age).

After the birth of a healthy baby girl, Mr. and Mrs. Harmon shared with the group their reflections. During the pregnancy and delivery of Tabatha, they had relived many turbulent memories and emotions associated with Aretha. It had been confusing and frightening to reexperience these thoughts, but ultimately enriching. They felt that they knew themselves better and in some strange ways were more available to love their children.

Third Year in the Program

By 2 years of age, Aretha was continuing to make progress in her development. The following factors were identified at this time as facilitating and interfering with her learning.

The factors facilitating learning were:

Increased interest in new and novel situations
Expanded self-comforting behaviors
Active exploration of her surroundings
Ability to participate in structured and unstructured tasks for short periods
Awareness of the moods of others
Imitation of simple, single actions
Engagement in spontaneous social interactions with adults

Awareness of peers and plays in close proximity
Communicative intent
Generalization of learning when guided by an adult

The factors interfering with learning included the following:

Inflexibility in adapting behavior to environmental demands
Low frustration tolerance with challenging tasks
Rigid persistence in getting own way
Functional skills limited by fine motor delay

Around this time, the Harmons were becoming increasingly worried and frustrated by Aretha's behavior. The mother said that "She is more active and interested in things, but oh so willful. My sweet pea has gone stubborn on me. It's like she is telling us: 'It's mine, I want it, get out of my way.' " The practitioner encouraged the parents to record what happened in a typical day and how Aretha acted. This log was useful in understanding the pattern of family life. It became clear that Aretha's occasional fretfulness and irritability were not erratic but tended to occur with predictable events: diaper change, finishing a meal, having the television turned off, and when asked to share anything in her possession. It was also evident that she was on her best behavior when her older brother Roy was present or when her infant sister Tabatha was absent.

The Harmons were quick to identify many of the dynamics that were occurring. Aretha was having sibling rivalry with the baby and was also entering a developmental period of questing for autonomy. She had a situationally effective coping style with particular circumstances being difficult to manage. The practitioner served as a resource to help the family determine a plan of action. Special attention was given to Mrs. Harmon, who had earlier identified on the IFSP a wish to increase her flexibility and problem-solving skills.

The parents developed and implemented many coping strategies to be responsive to Aretha's needs. A critical change was reframing the way they viewed her behavior from "terrible twos" to "terrific twos." This cognitive coping strategy prevented many power struggles from happening. A very successful action-oriented coping strategy was the creation of a game in which one parent would chase Aretha while saying, "I'm going to catch you and tickle you all over." When finally caught, the toddler would giggle with delight while being tickled. The "tickle game" built upon Aretha's most adaptive coping behaviors (enjoyment of touch, active exploration, social engagement) and also fueled her emotional need to be independent and adventurous. When indicated, the game was used by the parents as a reward for desired behavior. If, for example, Aretha did not resist having her diaper changed, they would play the tickle game.

At the age of 3, Aretha made the transition from the early intervention program to a special education preschool placement in the local public school. The following vignette is an excerpt from the progress summary and transition plan that was sent to the new school.

➡ Aretha has made solid progress in all areas of development but will continue to require special services to facilitate her growth. She is an outgoing, social child who initiates interaction in most learning situations. She is an active leader who is often motivated to communicate and explore, particularly when a novel experience is presented. However, Aretha's coping effectiveness can be restricted by her cognitive ability and inattention. She has good imitative skills (motor better than verbal), which can be employed to promote her learning (e.g., the use of adult modeling and demonstration as direct intervention strategies).

When stressed or not interested in a specific activity, Aretha attempts to avoid the situation by engaging in social distractions or by becoming passively resistant. Since the child has a short attention span and is easily distracted, she requires a great deal of external structuring, limit setting, and positive redirecting to remain focused. Aretha does, however, respond well to environmental cues and feedback. A predictable routine also helps her to know what is expected.

Follow-Up

The Harmons were interviewed 3 years after the pilot program as part of a follow-up study sponsored by the COPING Project. The interviewer was an outside consultant. A sample of the questions and responses are provided.

How would you describe Aretha now? Mr. and Mrs. Harmon reported that Aretha was very healthy and had many friends. She was happy, well-behaved, and very competitive for a 6-year-old child. Her father felt she was too friendly and must be watched very closely in public because she would go off with anyone. Mr. Harmon said Aretha played the role of "the informer in the house, snitching on anyone who misbehaves." She was stubborn and sometimes defied her parents, but this behavior was true of all their children.

Aretha was making progress in school and her teacher hoped to be able to mainstream her for reading and math at a later date. Currently, her acquisition of new vocabulary words seemed to have leveled off, possibly due to her short attention span. She was working on learning to tie her own shoelaces. Her parents rated her on the Coping Inventory as having a situationally effective coping style.

What important things have happened since the early intervention program? Aretha had been attending a self-contained special education class for the past 2 years. Six of the seven students in the class had Down syndrome. Mr. and Mrs. Harmon were happy with the program because it offered Aretha many varied experiences, including a weekend trip to Washington, D.C., the previous year. It was relatively easy for them to work with their school system, although they had some difficulties obtaining related services. The Harmons said that the "Transition to Preschool" workshop had prepared them to collaborate with the child study team at Aretha's school. The parents were not concerned with Aretha's lack of inclusion in the general education environment.

Other family events included the birth of another son and the death of Mr. Harmon's grandmother. Managing the birth was easy, but the death was a difficult event for all of them. Mr. Harmon believed it probably affected Aretha the least because she did not understand the significance of the death.

In addition, Mrs. Harmon had returned to school and obtained her license as a hair stylist. She started working more hours and felt that it was good for her mental state. Mr. Harmon reported enjoying the time spent with the children while his wife was working.

How has Aretha influenced the rest of the family? Mrs. Harmon reported that her mother accepted Aretha in certain ways but not in others. For example, she initially planned to cut the family out of her will if they did not have Aretha receive plastic surgery to eliminate the appearance of Down syndrome. Later she became more tolerant. Mr. Harmon's parents were sympathetic and treated Aretha basically the same as the other grandchildren.

The parents said that Aretha received no special attention from her aunts and uncles, except for Mr. Harmon's brother, who recently became somewhat more involved. After he had invited their other children to his house to sleep over, Mr. Harmon was disturbed that the offer was not extended to Aretha. He called his brother to ask why Aretha had been excluded; his brother then said she could come. It seemed that he was afraid it would be too difficult for him to handle her or that she would need some special type of care. After Aretha had slept there, the brother became more comfortable and emotionally close to her.

Reflections

Aretha and the Harmons are in sharp contrast to Elaine and the Merinos. In general, the Harmons had strong coping resources that included positive beliefs about themselves and a view of life as a challenge, not a threat. They were generally satisfied with their children and their station in life. To them, Aretha's disability did not define her as a person.

In contrast, the Merino family was more vulnerable and had more difficulty coping. They found it hard to see just Elaine and not her disability. The difference between the Harmons and the Merinos emphasizes the need to personalize services based on a family's concerns, priorities, and resources.

JIMMY DANVERS

Jimmy was the only child of a single mother. Ms. Danvers was granted custody of the boy when the father relocated to another state around the time of Jimmy's birth. The father, however, provided some financial support for his son. Ms. Danvers left her job as a graphic artist shortly before Jimmy was born. She came to the early intervention program soon after his first birthday due to her concern about his slow development. She was exasperated that the cause for the delay had not been medically identified.

First Year in the Program

In her initial meeting with the social worker, Ms. Danvers described her pregnancy as uneventful despite being involved in a stressful break-up of her relationship with the father. An issue had been his career-oriented drive, which he felt was incompatible with the responsibilities of raising a child. The delivery went smoothly, and Jimmy had a birth weight of 5 pounds, 2 ounces. He was a jittery newborn and had excessive calcium in his blood, but no special care was required in the nursery.

At the initial evaluation at 14 months of age, Jimmy's gross motor skills and level of play development were at the 6–7 month level. Cognitive and prelinguistic skills were in the 7–9 month range. His score on the Early Coping Inventory showed him to be minimally effective (an Adaptive Behavior Index of 2.3). His most successful coping skills were the ability to use vocalizations to indicate needs and to demonstrate feelings of pleasure, displeasure, and excitement. His least adaptive coping characteristics were difficulty with new routines, minimal self-protective behaviors to control the impact of the environment, and limited strategies to self-comfort. He was hypersensitive to sensory input, which resulted in restricted interaction.

Ms. Danvers was eager for her son to receive services and he was immediately placed in a program. In addition to developmental goals, short-term coping objectives were designed to increase self-initiated exploration with a variety of low-grade sensory materials and to acquire means for self-comforting. Ms. Danvers was very involved in Jimmy's intervention. However, she was so anxious about his unclear diagnosis and so motivated to help him to progress that sometimes her actions were misinterpreted by the staff.

Her persistent questioning generated tension. The practitioners started to feel that their expertise was being challenged. Consequently, they eventually viewed Ms. Danvers as "aggressive, difficult, and a trouble maker." There was much behind-the-scenes complaining about her "pushiness," and general concurrence that interaction with her was to be avoided. In contrast to the staff's perception, parents in the program found Ms. Danvers to be helpful and encouraging. In the support group she made insightful contributions to the discussion and her participation was valued.

It soon became evident that the staff had made the error of focusing on the child's development out of context of his family. They had not spent sufficient time getting to know Ms. Danvers and establishing a working relationship. It was therefore arduous for everyone concerned to recognize the other's point of view. As a result of this awareness, the social worker talked frankly with Ms. Danvers about the situation. They decided to take the time together to clarify priorities and resources.

Through mutual exchange the following information was shared. Ms. Danvers believed that she had strong coping resources. While Jimmy's developmental problems were stressful, she believed that the two of them could function well as a family. Although her separation from Jimmy's father had been traumatic, she had no regrets other than her son not having a male model during his formative years. She was in good health with lots of energy and would be financially secure when she returned to work, and would no longer need welfare assistance. Ms. Danvers was confident that, with the assistance of the early intervention program, she could "fix" Jimmy and learn to handle her "anxious personality."

The discussion regarding her anxiety level led to Ms. Danvers voluntarily completing two self-rated instruments—the Coping Inventory and the Belief Scale (see chap. 9, this volume). The insights from her responses to these measures had the most influence on expanding her coping effectiveness. She became aware that all of her energies were directed toward her child. She told the social worker, "I have put my life on hold and invested everything in Jimmy. His progress has begun to define my worth as a person." Around this time, she wrote the following entry into her diary and later shared it with the staff.

➡ I was initially surprised when I saw that the Belief Scale showed that I was overly focused on and emotionally attached to Jimmy. I didn't expect to find that there was a problem. Yet, I could also feel a deep sense of acknowledgement that I was more involved than I should be. I don't think I would ever have brought the issue up on my own. But having it presented as a result of a form that I filled out made it much easier for me to talk about it.

This experience was a turning point for Ms. Danvers that lessened her anxiety and enabled her to pursue part-time employment. The other significant event was a definitive diagnosis of Jimmy's condition. Ms. Danvers insisted at the time that her highest priority was to learn the cause of her son's developmental delays. In response, the program arranged for an evaluation at a tertiary medical center. After exhaustive testing they determined that he had a specific nonprogressive neurological condition.

Although the diagnosis was not easy to accept, Ms. Danvers found it comforting to know the reality of Jimmy's situation and to be able to establish more realistic expectations for his current program and future. There was a spontaneous improvement in the general climate. Ms. Danvers was more relaxed in her relations with the staff and trusting of their capabilities. The practitioners gained an appreciation of her many strengths and a respect for her persistence in seeking a definitive diagnosis. The staff became aware that the original breakdown in communication was due in large part to their lack of understanding about Ms. Danvers' concerns, priorities, and resources. They reacted to her anxious behavior in a defensive manner that undermined their ability to be of assistance to both Jimmy and Ms. Danvers.

By the end of the first year in the program, Jimmy's Adaptive Behavior Index had improved to 2.7. He was increasingly effective in his ability to play by himself for short periods of time and to initiate interactions with others. Progress in these areas had been facilitated by gains in gross and fine motor skills. Jimmy now responded to environmental demands with less hypersensitivity.

Second and Third Years in the Program

New coping-related goals were directed toward expanding Jimmy's attention span, as distractibility and perseverative behavior were starting to interfere with reactive and self-initiated learning. Another goal was to help him develop more purposeful strategies for managing stimulating and demanding situations. By the time he transitioned from the early intervention program, Jimmy was better able to screen out auditory and visual distractions and respond to simple verbal directions. He was starting to walk independently and play with different toys when given structure. Although he was significantly delayed, Jimmy was more competent in using his available skills functionally. Shortly before leaving the program, Ms. Danvers volunteered to write about her experiences in early intervention. The following vignette is the product of her recollections.

➡   My son entered the early intervention program when he was 14 months old. He was slow in attaining the expected developmental milestones. I was very concerned, particularly because there was no clear-cut medical problem to account for his delay. My doctor felt we should just let nature take its course. She felt Jimmy would eventually come along, but offered no explanation for his delays nor solace for my concerns.

My family also made me feel that I was overreacting. They felt Jimmy was an adorable, sweet, affectionate baby who shouldn't be rushed into growing up. They all seemed to know someone who didn't walk or talk until the age of 3 who turned out to be a genius. But I still wasn't satisfied. I felt there must be a medical professional somewhere who could thoroughly evaluate my son and provide some clue as to the cause of his developmental delays.

I finally learned of the existence of early intervention programs by contacting the local university medical center. The staff of the Pediatrics Department told me about the programs nearby. After doing research, I found this program to be the most highly recommended by people I trusted. Therefore, I called to find out how I could get my son into it.

A social worker affiliated with the program provided me with the necessary information. The best thing about that initial phone call was that this woman gave credence to my concerns. She made me feel I wasn't an alarmist and had made the right decision in contacting them. She arranged an appointment for Jimmy's initial evaluation.

Within 2 weeks of that time, Jimmy was involved in the program. Since then he has been getting an integrated program, including physical, occupational, and speech therapy, and is progressing well. Jimmy is now 33 months old. He is beginning to walk independently, but prefers walking while holding onto one of my hands. In addition, he started talking about 6 months ago, and already has a vocabulary of almost 100 words. He is combining words like "Hi Mommy" and "More cookie." However, it is quite apparent now that Jimmy's delays are significant.

Although some would say that he would have progressed anyway, I know that the early intervention program has made a tremendous contribution to his life and to our life as a family. It has provided me with a feeling that I can have some control over the situation. Before Jimmy started early intervention, I felt totally helpless in my endeavors to better understand the nature of his problem.

The medical staff provided us with the appropriate referrals, which eventually led to a conclusive diagnosis. Although it eliminated my hope that he would someday "catch up" to everyone else, I was finally forced to accept the reality. The diagnosis enabled me to work on improving his major deficits.

The staff contributed greatly to my sense that I could assist my son to become the best that he could be. They taught me techniques to help Jimmy at home. In addition, I worked jointly with them on establishing goals for each 6-month period. I was always consulted to determine which self-help skills could be emphasized to make our lives easier at home.

The weekly parent support group has been one of the most beneficial aspects of the program. There is tremendous value in knowing you are not alone. The group provides a forum for sharing experiences and feelings. I have become quite close to a few of the other mothers in the group. These are friendships that I treasure and hope to keep for a long, long time.

During the first months of our involvement I was asked if I wanted to complete several self-rated instruments. The Coping Inventory was instructive. However, the Belief Scale had the most significant impact on my life. This instrument, which assesses the parent's beliefs about his or her child, provided an invaluable insight into my relationship with my son. It revealed that my emotional involvement with Jimmy was at the maximum level on the scale. After I discussed this with the social worker during a home visit, I arrived at the conclusion that it would be helpful for me to become involved in some type of outside interest.

This discussion led me to start looking for a freelance job as a graphic artist, which I located in a short time. The early intervention staff then helped me to arrange for part-time day care for Jimmy at the childcare center affiliated with the hospital. After discussing the possible impact of this on Jimmy, I felt that it might help him to develop better social skills with other children.

Seven months have now passed since I first started working. Although the transition into child care was a little rough on Jimmy and therefore on our family life, he now seems very happy there. The most difficult part has been getting him through the illnesses that one inevitably catches when exposed to groups of children. Jimmy is beginning to interact with the kids more and more. He is now actively involved in the daily routine. He spent the first few months just watching all of the activity, but now he is obviously comfortable enough to act more like he does at home. He has also become much less reactive to loud noises that used to upset him.

The benefits I have reaped from my part-time work are many. I think before I found this job, I was beginning to feel having a child with a disability was limiting my ability to pursue a career. I could not trust anyone else to take him to his therapy because then I would be losing touch with the tools I needed to help him at home. With those restrictions on my time, how would I ever be able to fit a career into my life?

I feel so fortunate that I found a part-time job I can do near my home. It seems to be the ideal solution for me. I still can attend all of Jimmy's classes on the mornings that he is not in the child-care center. Then, on the other mornings, I have time to do work and also clear my mind of worries about Jimmy. I feel more like a total person again, not just being "Jimmy's Mommy."

Follow-Up

A follow-up study was conducted by a consultant of the COPING Project 3 years after Jimmy made the transition to a preschool program. Ms. Danvers confirmed that a significant change in their lives occurred when she realized the impact of her beliefs about herself and her role as a parent and then was able to modify them. She was pleased by the positive developments in her life and her growing sense of self.

How would you describe Jimmy now? Ms. Danvers stated that he was 6 years old and enrolled in a primary special class. Jimmy was making excellent progress and was involved in learning reading readiness skills and simple number concepts. He was able to function reasonably effectively within the group. Jimmy was doing much better than she had expected even one year ago.

Ms. Danvers had become active as a volunteer in a statewide parent advocacy group. In this capacity she had become enthusiastic about the virtues of inclusion. Consequently, she was working with the school system to help Jimmy make the transition toward an integrated environment. He was currently mainstreamed for a few activities. In the following year, he would be in a regular class placement supported by an aide and related services.

What important things have happened since the early intervention program? Many changes were reported. Ms. Danvers was now married to a man who was very family oriented and loving of Jimmy. They also had a 6-month-old son. The adjustment of a marriage and a new child was not easy, but Ms. Danvers felt they were coping productively with the many demands and enjoying it. She was on leave from her job to care for her baby but expected to return to part-time work in a few months.

This topic brought up the critical issue of child care. When Jimmy left the child-care center at the hospital, it was a challenge to find an alternative when he was not in school. In the beginning, Ms. Danvers' mother was reluctant to babysit. As Jimmy got older, she became somewhat more willing to care for him. Ms. Danvers constantly asked other people for recommendations of sitters in the area. She was finally able to find some help, but never a steady, reliable source. Now her need for child care had expanded even more with the addition of a second child and her approaching return to work.

Reflections

The following lessons were learned from the shaky start the early intervention program had with Ms. Danvers.

- It is very easy to rush into providing child-focused intervention and not dedicate sufficient efforts to develop a relationship with the family.
- The initially expressed concerns of parents may not hold true over time. With support and guidance, more emotionally laden issues that are difficult to confront may surface. It takes skill to assist parents to discover some of the issues that are unconsciously influencing their behavior and interfering with family life, and then to direct this new awareness into positive plans for action.
- Practitioners can readily lose perspective when working with challenging families and unknowingly acquire attitudes and behavioral patterns that are destructive to the meaningful provision of services. Families use their resources in idiosyncratic ways. Preconceived judgments of what is "right" are seldom useful.
- When conflicts arise, it is critical to address them early and openly in order to achieve a resolution and avoid lingering discontentment.
- Families and practitioners have a tremendous amount to teach each other for the common benefit of the children. A family-centered approach requires unhurried time and commitment to achieve trust and a shared agenda.

LUIS SUAREZ

Luis, an only child, was born 2 months premature at a weight of 4 pounds. He stayed in the intensive care unit for 30 days; when he was released, he weighed 5 pounds and 2 ounces. While in the hospital, Luis had an occurrence of apnea that nearly resulted in sudden infant death syndrome. At 8 months, when his parents brought him to the early intervention program, he was still on an apnea monitor. Luis had been referred by his physician because both the doctor and the parents felt he was clearly delayed and was difficult to manage. The lag time in referral was due to ambivalence by all of them that Luis "may just need additional time to catch up."

His medical diagnosis by that time was cerebral palsy with spastic quadriplegia and strabismus. Both parents, then in their early thirties, had degrees in health-related professions. The father was a pharmacist and worked full time; the mother was a medical technician and worked one day a week. At the initial meeting, the parents expressed concern that Luis was not able to hold his head up better and for longer periods of time, and that he was not rolling over in both directions. Mr. and Mrs. Suarez were frustrated that, despite their professional training and experience, they felt incapable of helping their own child. They expressed interest in therapy services and suggestions for home programming to foster Luis's development.

First Year in the Program

The initial evaluation over a few sessions indicated that Luis was delayed in all developmental areas. Three primary factors seemed to have the greatest impact on his ability to relate meaningfully and with satisfaction to his environment.

1. Increased muscle tone in all extremities combined with decreased tone in his trunk caused Luis difficulty in establishing the postural control necessary for developing stability against gravity and mobility skills. Movement patterns were incoordinated because they were influenced by a predominance of extensor muscle activity. The motor involvement interfered with Luis's ability to attend to his surroundings, engage in action, and respond in a timely fashion.
2. Luis had a minimally effective coping style (an Adaptive Behavior Index of 1.9). He demonstrated poor self-regulation and limited adaptability to novel events or changes in familiar surroundings. Thus, he was rigid and tended to have intense emotional reactions. Luis had a low tolerance level and would tantrum and cry uncontrollably when demands were placed on him. If upset, he had a poor ability to self-comfort and could not bounce back after the stressful event. Typically, Luis would cry excessively until his mother hugged and rocked him. When he was finally calm, he had no energy left for resuming interaction and would fall asleep.
3. Delayed cognitive skills inhibited Luis's development of strategies for acting on and responding to the environment. He had little awareness of cause-and-effect relationships and tended to play in a perseverative fashion with a limited repertoire for manipulating objects (e.g., shaking, banging, dropping). He demonstrated delayed communication and did not use acquired skills to solve problems. Interactions with him were frequently frustrating because of his resistance to change, his difficulty in communicating, and his negative mood.

During Luis's evaluation, Mr. and Mrs. Suarez talked freely about themselves and were pleased to be with professionals knowledgeable about cerebral palsy. Through informal conversation they provided the following information about their coping resources.

Beliefs and Values   The Suarezes had a number of beliefs in common. The parents reported a shared belief that the joint collaboration between themselves and professionals would best contribute to Luis's development. "God's will" would also play a role in his progress. They said that they had little feelings of guilt or burden regarding Luis's condition or care and that he was valued as a family member. However, they also stated that "raising this kid is no picnic," and "Luis has brought some meaning to our lives, I guess, maybe." There appeared to be an ambivalence in these reflections, suggesting mixed emotions.

Coping Style   Mr. and Mrs. Suarez described themselves as effective most of the time in coping with life. They identified few coping-related vulnerabilities and many strengths. Mrs. Suarez said that she was a "take-charge type of person," but had some problems handling stress. Mr. Suarez remarked that his least adaptive behavior was difficulty talking "one to one" about his thoughts and feelings.

Physical and Affective States   Both parents appeared to be in good health, but they complained that they had gained "a lot of weight since Luis came along." The father had a rather relaxed, casual disposition, whereas the mother was very energetic and tense in her demeanor.

Human Supports   The parents reported some differences in their perception of the quantity and quality of the social support available to them. Both partners described solid support from their relatives. Mr. Suarez identified few other supports, whereas Mrs. Suarez perceived their general network as adequate.

Material Supports   The Suarezes believed that their financial and material resources were generally adequate to meet their needs.

Despite the great demands associated with Luis's condition, the parents reported no special concerns beyond their son's development and his daily management. Their desired outcomes for participation in the program were to learn ways to manage Luis's behavior and care for him in the home. They requested a vigorous intervention schedule "to help make up for lost time."

After going through the personalized decision-making process for generating an IFSP, it was determined that Luis could handle an interdisciplinary infant "group." (In reality, the group structure for infants emphasized individual work with the child and parents. Group meant that a number of families attended the session and the parents participated in a support group.) Three intervention groups were considered appropriate, with each one having a somewhat different format, staffing pattern, and type of parent involvement (i.e., "Short and Sweet," "Little Rascals," and "Nighty Night Riders"). The Suarezs chose to participate in "Nighty Night Riders" because it met in the early evening twice a week and provided occupational, physical, and speech therapies. This allowed Mr. Suarez to attend sessions after work at the drugstore. In addition, a teacher would visit the home once a week to address child management issues.

Despite the collaborative IFSP process, staff members had an uneasy feeling that there were uncertainties pertaining to Luis and the dynamics of the family. Therefore, they requested that the IFSP be written for a 2-month period. After the 2 months, they all could evaluate how Luis was progressing and the appropriateness of the program. The parents readily agreed.

The staff's unsettled outlook proved to be well grounded. During the beginning sessions, Luis cried continually until he fell asleep. In an effort to calm or distract him, the practitioners changed his position, presented new and hopefully interesting toys, or attempted to quiet Luis by holding him. The team did not realize that expecting him to adjust readily to all these new people, new materials, and surroundings was inappropriate given his limited coping resources.

A case in point was the speech therapist, who was so confused by Luis's behavior that he became quite upset and driven to self-doubt. As a consequence, the demands he placed on Luis became increasingly inconsistent as he tried one thing after another. His response to Luis's lack of progress and crying was therefore not constructive. Mrs. Suarez became angry and frustrated with the therapist, and the therapist became further upset with the mother. Potential human supports became adversaries, with Luis the unwitting victim.

In addition, it was observed during home visits that Luis's typical day tended to be erratic and overstimulating. Mrs. Suarez, a friendly and outgoing person, did not hesitate to take Luis along on social outings or when running errands. Although the boy enjoyed riding in the car, he often became upset with the fast-changing pace of his mother's activity. When Luis was agitated, Mrs. Suarez could eventually calm him down. However, her strategy of always cuddling her son tended to reinforce his rigid use of hysterical crying as a coping effort, without supporting him to learn alternative means for self-modulation and self-comforting.

In response to the shared discomfort with this state of affairs, the service coordinator (teacher) and the parents talked about their perceptions and feelings. They decided that a meeting with the staff would be fruitful. At this meeting, the parents and practitioners discussed how they could help one another and help Luis. It was evident that they had misjudged the child's capacity to adapt to the home, center, and community. The impact of his minimally effective coping style was clear. The practitioners had overwhelmed the infant by constantly switching gears and trying too many new things. They needed to reduce the number of practitioners involved and make the intervention approach very predictable, consistent, and repetitious.

The parents came to realize that they also offered little consistency for Luis. The mother had no preplanned routine and took him everywhere and at any time. Mealtime, naptime, and playtime varied from day to day. Based upon this awareness, they decided to create more structure in their lives. For example, Mrs. Suarez planned to cluster her errands on the days she had a babysitter available so that Luis could stay at home. Mr. Suarez suggested other ideas, such as having daily rituals that guided Luis in knowing what to expect, thereby enabling him to feel more secure. For example, breakfast could always be introduced by placing the child in his adapted highchair, putting on his bib, and starting with his bottle.

The IFSP was revised at this time using the personalized decision-making process. Through analysis of the factors that could be changed, the parents and staff decided to:

Increase Luis's physical coordination with the use of adapted equipment and carefully selected physical handling.

Help Luis improve self-regulation by developing a more consistent routine at home.

Expand Luis's understanding of cause-and-effect relations through the use of battery-powered adapted toys.

Enhance his communication by introducing strategies for expressing needs and preferences.

Change their own expectations for Luis and alter their interactions with him accordingly.

These outcomes would help Luis relate more successfully with people and his surroundings, and improve the goodness of fit between demands and his coping resources. Thus, there would be a decrease in his unproductive behaviors, an increase in adaptive functioning, and more emotionally satisfying relationships for everyone involved. Teaching Luis communication skills was particularly important so that he could indicate his needs and have a way of controlling the influence of external events.

The staff realized that they could not focus on skill acquisition until Luis adjusted to the early intervention routine. The pace was slowed, with much repetition of consistent and familiar activities. Novel toys and equipment were introduced very gradually. The practitioners became more skillful in observing and responding to Luis's behavioral cues and in grading environmental demands.

Direct physical and occupational therapy were temporarily suspended as Luis was highly resistive to physical handling and interaction with so many adults. These therapists then served in a consultative role by giving suggestions to the parents, teacher, and speech therapist, as well as constructing adapted furniture. As Luis adjusted to the program, direct physical and occupational therapy were gradually reintroduced.

The following intervention sequence was used so that Luis would become more comfortable with Hector, his speech therapist, and would increase his tolerance for therapeutic involvement. Hector had to find a play medium that was nonthreatening and, if possible, soothing. He learned from the mother how much Luis enjoyed his bath. Water play seemed a perfect place to start, especially having Luis watch Hector pour water, because it capitalized on his strengths in visual and auditory awareness. Mrs. Suarez brought bath toys from home and taught Hector the games she played with her son while bathing him.

During water-play activities, Luis was initially positioned in an adapted floor seat. The water was placed in a clear tub in front of him to allow for maximum visibility. He babbled and cooed with delight as Hector poured water from various containers while singing familiar songs. The therapist repeated the child's vocalizations using a tone and pitch similar to the mother's voice. No other demands were placed on Luis. After several weeks of repetitive water play, Luis began to develop a more trusting relationship with Hector. The child was no longer fretful and gradually started to initiate interaction. Mrs. Suarez still had to remain in the room, but Luis tolerated having her sit to the side. Over the next few months, Luis became increasingly flexible so that more developmentally challenging activities were presented, and other therapists were able to work directly with him.

Second and Third Years in the Program

Intervention during the second year in the program continued to focus on building Luis's developmental skills and helping him apply them to coping efforts. At 26 months of age, his progress report indicated that he had improved the most in sitting balance and that he enjoyed this greater sense of control. Therapy emphasized expanding his play with familiar and novel objects in order to facilitate cognitive development and functional use of the hands. If given ample time, Luis would start to play independently with toys. His repertoire consisted of grasping, releasing, swatting, and poking. He was expressing his needs more consistently through vocalizations and gestures. While crying continued to interfere at times with his performance, improvement was noted in his tolerance level.

Mr. and Mrs. Suarez were active participants in the early intervention program and made numerous changes in their family life to accommodate to their son's special needs. As a result, there was less tension in the home. Although the Suarezes had many coping resources, the staff recognized that the mother in particular was very self-protective regarding the intensity of her feelings about having a child who not only had a severe disability but was very difficult to manage. Mrs. Suarez often used anger as a way of managing stress. For instance, at one point she became very angry and defiant at the suggestion that Luis be placed in a group that included some children with Down syndrome. Although these children were actually higher functioning than her son, she said that Luis was "not retarded like them." The staff appreciated that anger and denial are not pathological mechanisms, but important coping strategies for survival. They allow time for parents to adapt to their child's disability and their changed circumstances.

It was critical that the staff did not pressure Mrs. Suarez to "face the facts" or reach some artificial stage of "acceptance." Instead, the emphasis was on enhancing supportive resources. The success of this approach was revealed over time by her decreased stress level, greater comfort with her child, and openness to others.

As she developed more of a sense of well-being, Mrs. Suarez became a very active contributor in the parent discussion group. She was able to help other parents by sharing difficult personal experiences. She supported the parents with humorous or encouraging stories about raising a child with a disability.

As Luis neared his third birthday, significant behavioral changes had occurred, including a decrease in the frequency of crying. His Adaptive Behavior Index on the Early Coping Inventory had increased to 3.0, indicating that he was situationally effective in his coping style. Luis had made marked progress in his self-comforting skills as well as his ability to tolerate transitions between places without a warm-up period. He occasionally fussed during transitions from one activity to another but calmed quickly.

Although Luis was limited in his motor control and communication, he enjoyed being with the other children in the "Get Along Gang." This group program was the one that Mrs. Suarez had originally rejected because of the participation of children with Down syndrome. Approximately 6 months after the initial recommendation by the staff, Mrs. Suarez requested this placement because she was impressed by the stimulating verbal and social interactions of the children in this group.

At home and in the center, Luis used a battery-powered go-cart for mobility. It had been purchased at a discount store by his grandparents and adapted by the therapists to provide postural support. He became very adept at using the joy stick to drive the go-cart, which looked like a miniature sports car. This means of locomotion gave Luis a tremendous sense of autonomy, joy, and freedom. It helped him to work through developmental issues of separation and individuation with his parents, and therefore made a notable contribution to his social and emotional development.

During these years, the Suarezes struggled with the issue of whether they should have more children. They discussed this topic in the support group and also sought genetic counseling.

When Luis was 3 years old, he was enrolled in a preschool class at a special school run by the local United Cerebral Palsy Association. His school district provided the tuition and also supported supplemental physical therapy at the medical center.

Follow-Up

An interview was conducted with Mr. and Mrs. Suarez 3 years after Luis made the transition from the early intervention program. They shared the following information with an external consultant to the COPING Project. The parents were enthusiastic about the birth of another child 7 weeks earlier.

How would you describe Luis now? The Suarezes described Luis as easier to manage at 6 years of age than during his early years. He was better adjusted to new situations and socialized more actively with other children at school. Luis was starting to walk with the assistance of his physical therapist, but used a wheelchair for functional mobility. It was projected that in the future he would be ambulatory in the home and would use a wheelchair in the community.

Luis's verbal abilities had improved to the point that he used some words and signs. His receptive language was better than his expressive skills. The fact that he was the lowest functioning child in his class appeared to be motivating. His teachers encouraged Luis to be as independent as possible, despite his preference to have certain tasks done for him. He was essentially toilet trained at school, with infrequent accidents.

Luis's health was good and he had a strong appetite. Mrs. Suarez shared that a difficult challenge was keeping him on a routine. If his regular schedule was not followed for one day, it was very hard to get him back into the routine. As a result, he would wake up at 4 A.M. ready to start his day. It was a problem for both parents, especially because they now had a young infant in the house.

What important things have happened since early intervention? The Suarezes experienced several major events in the past 3 years. They moved into a ranch-style house to accommodate Luis's wheelchair. The house was also closer to the school that they had chosen for his next placement, which provided an after-school program as well as respite care services. In addition, Mrs. Suarez returned to her career. Employment was interrupted, however, when she injured her back on the job. She was hospitalized and then stayed at home for a total of 6 months. Her period of convalescence placed great stress on the family, but they were able to cope. Mrs. Suarez stated that she was taking 3 months off from work to care for the new baby before returning to her hospital position.

How has Luis influenced the rest of the family? The parents reported that Luis was well loved by their large extended family and was considered the special grandchild. Although his grandparents tended to minimize his developmental disability, they were always available as babysitters for Luis or to help them financially with medical expenses. Mr. Suarez believed that his son had a very positive effect on the nieces and nephews in the family. They enjoyed playing with him, took pride in his accomplishments, and considered themselves his "number one fan club."

Reflections

It is not only the availability of coping resources that is important, but how adequately they match the amount and intensity of the demands to be managed. In this instance, the Suarezes had generally abundant resources, but they faced a situation of extreme stress— the multiple demands of a child with a severe disability who was also very difficult to manage. It was a challenge for them to find a good fit between their demands and resources so that they could generate effective outcomes.

When a child has a minimally effective coping style, grading demands is a priority intervention option. These children readily become overloaded and consequently react with maladaptive behaviors, such as agitated crying, as in the case of Luis. Because these are very needy children, it is easy for parents and professionals to do too much, too fast with these children. A more careful, targeted, and integrated approach is required. Likewise, practitioners need to expect and respect the tendency of some parents to demonstrate denial, blaming, and anger. These strategies serve important survival functions as family members learn to cope over time with their new situation.

SUMMARY

This chapter highlights the experiences of four families who have children with minimally to situationally effective coping styles. Their participation and feedback in the pilot program were instrumental in the development of the coping perspective for intervention. In many ways, the work of the COPING Project was enriched most by experiences that did not progress smoothly. By analyzing relationships and activities that were difficult or challenging, the practitioners learned to embrace complexity and, therefore, learn from it.

CHAPTER 14

Staff Coping

Demands and Resources

For an early intervention program to be effective, staff members have to cope with a range of demands—providing services to children and parents; interacting with other practitioners, including supervisors and colleagues in the community; and managing the programmatic changes that are necessary to achieve best practices. Concurrently, staff members have to cope with the demands of their personal lives outside the program. What resources help to create a good fit between these many demands and the ability of practitioners to manage them?

Although demands and resources vary from program to program, many are similar. There is a need for knowledge and skills beyond those specific to one's discipline, for example, knowledge of families and how to work as a team member. Staff need to believe they are competent and that their efforts are valued. They need support from administrators and colleagues, both in routine activities and in situations that are difficult to handle, including the demand for change. Staff need a physical environment that is pleasant to work in and that provides the materials and equipment necessary for implementation of quality services.

This chapter addresses factors that contribute to successful staff coping. It applies the coping perspective to promote the functional well-being of practitioners. This chapter also describes ways for programs to manage the change involved in integrating this clinical frame of reference into their operations. It is essential that practitioners are able to work together in a group context and are clear about their roles; therefore, critical group functions and staff roles are initially addressed. Then, two additional aspects of staff coping are discussed: 1) the coping resources pertinent to working with colleagues and families in early intervention, and 2) coping with the demands of managing change within a program.

It is recognized that the realities of daily practice are often complicated and far from ideal. Many stressors are present. Early intervention programs are frequently underfunded so there is never enough time, staff, or resources to "do the job right." Many programs are run by administrators with limited managerial skills and no background in early childhood. Many practitioners have little formal preparation in applying their professional discipline to the unique needs of infants and their families. Some paraprofessionals essentially receive on-the-job training as their instruction. Furthermore, staff often have minimal experience working as a part of an interdisciplinary or transdisciplinary team. Given these realities, major attention needs to be committed to expanding the coping resources of the staff and program, as well as supporting the coping efforts of everyone involved (Turnbull et al., 1993).

WORKING EFFECTIVELY AS A GROUP

Regardless of the specific structure or philosophy of an early intervention program, a common need is for groups of people to work together in a way that is productive and personally satisfying. The groups may be composed of all staff members or all parents, a specific family and staff functioning as a team, or selected staff and parents joining together to implement an activity or project. In early intervention, groups may conduct a range of activities—interdisciplinary assessment of children, IFSP meetings, provision of intervention services, parent support groups, sibling programs, staff meetings, and inservice education programs. Awareness of the factors that generate productivity in any group helps those involved to observe the process and make modifications when necessary.

In a group there are continual transactions among the participants. Analysis of these transactions contributes to understanding why a group is or is not effective. Productivity of a group is dependent on its members performing roles and behaviors that support *task functions* (getting the work done) and *process functions* (maintaining relationships among people) (Dyer, 1987; Pryor, 1989). Behaviors to promote task functions are concerned with doing the job—accomplishing the task the group has before it.

Process functions concern what is happening to and among participants while the group is working. Two categories of behavior support process functions: group maintenance and meeting individual needs. Behaviors used for *maintenance* are directed toward facilitating group morale, enhancing harmonious working relationships, and fostering feelings that it is desirable to be a part of the group. Behaviors to *meet individual needs* are the personal actions or feelings of group members regarding their degree of acceptance and inclusion. These feelings are generated by their exchange with other members but are frequently not discussed.

Process functions involve awareness of group dynamics, such as emotions, tone, atmosphere, morale, norms, conflict, competition, and cooperation. In contrast, task functions are concrete steps for achieving the identified group objective. Figure 14.1 depicts the interaction of process and task functions. Optimal productivity is achieved by the group when all factors are considered.

The shifting, fluid nature of these dynamics is experienced when participating in any group. A case in point is the process of developing an IFSP with different families and practitioners. What happens when a professional feels that another staff member is taking over her role and is shutting her out? What happens when a parent feels that the group is not attending to his real concerns? What happens when two members distract the group with side conversations? It is critical that both process and task functions be actively monitored, particularly by a group facilitator.

Interdisciplinary or transdisciplinary teamwork is a sophisticated achievement, requiring staff training and close attention to group dynamics. The authors interviewed an early intervention staff that had failed to examine task and process functions in their daily transactions. As a result, the staff had many underlying issues that were sabotaging the program's operations. Some practitioners expressed strong feelings about staff meetings. One commented that he felt like "odd man out" because his comments were often ig-

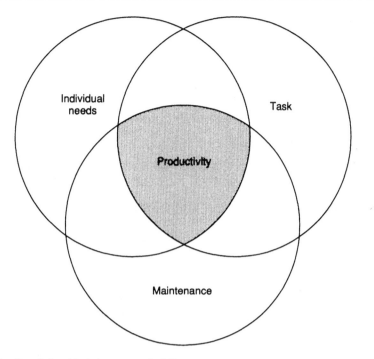

Figure 14.1. Functions that contribute to group productivity.

nored. Another professional reported that "when we are doing team planning, a certain individual always seems impatient. I don't know how to react to her."

Other staff members shared doubts about their competence in interacting with parents. One practitioner said, "I can't see that any of my formal training prepared me for having a parent break down in tears in front of me. Who was supposed to support whom? How was I to act, to respond? Was I appropriate?" Another staff member described her sense of futility in dealing with a mother who seemed depressed all the time, sitting at the side of the room and unable to get involved. She said, "I wanted to help but wasn't sure how, so I focused all my efforts on the child."

The situations that developed in this program are not unusual. They occurred in part because of the staff's inadequate understanding and management of task and process functions. Examples of these functions, as well as questions that are useful for increasing awareness of how a group is operating, are discussed.

Task Functions

The following are behaviors that participants can use to expedite achievement of the group's task.

Initiating   Proposing tasks, goals, or actions; suggesting a procedure
Informing   Offering facts; giving an opinion
Clarifying   Interpreting ideas or suggestions; defining terms; clarifying issues before the group
Reality testing   Making a critical analysis of an idea; testing an idea against some data; examining whether an idea will work

The following list of questions can be helpful for analyzing how the group is completing its task and achieving its goal.

Does anyone ask for or make suggestions as to the best way to proceed or to tackle a problem?

Does anyone attempt to summarize what has been achieved or what has been happening in the group?

Is there any giving of or asking for facts, ideas, opinions, feedback, or alternatives?

Who keeps the group on target?

Who prevents topic jumping, going off on tangents, or other distractions?

Process Functions: Maintenance

Participants can implement the following behavioral strategies to foster working relationships and help them feel satisfied with their participation in the group.

Harmonizing   Attempting to reconcile disagreements; reducing tension; getting people to explore differences

Gate keeping   Helping others to participate; keeping channels of communication open

Encouraging   Being friendly and respectful of others; demonstrating acceptance of others' contributions

Compromising   Admitting error; modifying one's initial statements to accommodate the group; compromising in times of conflict

The following questions are useful for analyzing the group's dynamics regarding maintenance of relationships among participants and feelings of group membership.

Who helps others to get involved?

Does anyone cut off others or interrupt them?

How clearly are participants communicating their ideas or expectations?

Are some members preoccupied and not listening?

Are there any attempts by group members to help others clarify their ideas or to support their activity?

How are ideas or behaviors rejected?

How do members react when their ideas or activities are not accepted?

Do members attempt to support the individual whose efforts are not accepted?

Group atmosphere and group norms are also related to process functions involved in maintenance. Every group generates an *atmosphere* that is reflected in the general climate and tone of the group. Individuals differ in the kind of atmosphere in which they are most comfortable. An awareness of the characteristic atmosphere of a group can be facilitated by addressing the following questions.

Which members seem to prefer a friendly, congenial atmosphere?

Which members seem to prefer an atmosphere of conflict and disagreement?

Is there any attempt to suppress conflict or unpleasant feelings?

Do participants seem involved and interested?

Is the atmosphere one of work, playfulness, satisfaction, taking flight, or sluggishness?

Norms are standards or ground rules that develop in a group and control the behavior of its members. They usually express the beliefs about behaviors that are or are not acceptable or the desires of the majority of the group members. These norms may be clear to all members (explicit), known or sensed by only a few (implicit), or operating completely below the level of awareness of any group members. Some norms facilitate group process; others hinder it. The following are questions to consider.

Are certain topics avoided in the group (e.g., discussion of parental concerns or talk about the program's administration)? Who seems to reinforce this avoidance? How do they do it?

Are group members overly nice or polite to one another?

Are only positive feelings expressed?

Do members agree with one another too readily?

What happens when members disagree?

Process Functions: Meeting Individual Needs

Individual needs are as diverse as the participants involved. Different patterns of interaction may develop in the group that provide clues as to how the group is meeting the needs of particular members. The following are questions to consider.

Are there any subgroupings (cliques)? Do two or three members consistently agree with and support one another or consistently disagree with and oppose one another?

Do some people seem to be "outsiders" in the group and others "insiders"? How are the "outsiders" treated?

Do some members move into or out of the group (e.g., lean forward or back in their chairs or move their chairs closer to or farther from the group)? Under what conditions do they move in or out?

What feelings are observed in group members (e.g., anger, irritation, frustration, warmth, affection, excitement, boredom, defensiveness, competitiveness)?

Effective group interaction does not occur automatically. The preceding sets of questions can be used to monitor and enhance group functioning and foster task achievement. The questions and related information can also be used for staff development. They assist group participants to observe, analyze, and evaluate what is occurring and to identify priorities for better teamwork. In the process, the staff has opportunities to share feelings and concerns about task functions, maintenance, and individual needs.

STAFF ROLES

Early intervention practitioners now assume expanded roles beyond being a direct service provider, including responsibilities such as service coordination. Dunst and his associates (1988) suggest that a staff member may need to function as a consultant, enabler, mediator, catalyst, and advocate. These roles place demands on professionals for knowledge and skills that often exceed their traditional training. Therefore, it is essential that programs provide inservice education activities that assist staff in understanding these roles and acquiring the ability to perform them successfully.

As consultants, staff members respond to requests for information that assist families in making informed decisions. As enablers, they support families in their efforts to develop their capacities for self-reliance. As mediators, practitioners help families, when necessary, to resolve conflicts within the program or community. As catalysts, staff assist families to identify and mobilize potential sources of support. As advocates, they share responsibility with families to know, protect, and expand the rights and opportunities of children with special needs. The necessity to shift among these diverse roles is challenging for staff members. Their individual and collective coping resources strongly influence how effectively they manage these demands.

COPING RESOURCES OF PRACTITIONERS

As in any group, staff members vary in their available resources to support coping efforts. In Chapter 2, these coping resources were described in detail. In Chapter 6, questions were presented that help to gain information about the resources of families. These questions are also useful for determining the coping resources of practitioners. Self-awareness is essential in becoming a competent professional and an effective team player. It is important for practitioners to be aware of how they cope and how their resources influence their transactions with each other and families. Such an appraisal can be accomplished in various ways, such as individual study, inservice training, continuing education workshops, and having a mentor. Probably the most desirable means is to have ongoing reflective supervision on the job.

Not only are each practitioner's coping resources influential, but there must be some compatibility or fit with those of other staff members and the families they serve. For example, recognition of the beliefs and values of individuals increases the probability of discovering common perceptions among those involved. Critical beliefs that influence service delivery are those related to each person's cultural background and socioeconomic status, the nature of a "helping" relationship, one's disciplinary perspective and sense of personal competence, as well as beliefs about disability and the potential for change. Likewise, clinically relevant values include priorities of how available time should be used and the importance of various outcomes for the program and families.

Another illustration is the need for practitioners to understand their own coping style and appreciate the styles of other staff members. This awareness can guide the program in making daily decisions, such as assignment of staff to specific families or tasks. A practitioner who is very flexible with a high tolerance for ambiguity and complexity may be a good fit for a particular family. In contrast, a practitioner who is highly structured, concrete, and focused may be a better match with another family. A similar investigation into the other coping resources of the staff, such as human and environmental supports, is equally helpful. Many early intervention programs may find it useful to design staff development activities around these concepts of individual and collective resources. In large part, they determine the effectiveness of service provision.

Within the coping resource of knowledge and skills, there are two abilities that are fundamental for all practitioners and often not adequately addressed in their professional education: 1) active and empathic listening, and 2) giving and receiving feedback. These skills are required for successful working relationships among staff members and for their interactions with families. Because of their special relevance, they are discussed in some detail. Both skills need to be practiced at staff meetings, during informal conversations, and during inservice training. Time spent in facilitating communication through activities such as role playing serves a dual purpose—developing the staff's skills and expanding their empathy toward other practitioners and families. For consistency of presentation, the discussion of listening skills focuses on family–staff interaction. Similar examples could be given for interactions among staff members.

Listening Skills

Active and reflective listening demonstrate empathy. They encourage family members to express and share their concerns. As an active listener, practitioners show interest in the family's priorities and how different family members perceive their circumstances.

> Example:
> You seem very concerned about your child's future. What types of things worry you?

As a reflective listener, practitioners can rephrase the family's statements to clarify exactly what is being said.

> Example:
> Do I understand you to say that you have doubts about your child's future and that this is causing you to feel "down" and depressed?

Listening is a more complex process than the physical act of hearing. Listening integrates physical, emotional, and intellectual inputs to determine meaning. Body language, eye contact, and voice tone may convey meanings different than implied by just the spoken word. Signs of tension may be shown in the degree of rigidity of various parts of the body or in their continuous motion, such as fidgeting hands or a swinging foot. Therefore, the listener needs to attend to both verbal and nonverbal messages.

The following list provides points to keep in mind for more effective listening.

Responses are timed so that the speaker believes he or she was listened to and that what was said was absorbed.

Judgments are not made prematurely about the content and meaning of the communication.

Distractions (e.g., noises, interruptions) are minimized so attention can be focused on the speaker.

The speaker's important themes are sought by listening beyond the spoken word for additional meaning.

Active and reflective listening enables the practitioner to respond in ways that generate meaningful communication. The following response techniques may be helpful.

Neutral Acknowledging Responses Neutral acknowledging responses convey interest and encourage the other person to continue talking.

> Example:
> I see. That's interesting. I understand.

Silence with accompanying behaviors such as eye contact or appropriate posture may communicate interest and concern. A more active response that offers an invitation to continue may be: "Tell me about it," or "I'd be interested in hearing what you have to say about . . .".

Questions that Seek Clarification, Additional Facts, or Opinions These questions are designed to gain better understanding of a situation, to request more information, and to solicit personal perspectives.

> Example:
> Why did that occur? *or* What do you mean by . . .? *or* Does that mean that . . .?

Paraphrasing   Paraphrasing is useful to check one's interpretation, to show understanding of what the other person is saying, or to clarify the other person's expectations or intentions.

Example:

As I understand it, you mean . . . . *or* Are you saying that . . .?

Perception Check   A perception check is a way to show that one understands how the other person feels at that moment or to check the accuracy of one's perception of the other's feelings.

Example:

You look pleased that . . . . *or* You're really angry about what happened, aren't you?

Summarizing Statements   Summarizing statements bring the whole discussion into focus or serve as a springboard for further discussion.

Example:

These are the main points as I understand them . . . . *or* Let me see if I can summarize what you've said.

Many people find it difficult to say what they mean or to express what they feel. They often assume that the other person understands what they mean, even if they are unclear in their speech. They seem to think people should be able to read each other's minds—"If it is clear to me, it must also be clear to you."

Virginia Satir, a pioneer in family therapy, has a story that shows the problem with that assumption (1972). She explained that a family ruckus occurred when the father sent his son to the lumber yard for a longer board. The child thought he knew what his father wanted and dutifully went to the lumber yard. But the longer board he brought back was still 3 feet too short. His father became angry and accused the boy of being stupid and not listening. The father had simply assumed that because he knew what he meant by "longer," his son would also know. He had not bothered to make himself clear or to check his meaning with his son. The son also assumed that he knew his father's meaning.

In early intervention an assumption is often made by staff members that their reporting of the child's progress is understood by the parent and other team members. Unless the developmental change is described in specific behaviors, others may assume the progress is greater or less than what actually occurred.

Giving and Receiving Feedback

Feedback is information offered to a person that is *in response* to something specific about that person. It is a way of helping others understand their behavior and make changes if indicated. In an early intervention program feedback can be provided in a variety of circumstances. A practitioner may need to give feedback to a colleague about his reaction to a discussion in a staff meeting. A clinician may need to give feedback to a parent about how she is putting on her son's braces. A parent may need to give feedback to a child about acceptable or unacceptable behaviors. Parents may offer staff members feedback about the effectiveness of a program component.

When it is constructive and supportive, feedback can generate two-way communication and can greatly increase an individual's awareness about his or her performance. This awareness, in turn, can motivate the individual and facilitate change. Thus, feedback should be helpful to the person receiving it. The receiver must be able to understand the information, accept it, and be able to do something about it. Certain types of feedback serve only the needs of the person giving it and not those of the person receiving it.

It is not easy to give feedback to another individual in such a way that the person will be strengthened by it and able to do a better job of handling a similar situation. It is not constructive if feedback is provided without considering whether the information is appropriate for the receiver, given the person's abilities, fears, or feelings of self-esteem. If the person receiving the feedback becomes defensive, the giver may try to argue or apply pressure. This situation can escalate into an argument or lingering resentment. Likewise, it is difficult to receive feedback. The receiver has to have enough trust to be open to what is said and willing to address potentially sensitive issues.

How to Give Feedback   Persons giving feedback should avoid making value judgments or suggesting specific changes in behavior (unless these are specifically requested). Changes in behavior as a result of feedback should be initiated by the person receiving the information. The following guidelines are suggested for giving feedback.

Choose constructive phrasing so that feedback is helpful.

Comment upon targeted, observable behavior and avoid generalizing concerns to other aspects of the individual. For example, to say that a person is "dominating" is not as useful as saying, "I feel that my opinions are not being considered when you do not let me speak in staff meetings."

Choose areas in which the person receiving the feedback can demonstrate some control over his or her behavior. Frustration is only increased when an individual is reminded of some shortcoming over which the person has no control.

Use nontechnical language as much as possible.

Point out strengths as well as areas of concern.

Provide descriptive, not evaluative feedback. By describing one's own reaction, the individual allows the receiver to be free in how the information will be used. The absence of evaluative language reduces the need for the receiver to react defensively. For example, "You are so messy" can be rephrased as, "I feel disorganized when materials in the staff office are not kept in their proper place."

Offer well-timed feedback. In general, feedback is most useful at the earliest opportunity after the given situation.

Discuss the feedback to ensure that both the giver and receiver agree on what is being communicated. One way of doing this is to have the receiver repeat the information to see if it corresponds to what the sender had in mind.

How to Receive Feedback   Practitioners can learn techniques of giving feedback, yet how to manage the feelings related to receiving it is a more sensitive issue. Personal experiences in receiving feedback can be used as a guide to understanding how others may feel when feedback is given.

Try to be open and nondefensive about the feedback. Avoid explaining it away by saying, "They don't understand."

Give a specific example that might clarify the meaning of feedback received if there is difficulty understanding it. Ask, "Is this what you mean?"

Share feelings and reactions about the feedback received.

Keep in mind that it is generally a personal decision to determine what changes, if any, are to be made in light of the feedback.

In summary, there is a need during supervision and inservice activities to increase awareness of the individual's coping resources and how they influence personal behavior and the group's functioning. Good fit among those involved does not mean sameness but rather recognition and respect for each person's uniqueness (Antonovsky, 1993). So far, this chapter has discussed issues faced by staff working together and with families in their multiple roles. Suggestions have been offered to promote group productivity and interpersonal communication. These skills are particularly relevant to practitioners and programs as they cope with change.

COPING WITH CHANGE

Early intervention is in a continuing process of change. Change may come from broad issues such as evolving public policy, legislation, and perceptions of best practices (see Figure 1.1, chap. 1, this volume). It can also come from local issues such as alterations within a program's budget, personnel, or population served. Whether for an individual or a group, change represents many challenges. Similar principles for managing change apply whether the needed change is a minor shift in staffing and routine or the more complex task of integrating a family-centered coping perspective into an early intervention program.

Change requires learning new skills and altering one's behavior and daily transactions; it moves one from the realm of the known into the realm of the less familiar and more risky. These demands can be viewed by individual staff members or programs as a challenge, threat, or some combination of the two. Personal beliefs about the meaning of the demands influences openness to change. When the staff is able to cope in ways that are personally and professionally satisfying, they are more motivated to do their job and feel pleased with the outcome. Because change usually occurs over time, staff must operate a program while acquiring the new skills needed to manage the desired change.

The following comments were made by staff members of early intervention programs when presented with the demand for moving toward a more family-centered orientation in their program.

I think involving families in early intervention is a wonderful idea.

Working with the family is the social worker's job.

I already work well with families and always teach them ways to work on therapy goals at home.

It is hard for me to find time to get to know the families well with my busy schedule.

My education and training have focused on assessment and treatment of the child's disability.

I am excited about learning new skills to help me relate better with families.

I feel pressured to get my paperwork done on time, and I am not up-to-date. It will be additional pressure to take on a lot of new and extra work.

Some of the families that I work with have more problems than I feel equipped or qualified to deal with. I do not want to get in over my head.

When I see the child and parents together, I feel that my intervention is more helpful and relevant.

The procedures we use now are working. I do not see how what I am already doing could be better. Families I work with are generally pleased with the services.

My own family is upset with me because I'm so wound up when I get home from work.

The successful implementation of change is dependent on the beliefs, coping abilities, and skills of the early intervention practitioners. They are the ones who have primary responsibility for the implementation of any programmatic change and are clearly the vital link in the service delivery chain. To the degree that planned change strengthens positive aspects of their experience, all involved individuals benefit—staff, children, and families. Staff are most likely to develop feelings of ownership and recognize the usefulness of new ideas when they are part of the planning process. Because every early intervention program has a unique blend of personalities, history, and organizational structure, a systems approach that recognizes these important components is essential for planning strategies for organizational change.

The purpose of this section is to address the critical question of how an early intervention program can best manage the change involved in integrating the coping perspective into its existing program. Factors are first reviewed that hinder or facilitate the successful introduction of programmatic change. Then strategies are outlined for planning organizational change. The personalized decision-making process is used as one example of how to plan for innovation. This information represents a blend of approaches from educational, organizational, community, and social psychology. The principles and procedures for incorporating coping concepts into a program can be adapted and applied to a variety of service environments.

A review of the literature about organizational change highlights two findings that underscore the importance of careful planning. First, most organizations, including early intervention programs, are structured in a way that resists change. Second, most plans for change do not result in true integration of desired activities and actions into daily practice. It is important to make the distinction between implementation and actual continued use of new actions, which the literature refers to as institutionalization. *Implementation* refers to the efforts of an organization to involve staff in training to put new procedures and skills into effect. Often these efforts include some mechanism for assisting staff to begin to use new approaches and ideas in their daily work. *Institutionalization* refers to the stabilization and practice of new program activities and skills as an ongoing, sustained part of a program and its policy (Feller, 1982). Clearly, it is the institutionalization of family-centered services with a coping perspective that is desired. Therefore, it is helpful to be aware of common factors that can hinder as well as support change.

Factors that Hinder Change

Change disrupts the existing expectations and routine of a program. If the staff have already developed what they believe to be productive and workable procedures, it is often difficult for them to be motivated to make the effort necessary to break old habits and form new ones. Individuals can also experience a loss of self-confidence when major organizational changes occur. The changes may be seen as devaluing the investments they have made in developing their knowledge and expertise through education and years of work experience. Change can also result in a shift of power and influence between individuals or groups in a program. An individual coping style that is rigid, intolerant of ambiguity, and low in risk-taking can also make new learning and change more difficult. In addition, in an environment undergoing changes that alter established working relationships and functions, the potential for unanticipated negative outcomes is increased.

Factors that Support Change

The key to successful change is that the people involved can develop ownership of the new methods. Thus, the question is: What contributes to the development of staff ownership? With this question in mind, six factors are presented that support effective change and each one is examined on the following pages. Staff are likely to adopt change when:

1. The climate of the program and its leadership actively support the change.
2. Individuals believe they will benefit in some way from the change.
3. Change is based on a tested model or innovation.
4. Plans for change begin small, with an overinvestment in the number of staff involved.
5. Training procedures and plans for innovation allow for skill development and change to occur over time.
6. Program staff have the internal and external resources needed to sustain their efforts.

The climate of the program and its leadership actively support the change. The philosophy and consistent behavior of key administrators and supervisors must support the staff in risk taking and learning new skills. Failure in implementing change is often due to an excessive value the American culture places on success and accomplishment. As a result of this value system, individuals tend to deny or whitewash efforts that are unsuccessful or in need of improvement. The failure of programs to consider both successful and unsuccessful experiences as legitimate parts of the learning process leads to an aversion to acknowledging errors and confronting mistakes. Yet, important discoveries and the development of more effective procedures are often the direct outgrowth of learning that takes place in an unsuccessful effort.

Program leaders can foster an environment supportive of change by adhering to the following guidelines.

Realistic expectations for change are identified so staff can feel more secure in trying new skills.

Staff are offered specific ways to acquire needed support and assistance if problems arise.

A climate is created in which new skills are actively acknowledged and appreciated. In such an environment, it is easier for staff to accept corrective feedback.

Problems are addressed as valuable learning experiences. This orientation facilitates problem solving and fosters a "learning by doing" policy that helps to develop or refine new skills.

The leaders are able to model in an honest fashion their own efforts that are less than successful. Their responsiveness to feedback and shared search for improvement can have a powerful influence in encouraging the staff to do the same.

Leaders have to trust the knowledge and expertise of the service delivery staff in their work with families, and they need to be realistic regarding logistical and situational constraints in the daily implementation of the program.

Program leaders can help maintain the innovations if they are open to the creative ideas of the staff and support them in working constructively to make necessary adaptations.

The specific characteristics of sound leadership are not easy to operationalize. As with all successful social interaction, it is person and situation specific; however, some generalizations can be made. The following elements seem relevant for effective leadership: listening skills, support and encouragement, interaction facilitation, goal emphasis, and work facilitation (Phillips & Elledge, 1989).

Listening fosters communication among members of an organization. As noted earlier, true listening involves not only understanding and remembering a delivered message, but in some way letting the speaker know that this has taken place. The feedback that is given, or the resulting action, is influenced by the message received.

Support and encouragement by leaders enhance the staff's feelings of personal worth and importance. Individuals are more likely to continue with behaviors—both personal and work-related—that receive positive feedback. In addition, when individuals receive praise and feel they are appreciated, it is much easier for them to accept constructive criticism. However, even positive feedback needs to be given with direction and sensitivity. An exaggerated expression of appreciation once a year is less meaningful to the receiver than intermittent, small compliments and positive signals over a period of time. Limiting positive feedback to those times when one is also meting out criticism creates resentment. The pairing of praise with a request is often viewed by the receiver as manipulation. Furthermore, going on and on with positive feedback to shy individuals can make them feel so uncomfortable that they may avoid doing what has been complimented.

Interaction facilitated by leaders tends to result in close, mutually satisfying relationships. Leaders can be an important influence in creating a warm social climate, fostering problem solving, and channeling constructive communication among staff.

Goal emphasis is achieved when leaders actively engage in behavior that stimulates an enthusiasm for meeting the group's goal or achieving excellent performance. In programs where efforts for change are successful, the goals are clear, staff are actively motivated to become engaged, and goal attainment is rewarded.

Work facilitation is generated by such behaviors as scheduling, coordinating activities, and planning. It is also essential to provide staff with the technical knowledge and tools necessary for implementing changes.

Individuals believe they will benefit in some way from change. Programs are most successful when staff believe that the new procedures offer them tools to achieve outcomes they not only believe in, but wanted to achieve *prior to* their introduction to the innovation. This statement does not necessarily mean they were actively requesting the change, but perhaps there was some awareness that this was an area of concern. It is also useful if training in new methods is linked to opportunities to advance professionally and increase marketable skills. Incentives can be introduced, such as allocation of time and supervision to acquire new skills, offering opportunities for promotion, and related strategies. Leaders who have little control over the work environment (e.g., salary, promotion) seldom achieve strong and consistent results.

Change is based on a tested model or innovation. Adapting a method that has proven successful in other early intervention programs and is recognized by professional organizations can promote a staff's sense of being up-to-date and responsive to identified needs. It is helpful when the envisaged change is congruent with the norms, goals, and values already evident in the program.

There is a somewhat paradoxical relationship between model demonstration programs and service delivery programs. Model demonstration programs are of little value without adaptation and use by direct service personnel. Yet, direct service staff are often the best equipped to make judgments concerning the most effective way to provide inter-

22

vention. The reality is, however, that front-line service staff are only occasionally (unless recruited to help with a grant-funded project) afforded the luxury of "stopping action" to research, plan, and develop new products and refine new procedures. The valuable resource of *time*, which is essential for creating the resources and materials needed to operationalize new ideas, is often the domain of individuals involved in model demonstration programs.

Plans for change begin small, with an overinvestment in the number of staff involved. One of the most consistent recommendations in the literature about organizational change is to begin small with a pilot project. This approach helps by providing staff with the opportunity to "work out the kinks" and experience key components of the plan for change before they are asked to make a large scale commitment. For example, in adopting the coping perspective, the staff may start by using the Early Coping Inventory as a way of appreciating the impact of the coping styles of children on their learning. Another way is to use the personalized decision-making process to develop an IFSP for one child and family before using it for all families. Overinvestment in the number of staff involved in pilot projects has been found to be particularly important. It fosters staff commitment and generates a strong core group who are involved in the initial stages of an innovation.

Training procedures and plans for innovation allow for skill development and changes to occur over time. Changes that threaten the role autonomy of staff, or that result in their feeling less effective, are likely to be resisted. For this reason it is essential to consider the training needs of the practitioners and encourage high levels of personal responsibility for learning. At the same time, there is need for a supportive structure that allows time for skill acquisition.

In most programs, the primary model for promoting change is to provide staff with inservice training and then wait and hope that individuals will independently decide to maintain, generalize, and transfer all they have learned into their daily practice. Such an approach seldom results in desired outcomes. Whereas many individuals can acquire understanding of a new concept in one or two learning trials, integration of the concept into applied skills usually develops more slowly.

As indicated earlier, training needs to be tailored to have realistic expectations for behavior change, with opportunities not only to practice new skills but also to acquire positive, corrective feedback on performance. Performance feedback should be immediate and frequent during the initial phase of applying new skills in daily work activities. Feedback can be given at less frequent intervals once the skill has been acquired.

Program staff have the internal and external resources needed to sustain their efforts. A critical aspect of the sustained effort needed for program change is the refinement of skills and methods to a point where: 1) service delivery procedures are realistic, workable, and effective; and 2) the changes initially desired have become integrated into ongoing routine activities.

Awareness of existing internal and external coping resources of staff members gives direction for planning and implementing change. The following questions are relevant for this issue.

Are there staff beliefs and values that are incongruent with program goals and could hinder staff motivation and commitment to change?
Are there staff coping styles that could hinder or facilitate program changes?
Do staff have in their repertoire the required skills for effectively implementing components of the desired change?

Are there additional skills (e.g., communication skills for handling difficult situations with families) whose acquisition would assist staff in successfully carrying out program changes?

Are there particular strengths in the staff that can be utilized to facilitate plans for program change?

Continuous assessment of progress can be achieved by developing specific plans for monitoring implementation. This need often requires altering job roles and scheduling time for performance feedback. Effective staff coping with new program demands can be achieved through clearly specified outcomes and planning ongoing opportunities for staff to attain the abilities necessary for reaching the desired goals for program change.

A Model for Planning

The personalized decision-making process is one model that can be used to plan and evaluate change. Any plan for change must be based on the expected outcome. In this book, a primary outcome is to incorporate a coping frame of reference into early intervention programs so that services enhance the adaptive competence and resilience of children and their families. The following questions can be considered when planning and implementing the changes necessary to reach this outcome. They are listed under the three decision-making steps of the process.

Collecting and Sharing Information

What are the existing program goals?

What program and service requirements are legally and institutionally mandated?

What physical, financial, and community resources are available to support program services?

What is the training, experience, motivation, and availability of staff?

What resources and incentives are available to facilitate and support change?

What overall characteristics, concerns, and priorities of families in the program have to be considered in planning change?

What service options are presently available for families within the program?

How are services delivered?

What is the present role of families in program planning?

Analyzing Information and Setting Long-Range Functional Outcomes

On the basis of the information collected, what factors facilitate and what factors interfere with making the desired changes?

Of the factors that interfere with achievement of the desired outcomes, which factors can be changed and which cannot (at least in the immediate future)?

Of the interfering factors that can be changed, which factors will contribute most to achievement of the desired outcome?

What new learning by the staff is necessary in order to implement the changes?

These questions help to establish priorities that can be translated into goal statements for change. They determine the steps or objectives that have to happen, and in what sequence, for innovation to occur.

Developing an Implementation Plan

What activities will be used to achieve the objectives—where, when, how, and by whom?

What procedures and record-keeping system are needed to evaluate the achievement of goals and objectives? (Very few programs have all the resources needed for the easy achievement of change.)

Staff members of an early intervention program used this decision-making process and gained insight into their functioning. As a result, a new direction was charted for the future. The following vignette summarizes their experience.

➡   The staff collected relevant information and analyzed the program's current status. The analysis identified that personnel problems generated its greatest vulnerability, making the implementation of any plan for change extremely difficult. There was a shortage of trained clinicians; and when the program was able to hire staff, they did not stay very long. As a consequence, the program was never able to implement its program effectively, let alone create change. This frustration led to staff burnout, which further exacerbated turnover of personnel. The administrators realized that unless this negative cycle was broken the program could not develop a true team approach to intervention. They set initial goals to utilize existing staff more effectively and invest in training less experienced staff. This commitment to team building ended the negative cycle and established a foundation for program development.

ACTIVITIES TO SUPPORT STAFF COPING

Early intervention programs vary in the time, knowledge, and structure available to support staff coping. Time is a particularly critical issue because learning cannot be achieved quickly. Although time has a very real and tangible cost for programs, scheduling needs to allow adequate opportunities for formal and informal support. The following activities, commonly used in the field, can be geared to promote the coping of individual practitioners and the staff as a whole.

Supervision—either individual or as a team in which reflection and collaboration are encouraged

Informal staff exchange—shared support and problem solving on a spontaneous collegial basis

On-site inservice activities—regularly scheduled events within the program or specially planned occurrences during which services are suspended

Staff library—relevant information shared through books, journals, videotapes, and related materials

Consultation—calling in an expert to meet a specific need

Visits to other programs—in the form of observation, sharing, and direct instruction; lends itself to a reciprocal arrangement

Courses, workshops, and conferences—offered by colleges, professional organizations, or qualified individuals

In addition to these generic options, there are specific activities that can help staff members become aware of and increase their own coping resources, resulting in more effective transactions. The following sample suggestions are designed to enrich the coping resources of staff.

Use the material in this book pertaining to the coping process for a lecture or group discussion.

Have staff complete the self-rated Coping Inventory and then discuss the results in a way that allows each participant to disclose only what he or she chooses.

Provide experiences that support or challenge existing beliefs and discuss personal reactions in a nurturing environment.

Offer opportunities to learn, try out, make mistakes, and receive supportive feedback.

Plan time for social activities and fun.

Provide a physical environment that facilitates coping (e.g., quality of light, temperature, and space).

Increase knowledge and skills through activities that emphasize not only acquisition but also generalization and fluency.

SUMMARY

In summary, this chapter highlights factors that need to be emphasized to support staff coping. It describes ways to enhance the productivity of group efforts and the significance of promoting the coping resources of the staff. Communication skills are targeted due to their primary importance. Guidelines for coping with change are presented to assist practitioners and programs to manage the challenge of integrating a coping frame of reference into their practice.

Case Report of a Parent Support Group

This case report documents the experience of a support group composed of four families during their first year of participation in an early intervention program. The families were predominantly middle class from diverse ethnic backgrounds. Because their children were infants, the parents were dealing with very new and emotionally charged changes in their lives. The group met in the evening at the program site on a biweekly basis. The group leader was a psychologist who was a member of the early intervention staff.

PHASE I (SIX SESSIONS)

The first phase of the parent support group lasted for six sessions. During this time, the parents became acquainted with each other. They described in detail the medical histories of their children, the circumstances surrounding their children's births and deliveries, and the discovery of their disabilities or delays. They began using the group as a forum to vent the rage, frustration, sense of futility, and confusion that they felt. During this "getting-acquainted" period of six sessions, there were group process issues of trust, resistance, and dependence on the leader.

At the opening session, seven parents attended—three couples and one mother. For all but two of the families, the child with a disability was their first born. The group began with introductions, then each family reported their expectations and hopes for the experience and the ways in which it could best serve their needs. Although each parent was animated and emotional when discussing his or her own child, there was a general "hands-off policy" adopted about commenting on other people's situations. As story after story evoked both anger and sad emotions, there were empathic nods, occasional cringes, and frequent looks that appeared to say, "Thank God my child is not that bad." Thus, the majority of time was spent recounting birth traumas, describing the shock of learning of a disability, and giving quick overviews of their present situations. The emotions displayed on this first evening were depression, frustration, and anger; yet, no one cried during this session. When frustration was displayed, it usually related to a lack of information about the status and prognosis of a child's condition and the inability to change it. It was this "gray area" of not having a definitive diagnosis that resulted in the most frustration.

During the next few sessions, there was intense interaction among the parents, almost to the exclusion of the leader. Most of the time was spent retelling their histories, ventilating pent-up emotions, and listening to how others attempted to cope and adjust to their situations. Several important issues surfaced—the first of which was denial by many of the families. Parents would blatantly denounce the findings of doctors as folly and guess-work, consider their children slow starters similar to them when they were young, and denounce the necessity of an early intervention program for their children. One father of a 1-year-old boy performing 8 months below age expectations repeatedly stated his son was "fine" and that his family would have the last laugh when the boy surpassed their other children. Gentle prods by the leader and occasional incredulous looks from other parents did not influence the denial. (Denial, anger, and blaming are understandable reactions to extreme stress and can allow time for individuals to organize their coping resources.)

A second issue was grief. Parents felt depressed and forlorn over the loss of their expected "normal" baby and the dreams they had for that child. The degree to which this grief existed was somewhat dependent on whether it was a first child or there were other siblings.

A third issue was raised that discussed the necessity for such a group. It became apparent that a number of parents interpreted the recommendation to participate in the parent support group as very threatening, and that it inferred that they were "head" cases because their children were born with developmental problems.

A fourth issue was a general feeling of isolation from friends and even relatives. This isolation and loss of social contact was universally experienced and appeared to be one of the most distressing issues because it symbolized the tremendous change in their lifestyle. The group became a place where these "isolated" individuals could gather, share, and receive support and guidance.

A fifth issue of this initial phase was the incessant blaming of the medical profession as the culprits behind the family's situation. Many lawsuits were in litigation at the time. Each family had a number of "doctor horror stories" that were shared during the sessions. Ironically, these anecdotes seemed to be important elements in generating the cohesiveness of the group.

Thus, this initial phase was characterized by parents becoming acquainted with each other, focusing on the histories of their children, projecting blame to healthcare workers, and expressing strong denial and difficulty in adjusting to their changed status. The group process was lively; by the end of this initial phase, interpersonal confrontations were not uncommon (i.e., "I used to be like you and it's infuriating to watch."). Whereas some members attended the group for support, others seemed more interested in venting emotions and trying to work through personal issues.

PHASE II (15 SESSIONS)

The second phase lasted from about the 7th through the 20th session. Whereas Phase I was basically introductory in nature with the focus on venting anger, grief, and blame, Phase II was characterized primarily by working through personal issues that were directly or indirectly related to their children with special needs.

The most frequent topic discussed during this phase was guilt felt by the parents. The first type of guilt expressed was that of feeling responsible for the child's developmental disorder because of: 1) potential side effects during the prenatal period (e.g., from medication, smoking), 2) failure to alert the medical staff when delivery problems seemed to exist, 3) being more than 35 years of age when having the child, 4) failing to have an amniocentesis, and 5) not being religious enough. The support group served the very important and effective function of encouraging parents to appreciate the reality that they were probably not responsible for their children's problems. For example, Chuck, the father of a 10-month-old boy who had spastic quadriplegic cerebral palsy, could not forgive himself for not allowing the doctor "to pull the plug on the respirator" when his son was a few days old. Chuck said he heard his son cry and believed he should live. This occurred just as he was preparing to sign the papers approving passive euthanasia. (This was a very emotional story for everyone in the group.)

The second type of guilt revolved around the parents' anger at their children for bringing such hardship to the family. The parents' ambivalence was incredibly painful for them. They felt "criminal" for blaming a helpless child for their aggravation. This type of guilt was frequently dealt with by compensating behaviors that prevented the child from experiencing any discomfort. One father wet his pants instead of putting his child down while she was crying.

A third type of guilt may be called the "tug"—so coined by Millie, a 36-year-old woman with an infant son with congenital blindness. The "tug," which all parents admitted to experiencing, was described as the guilt of being embarrassed or ashamed of the child, whom the parents both loved and wanted to hide. Frequently the parents would say they wanted to avoid embarrassment for the child; they would later admit the child was kept home so *they* would not be embarrassed. Parents claimed that it took months to get to the point where they could take their child to the supermarket and be able to handle the gawking glances from other adults and, especially, children. It was not uncommon in the group to hear the parents comment that they often had desires to "strangle" all children who were "normal." In the group, a significant amount of time was spent trying to understand the "tug."

Related to guilt feelings was the issue of self-esteem, which seemed to be dramatically lowered with the entrance of the child with disabilities. Some parents considered themselves failures as "baby-makers" and others as parents because they had produced a child who did not fit their script. One couple's self-esteem was absolutely shattered when they realized that their child was developmentally delayed. The reason became clear when the father noted that having a "handicapped child" made him a "handicapped person and parent." His image of himself as a parent was inextricably tied to the image of his child.

Self-esteem was also the basis of the maintenance of the "family secret" that had been propagated by several families—parents felt so fragile, insecure, and ashamed of themselves and their child that they refused to let anyone outside the immediate family know about the "problem." This resulted in social isolation. The support group helped parents give each other strokes to soothe bruised egos.

Another topic, a corollary to that of guilt and self-esteem, was that of problems with parenting. Many mothers and fathers stated that the special needs of their child precluded them from being "real" parents, imprisoned in a cycle of depression, guilt, overprotection, maintenance, and fatigue. A number of parents said that they were angry because they felt deprived of the freedom to pamper, play with, and discipline their child "as a normal kid." One couple cried as they shared their fear that they would never receive any joy from their child, only aggravation.

Some of the parenting problems centered around the inability to place any type of limits on their child; as a result the parents were being run ragged. Parents who had other children were particularly helpful, as they emphasized that they treated the child with a disability basically the same as the others (as much as possible) and did not feel guilty about restricting and molding their behavior. While parenting problems with the child with special needs was primarily a difficulty for parents with only one child, handling older siblings was arising as an issue for other families.

Issues of parenting led to discussions of marital stress and discord, with an emphasis on communication problems. For example, the wife may effusively recount the day's happenings to the husband (especially what transpired at the early intervention program) while the husband, drained from a full day of work, would courteously listen but remain removed. Helping the parents to speak to each other, to be honest about feelings, and to even cry together was a very important function of the parent support group.

In summary, it was during this second phase that the bulk of the problem-related work ensued. Parents seemed invested in the group; they were committed to coping with environmental, personal, and marital issues, and committed to returning their family life to as normal as possible. The parents seemed less burdened as they confronted their guilt feelings and learned to channel this energy for constructive purposes. The feelings of despondency were less intense, but nonetheless still present. Their moods were easily swayed, influenced by such factors as how the child "performed" in the program on that day, the findings of a new evaluation, or the comments of a neighbor.

PHASE III (EIGHT SESSIONS)

This final stage was characterized by the return to relatively stable family functioning, the experience of regular parenting, adaptation to the child's disability, and a slow decline of the group's cohesion. These parents needed approximately 9–12 months of consistent attendance in the support group and the other program activities before they were better able to cope with their child's disability. There was, however, a tremendous variability among the parents in their ability to manage their situations. This was frequently a function of their coping style, the severity of the child's disability, the quality of the marriage, the degree of identification with the child, the number of available social and emotional supports (especially friends), and the number of children in the family.

In this later time period, there seemed to be less investment in the group and increased focus on occupational and social activities that were important to them prior to the child's birth. The parents began to reintegrate into community life and into their marriages. Several parents at this stage spoke of the initial year as though it were a "blackout" period, forgetting much of the tumult and pushing events together. This happened in particular with families whose children were making progress in the intervention program. For those who had children with severe disabilities, adaptation was more difficult.

The most characteristic aspect of Phase III was that the parent support group appeared to outlive its usefulness for most of the parents. Most parents preferred to attend social events (e.g., sporting events, work-related functions, family affairs).

Early Intervention and Development and Coping with Transition Workshops

EARLY INTERVENTION AND DEVELOPMENT: A WORKSHOP FOR NEW FAMILIES

This workshop was developed based on feedback obtained from an interest survey of parents of children who were new to the early intervention program. The majority of parents indicated a need for developmental information and wanted a better understanding of how the early intervention program functioned. Informal discussion with parents prior to the workshop indicated confusion about their role in the intervention process.

The workshop, "Early Intervention and Development," was an educational program conducted over a 4-week period, one evening a week for 1½ hours. Members of the early intervention staff participated as speakers. Their familiarity with the children enhanced parental interest. Free babysitting was provided to encourage attendance. The sessions emphasized the importance of developmental skills for coping with the demands of daily living. Questions and general discussion were strongly encouraged throughout each presentation.

Session 1:   Early Intervention—What It Is and How It Works

Activities:

Identify factors that influence a young child's development as a way of introducing key
   elements of a family-centered approach to early intervention.
Present the personalized decision-making process as a method for facilitating parent–
   professional collaboration in intervention planning (the steps and teamwork involved in creating an IFSP).
Describe the roles and functions of the different early intervention practitioners in the
   program.
Discuss hopes and expectations for participation in early intervention.

Session 2:   The Development of Motor Skills in the Young Child

Activities:

Describe the components of posture and movement needed for the development of gross
   and fine motor skills (i.e., control of large body movements, as well as the arms and
   hands).

Discuss the relationship of motor control to the child's daily functioning.
Identify strategies and activities to assist the child to acquire motor skills.
Delineate ways to encourage the child's coping and learning in spite of a motor delay.

Session 3: Understanding Your Child's
Behavior—Early Communication and Cognitive Skills

Activities:

Define the terms *communication* and *cognition* as applied to the young child.
Give an overview of the sequence in which children learn to communicate.
Describe behaviors infants and toddlers use to communicate.
Review the early stages of cognitive development that form the foundation for thinking.
Discuss how play activities are used to enhance communication and help the child expand
    cognitive skills.

Session 4: Coping—How Children
Learn to Adapt to the Challenges of Daily Living

Activities:

Describe the coping styles of young children and the importance of coping transactions to
    their development and emotional growth.
Introduce the coping process as the vehicle for adaptive functioning.
Discuss the resources a child uses to cope with events and surroundings.
Describe intervention approaches that help the child with special needs to learn to cope.
Review the content of the workshop series and end with a general discussion.

COPING WITH TRANSITION WORKSHOP

A three-session workshop was developed to help parents cope with the transition of their
child from early intervention services to a preschool placement. Workshop content
evolved from the expressed needs of parents and the experiences of the staff and graduate
families. An interest survey, completed by each parent, addressed issues related to the law,
the school district, and general concerns regarding transition (see Figure 1). Based upon
results of the survey, content was modified to reflect interests of participating parents. In
general, the workshop was designed to meet the following educational objectives.
    As a result of attending the workshop, parents will:

Acquire an understanding of federal and state laws related to transition to preschool pro-
    grams, development of the individualized education program (IEP), and rights for
    appeal.
Learn about the roles and responsibilities of the school district.
Appreciate their own roles and responsibilities related to securing appropriate preschool
    services for their child.
Develop skills in analyzing preschool programs and matching them with their child's edu-
    cational needs.

Session 1: From Identification to Placement

Activities:

The director of special services from a local school district was invited to speak in the first
session on the topic "From Identification to Placement." This format provided an opportu-

Interest Survey
Your Child's Transition to Preschool

Please take a few minutes to rate the items listed below according to your interest in learning more about them. This information will help us to plan an educational workshop and other supportive services.

	No Interest	Some Interest	High Interest
The Law			
What are relevant federal and state laws?	1	2	3
What is an educational classification?	1	2	3
What are the criteria for determining eligibility for preschool services?	1	2	3
What are my legal rights and responsibilities?	1	2	3
What is an individualized education program (IEP)?	1	2	3
The School District			
Whom do I initially contact and when?	1	2	3
What questions should I ask?	1	2	3
What information will I need to provide?	1	2	3
How is the IEP developed and by whom?	1	2	3
What if I disagree with part of the process?	1	2	3
Can I choose the program my child will attend?	1	2	3
What do I do if my child is not eligible for services?	1	2	3
Will my child be classified forever?	1	2	3
What happens if my district has no program appropriate for my child?	1	2	3
How far away can my child be sent?	1	2	3
Coping with Transition			
How is the transition plan developed in the early intervention program?	1	2	3
How do I know if my child's special needs are being adequately addressed by the school district?	1	2	3
What can I expect (feelings, problems)?	1	2	3
What can I do to prepare myself for the change and ease the transition?	1	2	3
How do I evaluate my child's progress?	1	2	3

Figure 1.   Interest survey regarding transition.

nity for the parents to learn directly from a special educator about the relevant rules and regulations as well as steps in the transition process. The presentation clarified the roles and responsibilities of both the parents and the school district.

Time was spent discussing why this transitional experience is so emotionally laden for so many families. Some of the challenges of this new situation were identified. The children would be coping with: a new place and routine, new hours and schedule, new teachers and friends, and often a new mode of transportation. The parents would be coping with: separation and trust issues, an educational system with new people and new ways of doing things, and often less day-to-day involvement with their child and the program. Airing these issues and their associated feelings helped to place the transition into perspective and make it seem more manageable.

Session 2:   Rehearsing the Transition Process—Practice Makes Perfect

Activities:

The transition process was reviewed and the components of the IEP were explained. The early intervention staff facilitated a discussion regarding ways to make the IEP meeting collaborative, meaningful, and more comfortable. Some suggestions included: 1) make a list of questions or issues that you want addressed; 2) share pertinent information about your child's interests, strengths, and needs; 3) ask questions when any point or educational term is unclear; 4) consider the extent of your child's inclusion into regular school activities; 5) make sure that all necessary services are written into the IEP; and 6) spend time to reflect on whether the total plan really matches your child's ability.

To prepare for the transition, parents were invited to participate in role-playing activities. They identified the situations they wanted to rehearse. The early intervention staff then set the stage for the role play and served as the preschool personnel. Situations that the parents chose to practice included: the initial contact to their school district, the evaluation of their child and discussion of appropriate placement, and the IEP meeting. Involvement in the role play was voluntary. At first parents were tentative, but they became increasingly active as they participated. Each role play generated questions and lively discussion. The staff was prepared to perform the role plays in case the parents preferred to observe and comment rather than directly participate in them.

Session 3:   How It Worked For Us

Activities:

This session began with a discussion by the early intervention staff of the components of a quality preschool program. A handout described what to look for when visiting potential programs (see Figure 2). The importance of program observation was emphasized so parents could have adequate knowledge to make informed and comfortable decisions.

The key activity of the session was a guest panel of parents who had recently been involved in the transition of their children from early intervention to preschool. They shared their experiences and answered questions. These parents said that they believed time was an important factor in their adjustment to their children's new placements. They

---

Observing a Preschool Program

The Program

How many times per week does the program meet?
What are the hours?
What are the arrangements for transporting the children?
What do they expect the children to learn?
How are the children grouped? Does it vary with the activity?
What is the maximum number of children that the program will serve?
Will the program be personalized for all children? If so, how?
How are behavior problems managed?
What is the availability of related services such as physical and occupational therapy?
What is the parents' role in the program? Are there opportunities for observation and involvement?
How are school and home activities coordinated?
Is there a parent organization or parent support group available?

The Staff

What is the student–staff ratio?
What is the training and experience of the teacher and those who will provide supportive services?
How many aides and volunteers are used in the program?

The Facility

How many rooms are available for program use? Are they appropriately accessible?
Are the rooms spacious, bright, cheerful, and clean?
How is the environment organized? Is the room divided into activity areas?
Are the materials and equipment appropriate for the age and ability of the children?
Are the bathrooms easily accessible?

Figure 2.   A handout on what to look for when visiting a potential preschool program.

said they missed the active parent involvement in the early intervention program, but appreciated the greater flexibility of having their children in more extensive programs. All the parents expressed pride in their children's increased independence once they adapted to their new programs.

Experience with the workshop reinforced awareness of how stressful this transition is for many families. A feeling of anxiety and distrust was common. Some parents feared they might be in an adversarial relationship rather than in a collaborative partnership. The opportunity to meet preschool personnel and parents who had been through the process helped to reduce these feelings and to generate more confidence in the future.

—————————————————————————

Reflections of the Johnson Family

In Chapter 12 of this volume, the experiences of the Johnson family were introduced as an illustration of how the COPING Project initially developed IFSPs. As a result of feedback from parents, the project modified its approach to be more responsive to the concerns and priorities of individual families. When the Johnson family was leaving the early intervention program, Mrs. Johnson was asked to share her thoughts and feelings about the first years of Ruth Ann and Becky, her twins with cerebral palsy. Her reflections, presented in her own words on the following pages, provide rich insights from a parental perspective.

—————————

When we got the news that I was going to have a baby, both my husband and I were very delighted. We had planned this pregnancy and everything was going as expected. But 2½ months into the pregnancy, we found out I was carrying twins. The news was devastating . . . we hadn't planned on having twins but felt we no longer had a choice. We didn't know how it was going to change our lives. It would be a big enough change just having one child, and now we got the news we were going to have two. After a few months, we became used to the idea and were very happy and excited. Labor started about 29 weeks into the pregnancy, and the children were born 10 weeks premature. Ruth Ann, the second child born, had many complications associated with prematurity. The other twin, Becky, had virtually no problems apart from a slight heart murmur. She just needed to stay in the hospital to gain weight and get a little stronger.

The news about Ruth Ann was more upsetting. She had many things go wrong, including hydrocephalus, meningitis, and hemorrhaging in the back of her brain. Ruth Ann had a shunt placed and was later ready to go home. Before leaving the hospital, we had a conference with her doctors who informed us of the possibility that Ruth Ann might have cerebral palsy. My husband and I were shocked at this news . . . we thought that she had been through so much from birth [but] had pulled through with flying colors, [and] that she would surely grow up to be a normal, healthy, active child.

As it turned out, we noticed problems with her development at an early age. At around 5 months we decided to have her evaluated. It was a big move for us because finally we thought there was something wrong. As it turned out, it was the right move. She was diagnosed as having cerebral palsy. So now we knew and we could work from there. We entered the early intervention program and got into the routine of taking Ruth Ann for therapy. It became part of our lives.

Becky was growing up to be a beautiful little girl, perfectly formed like any other baby . . . to us she was the perfect child. We thought we were so blessed with having Becky. Although we loved Ruth Ann equally, there was always the extra work and the time and patience needed to manage her. As it turned out, as Becky got a little older, we had thoughts that there could possibly be something wrong. She was not doing some things, such as sitting on her own and maintaining her balance, and she was not trying to crawl or move around. She could roll, but that was all. We fought with the idea of getting her evaluated, but didn't dare do it for fear that we might find out the worst. I used to take Becky with me when I went with Ruth Ann for therapy. After a while, a few people called to my attention that there was a delay in Becky. So, now we had to confront that something was wrong. Until then we made excuses that Becky was simply lazy and just had no desire to do many things.

Once we had Becky evaluated, they gave us the news that Becky also had cerebral palsy. That news really set us back emotionally, as now we had two children with disabilities and our lives were again in turmoil. Although we had felt isolated when we had one child with cerebral palsy, we found things in common with others parents who had a disabled child. Now we were put in another situation. We knew no one else who had two children with disabilities, so we had to learn how to deal with situations all on our own. As the children got older, we had to learn how to cope with two of them getting therapy. And then as they got heavier, [we had to cope with] trying to carry both of them to the car to go visiting, or shopping, or whatever. As they get bigger and bigger, their weight is becoming one of the greatest problems.

The difficult situation we have been placed in is that of trying to decide if we want to have more children. We always planned on having three or four children in our family. We were greatly affected by the thought of whether the condition was hereditary and whether we wanted to risk having another child that may also have a disability. Through some genetic counseling, it was determined that the twins' problem was not hereditary. There was also the concern of whether we would be able to handle having to carry three children around while the third is still small. We have been waiting to see if one of the children will be able to walk. This would reduce the burden of having to carry three children and push them in a triple stroller. We have decided to go ahead and have more children as we don't want the fact of having children with disabilities change our thoughts about having more in our family. We're just hoping that it won't cut down on the attention and time we will be able to give Becky and Ruth Ann. Through the help of friends, family, and therapists, we should be able to handle the situation.

Also, another big factor of having two children with disabilities is the extra financial responsibility we have in paying for special equipment that the children need from day to day in order to make their lives easier. The children are 3 years old and it is only now that I have been able to get back into a normal way of life, or so-called "normal" way of life. We have many more years with Becky and Ruth Ann [and] trying to help them through the tough times. When they get older, they in turn will be able to help us through the tough times. This is something that we have accepted and have now come to understand. We are enjoying the children at last.

References

Allport, G.W. (1937). *Personality: A psychological interpretation*. New York: Holt, Rinehart & Winston.

American Psychological Association. (1985). *Standards for educational and psychological testing*. Washington, DC: Author.

Anderson, J., Hinojosa, J., & Strauch, C. (1987). Integrating play in neurodevelopmental treatment. *American Journal of Occupational Therapy, 41*, 421–426.

Antonovsky, A. (1979). *Health, stress, and coping*. San Francisco: Jossey-Bass.

Antonovsky, A. (1987). *Unraveling the mystery of health*. San Francisco: Jossey-Bass.

Antonovsky, A. (1993). The implications of salutogenesis: An outsider's view. In A.P. Turnbull, J.M. Patterson, S.K. Behr, D.L. Murphy, J.G. Marquis, & M.J. Blue-Banning (Eds.), *Cognitive coping, families, and disability* (pp. 111–122). Baltimore: Paul H. Brookes Publishing Co.

Bagnato, S.J., Neiwsorth, J.T., & Munson, S.M. (1989). *Linking developmental assessment and early intervention: Curriculum-based prescriptions* (2nd ed.). Rockville, MD: Aspen Publishers, Inc.

Bailey, D.B., & Simeonsson, R.J. (Eds.). (1988). *Family assessment in early intervention*. Columbus, OH: Charles E. Merrill.

Bandura, A. (1986). *Social foundations of thought and action: A social cognitive theory*. Englewood Cliffs, NJ: Prentice Hall.

Barber, P.A., Turnbull, A.P., Behr, S.K., & Kerns, G.M. (1988). A family systems perspective on early childhood special education. In S.L. Odom & M.B. Karnes (Eds.), *Early intervention for infants and children with handicaps: An empirical base* (pp. 179–198). Baltimore: Paul H. Brookes Publishing Co.

Barrera, M.E., & Vella, D.M. (1987). Disabled and nondisabled infants' interactions with their mothers. *American Journal of Occupational Therapy, 41*, 168–172.

Bates, J.E. (1987). Temperament in infancy. In J.D. Osofsky (Ed.), *Handbook of infant development* (2nd ed.) (pp. 1101–1149). New York: John Wiley & Sons.

Beck, A.T. (1976). *Cognitive therapy and emotional disorders*. New York: International Universities Press.

Beck, A., & Emery, G. (1985). *Anxiety disorders and phobias*. New York: Basic Books.

Beckwith, L. (1990). Adaptive and maladaptive parenting: Implications for intervention. In S.J. Meisels & J.P. Shonkoff (Eds.), *Handbook of early childhood intervention* (pp. 53–77). Cambridge, MA: Cambridge University Press.

Bertalanffy, L.V. (1968). *General systems theory*. New York: Braziller.

Bloom, L., & Lahey, M. (1978). *Language development and language disorders*. New York: John Wiley & Sons.

Bly, L. (1983). *The components of normal movement during the first year of life and abnormal motor development*. Chicago: Neurodevelopmental Treatment Association.

Bolles, R.C. (1974). Cognition and motivation: Some historical trends. In B. Weiner (Ed.), *Cognitive views of human motivation*. New York: Academic Press.

Brazelton, T.B. (1984). *Neonatal behavioral assessment scale* (2nd ed.). Philadelphia: J.B. Lippincott.

Brazelton, T.B. (1992). *Touchpoints*. Reading, MA: Addison-Wesley.

Brazelton, T.B., & Cramer, B.G. (1990). *The earliest relationship: Parents, infants, and the drama of early attachment*. Reading, MA: Addison-Wesley.

Bricker, D., & Cripe, J.J.W. (1992). *An activity-based approach to early intervention*. Baltimore: Paul H. Brookes Publishing Co.

Bridges, K.M.B. (1932). Emotional development in early infancy. *Child Development, 3*, 324–334.

Brinker, R.P., & Lewis, M. (1982). Discovering the competent handicapped infant: A process approach to assessment and intervention. *Topics in Early Childhood Special Education, 2*(2), 1–16.

Bristol, M. (1983a). The belief scale. In M. Bristol, A. Donovan, & A. Harding (Eds.), *The broader impact of intervention: A workshop on measuring stress and support*. Chapel Hill, NC: Frank Porter Graham Child Development Center, University of North Carolina at Chapel Hill.

Bristol, M. (1983b). Carolina parent support scale. In M. Bristol, A. Donovan, & A. Harding (Eds.), *The broader impact of intervention: A workshop on measuring stress and support*. Chapel Hill, NC: Frank Porter Graham Child Development Center, University of North Carolina at Chapel Hill.

Bristol, M., & DeVellis, R. (1982). *The definition scale*. Chapel Hill, NC: Frank Porter Graham Child Development Center, University of North Carolina at Chapel Hill.

Buss, A.H., & Plomin, R. (1984). *Temperament: Early developing personality traits*. Hillsdale, NJ: Lawrence Erlbaum Associates.

California State Department of Education. (1990). *Flexible, fearful, or feisty* (Video). Sacramento, CA: Child Care Video Magazine.

Campbell, P.H. (1987). Physical management and handling procedures with students with movement dysfunction. In M. Snell (Ed.), *Systematic instruction of persons with severe handicaps* (3rd ed.) (pp. 176–187). Columbus, OH: Charles E. Merrill.

Campbell, P.H. (1989). Posture and movement. In C. Tingey (Ed.), *Implementing early intervention* (pp. 189–208). Baltimore: Paul H. Brookes Publishing Co.

Cannon, W.B. (1953). *Bodily changes in pain, hunger, fear and rage.* Boston: Charles T. Branford.

Carey, W.B. (1986). The difficult child. *Pediatrics in Review, 8,* 39–45.

Carey, W.B., & McDevitt, S.C. (1978). Revision of the Infant Temperament Questionnaire. *Pediatrics, 61,* 735–739.

Carlton, S.B. (1988). *The relationship between temperament and coping in handicapped and nonhandicapped infants and young children.* Unpublished doctoral dissertation, Rutgers, The State University of New Jersey, New Brunswick.

Carter, B., & McGoldrick, M. (1989). The changing family life cycle: A framework for family therapy. In B. Carter & M. McGoldrick (Eds.), *The changing family life cycle.* Needham Heights, MA: Allyn & Bacon.

Center for the Study of Social Policy. (1992). *Kid count data book.* Greenwich, CT: Anne E. Casey Foundation.

Children's Defense Fund. (1990). *S.O.S. America! A children's defense budget.* Washington, DC: Author.

Children's Defense Fund. (1992). *Vanishing dreams: The economic plight of America's young families.* Washington, DC: Author.

Combs, A.W., Avila, D.L., & Purkey, W.W. (1978). *Helping relationships: Basic concepts for helping professionals* (2nd ed.). Needham Heights, MA: Allyn & Bacon.

Compas, B. (1987). Coping with stress during childhood and adolescence. *Psychological Bulletin, 101,* 393–403.

DeGangi, G.A. (1991). Assessment of sensory, emotional, and attentional problems in regulatory disordered infants: Part 1. *Infants and Young Children, 3,* 1–8.

DeGangi, G.A., Craft, P., & Castellan, J. (1991). Treatment of sensory, emotional, and attentional problems in regulatory disordered infants: Part 2. *Infants and Young Children, 3,* 9–19.

DeGangi, G., & Greenspan, S. (1989). *Test of Sensory Functions in Infants.* Los Angeles: Western Psychological Services.

Dember, W.N. (1974). Motivation and the cognitive revolution. *American Psychologist, 29,* 161–168.

Derogatis, L.R., Lipman, R.S., & Covi, L. (1975). *Symptoms checklist 90 revised (SCL-90R).* Baltimore: Johns Hopkins University, School of Medicine.

DiBuono, E. (1982). *A comparison of the self-concept and coping skills of learning disabled and nonhandicapped pupils in self-contained classes, resource rooms and regular classes.* Unpublished doctoral dissertation, Walden University, West Covina, CA.

Dohrenwend, B.P., & Dohrenwend, B.S. (Eds.). (1974). *Stressful life events: Their nature and effects.* New York: John Wiley & Sons.

Dohrenwend, B.S., Dohrenwend, B.P., Dodson, M., & Shrout, P.E. (1984). Symptoms, hassles, social supports, and life events: Problem of confounded measures. *Journal of Abnormal Psychology, 93,* 222–230.

Dollard, J., & Miller, N.E. (1950). *Personality and psychotherapy.* New York: McGraw-Hill.

Dunst, C.J., Cushing, P.J., & Vance, S.D. (1985). Response-contingent learning in profoundly handicapped infants: A social systems perspective. *Analysis and Intervention in Developmental Disabilities, 5,* 33–47.

Dunst, C.J., Johanson, C., Trivette, C.M., & Hamby, D. (1991). Family-oriented early intervention policies and procedures: Family-centered or not? *Exceptional Children, 58,* 115–126.

Dunst, C.J., Trivette, C.M., & Deal, A. (1988). *Enabling and empowering families.* Cambridge, MA: Brookline Books.

Dyer, W.G. (1987). *Team building: Issues and alternatives* (2nd ed.). Reading, MA: Addison-Wesley.

Elliot, G.R., & Eisdorfer, C. (1982). *Stress and human health.* New York: Springer-Verlag.

Ellis, A., & Grieger, R. (Eds.). (1977). *Handbook of rational emotive therapy.* New York: Springer.

Falicov, C.J. (1982). Mexican families. In M. McGoldrick, J.K. Pearce, & J. Giordano (Eds.). *Ethnicity and family therapy* (pp. 134–163). New York: Guilford Press.

Feller, I. (1982). Innovation process: A comparison in public schools and other public sector organizations. *Knowledge: Creation, Diffusion, Utilization, 4,* 271–291.

Fenichel, E.S., & Eggbeer, L. (1990). *Preparing practitioners to work with infants, toddlers, and their families: Issues and recommendations for the professions.* Arlington, VA: National Center for Clinical Infant Programs.

Fewell, R.R., & Kaminski, R. (1988). Play skills development and instruction for young children with handicaps. In S.L. Odom & M.B. Karnes (Eds.), *Early intervention for infants and children with handicaps: An empirical base* (pp. 145–158). Baltimore: Paul H. Brookes Publishing Co.

Fine, S.B. (1991). Resilience and human adaptability: Who rises above adversity? *American Journal of Occupational Therapy, 45,* 493–503.

Florey, L.L. (1981). Studies of play: Implications for growth, development and for clinical practice. *American Journal of Occupational Therapy, 35,* 519–528.

Foley, G.M., & Hobin, M. (1981). *The Attachment-Separation-Individuation Scale.* Reading, PA: The Family Centered Resource Project, Albright College.

Fraiberg, S. (1980). *Clinical studies in infant mental health: The first year of life.* New York: Basic Books.

Fullard, W., McDevitt, S.C., & Carey, W.B. (1978). *The Toddler Temperament Scale*. Unpublished manuscript, Temple University, Department of Educational Psychology, Philadelphia.

Fullard, W., McDevitt, S.C., & Carey, W.B. (1984). Assessing temperament in one- to three-year-old children. *Journal of Pediatric Psychology, 9*, 205–217.

Furuno, S., O'Reilly, K.A., Hosaka, C.M., Inatsuka, T.T., Allman, T.L., & Zeisloft, B. (1979). *Hawaii Early Learning Profile*. Palo Alto, CA: VORT Corp.

Gallagher, J.J. (1990). The family as a focus for intervention. In S.J. Meisels & J.P. Shonkoff (Eds.), *Handbook of early childhood intervention* (pp. 540–559). Cambridge: Cambridge University Press.

Gallagher, J.J., Beckman, P., & Cross, A.H. (1983). Families of handicapped children: Sources of stress and its amelioration. *Exceptional Children, 50*, 10–19.

Garland, C.W. (1993). Beyond chronic sorrow: A new understanding of family adaptation. In A.P. Turnbull, J.M. Patterson, S.K. Behr, D.L. Murphy, J.G. Marquis, & M.J. Blue-Banning (Eds.), *Cognitive coping, families, and disability* (pp. 67–80). Baltimore: Paul H. Brookes Publishing Co.

Garland, C.W., & Linder, T.W. (1988). Administrative challenges in early intervention. In J.B. Jordan, J.J. Gallagher, P.L. Hutinger, & M.B. Karnes (Eds.), *Early childhood special education: Birth to three*. Reston, VA: Council for Exceptional Children.

Garmezy, N., & Rutter, M. (Eds.). (1983). *Stress, coping and development in children*. New York: McGraw-Hill.

Gesell, A. (1940). *The first five years of life*. New York: Harper & Row.

Gibbs, E.D., & Teti, D.M. (Eds.). (1990). *Interdisciplinary assessment of infants: A guide for early intervention professionals*. Baltimore: Paul H. Brookes Publishing Co.

Gilfoyle, E.M., Grady, A.P., & Moore, J.D. (1990). *Children adapt* (2nd ed.). Thorofare, NJ: Charles B. Slack.

Goldsmith, H.H., Buss, A.H., Plomin, R., Rothbart, M.K., Thomas, A., Chess, S., Hinde, R.A., & McCall, R.B. (1987). Roundtable: What is temperament? Four approaches. *Child Development, 58*, 505–529.

Goldsmith, H.H., & Campos, J.J. (1986). Fundamental issues in the study of early temperament: The Denver twin temperament study. In M.E. Lamb, A.L. Brown, & B. Rogoff (Eds.), *Advances in developmental psychology* (Vol. 4, pp. 231–283). Hillsdale, NJ: Lawrence Erlbaum Associates.

Greenspan, S.I. (1981). *Psychopathology and adaptation in infancy and early childhood*. Clinical Infant Reports, No. 1. New York: International Universities Press.

Greenspan, S.I. (1992). *Infancy and early childhood: The practice of clinical assessment and intervention with emotional and developmental challenges*. Madison, CT: International Universities Press.

Greenspan, S.I., & Greenspan, N.T. (1989). *The essential partnership*. New York: Viking Press.

Grinker, R. (1968). Psychiatry and our dangerous world. In *Psychiatric research in our changing world: Proceedings of an international symposium, Montreal*. (Excerpta Medica International Congress Series No. 187). Amsterdam: Excerpta Medica.

Hagekull, B., Lindhagen, K., & Bohlin, G. (1980). Behavioral dimensions in one-year-olds and dimensional stability in infancy. *International Journal of Behavioral Development, 3*, 351–364.

Hall, S. (1990). Observation of sensorimotor development. In T.W. Linder, *Transdisciplinary play-based assessment: A functional approach to working with young children* (pp. 201–246). Baltimore: Paul H. Brookes Publishing Co.

Hanzlik, J.R. (1989). Interactions between mothers and their infants with developmental disabilities: Analysis and review. *Physical and Occupational Therapy in Pediatrics, 9*, 33–47.

Hildebrand, V. (1975). *Guiding young children*. New York: Macmillan.

Hines, P.M., & Boyd-Franklin, N. (1982). Black families. In M. McGoldrick, J.K. Pearce, & J. Giordano (Eds.), *Ethnicity and family therapy* (pp. 84–107). New York: Guilford Press.

Hobfoll, S.E. (1989). Conservation of resources: A new attempt at conceptualizing stress. *American Psychologist, 44*, 513–524.

Holahan, C.J., & Moos, R.H. (1990). Life stressors, resistance factors, and improved psychological functioning: An extension of the stress resistance paradigm. *Journal of Personality and Social Psychology, 58*, 909–917.

Holmes, T.H., & Rahe, R.H. (1967). The social readjustment rating scale. *Journal of Psychosomatic Research, 11*, 213–218.

Hoffman, M.S. (Ed.). (1992). *The world almanac and book of facts*. New York: Pharos Books.

Johnson, B.H., McGonigel, M.J., & Kaufmann, R.K. (Eds.). (1992). *Guidelines and recommended practices for the individualized family service plan*. Washington, DC: National Early Childhood Technical Assistance System.

Kennedy, B. (1984). *The relationship of coping behaviors and attribution of success to effort and school achievement of elementary school children*. Unpublished doctoral dissertation, State University of New York, Albany.

Kramer, P., & Hinojosa, J. (Eds.). (1993). *Frames of reference for pediatric occupational therapy*. Baltimore: Williams and Wilkins.

Lahey, M. (1988). *Language disorders and language development*. New York: Macmillan.

Lamb, M.E., & Bornstein, M.H. (1987). *Development in infancy: An introduction* (2nd ed.). New York: Random House.

Larson, J.G. (1984). Relationship between coping behavior and academic achievement in kindergarten children. (Doctoral dissertation, Fairleigh Dickinson University, 1984). *Dissertation Abstracts International, 45*, 2389A. (University Microfilms No. 84-15514, 147)

Lazarus, R.S. (1966). *Psychological stress and the coping process*. New York: McGraw-Hill.

Lazarus, R.S., Deese, J., & Osler, S.F. (1952). The effects of psychological stress upon performance. *Psychological Bulletin, 49*, 293–317.

Lazarus, R.S., & DeLongis A. (1983). Psychological stress and coping in aging. *American Psychologist, 38*, 245–254.

Lazarus, R.S., & Folkman, S. (1984). *Stress, appraisal, and coping.* New York: Springer-Verlag.

Lazarus, R.S., & Launier, R. (1978). Stress-related transactions between person and environment. In L.A. Pervin & M. Lewis (Eds.), *Perspectives in interactional psychology.* New York: Plenum.

Lerner, R.M., Palermo, M., Spiro, A., & Nesselroade, J.R. (1982). Assuming the dimensions of temperamental individuality across the life span: The dimensions of temperament survey (DOTS). *Child Development, 53,* 149–159.

Lewin, K. (1951). *Field theory in social sciences.* New York: Harper.

Lewis, M., & Michalson, L. (1983). *Children's emotions and moods.* New York: Plenum.

Linder, T.W. (1993). *Transdisciplinary play-based assessment: A functional approach to working with young children* (rev. ed.). Baltimore: Paul H. Brookes Publishing Co.

Lipsitt, L. (1983). Stress in infancy: Toward understanding the origins of coping behavior. In N. Garmezy & M. Rutter (Eds.), *Stress, coping, and development in children* (pp. 161–190). New York: McGraw-Hill.

Lipsky, D.K. (1985). A parental perspective on stress and coping. *American Journal of Orthopsychiatry, 55,* 614–617.

Loevinger, J. (1976). *Ego development.* San Francisco: Jossey-Bass.

Lynch, E.W., & Hanson, M.J. (Eds.). (1992). *Developing cross-cultural competence: A guide for working with young children and their families.* Baltimore: Paul H. Brookes Publishing Co.

Mahler, M.S., Pine, F., & Bergman, A. (1975). *The psychological birth of the human infant.* New York: Basic Books.

Mahoney, G., Powell, A., Finnegan, C., Fors, S., & Wood, S. (1986). The transactional intervention program. In D. Gentry, J. Olson, & M. Veltman (Eds.), *Individualizing for families.* Moscow: University of Idaho.

Maslow, A. (1954). *Motivation and personality.* New York: Harper & Row.

May, R. (1972). *Power and innocence.* New York: Norton.

McCormack, G.L. (1987). Culture and communication in the treatment planning for occupational therapy with minority patients. *Occupational Therapy in Health Care, 4,* 17–36.

McCubbin, H.I., & Thompson, A.I. (Eds.). (1991). *Family assessment inventories for research and practice* (FAIRP) (2nd ed.). Madison: University of Wisconsin-Madison.

McCubbin, H., Comeau, J., & Harkins, J. (1979). *FIRM: Family Inventory of Resources for Management.* St. Paul: University of Minnesota.

McCubbin, H., Wilson, L., & Patterson, J. (1979). *FILE: Family Inventory of Life Events and Changes.* St. Paul: University of Minnesota.

McGoldrick, M., Pearce, J.K., & Giordano, J. (Eds.). (1982). *Ethnicity and family therapy.* New York: Guilford Press.

Meichenbaum, D. (1985). *Stress inoculation training.* Elmsford, NY: Pergamon.

Meisels, S.J., & Shonkoff, J.P. (Eds.). (1990). *Handbook of early childhood intervention.* Cambridge: Cambridge University Press.

Minuchin, S. (1974). *Families and family therapy.* Cambridge, MA: Harvard University Press.

Moos, R.H. (Ed.). (1976). *Human adaptation: Coping with life crises.* Lexington, MA: D.C. Heath.

Murphy, L.B. (1991). Toddlers: Themes and variations. *Zero to Three, 11*(3), 1–5.

Murphy, L.B., & Moriarty, A. (1976). *Vulnerability, coping and growth.* New Haven, CT: Yale University Press.

National Center for Clinical Infant Programs. (1989). *Outreach junctures: Support for parents of children with special needs.* Arlington, VA: Author.

Owens, R.E. Jr. (1991). *Language disorders: A functional approach to assessment and intervention.* New York: Macmillan.

Pfeifer, J.W., & Jones, J.E. (1972). *The 1972 annual handbook for group facilitators.* Iowa City, IA: University Associates.

Phillips, S., & Elledge, R. (1989). *The team-building source book.* San Diego: University Associates.

Piaget, J. (1952). *The origins of intelligence in children.* New York: International Universities Press.

Piaget, J. (1960). *The psychology of intelligence.* Totowa, NJ: Littlefield, Adams.

Pryor, F.H. (1989). *How to turn your work group into a winning team.* Shawnee Mission, KS: Pryor Resources.

Public Law 90-538, Handicapped Children's Early Education Assistance Act. (September 30, 1968). Title 20, U.S.C. 621 et seq: *U.S. Statutes at Large, 82,* 901–902.

Public Law 94-142, Education for All Handicapped Children Act of 1975. (23 August 1977). 20 U.S.C. 1401 et seq: *Federal Register, 42* (163), 42474–42518.

Public Law 99-457, *Education of the Handicapped Act Amendments of 1986.* (22 September 1986). *Congressional Record, 132*(125), H 7893–7912.

Public Law 101-476, Individuals with Disabilities Education Act of 1990. (30 October 1990). Title 20, U.S.C. 1400: *U.S. Statutes at Large, 104,* 1103–1151.

Public Law 102-119, Individuals with Disabilities Education Act Amendments of 1991. (7 October 1991). Title 20, U.S.C. 1400 et seq: *U.S. Statutes at Large, 105,* 587–608.

Purkey, W.W., & Schmidt, J.J. (1987). *The inviting relationship: An expanded perspective for professional counseling.* Englewood Cliffs, NJ: Prentice Hall.

Rogers, C.A. (1961). *On becoming a person.* Boston: Houghton Mifflin.

Rosenberg, S.A., & Robinson, C.C. (1988). Interactions of parents with their young handicapped children. In

S.L. Odom & M.B. Karnes (Eds.), *Early intervention for infants and children with handicaps: An empirical base* (pp. 159–177). Baltimore: Paul H. Brookes Publishing Co.

Rothbart, M.K., & Derryberry, D. (1981). Development of individual differences in temperament. In M.E. Lamb & A.L. Brown (Eds.), *Advances in developmental psychology* (Vol. 1, pp. 37–86). Hillsdale, NJ: Lawrence Erlbaum Associates.

Rutter, M. (1983). Stress, coping, and development: Some issues and some questions. In N. Garmezy & M. Rutter (Eds.), *Stress, coping, and development in children*. New York: McGraw-Hill.

Sameroff, A.J., & Chandler, M.J. (1975). Reproductive risk and the continuum of caretaker casualty. In F.D. Horowitz (Ed.), *Review of child development research* (Vol. 4). Chicago: The University of Chicago Press.

Sameroff, A.J., & Emde, R. (1989). *Relationship disturbances in infancy*. New York: Basic Books.

Sameroff, A.J., & Fiese, B.H. (1990). Transactional regulation and early intervention. In S.J. Meisels & J.P. Shonkoff (Eds.), *Handbook of early childhood intervention* (pp. 119–149). Cambridge, MA: Cambridge University Press.

Satir, V. (1972). *Peoplemaking*. Palo Alto, CA: Science & Behavior Books.

Schaffer, M.P., & Schaffer, S.J. (1982). Stress related to organically-based learning disabilities. In A.S. McNamee (Ed.), *Children and stress: Helping children cope* (pp. 8–18). Washington, DC: Association for Childhood Education International.

Scherzer, A.L., & Tscharnuter, I. (1990). *Early diagnosis and therapy in cerebral palsy* (2nd ed.). New York: Marcel Dekker.

Schmitt, B.D. (1987). *Your child's health: A pediatric guide for parents*. New York: Bantam Books.

Seligman, M., & Darling, R. (1989). *Ordinary families, special children: A systems approach to childhood disability*. New York: Guilford Press.

Selye, H. (1974). *Stress without distress*. Philadelphia: J.B. Lippincott.

Selye, H. (1976). *The stress of life* (rev. ed.). New York: McGraw-Hill.

Shon, S.P., & Ja, D.Y. (1982). Asian families. In M. McGoldrick, J.K. Pearce, & J. Giordano (Eds.), *Ethnicity and family therapy* (pp. 208–228). New York: Guilford Press.

Simeonsson, R.J., Huntington, G.S., & Parse, S.A. (1980). Expanding the developmental assessment of young children. In J. Gallagher (Ed.), *New directions for exceptional children* (pp. 51–74). Washington, DC: Jossey-Bass.

Skinner, B.F. (1953). *Science and human behavior*. New York: Macmillan.

Spitz, R.A. (1945). Hospitalism: An inquiry into the genesis of psychiatric conditions in childhood. *Psychoanalytic Study of the Child, 1,* 53–74.

Stern, D.N. (1985). *The interpersonal world of the infant: A view from psychoanalysis and developmental psychology*. New York: Basic Books.

Sullivan, M.W., & Lewis, M. (1993). Contingency, means-end skills, and the use of technology in infant intervention. *Infants and Young Children, 5,* 58–77.

Teti, D.M., & Nakagawa, M. (1990). Assessing attachment in infancy: The strange situation and alternate systems. In E.D. Gibbs & D.M. Teti (Eds.), *Interdisciplinary assessment of infants: A guide for early intervention professionals* (pp. 191–214). Baltimore: Paul H. Brookes Publishing Co.

Thomas, A., & Chess, S. (1977). *Temperament and development*. New York: Brunner/Mazel.

Thomas, A., & Chess, S. (1980). *The dynamics of psychological development*. New York: Brunner/Mazel.

Thomas, A., Chess, S., & Birch, H. (1968). *Temperament and behavior disorders in children*. New York: New York University Press.

Turnbull, A.P., Patterson, J.M., Behr, S.K., Murphy, D.L., Marquis, J.G., & Blue-Banning, M.J. (Eds.). (1993). *Cognitive coping, families, and disability*. Baltimore: Paul H. Brookes Publishing Co.

Turnbull, A.P., & Turnbull, H.R. (1990). *Families, professionals, and exceptionality: A special partnership* (2nd ed.). Columbus, OH: Charles E. Merrill.

Uzgiris, I.C., & Hunt, J.M. (1975). *Assessment in infancy: Ordinal Scales of Psychological Development*. Urbana: University of Illinois Press.

Vaillant, G.E. (1977). *Adaptation to life*. Boston: Little, Brown.

Walsh, N. (Ed.). (1982). *Normal family processes*. New York: Guilford Press.

Werner, E.E. (1989). High risk children in young adulthood: A longitudinal study from birth to 32 years. *American Journal of Orthopsychiatry, 59,* 72–81.

Werner, E.E., & Smith, R. (1982). *Vulnerable but invincible: A longitudinal study of resilient children and youth*. New York: McGraw-Hill.

Werner, E.E., & Smith, R.S. (1991). *Against the odds: High risk children from birth to adulthood*. Ithaca, NY: Cornell University Press.

Williamson, G.G. (Ed.). (1987). *Children with spina bifida: Early intervention and preschool programming*. Baltimore: Paul H. Brookes Publishing Co.

Williamson, G.G. (1993). Intervention to promote adaptive behavior. In E. Vergara (Ed.), *Foundations for practice in the neonatal intensive care unit and early intervention: A self-guided practice manual*. Rockville, MD: American Occupational Therapy Association.

Williamson, G.G., Szczepanski, M., & Zeitlin, S. (1993). Coping frame of reference. In P. Kramer & J. Hinojosa (Eds.), *Frames of reference in pediatric occupational therapy* (pp. 395–436). Baltimore: Williams & Wilkins.

Williamson, G.G., & Zeitlin, S. (1990). Assessment of coping and temperament: Contributions to adaptive functioning. In E.D. Gibbs & D.M. Teti (Eds.), *Interdisciplinary assessment of infants: A guide for early intervention
   professionals* (pp. 215–226). Baltimore: Paul H. Brookes Publishing Co.
Williamson, G.G., Zeitlin, S., & Szczepanski, M. (1989). Coping behavior: Implications for disabled infants and
   toddlers. *Infant Mental Health Journal, 10,* 3–13.
Woodruff, G., & McGonigel, M.J. (1988). Early intervention team approaches: The transdisciplinary model. In
   J.B. Jordan, J.J. Gallagher, P.L. Hutinger, & M.B. Karnes (Eds.), *Early childhood special education: Birth to three.*
   Reston, VA: Council for Exceptional Children.
Zeitlin, S. (1981). Coping, stress and learning. *Journal of the Division of Early Childhood, 2,* 102–108.
Zeitlin, S. (1982). *Basic competencies for personnel in early intervention programs.* Westar Series Paper 14. Mon-
   mouth, OR: INTERACT.
Zeitlin, S. (1985). *Coping Inventory.* Bensenville, IL: Scholastic Testing Service.
Zeitlin, S., & Williamson, G.G. (1988). Developing family resources for adaptive coping. *Journal of the Division for
   Early Childhood, 12,* 137–146.
Zeitlin, S., & Williamson, G.G. (1990). Coping characteristics of disabled and nondisabled young children. *Amer-
   ican Journal of Orthopsychiatry, 60,* 404–411.
Zeitlin, S., Williamson, G.G., & Rosenblatt, W.P. (1987). The coping with stress model: A counseling approach for
   families with a handicapped child. *Journal of Counseling and Development, 65,* 443–446.
Zeitlin, S., Williamson, G.G., & Szczepanski, M. (1988). *Early Coping Inventory.* Bensenville, IL: Scholastic Testing Service.

Index

Page numbers followed by t *and* f *denote tables and figures, respectively.*

Physical disabilities, *see* Children with physical disabilities
Physical positioning
  as intervention, 108–112, 110*f*–112*f*
  see also Developmental skills, mobility
  and play, 113
Physical states
  child's
    assessment of, 71
    intervention to enhance, 90–91
  definition of, 17, 38
  family's, gathering information on, 74
Piaget, Jean, 3
Play
  and developmental assessment, 69–70
  as intervention, 112–117, 114*f*
Practitioner, *see* Staff
Practitioner–child relationship, 72
Practitioner–parent relationship, 52–57, 53*t*, 72
  and IFSP development, 158–159, 173, 177
Preschool, transition to, *see* Transition
Process functions, 270, 272–273
Productivity, group, 270, 271*f*
Public Law 90-538, *see* Handicapped Children's Early Education Assistance Act
Public Law 94-142, *see* Education for All Handicapped Children Act
Public Law 99-457, *see* Education of the Handicapped Act Amendments of 1986
Public Law 101-476, *see* Individuals with Disabilities Education Act (IDEA)
Public Law 102-119, *see* Individuals with Disabilities Education Act Amendments of 1991

Rogers, Carl, 11

Satir, Virginia, 276
Self-help skills (term), 5
Sensory experience, intervention to influence child's, 105–108
Services, in IFSP implementation plan, 188–189
Services for Crippled Children, 4
Skills
  definition of, 17
  family's, gathering information on, 74
  see also Developmental skills; Listening skills
Skinner, B.F., 3
Social Security Act of 1935 (Title V), 4
Staff
  coping in, 269–285
    activities to support, 284–285
  roles of, 273

see also Practitioner–child relationship; Practitioner–parent relationship
Stress
  definition of, 12, 233
  in family, workshop on, 142–147
  historical overview, 8–11
  in young children, 33–34
Stressors, classification of, 12–13
Summary matrix, for IFSP development, 168, 170*t*, 173, 174*t*
Support groups, 138–142
Swaddling, 106, 106*f*
Symptoms Checklist 90 (SCL-90R), 236*t*

Tactile defensiveness, 106
Task analysis, in IFSP implementation plan development, 186
Task functions, 270–272
Teamwork, among staff, 270–273
Temperament, 24–27, 133–134, 150
Test of Sensory Functions in Infants, 71
Toddler Temperament Scale, 26
Transaction(s), 19–22, 20*f*
  child–caregiver, 40–41
  components of, 19*f*, 76
  IFSP development and, 167*t*, 167–168
  intervention options based on, 81
  observation and analysis of, 76–79, 77*t*, 167*t*, 167–168
  see also Coping process
Transactional model, 9
  see also Coping process
Transformation, 33
Transition, from early intervention services
  planning of, 191–192
  workshop on, 292–295
Turntaking, 101–102

United Cerebral Palsy, 4
Uzgiris-Hunt Ordinal Scales of Infant Psychological Development, 165

Values
  definition of, 17
  establishment of child's, 70–71
  family's, gathering information on, 73–74

Workshops, family, 142–147, 146*f*–147*f*, 291–295, 293*f*–294*f*

Zero to Three/National Center for Clinical Infant Programs, 191

CPSIA information can be obtained
at www.ICGtesting.com
Printed in the USA
FSHW011142030920
73536FS